Economic Sentiments

ECONOMIC SENTIMENTS

Adam Smith, Condorcet,
and the Enlightenment

EMMA ROTHSCHILD

HARVARD UNIVERSITY PRESS

Cambridge, Massachusetts, and London, England

Library of Congress Cataloging-in-Publication Data

Rothschild, Emma, 1948–
    Economic sentiments : Adam Smith, Condorcet, and the
Enlightenment / Emma Rothschild.
      p. cm.
    Includes bibliographical references and index.
    ISBN 0-674-00489-2 (alk. paper)
    1. Economics—History—18th century.   2. Free enterprise—History—
18th century.   3. Liberalism—History—18th century.   4. Smith, Adam,
1723–1790.   5. Condorcet, Jean-Antoine-Nicolas de Caritat, marquis de,
1743–1794.   I. Title.

HB83 .R68 2001
330.15′3—dc21   00-053943

To Amartya

CONTENTS

Economic Sentiments

Introduction

This book is about laissez-faire when it was new. The half century from the 1770s to the 1820s was a time of enthusiasm and fear in economic life; of excitement over the projects of merchants and manufacturers, resentment over restrictions on buying and selling, confidence in the "liberal plan of equality, liberty and justice" to which Adam Smith looked forward in 1776, anxiety about what Napoleon in St. Helena, studying the *Wealth of Nations,* described in 1816 as the new system of "freedom of commerce for all," which had "agitated all imaginations" in the "furious oscillations" of modern times.[1]

Economic life was intertwined, in these turbulent times, with the life of politics and the life of the mind. Economic thought was intertwined with political, philosophical, and religious reflection. The life of cold and rational calculation was intertwined with the life of sentiment and imagination. The sources of economic opulence were to be found, it was thought, in political and legal institutions, and in the history of the human mind. They were to be found, most of all, in the dispositions or ways of thinking of individuals; in the disposition to discuss and dispute and to think about the future; in the unfrightened mind.

To look at the economic thought of the late eighteenth and early nineteenth centuries in the setting of the political, legal, and philosophical disputes of the times is to cast light, I hope, on the events and the dispositions of those times. It is to see the past more clearly; to glimpse a now unfamiliar landscape of economic and political life.

But the book is also about the present. For the disputes with which I will be concerned are in an odd and disconcerting sense the disputes of our own present times. They are disputes which have continued in one form or another—over laissez-faire and the state, over respect and disrespect for established institutions, over reason and faith—throughout the

1

entire period which separates Adam Smith's times and our own. They are even newly modern, in the new circumstances of the beginning of the twenty-first century. The rhetoric of freedom of commerce is as conspicuous now as it was in the period which preceded and followed the French Revolution. So is the sense of living in a society of universal commerce and universal uncertainty. It is this new world, too, with which the book is concerned.

The treatises and pamphlets of the late eighteenth century about the reform of commerce were considered, very soon, to be disquisitions of only limited and technical interest. The *Wealth of Nations*, Jean-Baptiste Say wrote in 1803, was a "vast chaos of just ideas, pell-mell with pieces of positive knowledge," overfull of historical digressions and "particular facts." Caroline, the ingenuous interlocutor in Jane Marcet's *Conversations on Political Economy* of 1817, complained that economic science "is about custom-houses, and trade, and taxes, and bounties, and smuggling, and paper-money, and the bullion-committee, &c," and that Adam Smith's work is no more than "a jargon of unintelligible terms."[2]

My objective, in what follows, is to look back, beyond the preoccupations of the early nineteenth century, at an earlier and more open political economy. I will be concerned mostly with two eighteenth-century writers—Condorcet and Smith—who have become emblems of the cold, hard, and rational enlightenment. They are opposite emblems in several respects. Condorcet has come to epitomize the cold, universalistic enlightenment of the French Revolution; the "utopian" enlightenment. Smith has come to epitomize the one-sided, reductionist enlightenment of laissez-faire economics; the "conservative" enlightenment. But both philosophers were preoccupied, as will be seen, with similar details of the regulation of commerce. Both were concerned with what Condorcet described, in 1790, as "the restoration of the most complete freedom" in commercial policy.[3] Both were also interested in economic dispositions, and in the politics of a universe of uncertainty. Both were interested in economic life as a process of discussion, and as a process of emancipation. To rediscover a different political economy, I will suggest, is also to rediscover a different, and more open, enlightenment.

Political economy, in the period with which the book is concerned, was seen already as a science of sorts. Condorcet indeed complained, as early as 1771, about the deluded use of "the language of geometry" in "the economic sciences," and one of Turgot's theological opponents wrote of "economic science," with its "useless, lewd, and twisted" views, that it was already, in 1780, "beginning to go a little out of fashion."[4] But the intertwining of economic, religious, political, and moral thought—the sense that there is only a shifting, indistinct frontier between economic and political relationships, or between economic life and the rest of life—is far more characteristic of the beginning of the period than of the end.

It was "since Adam Smith," in Jean-Baptiste Say's description, that political economy, defined "as the science concerned with wealth," had been distinguished from the quite different discipline of politics.[5] The economist George Pryme, the first professor of political economy at the University of Cambridge, looked back with some alarm, in 1823, at Smith's jumbling together of economic and political concerns. "Since his time the distinction between Political Economy and pure Politics, has been generally observed," Pryme wrote. Political economy had become an inoffensive and orderly subject; "though it may seem less interesting than Political Philosophy, its utility is more extensive, since it is applicable alike to a despotism and to a democracy."[6]

The new circumscription of political economy corresponded to the classificatory disposition of the times. It was suited to what Hegel described in 1807 as the "method of labelling all that is in heaven and earth" in the museum of science as in a "synoptic table like a skeleton with scraps of paper stuck all over it, or like the rows of closed and labelled boxes in a grocer's stall."[7] Condorcet himself contributed to the subsequent professional organization of political economy through his theory of social science, and through his projects of the 1790s (including those for the establishment of special chairs in the application of mathematics to the political and moral sciences, and in political economy).[8] Smith commented with characteristic coolness, a generation earlier, on the new taxonomic spirit; in an early draft of the *Wealth of Nations,* from the 1760s, he says of the subdivisions of modern philosophy—"mechanical, chemical, astronomical, physical, metaphysical, moral, political, commercial and critical"—that their effect is such that "more work is done upon the whole and the quantity of science is considerably increased by it."[9]

But the new circumscription and circumspection of political economy also corresponded to the exigent circumstances of post-Revolutionary politics. The context of political economy at the very end of the eighteenth century was the prospect, described by Malthus in 1798 in the first paragraph of his *Essay on the Principle of Population,* that the French Revolution would "scorch up and destroy the shrinking inhabitants of the earth."[10] The French economists were inculpated, as will be seen, in the anti-Jacobin and anti-philosophical writings of the 1790s. Like the supporters of political reform in Kant's *Contest of Faculties*, also of 1798, economic reformers were subject to the charge of "innovationism, Jacobinism and conspiracy, constituting a menace to the state."[11] The disposition of enlightenment, or the uncertain and insubordinate way of thinking of commercial society, was inculpated in the moral revolutions of the times.

The economic writings with which I will be concerned belong to a different, more innocent world. Smith and Condorcet, Hume and Turgot wrote, sometimes at great length, about freedom of commerce; none of them was a political economist in the professional sense that became familiar in the early years of the nineteenth century. All of them also wrote about philosophy, the history of science, the history of ideas, and about politics. All were, on occasion, public officials. Hume died in 1776, Turgot in 1781, Smith in 1790, and Condorcet in 1794, a few weeks before the end of the Jacobin Terror; they belonged to an earlier universe of thought. When Thomas Jefferson drew up "a course of reading" in 1799, he included Locke's *Essay Concerning Human Understanding,* Smith's *Wealth of Nations,* and Condorcet's *Esquisse d'un tableau historique des progrès de l'esprit humain.*[12] Condorcet's own objective, in the *Esquisse des progrès,* was to describe the history of ideas about the mind and morality and the law, from the earliest sages to "the profound analyses of the Lockes, the Smiths, the Turgots."[13] For Arthur Condorcet O'Connor, the Irish general who married Condorcet's daughter Eliza, "the Turgots, the Condorcets, the Smiths" were the "fathers of the science" of political economy, whose principles, including "the eternal principle of equality," had been overturned by the "new sect of *so-called* economists" of the post-Revolutionary reconstruction.[14]

It is this earlier world which I will try to describe. Chapter 1 is about late eighteenth-century descriptions of sentiments and dispositions in economic life, and the idea of an unfrightened mind; of a way of thinking of individuals, emancipated, at least from time to time, from fears of violence, injustice, and vexation. Chapter 2 is about Adam Smith's reputation following his death in 1790, including his reputation for an unseemly relationship to the principles of the French Revolution, and some of the ways in which the renown of political economy changed, in France, England and Scotland, over the decade of the 1790s. Chapters 3 and 4 are about two of the great controversies in economic policy which shaped subsequent views of eighteenth-century economic thought. The first, discussed in Chapter 3, is the dispute over free commerce in subsistence food, over the relations between commerce and government in the grain trade, and over the transition to commercial freedom. The second, discussed in Chapter 4, is the dispute over apprenticeship and mastership guilds: over laissez-faire in the market for labor, public instruction, and the relations between commerce and government in industry.

The idea of the "invisible hand," which was presumed, for much of the twentieth century, to constitute a unifying theme of Smith's economic thought, is the subject of Chapter 5. Smith's own view of the invisible hand, I will suggest, was different and more skeptical. It should be understood in the setting of other, and at the time more familiar invisible hands: the "bloody and invisible hand" of Macbeth's providence, or the "invisible hand" which rebuffs and then hovers over the unfortunate hero of Voltaire's *Oedipe*. The idea of the invisible hand raises troublesome questions both about the relationship between economic and religious thought and about the relationship between the political and economic choices of individuals; about the pursuit of self-interest within rules, and the transformation of wealth into political power, including the power to transform rules.

Chapter 6 is concerned with Condorcet's efforts, in his writings on economic policy, to explore closely related questions about the rules and the dispositions of competition, about buying and selling political influence, and about the depiction of discursive economic subjects. Chapter 7 is about some of Condorcet's criticisms of the cold, universal, and all-imbuing philosophy which has been seen as characteristic of the eighteenth-century enlightenment, and about an idea—the "indissoluble chain" of truth, virtue and happiness—which was taken, again for much of the twentieth century, as a unifying theme of Condorcet's political thought. In Chapter 8 I will look at theories of economic and political sentiments, and at the reflection of these theories in the politics of enlightenment, including the politics of an uncertain or fatherless world.

The detailed disputes in which Smith and Condorcet were engaged, over duties on salt or apprenticeship regulations or restrictions on the export of rams, are largely unfamiliar to readers today. The political relationships of the period—the identification of the reforming left and the conservative right, of the state and the market, of the disposition and the sect of enlightenment—are also unfamiliar. We still live, at the outset of the twenty-first century, in a world which is defined, in important respects, by the events of the French Revolution and of the post-Revolutionary restoration; by the coalition of laissez-faire economic policy and political conservatism which was established in opposition to the revolutionary violence of the 1790s, and which came to dominate nineteenth-century political institutions.

But we also live, in the new circumstances of the early twenty-first century, in a post-restoration world. Political institutions are more free of the fear of revolution now than at any time in the nineteenth or twentieth centuries. The rhetoric of the endlessness of commerce is more unquestioned. The political and economic thought of the late eighteenth century—the old, lost idyll of universal freedom—is itself, now, newly familiar. Condorcet wrote of the new society of the United States, in 1786, that "the spectacle of a great people where the rights of man are respected is useful to all others . . . It teaches us that these rights are everywhere the same." Of the French Revolution, he wrote in 1791 that it had "opened up an immense scope to the hopes of the human species . . . [T]his revolution is not in a government, it is in opinions and wills."[15]

The new prospects of the early twenty-first century have something of this vastness, this sense of an unbounded future. We may also have more sympathy, in our societies of universal commerce, for the endless uncertainty, the unquiet imagination, which were believed, in the late eighteenth century, to be the consequences of commercial freedom. The effort to look at eighteenth-century economic thought in its own context might also, in these circumstances, cast light on our context, and our economic politics.

1

Economic Dispositions

The "beauty of writing history," Adam Smith said in his lectures on rhetoric, in January 1763, consisted for Tacitus in a political theory of sentiments. Events, in Smith's description, have both external and internal causes, or causes to do with circumstances and causes to do with sentiments. It is the neglect of these internal causes, Smith says, which makes the writings of modern historians "for the most part so dull and lifeless." The ancient historians were preoccupied, by contrast, with "the feelings and agitation of mind" of individuals, or with "the motions of the human mind." Tacitus' plan, in Smith's conjecture, is to relate the history of public events by leading the reader "into the sentiments and the mind of the actors." Such a history, Smith says, "perhaps will not tend so much to instruct us in the knowledge of the causes of events; yet it will be more interesting and lead us into a science no less useful, to wit, the knowledge of the motives by which men act."[1]

The motions of the human mind were Smith's own preoccupation as well. Smith's lifelong study, his first biographer, Dugald Stewart, wrote in 1793, was of "human nature in all its branches, more particularly of the political history of mankind." He was concerned with the "principles of the human mind," the "principles of the human constitution," the "natural progress of the mind." His style, as in the *Theory of Moral Sentiments,* or "his copious and seducing composition," was at its best in his "delineations of characters and manners," or when "the subject of his work leads him to address the imagination and the heart."[2]

The *Wealth of Nations* is in Smith's description a "very violent attack . . . upon the whole commercial system of Great Britain."[3] But it is also a history of the "general disposition to truck, barter, and exchange," which is a "necessary consequence of the faculties of reason and speech."[4] It is a contribution to the history of the human mind. It is a description of the sentiments and agitation of mind of individuals in the ordinary events of life. Smith's epic begins, as in William Robertson's *History of Charles V,* with "the human mind neglected, uncultivated, and depressed," in the "thick and heavy" darkness of early feudal Europe.[5] It ends in a new, enlightened society of independent individuals, reasoning and disputing, trucking and exchanging, being fair and deliberate, seeing through their own prejudices, having conversations about vexation and oppression, reflecting on their own sentiments.

Economic life, in the disputes with which this book will be concerned, is described to a striking extent in terms of thought and speech. It is itself a sort of discussion. In Turgot's description, free commerce is a "debate between every buyer and every seller," in which individuals make contracts, listen to rumors, discuss the values of one another's promises, and reflect on "the opinion and the reality of risk."[6] Condorcet, in an essay of 1775 on monopoly and monopolists, evoked the scene at the outset of Laurence Sterne's *Sentimental Journey* in which Yorick, the sentimental traveler, and M. Dessein, the innkeeper, go forth into the street in Calais to converse about the purchase of a "sorry post-chaise." "He felt a secret hatred rising in his heart, against M. Dessein," Condorcet wrote; the traveler reflected on the hostility of the world; he chaffered about the price; he concluded with a twelve guinea bargain and an advantage, even, in the "balance of sentimental commerce."[7]

The source of opulence, Smith says at the beginning of the *Wealth of Nations,* is to be found in the trucking disposition which is common to the most dissimilar characters (a philosopher and a common street porter, for example), and which is itself a consequence of the faculties of reason and speech. The "fair and deliberate exchange" of civilized society is to be contrasted to the "servile and fawning attention" of relations between unequals (including between dogs and their masters).[8] In his lectures on jurisprudence, Smith describes exchange as a sort of oratory. "It is clearly the natural inclination everyone has to persuade," he says, which is "the principle in the human mind on which this disposition of trucking is founded"; "the offering of a shilling, which to us appears to have so plain and simple a meaning, is in reality offering an argument to persuade one to do so and so as it is for his interest . . . And in this manner every one is practising oratory on others through the whole of his life."[9]

Economic life is at the same time a matter of sentiment. "It is chiefly from this regard to the sentiments of mankind, that we pursue riches and avoid poverty," Smith wrote in the *Theory of Moral Sentiments*, of the desire to be attended to, and taken notice of, which is in his description the great object of worldly toil and bustle.[10] Sentiments are the objective of economic striving, and they are also the adjunct of economic exchange. The judgments of individuals, in the relationships of commercial life, are judgments, often, about one's own and other people's sentiments. All individuals, in their economic relationships as in the rest of their lives, are interested in what Smith describes as "the characters, designs, and actions of one another." They feel shame, and seek respect, and think about esteem. They have "anxious and desponding moments."[11] Tax reform, Condorcet wrote in his *Réflexions sur le commerce des blés* of 1776, would relieve "the sentiment of oppression," and freedom of commerce would reduce, for the poor, the horror of being ignored; "the idea of being counted for nothing, of being delivered up, without defense, to all vexations and all outrages."[12]

Sentiments influence reasons in economic life, and reasons influence sentiments.[13] Giacomo Leopardi said of the word "sentimental," in 1821, that it was one of the common European words, the *gallicismi* or *europeismi*, of a "philosophy which is part of ordinary conversation." The word "sentiment," too, was something other than what Leopardi called a term. It was not "naked" and "isolated"; it was one of the words which evoke "clusters of ideas" and "multitudes of concepts," vague, indefinite, and indeterminate.[14] But the indefinite idea of a sentiment was at the heart of Smith's and Condorcet's political and moral theory. Sentiments were feelings of which one is conscious, and on which one reflects. They were also events that connected the individual to the larger relationships in which he or she lived (the society, or the family, or the state).[15] The traffic or commerce of modern life was at the same time a traffic in opinions and sentiments. The "man of society," in Smith's translation of Rousseau's *Discours sur l'inégalité*, is "always out of himself"; he "cannot live but in the opinion of others, and it is . . . from their judgment alone that he derives the sentiment of his own existence."[16]

CIVILIZED AND COMMERCIAL SOCIETY

The discursive, reflective, self-conscious disposition, in the economic disputes with which this book will be concerned, is both a cause and a consequence of economic progress. The two most important conditions of commercial prosperity, for Smith and for Condorcet, are the improvement of political and legal institutions and the independence of individual dispositions. "Order and good government, and along with them the liberty and security of individuals," the circumstance which is for Smith at the heart of the progress of opulence, has the effect of making possible the enfranchisement of opinions and sentiments. Individuals are free of "servile dependency"; they exert their industry "to better their condition"; they are no longer "continually afraid of the violence of their superiors"; they have a sense of their own security.[17]

Free government is taken to be a necessary but not a sufficient condition for universal prosperity. It must be accompanied by certain dispositions and opinions, in Hume's description: "Liberty must be attended with particular accidents, and a certain turn of thinking, in order to produce that effect."[18] The only difficult question in relation to the abolition of all regulation of the commerce in subsistence food, Condorcet wrote in 1776, consists in "the prejudices of the people," including prejudices against "capitalists"; the only truly important transformation is in "public opinion," with respect to "freedom of commerce" and "respect for property."[19] The history of the rise of commerce, for Smith, is an epic of the emancipation of the mind. It is a story, as in the account of private credit and public debt in the *Wealth of Nations,* of "the operation of moral causes."[20] Individuals become independent in their lives and their opinions. They are freed, in particular, from superstitions and prejudices. Smith says, of the progress of opulence which he describes in Books 3 and 4 of the *Wealth of Nations,* that it is "interests, prejudices, laws and customs" which he will "endeavour to explain as fully and distinctly" as he can.[21]

Independence of mind is in turn a consequence, as well as a condition, of commercial prosperity. Commerce and manufactures gradually introduced order and good government, in Smith's description of late medieval European towns, and "this, though it has been the least observed, is by far the most important of all their effects."[22] Individuals become less dependent on their landlords and superiors, and are less subject to the fear of sudden destitution. These effects are even more pronounced when the benefits of opulence are extended to the greater part of the people, to "servants, labourers, and workmen of different kinds."[23] The great advantage of eighteenth-century England, for Hume, consists in the circumstance that "riches are dispersed among multitudes," and that the "high price of labour" is the source of "the happiness of so many millions."[24]

The high price of labor, for Smith, increases the industriousness and the "good spirits" of the laborer; it inspires "the comfortable hope of bettering his condition, and of ending his days perhaps in ease and plenty."[25]

The history of the human spirit, for Condorcet, was to be a history of the interior and private sentiments of millions of individuals; of the influence of the progress of the mind on "the opinions, the well-being of the general mass" of people in different countries. Until the late eighteenth century, Condorcet wrote, political history, like the history of philosophy and of the sciences, had been no more than the history of a few men. The history of the ideas and opinions of the mass of families—"the most obscure, the most neglected, and for which monuments offer us so little material"—was more difficult to write. Its neglect could not be ascribed only to the shortcomings of historians (the "bassesse des historiens"). It required quantitative information or observations. But it was the true object of philosophy.

This history of sentiments and thoughts was to be a history of "the law as it is written and the law as it is enforced; the principles of those who govern and the way in which they are modified by the spirit of those who are governed; institutions as they emanate from the men who shape them, and institutions as they are realised; the religion of books and the religion of the people; the apparent universality of a particular prejudice, and the real adherence it receives." It would end, as in the ultimate epoch of the *Esquisse des progrès*, in a society in which the "different causes of equality" reinforced one another. There would be greater equality of instruction, which would lead in turn to greater equality of industry and of wealth. There would be enough equality, at least, to exclude "all dependence," and to ensure that no one was obliged to depend blindly on others, in the ordinary business of life or in the exercise of individual rights.[26]

The rise of civilized and commercial society was by no means only beneficial, in Smith's and Condorcet's depictions. It can indeed be full of danger, under certain conditions, for the dispositions of ordinary people. The division of labor, in Smith's description, can "benumb the understanding" and lead the mind into a "drowsy stupidity." The individual "whose whole life is spent in performing a few simple operations" is "mutilated and deformed" in the "character of human nature," including in his capacity to enjoy "rational conversation" and to make judgments about private and public life. The progress of commerce and the mechanical arts can be an obstacle to human improvement, Condorcet wrote, citing Smith, and even a source of "eternal stupidity." But universal public instruction was for both Smith and Condorcet an efficient remedy, and the only remedy, for this evil. The eventual objective of a commercial society is not "equal enlightenment." It is the prevention, at least, of "that inequality which brings with it a real dependence, and which compels a blind confidence."[27]

THE UNFRIGHTENED MIND

The most heroic outcome, in this history of the human spirit, was to be the slow vanquishing of fear. The condition of uncivilized society, in Smith's description as in Hume's, is of the "lowest and most pusillanimous superstition."[28] Fear is the source of superstition for Hume, and superstition "steals in gradually and insensibly; renders men tame and submissive." The rise of commercial and civilized society is associated with the replacement of superstition by philosophy; in Smith's description, "when law has established order and security, and subsistence ceases to be precarious, the curiosity of mankind is increased, and their fears are diminished."[29] The highest calling of philosophy is to liberate the minds of individuals from terrors and apparitions and portents.[30]

Fear was for Smith and for Condorcet a natural condition of human life. It is "a passion derived altogether from the imagination, which represents, with an uncertainty and fluctuation that increases our anxiety, not what we really feel, but what we may hereafter possibly suffer," Smith wrote in the *Theory of Moral Sentiments*. For Hume, it is a passion associated with probability, or with a "wavering and unconstant method" of surveying the world.[31] It influences the way individuals think, for Condorcet: "We believe what we hope or what we fear, more forcefully than something which is indifferent."[32] It is even enticing, or at least interesting. We are interested in hope and fear and distress, Smith says. We are charmed by the *Phèdre* of Racine because of, and not in spite of, its "extravagance and guilt"; "her fear, her shame, her remorse, her horror, her despair, become thereby more natural and interesting."[33]

But fear is also a vast and insidious evil, even in modern societies. The superstitious fears of uncivilized societies, the frenzies and sacrifices and invisible beings, have been succeeded, in more recent times, by what Smith described, both in the *Wealth of Nations* and in the *Theory of Moral Sentiments*, as the "terrors of religion."[34] The feudal governments of Europe were founded on fear. In the unfortunate countries where individuals lived "under all the violence of the feudal institutions," tenants and tradesmen subsisted in continuing insecurity. Their leases were precarious. They were obliged to provide arbitrary and irregular services to their landlords and to the state. They found it prudent to conceal their stock, or to bury it in the ground. They were unwilling to take risks. The "irregular and partial administration of justice" in Spain and Portugal, which tended to protect the rich and powerful, makes "the industrious part of the nation afraid to prepare goods for the consumption of these haughty and great men."[35]

The progress of despotism, in Smith's description, or the absorption by the sovereign of all other powers, was an innovation in government by anxiety. Its consequence, for Condorcet, was to degrade the mind "under the weight of fear and unhappiness." Taxation, even in less despotic societies, was arbitrary, and individuals found themselves in the power of the tax collector, who can "either aggravate the tax upon any obnoxious contributor, or extort, by the terror of such aggravation, some present or perquisite to himself."[36] One's home, or one's inn, might be visited at any time by officers of the customs and excise. One was obliged, continually, to evaluate the most degrading and unsettling of probabilities: the prospect that the tax collector is a hard and unjust man, or that he is one's enemy; that the customer to whom one sells some damask is haughty, or that he is a friend of the king's prosecutor. The regulation of commerce, like the regulation of confession in the sixteenth- and seventeenth-century religious conflicts in England and France, was an authority of fear and anxiety.[37] As Smith wrote in the *Wealth of Nations* of the attempts of sovereigns to terrify the dissenting clergy, "fear is in almost all cases a wretched instrument of government."[38]

The corn trade in France, in Condorcet's description, was a scene of endless dread. The food riots, which were also riots against corn traders, were the work of people "agitated by a vague fear of scarcity," and guided by individuals who sought "to excite their fears, and to profit from them." The effect of free commerce was presented by these false guides, in a "frightening hypothesis," as being like the removal of a single loaf of bread from an enclosed population; individuals were "seized by terror; everyone believes that he will be the one who is destined not to eat." The rich in towns (the people who had windows to be broken) were meanwhile frightened of the riots. The fears of the poor and the fears of the subaltern magistrates eddied together and augmented one another. "Fear is the origin of almost all human stupidities, and above all of political stupidities," Condorcet wrote in his article on monopoly and monopolists. It is a means of political and moral oppression: "One is more sure of subjugating people's minds by frightening them, than by speaking to them of reason; for fear is an imperious passion."[39]

The great promise of commercial and liberal society—of the liberal plan of equality, liberty and justice which had been rejected in seventeenth-century France, in Smith's description—is that the minds of individuals will be less frightened, and their lives less frightening. Commerce will flourish only in a state with a regular administration of justice, or in which there is a "certain degree of confidence in the justice of government."[40] The flourishing of commerce and opulence is in turn a source of confidence, in that people are less afraid of falling into destitution at the slightest accident. They are confident of ending their days in comfort.

Contracts and obligations, the acts which are at the heart of commercial society, are counterposed, by law, to fear and duress. "All fear in the parties renders the obligation they have entered into void from the beginning," Smith said in his lectures on jurisprudence, and "with respect to what is done through fear . . . a bond given from this principle is not binding." Like a contract entered into on behalf of an unknown posterity—the individual is "not conscious of it, and therefore cannot be bound by it"—a contract entered into out of fear is unjust, the outcome of a *metus injustus*. The essential condition of civilized and commercial life, for tenants and for the cooks and upholsterers who sell to the rich, is to be able to form "reasonable hopes, imagination or expectation."[41]

Understanding and enlightenment, like the curiosity of individuals in uncivilized societies, are in these circumstances a source of security. The uncertainty and difficulty of providing for one's subsistence, Condorcet wrote in the *Esquisse des progrès*, leave one with no free time in which to think about one's ideas. But to be in a position to reflect on new ideas, to be instructed and to have time to think, is to be independent of chimerical hopes and fears. It is to be someone who can "separate himself from his needs, from his interests, from his dangers, from his deprivations, from his anxieties, from his sorrows, and, so to speak, from himself."[42] It is also to be someone who can form expectations about his own future, and the future of others. It is to be free of the "painful anxiety which is associated with being aware of one's own ignorance, and which produces the vague fear of not really being in a position to defend oneself against the ills by which one is threatened."[43] It is to be free even to question one's own understanding, and one's own education. One would be free to doubt, and to enter into obligations, and to take risks. There would be a good uncertainty, that is to say, an uncertainty without subjugation, and without fear.

TWO KINDS OF ENLIGHTENMENT

Enlightenment, in the late eighteenth century, was considered to be a disposition, and also a sect. In the first sense, it was a way of thinking and seeing. It was a condition of the human mind, undepressed and unneglected. It was a *mentalité*, a *Denkart*, a "disposition des esprits," in the phrase that Condorcet used in his *Vie de Voltaire*.[44] It was a "reform in ways of thinking" or a gradual change in "the mentality of the people," as in Kant's *What is Enlightenment?*[45] The word *Aufklärung* was indeed translated by the Austrian reformer Windisch-Grätz, in a text that he sent in 1788 both to Condorcet and to Smith, as *"populorum cultura."*[46] As in Hegel's "struggle of the enlightenment with superstition," in his *Phenomenology of Spirit* of 1807, enlightenment was the dominion of *"pure insight* and its diffusion," and it seeped into men's thoughts like a "perfume," or like an "infection."[47] It is this kind of enlightenment with which I will mostly be concerned; with the disposition of enlightenment, in economic and in political life.

In the second, later, and by now far more familiar sense, the enlightenment was a society of philosophers and literary men. It was composed of individuals who were theorists, or historians, of the change in ways of thinking, and who were also its apostles. Almost everyone who described the political (or economic) life of the late eighteenth century identified some version of what Johann Gottfried Herder, in 1769, called the "neue Denkart" of Europe, or of what the poet Robert Southey described as the "tremendous change" in "the character of the lower orders" in England which began in the 1770s, of which the *Wealth of Nations* was the "code," and which constituted a "great moral revolution, for such it may truly be called."[48] The sect of enlightenment, or of the philosophers, was constituted by men who enjoyed, glorified, and conspired in this new disposition. The enlightenment in this sense was a fairly small group of eighteenth-century men of letters, a movement or a campaign, most of them in or connected to France, and almost all of them interested in the minds and dispositions of other men.

In his book *Sökandet efter Upplysningen*, on the thought of the Swedish enlightenment, Tore Frängsmyr distinguishes three senses of enlightenment, as a philosophical attitude, as a period in time (an "age"), and as an intellectual movement, centered in France; he, like Franco Venturi, adopts the third and least imprecise sense. This is also Robert Darnton's "deflationist" sense of the enlightenment as "a campaign to change minds and reform institutions." J. G. A. Pocock has by contrast emphasized the plurality of "enlightenments," as a series of programs for the reform of the relationships between religious and political institutions.[49] My concern will rather be with enlightenment in a fourth sense, of a universal, or potentially universal, disposition. This is connected to but distinct from the sense of a (Baconian or Newtonian) philosophical attitude. It is in particular a disposition of everyone, or of everyone with some minimal instruction and time to think. It is not a characteristic only of philosophers (although one of the habitual assertions of the sect or movement of enlightenment, as of Smith and Condorcet, was that everyone, without exception, has the natural capability to be a philosopher). It is a condition of the minds which are to be changed, an outcome of the programs of reform.[50]

Economic thought was conspicuous in all these kinds of enlightenment. Political economy was engaged, to an extent that is unfamiliar today, in the great philosophical disputes over public enlightenment. Johann Georg Hamann, in Königsberg, translated Galiani's *Dialogues on the Corn Trade*, and the aspiration of the young Herder, in Riga, was to be for Russia what the abbé Morellet—with his criticism of the East India Company—had become for France. He was determined to think of everything "from the point of view of politics, the state, and finance," and to put forward "some proposals for the new economic society, more suited to the spirit of the Russian economy."[51] Diderot denounced the regulation of lending at interest, and defended the regulation of the corn trade.[52] Kant, in the Third Antinomy in the *Critique of Pure Reason*, of free will versus determinism, named the determinist position (for Quesnay) as "Transcendental *Physiocracy*."[53] He said of the attributes of individuals in the "kingdom of ends" (in the *Groundwork of the Metaphysic of Morals*) that they have either a "market-price," a "luxury-price," or "an intrinsic value—that is, *dignity*."[54]

The disposition of universal discussion—the unending, discursive process of public altercation which was so admired, and so execrated, for much of the eighteenth century—was concerned, often, with economic policy. "From the scholastic disputes of theologians to matters of trade," d'Alembert wrote, "everything has been discussed and analyzed, or at least mentioned."[55] For Edmund Burke, "it has been the misfortune (not as these gentlemen think it, the glory) of this age, that everything is to be discussed"; the age was one of "oeconomists, and calculators."[56] Taxes and regulations, guilds and excise inspections, were a principal preoccupation, together with religion, of enlightened opinion. Adam Smith's most serious offense, for his Edinburgh contemporary the Reverend Alexander Carlyle, consisted in "introducing that unrestrained and universal commerce, which propagates opinions as well as commodities."[57] The commerce in opinions was itself, in large part, a commerce in opinions about commerce, or about commercial policy. The "focal point of enlightenment," Kant says in *What is Enlightenment?*—the subject to be disputed, in the imperative to "*argue* as much as you like and about whatever you like"—consists in matters of religion. But economic matters are also a subject of enlightened discussion in Kant's description; the tax official says, "'Don't argue, pay!'" and the cosmopolitan citizen "publicly voices his thoughts on the impropriety or even injustice of such fiscal measures."[58]

The enlightened disposition, and the philosophical history of the commercial mind, were the preoccupation, even, of commercial men themselves. When the editor and economist James Anderson introduced his short-lived Edinburgh journal, *The Bee,* in 1791, his "General Queries to Foreign Correspondents" were concerned to a striking extent with opinions and ways of thinking. Of religious establishments, he asks what are "their effects on the conduct and disposition of mind of certain classes of people?" "What sorts of business usually fall to the share of women among the lower ranks?" he asks. "What is the state of the country in regard to the *liberty of the press?*" In relation to the conditions imposed in leasehold tenancies, he asks, "May they be loosely and *generally* expressed?" Of excise duties, he asks, "Are they levied in a loose and arbitrary manner?" Of tax collectors, "Are they tied down by rules so clear and definite, that they cannot transgress them without being *evidently* culpable?" "What kinds of theft are here accounted as of least importance; and what kinds of it are reckoned heinous crimes by the common people?" he inquires. His general instruction to his correspondents, or his commercial travelers, is imposing enough; it is "to illustrate the history of the human mind."[59]

THE DEVIL HIMSELF

Enlightenment in the sense of a sect—which was the sense, in general, of the enlightenment's enemies—was widely associated, especially in the anti-Revolutionary and anti-philosophical writings of the 1790s, with the activities of economists. Burke, in the *Reflections on the Revolution in France*, finds the origins of "this enlightened age," "this new conquering empire of light and reason," this epoch of "*'enlightened'* usurers," in the "cabal, intrigue, and proselytism" of a society of "philosophic financiers," in connection, his editors added in 1803, "with Turgot and almost all the people of the finance."[60] The abbé Barruel, in his *Histoire du Jacobinisme*, published in 1797, said of Turgot, in his economic reforms of 1774–1776, that "as much as was within his power, he made a Jacobin out of the young King." Condorcet, for Barruel, was "the Devil himself," "the monster Condorcet," "the most determined of the conspirators," "a Devil named Condorcet."[61] William Playfair, who also wrote a *History of Jacobinism*, set out in his "eleventh edition" of the *Wealth of Nations*, published in 1805, to explain "the acquaintance between Mr Smith and D'Alembert, &c.," and Smith's "coincidence of reasoning with the French Oeconomists." The "infamy" of the economists had now been discovered, together with various secret meetings of Quesnay, Turgot, Condorcet, and Diderot, which Playfair described as "the conduct of the sect, when acting in a Jacobin direction"; "I must, and do attribute to them, and those with whom they associated, most of the terrible transactions of the last sixteen years."[62]

This is the prosopography of the examining magistrate, and economists, or the theorists of economic reform, are prominent within it. But the economic thought of the mid-eighteenth century was also inculpated, a generation after Barruel and Playfair, in one of the most profound evocations of the philosophical and administrative origins of the French Revolution. "It is above all in their writings that one can best study the true nature" of the French Revolution, Alexis de Tocqueville wrote in *L'ancien régime et la Révolution,* of the *Économistes* or Physiocrats of the mid-eighteenth century, of Quesnay and Letrosne and Morelly and Mercier de la Rivière. The "Economists have had less brilliance in history than the philosophers," he wrote; they nonetheless express, even more than the philosophers, the "single notion" in which "the political philosophy of the eighteenth century consists." This is the idea that it is appropriate "to substitute simple and elementary rules, derived from reason and from natural law, for the complicated and traditional customs" of particular societies at particular times. The past, for the *Économistes,* was "the object of a limitless scorn." They argued for the abstract and the general; for administrative simplicity, for "public utility" without "private rights," for "laisser faire" or "the free exchange of commodities" without "political freedoms." They conceived the duty of the state, in Tocqueville's description, as being to enlighten the mind of the people by an education founded on its own principles of natural order; "to fill it with specific ideas and to furnish their hearts with specific sentiments which it judges to be necessary."[63]

The economic disputes with which this book is concerned were the expression of a different political philosophy, and a different conception of enlightenment. They show both the diversity of the sects or movements of the enlightenment, and the extent to which the philosophy of enlightenment changed—and became less despotic—at the end of the ancien régime. Turgot was to be distinguished from all the other supporters of economic reform in France in the middle decades of the eighteenth century, Tocqueville wrote, by the greatness of his spirit and the qualities of his genius; even the "taste for political freedoms" came to him at last, late in his life.[64] But the disputes over economic policy of the 1770s and 1780s were also the occasion for a much more general transformation in political ideas. The change was apparent, as will be seen, in the criticisms by Turgot and Smith and Hume, by Diderot and Condorcet, of the political principles of the *Économistes* or Physiocrats; in the repudiation, well before 1789, of the administrative despotism of the "first" French revolution which Tocqueville described.[65] It was also apparent in the odd conception of the unfrightened and enlightened disposition, in ordinary or economic life.

The figures with whom this book is mostly concerned were all participants, to different extents, in the tractations of the sect of enlightenment. Condorcet and Turgot were intimate friends, as were Smith and Hume; the relationships between Smith and Condorcet, or Smith and Turgot, were ones of correspondence, or reciprocal study, or distant regard. They were all deeply interested in the disposition of enlightenment, or in the history of the human mind. But they were all skeptical, at various times and in different ways, about the campaign of changing or reforming other people's minds. Smith does not use the word "enlightenment," and he uses the word "enlightened" in only the most capacious of senses; Scipio's unbellicose view of Carthage, for example, is the "liberal expression of a more enlarged and enlightened mind."[66] Condorcet uses the phrase "les lumières" mostly in his projects of public instruction, and to denote knowledge; he was by the end of his life, as will be seen, profoundly opposed to the "enthusiasm" of public enlightenment, and of public education. Independence of mind, the condition to which the *Économistes* and the men of letters of the 1750s were least attracted, in Tocqueville's description, was for Condorcet a paramount good. To impose enlightenment was sometimes a form of despotism, "dazzling men instead of enlightening them." The eventual prospect, for individuals, was to be free of "submission even to the authority of enlightenment."[67]

HEROIC DISPOSITIONS

The disposition of enlightenment, like the sect of philosophical enlightenment, was intimately intertwined with economic thought. In the disputes over economic reform of the 1770s and 1780s, it was seen as a condition of individual men and women, in their usual and local lives. They were unfrightened, and disposed to form their own judgments. "Every individual, it is evident, can, in his local situation, judge much better than any statesman or lawgiver can do for him," Smith says in the *Wealth of Nations*.[68] The entire system of freedom of commerce, Turgot wrote some years earlier, or of "leaving each person free to do what he wants," is founded on the presumption that "each individual is the only judge of the most advantageous use of his land and his labor. He alone has the local knowledge without which the most enlightened man reasons only blindly." "Laissez-nous faire," Turgot describes the merchant Le Gendre saying to Colbert; let us be the judges of what to do. "Laissez-les faire," Turgot himself says, of educational foundations; let families choose the education of their children.[69]

"The cart drivers, the millers, the bakers are for them a class of heroes," the Chevalier says of the exponents of commercial freedom, in Galiani's *Dialogues sur le commerce des blés;* "everything is painted in smiling colors in this picture of the world which they have in their imagination . . . [T]he vices, the unjust passions have disappeared from it."[70] The economists ignore "the deceits, the passions, all the ruses of avidity, all the ruses of fear," Diderot added in his "Apologie de l'abbé Galiani"; the "tranquil flow" of economic forces is rather "a tumultuous conflict of fear, of avidity, of greed."[71] William Playfair, in his eleventh edition of the *Wealth of Nations,* says that Smith "makes a love of traffic the basis of all wealth," and, "in so many instances, is for confiding in the sagacity of individuals."[72]

This idyll of individual understanding was at the heart of the new philosophy of enlightenment in Turgot's and Diderot's France. The enthusiasm for enlightenment in the sense of scientific knowledge—for *les lumières*—was by the 1750s, in France, the subject of extensive derision.

Jean-Jacques Rousseau's *Discours sur les sciences et les arts* of 1750, with its sarcastic evocation of the spectacle of man "dissipating, by the enlightenment of his reason, the darkness in which nature had enveloped him," its depiction of political figures who "speak only of commerce and money," and its peroration against the "republic of letters," was an early, influential criticism of the sect of enlightenment. It was countered, by d'Alembert and Diderot, with an ideal of (virtually) universal enlightenment. To Rousseau's simple and rustic man of virtue, uncorrupted by luxury, there was opposed a busy, industrious scene; a prospect of flower sellers and laundresses, schoolchildren and booksellers and cart drivers. If the times are still corrupt, for d'Alembert, it is because "enlightenment, there, is too unequally diffused; because it is crowded and concentrated in too small a number of minds." "Our existence is poor, contentious, unquiet," for Diderot; "we have passions and needs." But to reason is nonetheless the condition and the nature of all individuals.[73] The promise of commerce and industry, knowledge and refinement, Hume wrote in response to Rousseau, is that the "minds of men" are roused and "put into a fermentation." "They flock into cities; love to receive and communicate knowledge"; they resist despotism and have conversations with women; "both sexes meet in an easy and sociable manner."[74]

The discovery of individual and local judgments—of the universal disposition of enlightenment—was itself a discovery of "nature." The division of painting into the depiction of history and the depiction of *genre*, or generic subjects, of flowers, fruit, animals, the "scenes of common and domestic life," was unnatural, Diderot wrote in one of his essays on painting, in 1765. The domestic subjects of Chardin and Greuze, as much as the heroes of historical scenes, are "beings who live, feel, and think."[75] The philosopher of enlightenment, like Greuze in Diderot's description, is "endlessly an observer, in the streets, in the churches, in the markets, in the theaters, in the promenades, in the public assemblies." His subjects are sometimes busy and calculating, as in Greuze's scene of a village dowry, where one cannot quite tell who is a sister and who is a servant, who is sly and who is honest, who is a peasant and who is a flower seller from the Paris market. They are sometimes reflective, quiet, in repose, as in the scenes of Chardin, the painter Diderot most admired. The laundress, the woman peeling turnips, the nurse with a pink apron, the boy memorizing his lessons, the musical instruments, the jars of olives and porcelain dishes and baskets of plums; the woman who has come in from the market with loaves of bread: this is the imitation of a "low, common, and domestic nature." It is a nature in which everyone, without exception, is deep in thought.[76]

Turgot's reform edicts of 1776, which were presented by the young Louis XVI at Versailles, in a *Lit de Justice* which was one of the great set pieces of late eighteenth-century European politics, were a eulogy, in this spirit, to the independence of mind of the people. Adam Smith wrote some years later, of his copy of the *Procès-Verbal* of the transactions, that it was a "most valuable monument of a person whom I remember with so much veneration," the "ever-to-be-regretted Mr. Turgot"; Goethe described reading in the Frankfurt newspapers of the "new and benevolent sovereign," whose noble ends consisted "of introducing a regular and efficient system of political economy, of dispensing with all arbitrary power, and of ruling alone by law and justice."[77] Turgot and Louis XVI invite their listeners to think themselves into, or sympathize with, the sentiments of the cultivator oppressed by subaltern officials of the administration of roads, the seamstress excluded from joining a corporation, the independent flower seller, the carrier who is forbidden to untie his sacks of grain in the street, the trader whose house is searched by magistrates.

The object of the reforms, Louis XVI declares (in the edict for the suppression of the *jurandes,* or mastership guilds), is to protect the "rights" of all his subjects, and especially of those who have no property other than their own labor and industry. He wishes to "enfranchise" his subjects from "all the assaults" on the "inalienable right of humanity" to choose where to work, and to abolish the "arbitrary institution" of the guilds, together with their "obscure codes, drawn up by greed, adopted without scrutiny in ages of ignorance." The *corvée* which obliges laborers to work on the construction of roads is a "form of crushing servitude." The king is concerned (in the edict on the regulation of the grain trade) with restrictions which are "inconvenient and disheartening for the trader, who is exposed to being disquieted, and perhaps unjustly punished." He insists (in the edict on the regulations concerning suet and tallow) on the rights of butchers to buy and sell freely, and of candle makers to make judgments about their own needs. The effect of the *jurandes,* he says, had been to "force the poorest members to submit to the law of the rich."[78]

A SORT OF INNER SHUDDERING

The idyll of individual independence was for the opponents of economic reform the most fearsome of prospects. For Turgot's principal adversary in the *Lit de Justice*, the advocate-general Antoine-Louis Séguier, to abolish regulations would be to "abandon the certainty of the present for an uncertain future." It would be to threaten both commerce and the way people think about themselves: "Every manufacturer, every artisan, every worker will regard himself as an isolated being, dependent on himself alone, and free to wander in all the discrepancies of an often disordered imagination; all subordination will be destroyed." "This sort of freedom is nothing other than a true independence," Séguier said, and "independence is a vice in the political constitution"; "this freedom would soon transform itself into license . . . this principle of wealth would become a principle of destruction, a source of disorder."[79] As J.-E.-M. Portalis, Napoleon's minister of religion, wrote in a eulogy to Séguier, the period of Turgot's reforms was an epoch in which traders had "a great idea of their independence and their strength," and in which "industry was great, but disquiet was greater still." "The spirit of discussion and criticism" had "incredible effects," and "there was nothing constant except the perpetual change in everything."[80] In the *Lit de Justice*, the last poignant words were the king's: "My intention is in no way to confound the conditions of men; I wish to reign only by justice and laws."[81]

The people have no more than "a single sentiment," Jacques Necker wrote a few months before the *Lit de Justice*, in opposition to Turgot's economic policies and to the prospect of universal enlightenment. "The bread which nourishes them, the religion which consoles them; these are their only ideas," he wrote; "they are connected to society only by their pains, and in all this immense space which is called the *future*, they never see more than tomorrow." Necker was unconvinced, in these circumstances, of the advantages of "an increase in enlightenment"; while landowners were interested in the right to property, and merchants in the right to liberty, the interest of the people was in no more than humanity.[82] For Condorcet, by contrast, liberty and the security of property were of intense interest to the poor as well. "You exaggerate the stupidity of the people," he wrote to Necker in 1775, in the assumed personality of a laborer from Picardy; the people, like everyone else, want property rights, justice, and personal security. It is not "alms" that they want, but good laws. Until Turgot's economic reforms, Condorcet wrote, "no one had yet deigned to treat the people as a society of reasonable beings."[83]

The "social economy" of mid-eighteenth-century France, in Tocqueville's description, was characterized by "a sort of inner shuddering," in which "each individual is disquieted and agitated in his condition, and tries to change it." Tocqueville's journey, in *L'ancien régime et la Révolution*, is into the tomb of the "France which is no more." He is concerned with the "details" of the "administrative and financial history of the ancien régime." His object is to understand the origins of the Revolution of 1789, in the "sentiments, the habits, the ideas" of the old society which the Revolution destroyed. He wishes to understand, in particular, why it was that a revolution which was in preparation, in the 1770s and 1780s, "across almost the entire continent of Europe" came to pass in France, and not elsewhere. He is interested, like Condorcet, in the political history of the sentiments of millions of people: in "the manner in which business was conducted, the true practice of institutions, the exact position of classes in relation to one another, the condition and the sentiments of those who still could not make themselves understood or seen."[84]

There are two great spectacles in Tocqueville's history of eighteenth-century sentiments, and both are displayed in the details of administrative and economic life. The revolution in individual dispositions, or the "new spirit" of the French economy, was associated, for Tocqueville, with the new "public prosperity" of the second half of the eighteenth century. There was a transformation in "the spirit of those who are governed and those who govern." Individuals became "more industrious, more enterprising, more inventive." At the same time, public discontent was more bitter, people seemed more uncomfortable and more disquieted, and the "hatred against all old institutions" continued to grow.[85] But this new spirit was characteristic, eventually, of much of the rest of Europe as well. In Germany, Tocqueville wrote in his notes for *L'ancien régime et la Révolution*, and especially in "the most commercial cities of Germany, in Hamburg, in Lübeck, in Dantzig," the period of great prosperity which preceded the French Revolution was also one of a "strange social upheaval." There was a "vague agitation of the human mind"; a "universal idea of change which occurred to all minds without being sought out, and although nobody yet imagined how one might change."[86]

The other great spectacle—or Tocqueville's "first" French revolution of the 1760s and 1770s—was idiosyncratically French. It was a transformation in the rules and the habits of administrative life. It, too, was a transformation in economic relationships. It was influenced by what Tocqueville described as the "language of politics": the "dangerous language" of the reform edicts of Louis XVI, inspired by Turgot, with their references to the rights of man, the "perilous" words of the edict on the suppression of *jurandes*. It was also influenced, as has been seen, by the theories of the philosophers and economists of the times; of the sect of enlightenment.

The slow revolution in individual dispositions, with its "burning desire to become rich" and its "burning desire to change one's position," had prepared the human mind, in Tocqueville's description, for these dangerous and despotic doctrines.[87] The great drama of the late eighteenth century was indeed, for Tocqueville, a conflict over the meaning, and the consequences, of the new, universal disposition. The "desire of bettering our condition," which is also the desire of changing one's condition, was in Adam Smith's description "uniform, constant, and uninterrupted," or "universal, continual, and uninterrupted." It was a universal principle of the human mind, and the principle which inspires saving and enterprise.[88] But it was also, under certain circumstances, a principle of political upheaval. The Revolution was not caused by the prosperity of mid-eighteenth-century France, Tocqueville wrote, in a note on Dupont de Nemours's edition of Turgot's writings. But the "spirit which was to produce the Revolution" was also the inspiration of commercial prosperity: "This active, unquiet, intelligent, innovative, ambitious spirit, this democratic spirit of new societies, began to animate everything, and before overturning the society for a moment, was already sufficient to shake it, and to develop it."[89]

THE COLD LIGHT OF REASON AND THE WARMTH OF ECONOMIC LIFE

The landscape of late eighteenth-century economic thought is at times uncomfortably unfamiliar. Smith and Condorcet, Burke and Necker, are so like us, and also so unlike. They think and write about self-interest and competition, about institutions and corporations, about the "market" and the "state." But the words mean different things to them, and their connotation is of a different, and sometimes of an opposite, politics. Even the most imposing dichotomies of the post-Revolutionary world—of "cold," rational, and reflective calculation as opposed to "warm" and instinctive sentiment, and of the all-controlling, all-reforming state as opposed to the unintended and unimposed diversity of civil society—are virtually unrecognizable in the political economy of the 1770s and 1780s. It is as though the two sides in subsequent political philosophy lie strewn, like Burke's disbanded *moleculae*, across the entire landscape of the old Europe.[90]

The opposition between cold and warm thought was a commonplace of the popular philosophical opinion of the mid-eighteenth century. For Herder, on his journey of 1769 from Riga to Nantes, the spirit of France was to be found in its "cold language and mentality," its "cold reason," its "cold blood," its "politeness," and its "spirit of prosperity."[91] The new mentality of Europe was divided, in turn, into two principal varieties of cold philosophy. There was the coldness of calculation of interest: the "corpselike souls" of Helvétius's *De l'Esprit,* as Rousseau wrote in *Émile,* or the "secret egotism" of the man who "is already dead," and whose "frozen heart no longer palpitates with joy." But there was also the coldness of duty. Rousseau opposed the "great and powerful passion" of fanaticism, also in *Émile,* to the "reasoning and philosophical spirit," with its "philosophical indifference" which constitutes the "tranquillity of death."[92] Hamann speaks of the "indifferentism" of the *Critique of Pure Reason,* and says of Kant's man of enlightenment that he is the "man of death." The public use of reason in *What is Enlightenment?* was nothing more, for Hamann, than an aurora borealis or "northern light," "a cold and sterile moonlight" which provides no enlightenment for the "weak and indolent understanding," and no "warmth for the weak will."[93]

This conflict of political thermometers was transposed, in the period following the French Revolution, into a momentous struggle of faith and death. The perfume of enlightenment, in Hegel's description, is doubly cold. It divides itself into two unpleasant forms of consciousness, a "discrete, absolute hard rigidity and self-willed atomism" and a "simple, inflexible cold universality." On the one hand, that is to say, enlightenment leads to the cold "utility" of bourgeois society, in which the objective of individuals is the exchange of "money for butter and eggs," and "these persons as such have in their consciousness and as their aim not the absolute unity, but their own petty selves and particular interests." On the other hand, it leads to the Terror of the French Revolution: in Hegel's words, "the coldest and meanest of all deaths, with no more significance than cutting off a head of cabbage."[94]

Adam Smith, for the enemies of enlightenment, was the emblem of the first sort of consciousness, and Condorcet of the second. Louis-Gabriel-Ambroise de Bonald said of Condorcet's *Esquisse d'un tableau historique des progrès de l'esprit humain* that it helped him to understand the "inconceivable phenomenon" of the revolutionary state, in which men "coldly commanded their destructive hordes to the desolation and the death" of their fellow citizens; it was the "final *production*" of the destructive philosophy of the eighteenth century, or "the *Apocalypse* of this new *Gospel.*"[95] But Adam Smith was almost as frightful. The *Wealth of Nations,* Bonald wrote, was destructive of the entire "moral wealth" of society. It too was a source of desolation. War, plague, and famine cannot destroy the force of public society, Bonald said in his observations on Smith, but "a book is enough to overturn it." The effect of political economy is to distract the state from the "morality of society," which cannot be maintained without the "continual action of governments. The administration of things has thus led them to lose sight of the direction of men."[96]

Condorcet and Smith have been seen, ever since, as the precursors in two great diachronic processions, trudging across the nineteenth century toward the universal state, or toward the desolation of market relations. It is these processions, as will be seen, which are so difficult to recognize in the economic thought of the 1770s and 1780s. For economic life is itself, in Condorcet's and Smith's descriptions, a place of warm and discursive emotions. Smith sees self-interest, or self-love, as a characteristically warm (and confusing) sentiment; he speaks in the *Theory of Moral Sentiments* of the "fury of our own passions," or the "heat and keenness" in which "everything appears magnified and misrepresented by self-love." Like moral judgments, commercial judgments are a combination of reasons and sentiments.[97] Mercantile policy, in the *Wealth of Nations,* is, like the "corporation spirit," a matter of "jealousy" and "animosity," inflamed, from time to time, "with all the passionate confidence of interested falsehood." The projectors, or entrepreneurs of new ventures, are men of "imagination" and "passion" more than of "sober reason and experience," entranced by the "golden dreams" of mining, empire, and capital investment.[98]

Interference with the freedom to buy and to sell and to work is for Smith a form of political oppression. It is also, from time to time, intense and emotional. Freedom of commerce, in the *Wealth of Nations,* is an emancipation from personal, political, and sometimes physical oppression. The poor are oppressed by the laws of settlement; the French are oppressed by the *taille;* the Germans are oppressed by having to feed sovereigns' horses; small wine sellers are oppressed by licensing regulations; the tenants of great proprietors are oppressed by "factors and agents"; people who try to export sheep are oppressed by laws "written in blood"; apprentices are oppressed by corporations; clothiers are oppressed by the Hamburg Company; the Javans are oppressed by the Dutch East India Company; and almost everyone, including their own inferior servants, are oppressed by the East India Company in Bengal.[99]

Oppression is a relationship, in many of these instances, between one individual and another; it is an abuse of political power. It is connected to the petty and personal despotism which was a continuing obsession for Condorcet and Turgot, as well as for Smith, and which they described as a form of "vexation." Smith thus refers repeatedly, in the *Wealth of Nations,* to the "mortifying and vexatious visits of the tax-gatherers," to the "trouble or vexation" to be expected from the "custom-house officer." Vexation is the sort of oppression which flourishes in the circumstances of an uncertain jurisprudence, in which men use the power of their offices to pursue their personal grievances. It is the oppression in which one's oppressor knows one's name, and one's weaknesses, and where one lives. Customs officers are obliged "to be frequently very troublesome to some of their neighbours," Smith says. Their visits expose people "to much unnecessary trouble, vexation, and oppression; and though vexation is not, strictly speaking, expence, it is certainly equivalent to the expence at which every man would be willing to redeem himself from it."[100]

The personal and the commercial, the economic and the political, the rational (or calculable) and the emotional (or intuitive) are here intimately interrelated. The consequence of laws regulating interest and usury, Turgot wrote in 1770, is to expose individuals to odious and dangerous vexations. "The destiny of citizens is abandoned to an arbitrary and fluctuating jurisprudence, which changes with public opinion," he said in his "Mémoire sur les prêts d'argent"; he describes the "vertigo" and "terror," the "denunciations" and "vengeance," which were the consequence, in the small provincial town of Angoulême, of prosecutions for usury. People have become "heated," from one end of the town to the other, and officers of justice have themselves adopted "cette chaleur." It is essential, he told the authorities in Paris, to put an end to "a sort of vexation which is so odious, and which is even more dangerous to the extent that it covers itself in the appearance of zeal for the observation of the law."[101]

The regime of regulation, Condorcet wrote in his *Réflexions sur le commerce des blés* of 1776, is a society of "ruses and oppression," in which farmers become dependent on "the inspections, the prohibitions, the condemnations, the vexations" which are characteristic of city life. They have to study the ruses of "subaltern" officials, and to learn how to seduce them. They lose even the independence which is the greatest advantage of agricultural life: "Man prefers to depend on nature than on other men; he suffers less if he is ruined by a hailstorm than by an injustice; it is that which attaches him to agriculture." The reform of the fiscal regime of indirect taxation is itself, for Condorcet, a question of sentiments: "It would deliver the people from the vexations, the terrors under which they are groaning in the present regime; it would relieve them of the sentiment of oppression, a thousand times more painful than that of misery."[102]

SEEING THE STATE AS IN A PICTURE

Even the "state" and the "market," in these warm and discursive societies, are intricately interconnected. Late eighteenth-century economic thought is now so unfamiliar, in part, because of the subsequent transformation in political positions: in the politics of economic reform and also in the depiction of the state. It was the "left," in the period with which this book is concerned—the friends of enlightenment, the sympathizers of revolution—who were the most severe critics of the economic, political, and religious state. Thomas Paine, praising Smith and criticizing Burke, described "the greedy hand of Government thrusting itself into every corner and crevice of industry," and called for "lessening the burden of taxes," in particular through a plan for reducing taxation which would limit civilian government spending to less than 1 percent of national income.[103]

Condorcet's idyll of future progress, in the work described by Bonald as the apocalypse of the revolutionary gospel, was of an "indefinite freedom" of commerce and industry, in which people would be liberated, at last, from the "destructive scourge and the humiliating yoke" of "tyrannical fiscality."[104] The object of fiscal reform, for Condorcet in 1793, should be to establish direct and minimal taxation; to avoid the marginal disincentives of "progressive taxation," such that "it should not become useless, for an individual, to acquire a new piece of land, or to invest a new capital sum." The object of politics should be the "virtual nonexistence" (the "presque nullité") of the state; people need "laws and institutions which reduce to the smallest possible quantity the action of government."[105]

The "right," or the opponents of revolution, were the defenders of the state. "It is these obstructions, these fetters, these prohibitions which make the glory, the security, the immensity of the commerce of France," the advocate-general Séguier argued, against Turgot, in 1776.[106] For Burke, "the provision and distribution of the public wealth" were essential for the "prosperity and improvement of nations." A society which destroys the fabric of its state would soon be "disconnected into the dust and powder of individuality." It is the poor, above all, who would suffer most, for the state "nourishes the public hope. The poorest man finds his own importance and dignity in it." The "truly public" state should be looked on "with pious awe and trembling solicitude." But the fiscal state is itself an object of reverence. "The revenue of the state is the state . . . [F]rom hence not only magnanimity, and liberality, and beneficence, and fortitude, and providence, and the tutelary protection of all good arts, derive their food, and the growth of their organs."[107]

Revolutionary and imperial politics were associated, throughout Europe, with the reform and deregulation of economic policies. Coleridge described Napoleon as a follower of the *Économistes*, committed to the view that government should "preserve the freedom of all . . . Whatever a government does more of this, comes of evil: and its best employment is the *repeal* of laws and regulations, not the establishment of them."[108] In one of the comic set pieces of *War and Peace*, in the Moscow occupied by Napoleon's troops, the new French-supported municipal authorities proclaim that "markets have been organized in the city where peasants can bring their surplus produce," to be sold "with no hindrance," and "at prices agreed upon between seller and buyer."[109] "Adam Smith's cosmopolitan views and his concept of freedom could only bring happiness at the moment of greatest decline for all nationalities in Europe," the German "romantic" economist Adam Müller wrote in 1810. The ideal of those who conceived, like Smith, of the state as a "useful enterprise," Müller said, was of a nation of individuals, without reverence and without illusion: of the state as a *wilde Ehe*, a "wild marriage."[110]

The political rhetoric of economic reform is virtually the opposite, here, of the rhetoric of subsequent politics. So too are the political friendships. The coalition of laissez-faire economic policy and political conservatism is in particular, as will be seen, the outcome of post-Revolutionary and post-Napoleonic politics. Napoleon himself studied the *Wealth of Nations* in St. Helena, and the protected monopolies of the "old systems" (such as the East India companies); his conclusion, as reported by Las Cases, was that free commerce "agitated all imaginations, shook an entire people; it was entirely identical with equality, led naturally to independence, and, in this respect, had much more to do with our modern system . . . I pronounced in favor of free commerce, and rejected the companies."[111]

The politics of late eighteenth-century economic thought is unfamiliar in a more profound sense as well. For the "state" and the "market" were not yet understood as the two imposing and competing dominions of society, and they were indeed interdependent. Markets were established by states, or imposed by them upon recalcitrant traders. States were great rambling societies, which include the governments of parishes, guilds, incorporations, and established churches. Even the words in which the two dominions were described are now unfamiliar, changing from abstract to concrete, and from concrete to abstract. A market is thus an order of which the "principles" can be "subverted," as Burke wrote; it is also a collection of physical structures, at a particular time and with particular rules.[112] Burke describes the state, in the *Reflections,* as "a partnership in all science; a partnership in all art; a partnership in every virtue, and in all perfection"; he also says, of the "mere country curates" in the National Assembly, that they were "men who never had seen the state so much as in a picture."[113]

Condorcet described the ideal of economic relations, in 1775, as a setting in which "the avarice of buyers and the avidity of sellers counterbalance each other, without anyone interfering."[114] But markets were at the same time an obstruction imposed by oppressive and prohibitive legislation. Colbert's code for transactions in salt in Brittany is an example, in Condorcet's description: the sale of salt was to be permitted only, subject to five years' hard labor, "in the market hall, on the days and at the hours of the market, and to people domiciled in the province."[115] Turgot distinguished between markets, which developed out of reciprocal interest, and the "fairs," which were organizations of privilege and regulation; some governments, however, went so far as to "use the intervention of the police to establish markets."[116] One of Turgot's edicts of 1776 abolished the obligation on merchants who brought grain into Paris to sell it "before the third market" (with the "interval between three markets being only 11 days").[117] There is sometimes as much as "five to six leagues from one market to the next," Condorcet said, against Necker's defense of the obligation that merchants should sell only in markets. When Necker promised that the law would not be used against small, local transactions, he was promising no more than an "arbitrary tolerance," in which officials could choose to "close their eyes, or to ensure the execution of the law, according to their interest or their whim."[118]

In the Prussia of the *Régie* established by Frederick the Great with the help of Helvétius, and in which Hamann was an inspector of excise duties, the towns where market transactions took place were "islands of protective tariffs, in a sea of rural free trade."[119] Towns were where people met to buy and sell in markets, but also, Condorcet said, to become dupes of "ruses and oppression." Even in England, or at least in the incorporated towns which Smith so disliked, towns were the locus of buying and selling, of industry, and above all of regulation. They were places of rhetoric and of the exchange of information; for Turgot, the formation of prices was the consequence of a debate between buyers and sellers. But the conversation turned inevitably, in market towns, to rules and to taxes. Officials lived side by side with merchants; and they were sometimes the same people as the merchants: "the government of towns corporate was altogether in the hands of traders and artificers," Smith wrote (and compared Norwich and Sheffield, both corporate towns, most unfavorably with Manchester, Birmingham, and Wolverhampton).[120]

The idea of a purely political government is as elusive, here, as the idea of a purely economic market. The "constitution of the state," for Smith, is composed of the government of the church, of local and municipal councils, of the kingdom, of parishes, and of guilds and corporations.[121] The British state, in the *Wealth of Nations,* is also Namier's state: it incorporates "the contracts, the jobs, the subscriptions, the loans, the remittances &c., &c." described by the amanuensis of Lord Bath in 1761.[122] Its policies are directed, Smith said, "by the clamorous importunity of partial interests." Of Smith's great diatribes in the *Wealth of Nations,* only one is concerned with what would later have been understood as a principally economic activity of national government. This is his criticism of the restrictions on imports and bounties on exports imposed by partial legislatures, intimidated as they often are by an "overgrown standing army" of interested monopolists.[123] His other principal objections are to the policies of parish councils and churchwardens (the laws of settlement restricting the freedom of movement of the poor); of corporations and guilds (apprenticeship regulations); of incorporated trading companies (the East India Company); and of religious incorporations.

"Church and state are ideas inseparable in their minds," Burke said of the people of England in the *Reflections,* and they consider the church as "the foundation of their whole constitution."[124] For Smith, too, "ecclesiastical government" is part of the constitution of the state, and it is indeed the subject of some of his most devastating criticism. He uses the language of economic obstruction in describing official religions: "The clergy of every established church constitute a great incorporation. They can act in concert, and pursue their interest upon one plan and with one spirit." His own proposal is for the competition of "two or three hundred, or perhaps . . . as many thousand small sects," as had been favored in England toward the end of the Civil War; a "plan of ecclesiastical government, or more properly of no ecclesiastical government."[125]

The interdependence of commerce and government, in this setting of regulated markets and interested officials, is at the heart of Smith's theory of economic reform, as it was for Turgot and for Condorcet. Manufacturers are churchwardens and aldermen and the counsellors of legislators, as well as people who buy wool and sell coats; "whenever the legislature attempts to regulate the differences between masters and their workmen, its counsellors are always the masters," Smith says.[126] Condorcet made an effort, both in the *Réflexions sur le commerce des blés* and in his *Vie de M. Turgot,* to distinguish between true and political entrepreneurs: between "true merchants" and "accredited" traders, who pursue their own interests by conniving in government regulations, thereby avoiding "the competition of traders who are not rich enough to have patrons."[127] But the choice for the merchant, in general, was between different, more or less regulated markets, and between different, more or less "political" strategies for pursuing his interests. Even his interests were political as well as economic, and political influence was itself a form of consumption. As Condorcet wrote, arguing against the taxes on luxury consumption which Smith supported, "Instead of buying horses, people will buy hangers-on and positions; for expenditures on taste . . . they will substitute expenditures on intrigue."[128]

The idea of vexation, which was of such central importance to Smith's, Turgot's, and Condorcet's descriptions of the sentiments of economic life, is similarly important to their theories of the state and of political oppression. Vexation is indeed a particular, personal form of the abuse of power, characteristic of the enforcement of commercial and fiscal rules. There are other (and worse) abuses: when Smith says of religious incorporations that they use the fear of eternal misery, or all the terrors of religion, to protect their own interest, then he is talking about the abuse of spiritual power; when Condorcet speaks of the "inequality of rights" within families—an inequality, in his words, "between the two sexes"—then he is talking, as he explains, about the "abuse of force."[129] But the particular circumstances of vexation arise because of the interrelatedness of political and economic life, of the dominions of government and of commerce. Economic life is not a distinct universe, a "side" of life. People have the same personalities, or the same sentiments, in their economic lives (their lives as merchants or customs officers) as in the rest of their lives. They bring their fears and their enmities with them, from one side of their social relationships to the next.

The most oppressive of all institutions, for Smith and Turgot, are the incorporations and communities of civil society. The mastership and apprenticeship guilds were considered to be little hells of vexation. They provided a propitious setting for the abuse of personal power; they were private associations, protected by the inexact and arbitrary force of public law. Turgot's edict for the suppression of the mastership guilds, in 1776, described the regulations of the guilds "as bizarre, tyrannical, and contrary to humanity and morality." For the advocate-general Séguier, as for Burke in 1790, the effect of reform would be to undermine (rather than to "repair") the "ancient foundations of the state," or the "very edifice of the political constitution." The communities were like "little republics" within the state, Séguier said, in which each worked for the good of all, and without which no artisan would be more than "an isolated being."[130] But it is just this power, of a republic within the republic, that was for Smith so insidious. The apprenticeship guilds, in Smith's description, were enclosed worlds of oppression, whose bylaws were supported by the "public law of the kingdom."[131] They were places of fluctuating jurisprudence and unpredictably enforced laws. The institutions which flourished in the common dominions of states and markets, that is to say, were no more free, and no more enlightened, than the institutions of the political "edifice" itself.

INDULGENCE AND INDIFFERENCE

The distinction between the enemies and the enthusiasts of enlightenment is itself unfamiliar, in these disorderly times. It is different and less constant than it came to seem in the post-Revolutionary world. The sense of the enlightenment as a society or sect was conspicuous, as has been seen, in the polemics of the 1790s. It is also at the heart of one of the most profound charges against enlightenment thought. The philosophers and the economists were telling a great lie, in the view of their critics, when they said that they were concerned with the dispositions, or the spirit, of millions of men and women. They were in truth concerned with no more than their own dispositions, and their own schemes. They wanted a people who would obey their own, tutelary authority. They were a sect, and they pretended to be the theorists of a new world of public understanding.

This is the charge, at its most coruscating, of duplicity in the sight of eternity: Lamennais's charge, against Voltaire, of a double indifference, in which religion is an amusement for men of letters, and necessary only for the people.[132] It is Tocqueville's charge, against the *Économistes*, against Quesnay and Letrosne and Mercier, of wishing to reconstruct the spirit of individuals to fit their own "model" of "essential order," or their own "imaginary society." The role of the state, for the *Économistes*, was in Tocqueville's description "not only to command the nation, but to shape it in a certain way"; to "form the spirit of the citizens," to imbue them with the "ideas" and "sentiments" which the state itself deems necessary: "It does not simply reform men, it transforms them."[133]

One crime of the enlightenment, in the view of its early critics, was to have led other people into sin, in a frivolous, sometimes demonic unconcern with the consequences of one's own policies. "I sent some books to my binder, among others the *Système de la Nature*," Madame La Baronne writes at the outset of the abbé Barruel's anti-philosophical novel *Les Helviennes*, published shortly before the Revolution. The binder's apprentice "spent the night leafing through these books, and took some liberties with his master's daughter," to whom he said confidently "that there was no hell, and he had just read it in one of Madame La Baronne's books."[134] The advocate-general Séguier, in his oration in defense of the *jurandes*, imagined that Paris would be overwhelmed by a crowd of apprentices "escaped from the workshops," in whom the "spirit of subordination will be lost." Of Turgot's (and Louis XVI's) description of guild regulations as bizarre and contrary to morality, he said that he could not repeat it without "a sort of trembling."[135]

The crime of wishing to reconstruct the minds of other men was in a different version more sinister. For it was to make a religion out of irreligion. A subset of the "sect of philosophers" were in Lamennais's description "apostles of impiety." Voltaire was for them "the priest of reason"; they were willing, in their "blind fanaticism," to sacrifice entire societies to their principles.[136] This was the quasi-religious spirit of the *Économistes* or Physiocrats, for Tocqueville, and the spirit of Jacobin principles. It was the spirit of Robespierre's religion of the Supreme Being, and of the revolutionary project (Talleyrand's project, in his revolutionary period) of a public education which would "imprint, for ever, new sentiments, new morals, new habits."[137] But the crime of moral despotism was also one with which several of the philosophers of the 1770s and 1780s—of the generation younger than Quesnay and Mercier—were themselves preoccupied. Condorcet said of Voltaire, in words that were more appropriate to his own changing view of knowledge, that he became truly enlightened only when he visited England: he saw that "truth is not made to remain a secret in the hands of a few philosophers, and of a small number of men of the world instructed, or rather indoctrinated by the philosophers; laughing with them at the errors of which the people are the victim."[138]

The system of unsecret truth is opposed, here, to the "laws of order" of the *Économistes* or Physiocrats. Turgot described the reproach, against the *Économistes*, of adopting the "tone of a sect" as "just, and too just": "Oh! spirit of sect!" He objected vigorously, in 1770, to Dupont de Nemours's efforts to turn him, by editorial emendation, into an Economist. He would never, he wrote, refer to "the laws of order"; his own principle was of "the rights of humanity," and he considered that the Economists' concept of "tutelary authority" was a "dishonor" to their doctrine, in that "men do not need tutors. When they are reasonable, they know how to understand one another."[139] Hume described the *Économistes,* in 1769, as "the set of men the most chimerical and most arrogant that now exist," and urged Morellet, in his projected *Dictionnaire du Commerce,* to "thunder them, and crush them, and pound them."[140] Smith said of Quesnay and his "sect" that their "exact regimen of perfect liberty and perfect justice" disregards the diversity of individual lives. Of their view of taxes on land, he said that he prefers to review it "without entering into the disagreeable discussion of the metaphysical arguments by which they support their very ingenious theory."[141] Condorcet said that the "generality of their maxims, the inflexibility of their principles," was such that they seemed "to forget the interests of political freedom for those of freedom of commerce." To impose the ideas and the sentiments of the legislator in a system of public education, Condorcet wrote, is "a true tyranny."[142]

The mid-eighteenth-century prospect of moral or psychological modernization—of compulsory enlightenment—was a version of a much older enterprise. "It is necessary to change the taste and the customs of an entire nation," Mentor (or Minerva) says in Fénelon's *Aventures de Télémaque* of 1699, of which more than two hundred editions were published in the course of the eighteenth century; the people of Ithaca might then be like the people of Tyre, "industrious, patient, hardworking, clean, sober, and cautious; they have an exact system of regulations; they are in perfect agreement with one another; no people has ever been more constant, more sincere, more faithful, more secure."[143] The psychological reform of Phoenician cities was indeed a model of commercial policy for much of the eighteenth century. The emperor Peter sought to suppress willfulness in the Russian people, and to transform "harm into benefit, laziness into diligence."[144] The empress Catherine, advised by Voltaire, wished to "exterminate laziness in the inhabitants," and to be rid of "supineness and negligence" and "disregard for everything."[145] The "business of a statesman," for Sir James Steuart, was "to model the minds of his subjects," or to model "the spirit, manners, habits, and customs of the people." "By properly conducting and managing the spirit of a people, nothing is impossible," Steuart said, although he conceded that "it requires a particular talent in a statesman to dispose the minds of a people."[146]

The minds of the people, in the political economy with which this book is mostly concerned, were far more resilient. "Man is generally considered by statesmen and projectors as the materials of a sort of political mechanics," Smith wrote in a manuscript of 1755, quoted by Dugald Stewart; his own preference, rather, was for no more than "fair play."[147] "Sovereigns must take mankind as they find them, and cannot pretend to introduce any violent change in their principles and ways of thinking," Hume wrote in his essay "Of Commerce." There is a psychological laissez-faire, that is to say, which is the complement to laissez-faire in commerce. There is a freedom of the soul, which is the complement to economic freedom. Commercial life is itself a disorderly, discursive, uncertain business, in Hume's description; and when someone "forms schemes in politics, trade, economy, or any business in life, he never ought to draw his arguments too fine, or connect too long a chain of consequences together. Something is sure to happen, that will disconcert his reasoning, and produce an event different from what he expected."[148] This was Smith's view of commerce (and politics) as well, and it was also Condorcet's, by the end of his life.

The enlightened disposition, for Smith, which is also the disposition of commercial life, is a universal condition of all individuals. It can be obstructed (by prejudice, or fear, or the mutilation of ignorance). It can be set free. But it is not something in which people can be instructed, or conducted, or with which they can be imbued. Smith's view of economic sentiments is very different, in this respect, from Steuart's, or from Montesquieu's, including in the theories of the "political" justification for commerce which are the subject of Albert Hirschman's study *The Passions and the Interests*.[149] For the view of individuals' passions as something to be "tamed," or "harnessed," is the view of the sovereign. Smith's point of view, like Condorcet's, is in general the view of the individuals themselves, or of the unheroic heroes of commerce.[150] They were concerned, like earlier writers on commercial policy, to provide advice to sovereigns (and to legislatures). But they are unrelentingly skeptical with respect to the wisdom of these sovereigns and statesmen. Their advice, again and again, is that sovereigns should try to see the world from the point of view of their subjects; that they should be willing, unlike Colbert, in Smith's description, to allow "every man to pursue his own interest his own way, upon the liberal plan of equality, liberty and justice."[151] The greatest folly of the statesman, for Condorcet, is to think of societies as an "undivided whole"; to seek, like Colbert in Necker's "Éloge de Colbert," to "envelope them in one's thought."[152]

There is no certainty in such a view of the world; there is only the consonance, or the conflict, of individual lives. Lamennais indeed identified Condorcet's view of society with yet another, and in some respects even more frightening version of the crime of enlightenment. This was the crime of a "dogmatic indifference" to religion. Condorcet understood, Lamennais wrote, that religion could not persist if it were reserved for the people alone. Society would then be abandoned to a morality without foundation, and to a universe without certainty. The human spirit, as in the later Roman Empire, under the influence of Epicurus, would be "deprived of its beliefs and even of its opinions, it would swim, at the mercy of chance, in an immense ocean of uncertainties and of doubts." The universe would be one in which the individual was endowed with "absolute sovereignty over himself"; a "horrible anarchy of contrary wills and opposed interests, of unequal forces and unequal desires," an "orgy of doctrines, [a] confused shock of all the interests and all the passions."[153] This was indeed the condition of France in the 1760s, Lamennais wrote, under the influence of a modern philosophy, a "monstrous chaos of incoherent ideas," which "imagines that one can do everything with money"; a condition in which all relations between persons were inverted, in which women pronounced solemn dissertations about science and military men embroidered, in which the old were silent and children insolent.[154]

The economic writings with which this book is concerned are a description, above all, of opposed interests and unequal desires. They express an extraordinary tolerance for uncertainty, and for doubt. Condorcet's view of enlightenment, like Smith's, was close to the Epicurean prospect, as described by Lucretius, in which men and women no longer tremble like children in the dark, and the "terror of the mind" is dispelled by understanding; or as described by Lucian, in which men are freed "from terrors and apparitions and portents, from vain hopes and extravagant cravings."[155] But they also believed that the process of understanding is slow, uncertain, and subject to error, chance, and the likelihood of being disconcerted. One source of uncertainty is that individuals will not understand their own interests very well; or that they will understand their own "local situation" so well that they will choose to pursue their interests by the "ruses of fear," or by political intrigues. A different source of uncertainty is the one which Lamennais found so fearsome; it is that the new, enlightened society will be without foundation, and without providence. There is an even more disturbing prospect; it is that a life of uncertainty will itself, eventually, be a source of strength, or of virtue. The challenge of laissez-faire—that is to say, of psychological laissez-faire, as well as of laissez-faire in the relations of commerce—is to live without certainty, including certainty about the truth of one's own dogmas.

"I do not believe that morality in itself can ever be local," Turgot wrote to Condorcet in 1773, against the philosophical system of Helvétius, in which morality is founded on interest. But "the judgment to be made on the actions of individuals is a much more complicated problem":

> I am, in matters of morality, a great enemy of indifference and a great proponent of indulgence . . . It is, I think, because of not distinguishing adequately between these two points of view about ways of judging the morality of actions, which are so different, that some have given way to an excessive rigorousness, in judging individual actions on the basis of general ideas of morality, without regard to the circumstances which excuse the individual; and that others regard all actions as indifferent, and see in them no more than physical facts, because there is very little that cannot be excused in some given circumstance.[156]

This morality of indulgence, or of respect for principles and of respect, too, for the circumstances of individuals, is also the morality of a certain kind of enlightenment. Condorcet was opposed, throughout his life, to the enemies of universal enlightenment; to Necker, who wrote in 1775, in his *Sur la législation et le commerce des grains*, that the people were like children, who act "without reflecting, but enlightened by their instinct, commanded by their needs"; that they were a "blind and wild multitude," who "will be the same for all time."[157] But he was even more powerfully opposed, late in his life, to the enthusiasts of enlightenment and of reason; to the "supposed philosophers" who were as certain of their own "political truths" as "the fanatics of all sects," and who sought to impose political commitment as a "blind sentiment," by "all the follies of enthusiasm, all the ruses of proselytism." To teach even a free constitution as "a doctrine which conforms to the principles of universal reason, or to excite in its favor a blind enthusiasm which makes citizens incapable of judging it," would be "to violate freedom in its most sacred rights, under the pretext of teaching how to cherish it."[158]

THE LIGHT OF HISTORY

This is a book about history; about how people once thought. Its objective is to cast light on eighteenth-century economic thought (by looking at it in the setting of disputes over enlightenment), and on the enlightenment (by looking at economic disputes). To see the controversies over the *jurandes* and over the commerce in suet, over bounties and excise duties, as being of intense and political interest—to see them as they seemed to people at the time—is to have a richer insight, I hope, into the circumstances of an earlier and different world. Economic history has been at a distance, for some time, from the history of economic thought, and from political history. In the disputes with which I am concerned, the emancipation of the mind, and of political and legal institutions, was by contrast at the heart of economic improvement. Economic reform and political reform, the economic thought of philosophers and the economic thoughts of flower sellers, were thought to be closely intertwined; it is these circumstances which I hope to describe.

I am less concerned, in general, with what Tocqueville, writing of the Revolution of 1848 in France, described as "this false light [*cette lueur trompeuse*] that the history of past facts casts on the present."[159] But the events with which I am concerned have been the subject, to a disconcerting extent, of a sort of diachronic *son et lumière,* in which the past illuminates the present, and the present illuminates the past. Woodrow Wilson wrote of Adam Smith, in 1893, that his "philosophy has entered everywhere into the life of politics and become a world force in thought."[160] Tocqueville himself said, of Quesnay and Morelly, that "of all the men of their times, it is the Economists who seem the least out of place in ours." The *Économistes* and the socialists of the nineteenth century were close relations, in Tocqueville's description: "They have a false air of contemporaries . . . [W]hen I look through the books of the Economists, it seems to me that I have lived with these people, and that I have just been debating with them."[161]

The history of economic thought has been characterized, for most of the nineteenth and twentieth centuries, by a continuing preoccupation with present times. Like the history of education, in Bernard Bailyn's description, the history of economic thought has been written by professionals within the discipline itself, "impelled to search the past for the seeds, the antecedents, of the present."[162] It is a story of influential men and influential doctrines; a *Dogmengeschichte.* It is uninterested in the intentions and errors and distractions of the past. Like the history of chemistry, to which Jean-Baptiste Say compared the history of economic science, it is a history which should become shorter as science itself progresses. For "what could we gain by collecting absurd opinions," Say asked, or "doctrines which have been discredited and which deserve to be so?"[163]

The history of the enlightenment, too, has often been a search, of a far more imposing sort, for the seeds of present discontents. The French Revolution, Jacques Necker wrote in 1796, could be seen as something like the Flood, a consequence of the "monstrous union of philosophical ideas with the most violent passions, a union which seems to recall the criminal pact of which the Bible tells us, the marriage of angels with the daughters of men." It was "the political system of the philosophers of France," with its "ideal abstractions" and its "diverse metaphysical principles," which had "the effect, in our times, of shaking the world."[164] The principles of the sect of enlightenment have been seen, ever since, as the antecedents, or precursors, of modern times. The philosophers are conspirators in turbulent change (as in the anti-Jacobin prosopography of the 1790s). They are the inspiration of continuing turmoil (as they were for Necker). They are, at the very least, "world forces in thought." Rabelais, Lucien Febvre wrote in his study of sixteenth-century religious disbelief, has been seen as the "first in a linear series, at the end of which we place the 'free thinkers' of the twentieth century": "'That Rabelais! A free thinker, and so early on!'"[165] The diachronic procession which begins with Condorcet, or the linear series of cold, universalistic reason, comes to an end, in much the same way, in the socialist calculation of the twentieth century. Smith's lineage is supposed to end in the cold and unforgiving competition, the one-sided calculation of self-interest, of the twenty-first-century world economy.

I hope, in what follows, to avoid at least some of this processionalism. Like Keith Baker, I will try to see Condorcet in the context of "the Enlightenment he knew," or of "the philosophes as they lived and thought"; like Donald Winch, I will try to imagine "what it would be conceivable for Smith" to have conceived, or to have thought.[166] I will try, in particular, to convey Condorcet's and Smith's own sense of the past (of their own past, or of an earlier history). I said earlier, of the landscape of late eighteenth-century economic thought—its states and markets and corporations, its cold and warm dispositions—that it is uncomfortably unfamiliar. It is unfamiliar, in part, because of the persistence in eighteenth-century economic life of regulations and customs which were even then archaic. Smith describes the Elizabethan laws, still unrepealed, under which the export of "sheep, lambs or rams" was punishable by mutilation and death ("Like the laws of Draco, these laws may be said to be all written in blood"); the Hanoverian legislation which prescribed imprisonment and loss of all property for "artificers" practicing their trade in foreign countries; the Elizabethan statute of apprenticeship.[167] Condorcet describes the penalties of death and deportation to the galleys imposed under the French regulation of salt (of which Smith says that "those who consider the blood of the people as nothing in comparison with the revenue of the prince, may perhaps approve of this method of levying taxes").[168]

Turgot's *Lit de Justice* of March 1776, so renowned across Europe, was a dazzling illustration of the intermingling of the present and the past. It was a ceremony of the reform of ceremonies. Louis XVI was seated, for the occasion, on a "carpet of violet velvet, sprinkled with gold fleur-de-lys," surrounded by ecclesiastical and secular peers, counsellors in "black satin," a legal adviser "in his red robe with his stole," three aides "each having before him a desk covered in violet taffeta." The reform edicts—one, on the *corvées*, is concerned with the "vexations" of a tax in whose administration "distributive justice loses itself in a multitude of details," and another, on the *jurandes*, seeks to abolish the obscure codes by which the guilds and corporations impose "frequent rights of visitation" and "expenses for ceremonies, holidays, assemblies, procedures," whose effect is to force the poorest members to submit to the law of the rich—are sealed "with the great seal of green wax, on a background of red and green silk." Turgot's opponent, the president Miromesnil, is "dressed in a robe of violet velvet, lined with crimson satin." But the mood is described, by Miromesnil, as grim: "Today, a gloomy sadness presents itself everywhere to Your Majesty's august regard."[169]

The philosophical universe of late eighteenth-century economic thought, too, is turned toward the past. It was profoundly influenced by older Christian philosophy, in a way that is now quite unfamiliar. Smith, Turgot, and Condorcet were immersed, from their earliest schooling, in Latin and Hellenistic writings. Their references, like those of Rabelais, were to Tertullian and Lactantius, to Lucian and Cicero. Church power was ubiquitous, still, in the events of life and death; Smith's only notoriety, in his lifetime, was over his description of Hume's tranquil and un-Christian death, and it was Condorcet's role in the circumstances of d'Alembert's un-Christian death which convinced Barruel that he was indeed a demon in human form.[170]

Ecclesiastical power was ubiquitous in economic life as well, from the administration of the English poor laws to the jurisdiction of the parliament of Paris. The merchant contemplating lending money in France was surrounded by the distinctions described in the *Dictionnaire des cas de conscience* of the theologians Lamet and Fromageau: usury is "real and mental," "express" and "palliated," "active and passive," "*lucratoriae, punitoriae,* and *compensatoriae.*"[171] One of Smith's great diatribes, in the

Wealth of Nations, is directed against the English laws of settlement, whereby the "independent workman" is subject to removal "at the caprice of any churchwarden or overseer"; the duties of churchwardens, according to Richard Burn's *Justice of the Peace,* which was Smith's principal source, included levying penalties for "selling corn by a wrong measure," "eating flesh on fish days," "exercising their worldly calling on the lord's day," and "not coming to church."[172] Turgot's interlocutors, in his memoir on free competition in lending at interest, were the legal experts "who have taken so much effort to obscure simple notions of good sense," led down this "false road" by "scholastic theologians," and the "rigorist theologians" who have read five words of Saint Luke ("mutuum date nihil inde sperantes") "with the prejudices they derive from a false metaphysics."[173]

The conceptual and scientific world of eighteenth-century political thought is itself often unfamiliar; particularly unfamiliar, in fact, in relation to the "science" of dispositions and sentiments. Smith himself uses a dizzying sequence of nouns to denote psychological conditions; he refers in the first few lines of the *Theory of Moral Sentiments* to emotions, sentiments, senses, sensations, and faculties, and to both the principles and the passions of human nature.[174] He says later, of the controversy between Hobbes and the theologian Ralph Cudworth over reason and sentiment, that it unfolded "at a time when the abstract science of human nature was but in its infancy, and before the distinct offices and powers of the different faculties of the human mind had been carefully examined and distinguished from one another."[175] But this science of the mind is scarcely more familiar now than Cicero's, or than that of the author of a slightly earlier *Théorie des Sentimens Agréables,* Levesque de Pouilly, who set out to describe "the laws of sentiment" with the help of a "microscope of the spirit."[176]

The idea of a history of sentiments—a Tacitean or inner history, in Smith's description, or Condorcet's history, of opinions and prejudices, well-being and institutions, economic theories and the enforcement of laws—is also unfamiliar.[177] For François Guizot, in 1828, the great crises of civilization were "always crises of individual or social development, facts which have changed the interior man, his beliefs, his morality, or his exterior condition, his situation in his relations with those around him." The historian must choose, Guizot said, between "describing the vicissitudes of the ideas, of the sentiments of the individual being," and describing "exterior facts, events, changes in the social condition."[178] Like Guizot himself, subsequent historians have chosen, mostly, to describe the exterior events of life. The history of economic relationships has come to be seen, in particular, as a matter of quantities and commodities, of canals and paper money and the bullion committee. Economic thoughts (the thoughts of economic theorists, and of public officials, and of individuals in their economic lives) have come to be seen as something less than events.

Our sense of the familiarity of eighteenth-century thought is an illusion, above all, because of our own unequal knowledge. This asymmetry of information is one of the most troublesome difficulties of the political and intellectual historian: that he or she knows how the story ends, or the outcome of the events in which her subjects are engaged, and to which they look forward in fear or hope or indifference.[179] The difficulty is particularly intense in relation to a period, such as the half century before and after 1800, which was, and which seemed at the time to be, one of intense and violent change. Is the historian to read Louis XVI's words of 1776 and to say to herself that she knows nothing of his subsequent destiny? Is she to presume that Goethe's memory of the unsuccessful economic reforms of the 1770s, as he looks back a generation later, is uninfluenced by his knowledge of subsequent events? Is she to feel no frisson when Dupont de Nemours writes to Adam Smith in June 1788, of the disputes over the Anglo-French Commercial Treaty and over Turgot's suppression of the *corvées,* that "these storms are not as harmful as they seem," that "we are moving rapidly towards a good constitution," and that "you have done much to hasten this useful revolution"?[180]

The course of legal and economic reform was itself a matter of the greatest uncertainty. Smith and Condorcet died during a period of economic as well as political revolution; like the bankers Turgot described in Angoulême in 1769, who were suddenly prosecuted under old, somnolent statutes against lending at interest, they did not know what would happen to the incipient industrial and commercial revolution of the eighteenth century. They did not know whether the apprenticeship guilds would be reformed, or abolished, or revived. They did not know whether the doctors of the Sorbonne, or the parliaments of Paris and Toulouse would take hold once more of economic regulation. They did not know what would happen to the new dispositions of the human mind: whether the "next epoch" would not, against Condorcet's own expectation, bring "one of these oscillations which must return it to barbarism, to ignorance, to slavery."[181]

Smith and Hume, Turgot and Condorcet did not know, disconcertingly, what would happen to their own principles. They were used enough to editorial obstruction in their lifetime, and to the oddness of the public. "You have caused me real pain," Turgot wrote to Dupont de Nemours in 1770, of Dupont's editorial changes to the text of his *Réflexions sur les richesses*, "above all by adding things which are neither in my tone, nor in my way of thinking . . . I absolutely demand that in future you conform to my manuscript."[182] Smith's works, like Hume's *Dialogues concerning Natural Religion*, in Hume's own description, were written most "cautiously" and "artfully." But Smith, too, found that the destiny of his writings was not as he had expected. "I am afraid I am not only your best, but almost your only customer" for the revised edition of the *Wealth of Nations*, he wrote to his publisher in 1780. The *Wealth of Nations*, he wrote in the same year, had attracted less public criticism than his short description of Hume's death: "A single, and as, I thought a very harmless Sheet of paper . . . brought upon me ten times more abuse than the very violent attack I had made upon the whole commercial system of Great Britain."[183]

Within a few years of Smith's death, his writings, and their reception, had been transformed far more profoundly. William Playfair's eleventh edition of the *Wealth of Nations*, published by Smith's own publishers in 1805, and of which the *Edinburgh Review* wrote that "in the whole course of our literary inquisition, we have not met with an instance so discreditable to the English press," is only an extreme example; it was augmented by six "supplementary chapters" (printed "in the same types," the *Edinburgh Review* pointed out) and several hundred carping footnotes, many of them along the lines of: "In this particular assertion, Mr. Smith is certainly entirely wrong."[184]

"What is money? . . . What is a book?" Kant asked in one of his last and oddest works on the metaphysics of morals, and his answer, invoking Smith, was that both books and money were the universal instruments of exchange: the exchange of thoughts, in the case of books. A writing, Kant says, is a "discourse addressed in a particular form to the public"; it is "not an immediate direct presentation of a conception," unlike a bust or a cast by a sculptor, and its misappropriation is an affront to the "personal right" of the author.[185] Smith's own conceptions, like Condorcet's, or like Kant's, have been appropriated, and misappropriated, in the universal exchange of subsequent thought.

Our unequal knowledge is disconcerting, above all, with respect to the history of the human spirit. The period with which I am concerned was one of intense, self-conscious interest in the vicissitudes of sentiments and opinions. This is what individuals remembered of the period, when they looked back, or what they imagined when they tried to reconstruct the lives of their fathers and grandfathers; when they tried to make sense out of or explain the events of their own, tumultuous times. "The Revolution was in the minds of the people, and this was effected, from 1760 to 1775, in the course of fifteen years before a drop of blood was drawn at Lexington," John Adams wrote to Thomas Jefferson in 1815, in a comment on the recent histories of the American Revolution; it was a change, he wrote later, in the "principles, opinions, sentiments, and affections of the people."[186] Tocqueville, in his notes for *L'ancien régime et la Révolution,* described the "ten to fifteen years which preceded the French Revolution" as a time in which "an inner movement, without any motor, seemed all at once to disturb the entire public life of societies, and to displace the ideas and the habits of all men." His own historical enterprise, in the words of his correspondent Harriet Grote, was to explain "how feelings, sentiments, prejudices and passions work their way into common action."[187]

The sense of a continuing change in opinions was omnipresent to observers at the time as well. It is what the opponents of economic reform anticipated, as a consequence of the abolition of established regulations; Séguier's prospect in the 1770s, and Necker's, of an enfranchisement of dangerous principles. Even Smith, for whom the progress of the human mind was a slow, uneven emancipation of universal dispositions, was meticulous in identifying events in time; the *"present state of things,"* he wrote in his advertisement to the third edition of the *Wealth of Nations,* refers to "the year 1783 and the beginning of the present year 1784."[188] But this sense of incipient and continuing uncertainty is itself, for the historian, an elusive condition. For the preoccupation of individuals in the late eighteenth century with changes in sentiments was also, to some extent, a consequence of their own sense that they lived in times which were not in fact disorderly. "We are for sentiment in the same way that the avaricious are for wealth," Condorcet wrote to Amélie Suard, in 1771, from the "small provincial town" in which he was spending a quiet summer with his mother.[189] Smith imagines Tacitus determining on his "plan" of a history of sentiments and motives, because it would be suited to the preferences of the Romans in the tranquil and secure times of the emperor Trajan; "sentiment must be what will chiefly interest such a people."[190]

The philosophers of economic reform of the 1770s and 1780s with whom I am concerned were interested, for several different reasons, in the prospect of uncertainty. They were obliged, by their political opponents, to think about the insecurity of a world with very much less government restriction. They were subject, in their own lives, to continuing uncertainty, from the possibility of sudden imprisonment (the arbitrary justice of the ancien régime in France) to the fluctuating jurisprudence of excise duties on imported commodities.[191] They lived, above all, in a world of religious and moral and metaphysical uncertainty; a fatherless world. But they did not know, as we know now, that they were also living in a world which was about to come to an end, in an epoch of insecurity, and of revolutionary transformation in sentiments and opinions, beyond their own most fearful expectations. It is this insouciance, this confidence in an uncertain future, which is now so difficult to imagine.

THE ENLIGHTENMENT AND THE PRESENT

"It is impossible to understand the past without orienting oneself to the present," Marc Bloch wrote in *L'étrange défaite,* and it is also difficult to understand the present without the orientation, the "criticism" and the "observation," of the historian.[192] The historian's regard is distant, an "eagle's-eye view," as Herder said of eighteenth-century political science.[193] But it is not a view from nowhere. Like Smith, in the *Theory of Moral Sentiments,* who sees in his little window "an immense landscape of lawns, and woods, and distant mountains," and who seeks to transport himself, "at least in fancy," to a position in which he can see his own position, the historian has to observe, and to criticize, her own *Adlersblick.*[194]

I will be concerned with the present, in this book, in two different respects. I will try to observe some of the present uses of eighteenth-century thought, and in particular of eighteenth-century political economy; some of the purposes that Smith's and Condorcet's ideas have served in subsequent political disputes. The book is not a history of the reception of enlightenment ideas in the nineteenth and twentieth centuries. But it is influenced, at several points, by a view of these receptions (and receptions of receptions). I do not believe that to look at eighteenth-century political economy in the setting of the eighteenth century is to renounce the now unfashionable possibility of using the past to illuminate the present. To see past writings in their own context—the economic disputes of the late eighteenth century in the context of disputes about church and guild property, for example, or of legislation about customs and excise, or of theories of the progress of the mind—is rather to have a better understanding of these disputes, and thereby to be in a better position to understand their importance for the present.

I will make a stronger claim as well. It is that some of the disputes of the late eighteenth century are important, in the twenty-first century, because they are also our own disputes. They are not disputes which are repeated over time, or which can illuminate our times. They *are* our disputes. They are part of our historical context, as much as of the context of the past. It is possible for individuals to live in multiple contexts—this is Hume's prospect, in which one is influenced by where one lives, and who one's friends are, and the constitution of one's country, and the music one listens to, and one's philosophical tastes—and societies, too, have many sorts of lives. Our own disputes, at the beginning of the present century, can thus be set in many different contexts, some of which extend very much further over time than others. These disputes unfold at a very different pace, and persist over very different periods. As Smith wrote in the *Theory of Moral Sentiments,* well-fancied coats last for a year, fashionable furniture lasts for five or six years, well-contrived buildings last for many centuries, and a well-written poem may last as long as the world.[195]

Our context and the context of late eighteenth-century political economy are the same in the literal sense that we share at least some of our public and constitutional texts. The documents of the American Revolution of 1776 and of the French Revolution of 1789 are still the texts of much of public life in innumerable countries. The Declaration of the Rights of Man of 1789—in Thomas Paine's translation, of "Liberty, Property, Security, and Resistance of Oppression," culminating in "the right to property . . . inviolable and sacred"—is the basis for the universal rights of the post–Second World War settlement.[196] Some of the institutions and constitutions of the late eighteenth century are still in use; other institutions draw explicitly on the texts and the principles of the 1770s and 1780s.

The grand political coalition of the period which followed the French Revolution, to take a different example, has remained the same, in very general terms, for almost two centuries. The politics of economic reform, of individual rights, of rights to property, were linked, in the 1770s and 1780s, to the objective of constitutional change, in Paine's politics, or in Condorcet's. But the events of the Revolution destroyed the possibility of political coalition between the supporters of market freedom and the supporters of Revolutionary freedom. The obvious coalition for economic and political "liberals" by the end of the 1790s, at least in England and France, was with the "conservative" opponents of the Revolution. In a conflict between gradual change and Revolutionary violence, the liberals were on the side of the slow and the consensual; in a conflict between freedom of individual property and violent expropriation, they were on the side of property. This taking of sides has lasted ever since; it lasted, at least, until the eventual end, with the overthrow of communist power in Eastern Europe and Russia, of the epoch of European revolutions.

There are disputes in political and economic theory, too, which last for a very long time, and it is with these that I am principally concerned. They are disputes, above all, about the political theory of people who themselves have theories. The idea of a universal disposition of enlightenment, or of a discursive, disputatious, theorizing way of life, which is also a way of life for everyone without exception, has been the subject of virtually uninterrupted discussion over the course of the past 250 years. It is this continuing discussion to which the book is a contribution, and in respect of which the past of political economy (or the early reaches of the present) seems to me to illuminate the disputes of our own times.

The difficulty, in very general terms, is of the depiction of complicated and self-conscious lives. Everyone knows, by introspection or imagination, that individuals have different, conflicting desires; that they have needs, and they also have opinions about needs; that they have political, economic, and spiritual sentiments; that they want commodities, and power, and they want to avoid being vexed. It is easy enough to describe (or to hint at) all this in one's own life, or in the tragedy of Oedipus, or in the biography of Voltaire. The great difficulty, for the political theorists of the enlightened disposition, was how to describe a universe, or a society, in which everybody has opinions and theories and conflicting, changing desires. It was to make a "system" out of the innumerable, swerving *moleculae* of individual reflections and sentiments.

There is a beautiful moment in one of the last passages Smith added to the final, sixth edition of the *Theory of Moral Sentiments,* published shortly before his death, where he says, of the "man of system," that "he seems to imagine that he can arrange the different members of a great society with as much ease as the hand arranges the different pieces upon a chess-board. He does not consider that . . . in the great chess-board of human society, every single piece has a principle of motion of its own." This is a characteristic of imperial and royal reformers; it is also, or can also be, characteristic of the theorists of human societies.[197] For if everyone has his or her own principle of motion, then it is difficult to think of their union as a system, or a society. If everyone has the same principle of motion, then the system is too simple; it does less than justice to the subtlety of individual lives. If everyone has a theory of society, or an opinion about the principles of motion of other individuals, then the system must be a theory of people with theories.

The disputes of the late eighteenth century are particularly evocative now because they took place at a time when the prospect of an entire society of self-conscious individuals was quite new, and when the frontier between the economic and the political, or between economic and political sentiments, was still quite shifting. They are antecedent, that is to say, to the systematization of economic thought in the early decades of the nineteenth century, and to the vast self-abnegation whereby political economy defined itself (in John Stuart Mill's words of 1836) as the science of man considered "solely as a being who desires to possess wealth . . . It makes entire abstraction of every other human passion or motive."[198] These earlier disputes are concerned, rather, with economic subjects who pursue their objectives sometimes by producing goods, sometimes by trying to influence regulations, and sometimes by seeking the friendship of officials; whose objectives are sometimes to become rich, sometimes to be revenged, and sometimes to live in a more just society.

The eighteenth-century disputes are evocative, too, because they took place at a time when sentiments and objectives were changing very rapidly, or were at least thought to be changing rapidly. "All centuries, more or less, have been and will be centuries of transition," Tristan says in one of Leopardi's dialogues of 1834.[199] But the later part of the eighteenth century, like the end of the twentieth century, was a period of peculiarly self-conscious preoccupation with change in the rules, norms, and institutions of economic life. It was not a time of which one might say, as Mill said of Victorian England, that "serious controversy" had ceased on one subject after another, that industry flowed into "an apparently stagnant sea," and that people did only that which was suitable; that "it does not occur to them to have any inclination except for what is customary."[200] The tendency which so concerned Turgot, Smith, and Condorcet, of the shifting jurisprudence of unenforced laws, was one illustration; so was the rapid change in economic regulation. It is not only theorists, in such a period, who have to think about cases of conscience in economic life, and to form expectations about continuing changes in economic policy.

My suggestion, for all these reasons, is that the economic thought of the late eighteenth century, including thought about the disposition of enlightenment, can indeed cast light on present disputes, in political theory, in political economy, and in politics. For the old disputes were concerned, at their most general, with two very large and very lasting difficulties. One has to do with the pursuit of self-interest subject to rules, and in particular with the pursuit of economic interest subject to changing political regulations and norms; with the transformation of money into power, including the power to influence rules. The other has to do with public opinion and public instruction; with the disposition of individuals to subject themselves to and to try to influence rules, and with the power of other individuals to influence this disposition. The two difficulties were of continuing importance, as will be seen, both to Smith and to Condorcet. They are the difficulties, in particular, of living with uncertainty. They are difficulties of the present as well.

2

Adam Smith and Conservative Economics

THIS FAMOUS PHILOSOPHER

Adam Smith died in Edinburgh in July 1790, at the beginning of the revolutionary period in Europe.[1] He was remembered, until the mid-1790s, as a subversive and as a friend of French philosophy; by the end of the century, he had been rediscovered as a theorist of established institutions. The odd story of Smith's posthumous decline and rise is the subject of this chapter. It will be concerned with three successive episodes: with the period of Smith's renown as one of the inspirations of the French Revolution, and his reputation for promoting unseemly popular discussion; with the effort of his first biographer, the philosopher Dugald Stewart, to defend Smith's memory by redefining his view of freedom; and with the policy disputes, over scarcity and wages, in which Smith was first invoked as a conservative philosopher.

Smith's death was the subject of rather little interest, in England and even in Scotland. The published obituaries were exiguous, and also disobliging. The *Annual Register* devoted twelve lines to Smith in its chronicle of deaths, and sixty-five lines in the same section to a Major Ray, a deputy quartermaster general with an interest in barometers. The notice in the *Scots Magazine* ran for only nine lines.[2] The first comment in the *Times* referred snidely to Smith's friendship for the skeptical Hume.[3] The second, biographical notice was also concerned with irreligion and with French influence: "The church seemed an improper profession, because he had early become a disciple of Voltaire's in matters of religion." Smith was said to have drawn attention to "subjects that unfortunately have become too popular in most countries of Europe.—Dr Smith's system of political oeconomy is not essentially different from that of Count Verri, Dean Tucker, and Mr Hume."[4] The *Gentleman's Magazine,* which reprinted the

Times notice, added that the *Wealth of Nations* had been quoted in Parliament and the French National Assembly, and "contributed to that spirit of liberty which at present so much prevails."[5]

In France itself, Smith's loss was far more keenly felt. The Revolutionary *Moniteur Universel* wrote that "Europe has just been deprived of this famous philosopher." It welcomed a new translation of the *Wealth of Nations*—with a promised volume of notes by Condorcet—as especially opportune in France, "since every citizen can have a part in government." "One can scarcely believe," it added, that pre-Revolutionary editors were too timid to publish Smith's work; "today it is no longer an act of daring." Condorcet's notes—on what the *Moniteur* described as "a text which he could have composed himself"—were never published.[6] But Condorcet did publish a 220-page summary of the *Wealth of Nations* in his *Bibliothèque de l'homme public* of 1790–91, identified as one of the works "which does most honor to Great Britain."[7]

The "war of ideas" over the French Revolution blazed into intensity in England and Scotland in the months after Smith's death.[8] Dugald Stewart later wrote in self-exculpation that "no reference has been made to my opinions (so far as I have been able to learn) by any of the inflammatory writers of the times."[9] But the same could not be said of Smith himself. Thomas Paine compares Burke unfavorably with Smith in 1791 in *The Rights of Man*, his answer to Burke's *Reflections on the Revolution in France*.[10] Mary Wollstonecraft quotes Smith at length in her *Vindication of the Rights of Woman* of 1792, and uses the language of the *Theory of Moral Sentiments* in her own first answer to Burke, in 1790.[11] James Mackintosh refers admiringly to Smith in *Vindiciae Gallicae* in 1791.[12] William Godwin uses phrases which are close to Smith's in *Political Justice* in 1793; a study of Godwin's text led Elie Halévy to ask, "How then can the same ideas, expressed in almost the same terms, end with different authors in such different consequences?"[13] The minor pamphleteers, too, were inflammatory enough; one defended Smith as the enemy of feudalism in France, or of "pale Despotism, with her haggard train of pampered lusts."[14]

Burke himself makes no reference to Smith in the *Reflections*. But much of the book consists of an attack on Smith's friends, and on the language of at least part of the *Wealth of Nations*. Burke's changing relationship to Smith's ideas is of considerable importance, as will be seen, to the subsequent changes in Smith's repute. In the *Reflections*, Burke's eulogy of the state extends to government expenditure ("it is the publick ornament"), government revenue ("the revenue of the state is the state . . . in its administration the sphere of every active virtue"), and government officials ("they stand in the person of God himself").[15] The French "Oeconomists" and "philosophers" whom Burke denounces were Smith's acknowledged inspiration.[16] His perfidious noblemen were Smith's patrons.[17] Condorcet was for Burke the leader of the "sect of Philosophic Robbers and Assassins," and a "turbulent and seditious Libeller."[18] "Prejudice," which Burke defends, is Smith's consistent term of abuse, throughout the *Wealth of Nations,* and in the last passages he wrote.[19] "Superstition," which Burke also defends, is the term which Smith (like Hume) uses of the Anglican establishment which Burke wishes to "consecrate" or "oblate."[20] "We are not the disciples of Voltaire," Burke says of the men of England, in the words that the *Times* (and the *Gentleman's*) use of Smith.[21]

As late as 1793, the former prime minister, Lord Lansdowne, claimed Smith as the inspiration of French policy. "With respect to the principles of France," he said in the House of Lords, "those principles had been exported from us to France . . . [and were] generally inculcated by Dr. Adam Smith in his work on the Wealth of Nations."[22] Smith's old Edinburgh friend Lord Loughborough did then defend him, asserting that the *Wealth of Nations* was not "inimical to the principles of civil government, the morals or religion of mankind."[23] But Smith was reported, meanwhile, to have spoken of Rousseau "with a kind of religious respect"; to have revered Voltaire, "who has done much more for the benefit of mankind than those grave philosophers whose books are read by a few only"; to have been "not a Christian"; and to have "approached to republicanism in his political principles."[24]

Smith himself wrote nothing that was concerned explicitly with the Revolutionary events in France. He was well informed about French politics until the end of his life. Dupont de Nemours wrote to him in June 1788 about the political "revolution" under way, and about Smith's own influence upon it: "We are moving rapidly towards a good constitution . . . You have done much to speed this useful revolution, the French *Économistes* will not have harmed it."[25] Smith even seems to have owned four pamphlets by Condorcet on constitutional reform in France, written as late as September 1789; in one, Condorcet proposes a second chamber of distinguished citizens of whom, "in England," Locke, Hume, Smith, and Price would have been the first to be chosen.[26] But these interests are reflected only indirectly in Smith's last political writing.

The sixth, extensively revised edition of the *Theory of Moral Sentiments* was published a few weeks before Smith's death, and the new sections are concerned to a substantial extent with theories of political justice. They are written in a tone of sometimes powerful indignation, as when Smith speaks, for example, of the "mean principle of national prejudice," or of the "corruption of our moral sentiments" which follows from the disposition "almost to worship, the rich and the powerful."[27] They also are distinctively influenced by French ideas, in the sense that Smith refers frequently to Voltaire and Racine. But no more than a few paragraphs are concerned with current political events.[28] Some—about the circumstances in which "even a wise man may be disposed to think some alteration necessary in [the] constitution or form of government"—seem to be influenced by French disputes, and by Dupont's letter.[29] They may also reflect the English constitutional crisis over George III's illness in 1788–89.[30] Others—the most impassioned—seem to be about the "systematical" Prussian despotism of Frederick II.[31] Smith has been interpreted, on the basis of these pages, as criticizing the early Revolutionary events in France. He can also be seen as a friend of reform.[32] But his turbulent reputation, in either case, was based on far more than a few comments on current policy. He belonged to neither side in the Anglo-French pamphlet wars of 1790–1792, and the side which claimed him was Wollstonecraft's and Paine's.

SCOTLAND IN THE 1790s

By 1792, Smith's new principles were seen as virtually seditious, in the juridical sense of tending to inflame public opinion. Scotland itself was considered to be on the verge of revolution, and Smith's ideas were thought to have inspired popular discussion, opposition to war, and discontent with English government. Smith, like Hume, had been considered in Scotland to have been influenced by French skepticism. Boswell urged Johnson to "knock Hume's and Smith's heads together, and make vain and ostentatious infidelity exceedingly ridiculous."[33] Like Hume, Smith was thought to be hardly capable of writing English.[34] The *Wealth of Nations* was "tedious and full of repetition," according to Alexander Carlyle, a leading conservative divine; "on political subjects his opinions were not very sound," he had once said "Bravo!" about John Wilkes, and he was "prejudiced in favour of the French tragedies."[35] Carlyle later described a malevolent little vision in which Hume and Smith "were shrunk into a nutshell" as retribution "for having contributed their share to the present state of the world": "the one, by doing everything in his power to undermine Christianity, and the other by introducing that unrestrained and universal commerce, which propagates opinions as well as commodities."[36]

The divisions in Scotland increased dramatically after 1789. "How they raved!" Lord Cockburn wrote of his conservative family's conversations about the French Revolution. "Everything, not this or that thing, but literally everything, was soaked in this one event." Smith was the hero of the "liberal young of Edinburgh."[37] But he was the object of deep suspicion for many others, including former admirers. Dugald Stewart looked back in 1810: "The doctrine of a Free Trade was itself represented as of a revolutionary tendency; and some who had formerly prided themselves on their intimacy with Mr. Smith, and on their zeal for the propagation of his liberal system, began to call into question the expediency of subjecting to the disputations of philosophers, the arcana of State Policy, and the unfathomable wisdom of the feudal ages."[38] To be praised by Paine and translated by Condorcet was fearsome, in the Scotland of 1793. "Scotland was at nearly the lowest point of political degradation," Lord Cockburn wrote; he described a scene of "absolute power . . . exercised in a small and poor country," which could be compared to a "province of Austria or Russia."[39]

The famous Scottish sedition trials began early in 1793, and they were concerned with words which were ominously close to Smith's. The most publicized trial—of Thomas Muir, a lawyer who was sentenced to fourteen years' transportation in August 1793—was over the crime of "exciting disaffection to government." In the words of the prosecution: "He said, that their taxes would be less if they were more equally represented; and that from the flourishing state of France, they could not bring their goods to market so cheap as Frenchmen. What could possibly be more calculated to produce discontent and sedition?" The judge's summing up was forthright: "I never was an admirer of the French; but I can now only consider them as monsters of human nature."[40]

In another trial, Thomas Palmer, a Unitarian clergyman, was indicted for such crimes as saying, of the war with France, that "by it your commerce is sore cramped and almost ruined." Palmer's counsel referred to the views of Smith, and of Hume, on the liberty of the press. The great issue, for the defense, was the freedom of even the poorest subjects to discuss reform: "The beggar in rags has a right to give his opinion upon the most important of our affairs." But Hume, Smith, and Milton were of little use, and Palmer, too, was transported, for seven years.[41] William Skirving, a farmer, invoked Smith's views on the burden of public credit, and was transported for fourteen years. Maurice Margarot spoke in court about the commercial treaty between France and England, and criticized, as Smith had, the "idea, that they were natural enemies, and should go to war on every trivial occasion"; he too was transported for fourteen years.[42]

Dugald Stewart himself was forced into an extraordinary act of recantation over a modest little reference to Condorcet in his *Philosophy of the Human Mind*. Two of the Scottish Law Lords concocted a classic text of persecution in a letter sent to Stewart early in 1794. They expected "that you would embrace the earliest opportunity of retracting in an open and manly manner, every sentiment you had ever entertained, and every word you had ever uttered, in favour of doctrines which had led to so giant a mischief." Stewart's answer was fairly dignified. He denied any "wish to encourage political discussions among the multitude," supported the "Economists" but not the "French philosophers," and said that he had spoken with political "warmth" only against the slave trade ("and even these expressions I dropped from my course, as soon as it became matter of popular discussion"); he did add that "I shall ever regret that I dishonoured some of my pages by mentioning with respect the name of Condorcet."[43]

ECONOMIC AND POLITICAL FREEDOM

Stewart's "Account of the Life and Writings of Adam Smith" must be set within this frenzied scene. It is by far the most important biographical work about Smith, and an early source of Smith's subsequent conservative renown. But it was read to the Royal Society of Edinburgh in the same weeks that the sedition trials began in 1793, at a moment of what Stewart described in a private letter as "infatuation . . . beyond belief," in which "all freedom" had been "suspended." Stewart indeed refers to the memoir in his answer to the Law Lords; it should be seen as a defense of Smith, and of himself, against the terror of the times.[44]

Only a few pages of the memoir are concerned with the *Wealth of Nations,* for "reasons which it is unnecessary to mention here"; Stewart explained in 1810 that he was hinting, in this comment, at the contemporary tendency to confound "speculative doctrines of Political Economy, with those discussions concerning the first principles of Government which happened unfortunately at that time to agitate the public mind."[45] But Stewart does try to describe Smith's intentions. Smith, he says, was concerned only with those "speculations . . . which have no tendency to unhinge established institutions, or to inflame the passions of the multitude." His objective was that of "enlightening the policy of actual legislators." He was abundantly aware of the dangers of "rash application of political theories." He was concerned only with "the ultimate objects" of policy.[46]

Stewart's conclusion, in the memoir, is that Smith's reputation for "extreme" judgments was undeserved. "In the thoughtlessness and confidence of his social hours," he would sometimes "hazard" opinions on "questions of speculation," in contrast to "those qualified conclusions that we admire in his writings." But his thoughtless remarks (as "retailed" by occasional visitors) suggested "false and contradictory ideas of his real sentiments."[47] The "real" Smith, according to Stewart, was the sober public philosopher, and not the private man who spoke to friends about religious prejudice, Voltaire, and the madness of modern wars.

Smith is a sort of defendant, in these passages, and Stewart is his counsel. Stewart's language is indeed very close to that of the standard legal texts of the time, in which jurists attempted to explain the relationship between "speculative remarks" and the "criminal libel of the constitution." The defendant, in a sedition trial, was required to show that his writing was not "calculated" to "inflame," and that his intention was only the modest one of "pointing out to those *who have political power,* how it may best be exerted for the benefit of the State." Lord Cockburn, who quotes these texts, is thoroughly skeptical: "Who is to judge of all this?" But Edinburgh was "sincerely under the influence of fear." Stewart's memoir is evidence of the effort to present Smith as a conservative; more than of Smith's own conservatism.[48]

Stewart's defense of Smith was part of a far more extensive discussion, in the mid-1790s, about the distinction between politics and political economy, and about the definition of freedom. His object, in the memoir, seems to have been to show that political economy was an innocuous, technical sort of subject. Smith was a retiring, innocuous sort of person, quite unconcerned to influence public opinion, and interested only in offering hints on policy to "actual legislators." "Political freedom," Stewart says in his comments on the *Wealth of Nations,* was of value chiefly "from the facility which it is supposed to afford" for legislative improvements. If the laws themselves are satisfactory, then people "have little reason to complain, that they were not immediately instrumental in their enactment." Under certain circumstances, political liberty can indeed be "the means of accomplishing their own ruin."[49]

Stewart's description of the instrumental value of freedom corresponds to very little which Smith himself wrote. It is also in quite striking contrast to Stewart's own earlier (and indeed later) views. But it does reflect an intense public discussion, in Edinburgh, Paris, and London, about the words "freedom" and "liberty."[50] Thomas Muir, in his courtroom in 1793, predicted that "the word 'freedom' is soon to be proscribed from our language; it carries alarm and sedition in the sound."[51] What happened, instead, was that the seditious word was redefined, and divided into seemly new sub-senses.

Stewart's account suggested that there were two spheres of life, the commercial and the political. Political economy was concerned with commercial or economic life. Freedom, for the purposes of political economy, could therefore be defined as "freedom of trade and industry," "free circulation of labour and of stock," and "the freest competition" between individual citizens.[52] These freedoms, in turn, were valued as the instruments of "national wealth." "Political freedom," by contrast, was an attribute of political life, and was outside the scope of political economy. But it too was of intermediate value: an "instrument," "means," or "facility" of justice.

Freedom, under these circumstances, could be spoken of with more confidence in Scotland. It was to be found within the sphere of commerce; it was freedom of property. The word "equality," oddly enough, was meanwhile being divided in the opposite way. The minutes of Muir's "Convention" in December 1792 show a precision worthy of Stewart himself. One delegate complained that the "Friends of the People were calumniated with entertaining notions of Liberty and Equality inimical to property." He therefore moved that "an addition should be made to the resolution explaining what was meant by the word 'Equality'—that it was only political equality that was wanted."[53] Freedom belonged to one sphere of life, equality to another, and both were useful for national prosperity.

The redefinition of freedom proceeded in much the same terms in London. Coleridge tells the story of a shipowner in 1798: "An acquaintance of mine (least of all men a political zealot) had *christened* a vessel which he had just built—THE LIBERTY; and was seriously admonished by his aristocratic friends to change it for some other name. What? replied the owner very innocently—should I call it THE FREEDOM? That (it was replied) would be far better, as people might then think only of Freedom of Trade; whereas LIBERTY has a *jacobinical* sound with it!"[54] The solution turned out to be very much the same as Dugald Stewart's. Freedom was a sort of intermediate good, or necessary evil, to be used in the production of prosperity. The friends of Coleridge's acquaintance thought that the ship was beautiful, but the name *"obnoxious"*: "Liberty = Freedom?—No! No! No!—Not at present, You *may* use the latter without heinous offence, if you take care to show that it is necessary to the prosperity of Trade and Commerce, a *necessary Evil* in the process of moneygetting."[55]

In Paris, over the same period, the economic and the political were divided off in opposite and symmetrical respects. The old inclusive view of freedom survived, like Smith's revolutionary renown, until the beginning of the Jacobin ascendancy. To see economic freedom as a component of revolutionary freedom was indeed one of the distinguishing principles of Girondin policy. Condorcet argued, as late as March 1792, that a completely free domestic commerce was the best way to avoid scarcities of subsistence grains.[56] In June 1793 he still supported the principle of "unlimited freedom for the grain commerce," except under such extreme circumstances as military blockade.[57] But for the Jacobins, as for the established powers in London and Edinburgh, the definition of freedom was beginning to change by 1793.

Economic and political freedom were divided, in France as in Scotland. But where economic freedom was seemly in Edinburgh, it was subversive in Paris. Political freedom was subversive in Edinburgh and useful in France. Smith's acquaintance and translator, the abbé Morellet, described the transformation in the memoirs he published during the restoration. The process began, he said, in the summer of 1789. He was staying at the time with Mme. Helvétius. Until then, "freedom, tolerance, the horror of despotism and superstition, the desire to see abuses reformed, were our common sentiments. But our opinions began to be a little divergent toward the month of June 1789."[58]

Morellet remained in Paris during the Terror, and he was denounced in September 1793. He then needed a certificate of "civism," so he went to see his denouncer with a large bag containing his works. His account is in much the same words that Stewart and Coleridge use, and it suggests the turbulent destiny of political economy in the 1790s:

> This book, I said to him, putting into his hands a quite large volume, *The Refutation of Galiani's Dialogues,* is also in favor of freedom of commerce. Oh! he said, one should not mention that one. Do you not think, I said to him, that freedom is the only means of preventing famines and high prices for subsistence grains? Is it not the case, I

added slyly, that freedom is always good, and good for everything? I saw that my praise of freedom embarrassed him, and that he did not dare to argue with it. All in good time, he said to me. But today, the anxieties are too great, and one cannot speak of that sort of freedom.[59]

THE LIBERAL REWARD OF LABOR

The disjunction of economic and political freedom was the necessary condition, in the 1790s, for the transformation in Smith's own reputation. The decisive issue of policy, in England as in France, was the connection between food and economic freedom. Smith's renown as a cold-souled enemy of the poor has been justified, for almost two centuries, by reference to his presumed "general principles" of scarcity and famine. These principles were discovered during the English food crisis of the mid-1790s, and they mark the beginning of the long rise of Smith as a conservative theorist.

In 1795–96, and again in 1799–1800, sudden increases in food prices set off an intense discussion in England of wage rates and poor relief.[60] One episode—Samuel Whitbread's proposed minimum wage legislation of 1795—provides a particularly clear illustration of the changing interpretation of Smith's ideas. Whitbread was a reform M.P., and his bill would have given magistrates powers "to regulate the wages of Labourers in Husbandry" by fixing minimum wages.[61] He was strongly influenced by Smith, and introduced the Commons debate on the bill by explaining that "he felt as much as any man . . . that the price of labour, like every other commodity, should be left to find its own level."[62] But he was prepared to countenance some "legislative interference" to protect the "rights" of the poor.

Whitbread followed the *Wealth of Nations* closely in his parliamentary presentation. Smith himself was tolerant, after all, of some wage regulation: "When the regulation . . . is in favour of the workmen, it is always just and equitable; but it is sometimes otherwise when in favour of the masters."[63] Smith says of existing regulations to fix maximum wages that they were "in favour of the masters"; Whitbread adds that they gave magistrates "the power to oppress the labourer."[64] Smith argued for high wages, more generally, on grounds of equity: "No society can surely be flourishing and happy, of which the far greater part of the members are poor and miserable. It is but equity, besides, that they who feed, clothe and lodge the whole body of the people, should have such a share of the produce of their own labour as to be themselves tolerably well fed, clothed and lodged." Whitbread's object was similar: "To enable the husbandman, who dedicated his days to incessant toil, to feed, to clothe, and to lodge his family with some degree of comfort . . . by giving him a right to a part of the produce of his labour."[65]

Whitbread's Smith-inspired rhetoric was greeted, however, with a quite different interpretation of political economy. Pitt answered Whitbread with a resounding defense of the "unassisted operation of principles." He invoked "the most celebrated writers upon political economy" as testimony that the House should "consider the operation of general principles, and rely upon the effects of their unconfined exercise." His solution was to remove restrictions on the free circulation of labor, and to begin reform of the laws of settlement (the poor laws). Whitbread and his friends pointed out that such reforms "would take a considerable time"; a barley loaf, meanwhile, cost rather more than "the whole of the labourer's daily wages." But "the present case," for Pitt, was not "strong enough for the exception."[66]

There is something of Smith on both sides of the parliamentary debate. Like Pitt, Smith thought that wages in England and Scotland were high (at least until the early 1780s).[67] The regulations he considered equitable were more limited than those proposed by Whitbread.[68] But his description of them was closer to Whitbread's than to Pitt's, as Pitt's opponents pointed out.[69] His view of general principles was quite unlike Pitt's. He was opposed to the zealous application of "systematical" policies; Dugald Stewart interpreted Smith's strictures as "cautions with respect to the practical application of general principles," and notably to "the unlimited freedom of trade."[70] His principles of commerce are always circumscribed by other laws of justice and equity. High wages are good for prosperity, and for "equity, besides." Wages are determined by supply and demand, and are also "regulated" by "common humanity."[71]

Smith was considered, like Whitbread, to be a friend of the poor. In the *Wealth of Nations* he describes the "liberal reward of labour" as the "necessary effect and cause of the greatest public prosperity"; in the "Early Draft" of the work, he had written that a "high price of labour" was the "essence of public opulence."[72] Malthus, in his 1798 *Essay on the Principle of Population*, reproves Smith for the "error" of mixing two distinct inquiries: into "the wealth of nations" and into "the happiness and comfort of the lower orders of society."[73] In his *Principles of Political Economy*, Malthus identifies more of Smith's infelicities, including using "exceptionable" language about landlords, considering profits as "a deduction from the produce of labour," underestimating "the production contributed by the capitalist," and talking about humanity; "if humanity could have successfully interfered," Malthus wrote, "it ought to have interfered long before . . . But unfortunately, common humanity cannot alter the resources of a country."[74]

Smith's language, more generally, is quite different from Pitt's. Pitt followed Smith in criticizing the law of settlements. But where Smith described an "evident violation of natural liberty and justice," by which the "poor man" feels himself to be "most cruelly oppressed," Pitt saw no more than a "grievance": "instances where interference had shackled industry."[75] Whitbread and his friends, like Smith, wished "to rescue the labouring poor from a state of slavish dependence." The laborer should not "receive his due as an eleemosynary gift"; the dependence of the poor was especially evil because people who had received relief were excluded from the franchise, and thus from their constitutional rights. But for Pitt, the poor were concerned with prices and not with rights; the workman was prevented, at worst, "from going to that market where he could dispose of his industry to the greatest advantage."[76]

The 1796 debate can be interpreted as a conflict between two different "Smiths": Whitbread's and Pitt's. Whitbread's Smith is in many respects closer to the "real" Smith, or to the real *Wealth of Nations.* But by the second food crisis of 1800, Pitt's Smith had won overwhelmingly. Edmund Burke's changing economic views provide a striking illustration. Smith and Burke were on friendly terms, as least for a period in the early 1780s.[77] But in the *Reflections,* as has been seen, Burke's view of government was very different from Smith's, with respect, for example, to the good commercial consequences of national expenditure on bridges, religion, and public reverence.[78] By 1795, Burke had become doubtful about what he now called government "interference." A paper which he prepared for Pitt may indeed have influenced the parliamentary criticism of Whitbread. "What is doing supposes, or pretends," Burke says, "that the farmer oppresses the laborer." But the "principles of market," or the "principles of general policy," do not admit of deviation. Providence sometimes withholds "necessaries" from the poor; "it is not in breaking the laws of commerce, which are the laws of Nature, and consequently the laws of God," that divine displeasure is to be softened.[79]

Burke's paper was first published in 1800, together with another "memorial," as part of the posthumous pamphlet *Thoughts and Details on Scarcity*. It is close, at several points, to being in open opposition to Smith. Burke does not mention Smith in the pamphlet. But he paraphrases the *Wealth of Nations* at some points, and contradicts it at many others. "Nothing can be so base and so wicked," he says, "as the political canting language, 'the laboring *poor*'"; Smith uses the phrase six times in a few paragraphs of his chapter on wages. Smith says that wages are determined in contracts made between "two parties, whose interests are by no means the same"; Burke says that "in the case of the farmer and the laborer, their interests are always the same." Burke saw the first duty of the state as "the exterior establishment of its religion"; Smith favored the competition of some "thousand small sects." Monopolies, for Smith, were a wretched derangement of natural order; for Burke, "the monopoly of capital . . . is a great benefit, and a benefit particularly to the poor." Smith thought that the children of the poor should be educated to take part in political discussions; for Burke, they were no more than "present drains and bloodsuckers," although "growing from less to greater utility."[80]

By 1800, however, Burke's pamphlet was received as little more than an exposition of Smith's "principles." The editors claimed in their introduction that Smith paid "the greatest deference" to Burke's views in the *Wealth of Nations*.[81] It was as though all the different Smiths—Whitbread's Smith, with his right to the produce of labor, or the quasi-French, quasi-atheistical, quasi-revolutionary "Oeconomist"—had vanished into the simple prescription of economic freedom. The laconic review of Burke's pamphlet in the *Gentleman's Magazine* was characteristic: "This celebrated author proceeds on the principles of Dr. Adam Smith, that all trade should be free; and that government should not interfere by compulsory acts and regulations, particularly in grain and agriculture. He was equally averse to public granaries." The *Monthly Review* identified five separate pamphlets, including Burke's, which were concerned with "the principle of Dr. Adam Smith, that all trade should be free"; one of the authors was even described as "Smithian."[82] Burke and Smith were no longer seen as opponents by the end of the century; they were equivalents, and economic conservatives.

ONE-SIDED RATIONALISTIC LIBERALISM

Smith had been transformed, by 1800, into the modern hero of commerce. This is not to say that the conflict over interpretations of his ideas came to a sudden end. The old subversive Smith of the early 1790s survived well into the Victorian period in Britain. The economist Thomas Hodgskin defended Smith in the 1820s against the errors of his "commentators and disciples"; Smith, he said, never confused the laws of nature with the artificial laws of property, and he never extended the doctrines of political economy to "all the relations of social life."[83] Lord Acton, as late as 1881, concluded that "government with the working class" was the irresistible consequence of Smith's ideas of freedom of contract, and of labor as the source of wealth: "That is the foreign effect of Adam Smith—French Revolution and Socialism."[84] Beatrice Webb looked back in 1886: "The Political Economy of Adam Smith was the scientific expression of the impassioned crusade of the 18th century against class tyranny and the oppression of the Many by the Few. By what silent revolution of events, by what unselfconscious transformation of thought did it change itself into the 'Employers' Gospel' of the 19th century?"[85]

In Germany, the process of transformation was even slower. There was no German Burke to claim freedom of commerce as the fulfillment of feudal wisdom; one great division, in nineteenth-century German economic doctrine, was indeed between the "Burke-Savigny" school of historical jurisprudence and a Kantian *Smithianismus* of cosmopolitan reform. Carl Menger in fact commented in 1883 on Smith's lack of conservative sentiment. Smith had no understanding of organic social structures, and therefore "was nowhere concerned to conserve them": "What characterizes the theories of Adam Smith and his followers is the one-sided rationalistic liberalism, the not infrequently impetuous effort to do away with what exists . . . [which] inexorably leads to socialism."[86] In a later article, Menger defended Smith as a friend of the poor, and noted that he was quoted frequently by Louis Blanc, Ferdinand Lassalle, and Karl Marx: "A. Smith placed himself in all cases of conflict of interest between the poor and the rich, between the strong and the weak, *without exception* on the side of the latter. I use the expression 'without exception' after careful reflection, since there is not a single instance in A. Smith's work in which he represents the interest of the rich and powerful as opposed to the poor and weak."[87] Menger's brother, the jurist Anton Menger, meanwhile claimed Smith—on the basis of the same passages which Whitbread used in 1796—as the precursor of a socialist jurisprudence: "The Right to the Whole Produce of Labour."[88]

Smith's old renown persisted even into the early decades of the twentieth century. The Smith scholar James Bonar addressed the National Liberal Club, in 1924, on what he called "The Revolutionary Element in Adam Smith." This extended from "first principles," including the rights of labor, to "emotional appeals" on behalf of the suffering, and to "reforms of detail." "The charge is no novelty," Bonar said, "but economists do not love to dwell on it"; "it strikes everyone who reads him for the first time; and then, as a rule, the reader finds himself taking it as covered up or explained away, and he generally leaves it out of his thoughts."[89]

SMITH'S REAL SENTIMENTS

The year 1800 is a turning point, still, for Smith and the different "Smiths." There seems to be little merit in trying to answer the counterfactual questions: What would Smith himself have thought about his changing reputation, or about the French Revolution? But it may be useful to conclude with some observations about what Dugald Stewart called Smith's "real sentiments," and why it is that they can have been understood in such widely different ways.

There are great difficulties in trying to interpret Smith's politics, as Donald Winch and others have emphasized.[90] One reason is that Smith himself went to considerable lengths to obscure his opinions. He is extraordinarily cautious and elusive when he writes about current policies in the *Wealth of Nations*. In his letters and conversations, he seems to have several more or less distinct personalities. It was this multiplicity which led to the tension, described by Dugald Stewart, between the qualified public Smith and the private Smith who revered Voltaire in his supposedly thoughtless social hours.

Smith's real sentiments, according to Stewart's memoir, were those of the prudent public man. Yet the same tension was interpreted by Smith's French friends in exactly the opposite way. Dupont de Nemours thus suggested after Smith's death that the real "spirit" of Smith was to be found in the private man, or the unqualified friend of freedom. The public Smith was hiding his real sentiments from conservative public opinion. In his comments on Turgot and Smith, Dupont is critical of Smith's permissive attitude, in the *Wealth of Nations*, to some government interference, and especially to indirect taxes. But he explains Smith's "error" by the fact that he "appears to have been frightened by the severe judgment which his entire book suggests" in relation to British policy. Smith's errors were therefore no more than "a sacrifice which he thought he must make to the popular opinions of his country"; "Smith in freedom, Smith in his own room or in that of a friend, as I saw him when we were disciples together in the home of Mr Quesnay," would never have said such things.[91]

Smith's caution, on this "French" view, is that of someone who must obscure his real and severe opinions in public. He is seen as a reformer who sometimes compromises, and not as a conservative who is sometimes systematic. Like Turgot or Condorcet or Gibbon, he writes in a sort of code; like Quesnay, whose *Physiocratie* was published in "Peking" to avoid French censorship, he lives in a society of absolute power.[92]

Dupont's interpretation is supported by much of Smith's correspondence, and by the revolutionary side or element of his published and unpublished work. But Smith's compromises with conservative opinion were not simply a matter of expediency. To respect public opinion was of central importance to Smith's political philosophy, as it was to Condorcet's. To act "slowly, gradually, and after a very long warning" was not to be conservative.[93] It was rather to put popular ideas—in Smith's words, the "judgment which the people may form" of government—at the center of the political process.[94] It was to change society by public consent. Smith's most profound criticism, in his last writings, was of Frederick the Great: of the imperial reformer who seeks "to erect his own judgment into the supreme standard of right and wrong," and to dispose of individual beings "as the hand arranges the different pieces upon a chess-board." The man of humanity, by contrast, was more like Smith himself: cautious, accommodating, and respectful of the prejudices of the people.[95]

Smith's preoccupation with public opinion was indeed one of the charges made against him in the 1790s. He was subversive, according to the Reverend Mr. Carlyle, because he wished to propagate opinions. His humanitarian reformer was Burke's (and also Robespierre's) anathema: the man without prejudice, "hesitating in the moment of decision, sceptical, puzzled and unresolved."[96] Even Dugald Stewart's tribulations were brought on, as was seen earlier, by the indiscretion of having quoted Condorcet's views on public education. He was obliged to retract gradualism itself: "If I have dwelt long on the expediency of a slow and gradual accommodation of laws to the varying circumstances of a people, it was not from a wish to encourage political discussions among the multitude, but from an anxious desire to prevent the danger of such an evil."[97]

Smith's real political sentiments have been obscured, more generally, by the very disputes which have been described here. The *Wealth of Nations* was reduced, in the reviews of 1800, to little more than a single "principle," and Smith himself to a zealot of "Freedom of Trade."[98] Yet the most subversive parts of the *Wealth of Nations* and the *Theory of Moral Sentiments*—the passages which inspired Wollstonecraft and Sieyès, and which horrified the Scottish Tories—were not even concerned with commercial policy. The occasions when Smith becomes most indignant are the very moments which were "covered up or explained away" (to use Bonar's phrase) in the 1790s.

The *Wealth of Nations* is, in Nathan Rosenberg's words, "a systematic critique of human institutions."[99] It is thereby among the objects of Burke's obloquy: "Instead of quarrelling with establishments, as some do, who have made a philosophy and a religion of their hostility to such institutions, we cleave closely to them . . . It has been the misfortune (not as these gentlemen think it, the glory) of this age, that everything is to be discussed."[100] Smith described the ill effects of institutions on commerce. But he was concerned with their other effects as well. At one point in his memoir, Dugald Stewart makes an odd comment about Smith's criticism of merchants who precipitate discord between nations. Smith's remarks, he says, "are expressed in a tone of indignation, which he seldom assumes in his political writings."[101] This is true when political writings are taken to be concerned with commerce, or with wealth. Smith is not particularly outraged about prices, or investments, or even about the level of taxes. But indignation is nonetheless one of the most powerful tones in his writing, and it is used, above all, of the injustice of political and religious institutions.

Smith's subversive renown was founded, to a great extent, on his criticisms of established religion. He was most objected to, in his lifetime, for his friendship with Hume; some of his boldest proposals in the *Wealth of Nations* are to limit the "great incorporation" of the established church, and to promote science as an "antidote to the poison of enthusiasm and superstition."[102] The *Theory of Moral Sentiments* was read by many, at least in France, as a protracted attack on religious prejudice. This was one of its attractions for Condorcet's wife, Sophie Grouchy, who translated the last edition during the Revolution: Smith was thought to have "laicized morality, and removed it from all dependence" on religion.[103]

The other great source of Smith's dangerous reputation was his opposition to national prejudice and foreign military expenditure. His description of the sentiments of empire—"the amusement of reading in the newspapers the exploits of their own fleets and armies," the "thousand visionary hopes of conquest and national glory"—was already suspect in the *Wealth of Nations*. He admired martial virtues, and was tolerant of standing armies. But he was fiercely critical of "wantonly undertaken" and "expensive and unnecessary wars." He cited "a great ecclesiastical establishment, great fleets and armies," as instances of "public prodigality and misconduct."[104] His last comments in the *Theory of Moral Sentiments* were even more forceful. "The mean principle of national prejudice," he said, was often "malignant" and "savage"; it was weak and foolish to "call the French our natural enemies"; "great warlike exploit" was contrary to justice and humanity, and conducted by "very worthless characters."[105]

Smith's language was close, in fact, to that of the friends of France whom Burke attacked in the *Reflections*.[106] His arguments about military expenditure were invoked, against Burke, by opponents of the French wars. Pitt indeed became exasperated, as the wartime prime minister, with having Smith quoted against him on the costs of foreign policy: "Much as he respected the opinions of that great writer . . . he could not help dissenting from several maxims which he had advanced. He thought that great author, although always ingenious, sometimes injudicious."[107] Yet by the end of the century, at least in England, these unwarlike maxims were widely ignored. Smith's cosmopolitan principles, like his opposition to established religion, had been subsumed in the single-minded theorist of commerce.

Smith's real sentiments about poverty, too, were disregarded by 1800. He is indignant in the passages about wages which inspired Whitbread, and far more so in his unpublished works: as when he says, in the lectures on jurisprudence, that the poor laborer "supports the whole frame of society," yet is "himself possessed of a very small share and is buried in obscurity"; that "it may very justly be said that the people who clothe the whole world are in rags themselves"; or that "laws and government may be considered . . . in every case as a combination of the rich to oppress the poor."[108] He is tolerant in his view of government interference, especially when the object is to reduce poverty. One example is his remark about equitable wage regulations; another is his support for progressive taxes on carriages, such that "the indolence and vanity of the rich is made to contribute in a very easy manner to the relief of the poor."[109] Yet these passages, too, were virtually ignored in the interpretation of the *Wealth of Nations* as a book with a single principle, "that all trade should be free."

Smith's support for free trade in corn was of great importance to his nineteenth-century renown as an enemy of the poor. But his own argument was that free trade would prevent famine and palliate scarcity.[110] He was not concerned, here, with exceptions to a supposedly cruel "system of freedom"; he believed, as did Turgot and Condorcet, that freedom is much less cruel for the poor than the policies of oppressive and ill-informed governments. Like Turgot, as will be seen in Chapter 3, Smith considered free trade in corn to be a "preservative against scarcity"; like Condorcet, he believed that it was a way of assuring "more equal" subsistence.[111] He wrote very little about famines in free countries. But there is no reason to suppose that he disagreed with Turgot's policy, in times of scarcity, of free commerce in food combined with government projects to provide wages for the indigent.

Even Smith's sentiments about freedom were submerged by 1800. The idea of freedom is central to everything Smith wrote. But the distinction between "economic" freedom as an end, and "political" freedom as a means—as in Dugald Stewart's memoir, or for the friends of Coleridge's shipowner—is entirely missing. The burghers of medieval cities "became really free in our present sense of the word Freedom," Smith wrote, when villanage and slavery were taken away. Commerce and manufactures introduced "liberty and security of individuals." "This, though it has been the least observed, is by far the most important of all their effects."[112] Freedom, for Smith, is an end in itself, of a self-evident sort. It is a sort of feeling: in the words of the *Theory of Moral Sentiments,* to "breathe the free air of liberty and independency."[113] This is very much Turgot's or Condorcet's sense. "To feel the sweetness of liberty" is Condorcet's phrase in his *Réflexions sur le commerce des blés;* he criticizes the *Économistes,* in his *Esquisse des Progrès,* for "seeming to forget, in the interests of freedom of commerce, those of political freedom."[114] Sophie Grouchy writes in her postcript to Smith that "liberty is the first need of the human heart."[115]

Smith believed that freedom was good, and also, as he argued throughout the *Wealth of Nations,* that it was good for prosperity. But he distinguished meticulously between the two sorts of argument: between what was "impolitic" in relation to commercial policy and what was "unjust," or between prosperity and "equity, besides." This, too, was the conventional distinction of the later French enlightenment. "The goods which liberty confers are of two sorts," Condorcet wrote: "first, there are the advantages of liberty; then, there is the pleasure which one feels in being free." Servitude, correspondingly, is evil both because of the ills which it engenders, and because of the "feeling of dependence, the spectacle of human degradation."[116] The effect of the disputes of the 1790s was to confuse the two sorts of goods, and eventually to diminish the importance, at least in political economy, of intrinsic goods and evils. But this was not Smith's view of freedom, and not his politics.

Smith's real sentiments were obscured by Smith himself, and by his friends and followers after his death. But they amounted, during his lifetime, to a cluster of beliefs which were distinctively influenced by French ideas.[117] He was critical of religious establishments, of war, of poverty, and of the privileges of the rich. He was in favor of public discussion. There is nothing in Smith's politics to bely his early Revolutionary reputation as a friend of freedom, and of France.

Freedom consisted, for Smith, in not being interfered with by others: in any of the sides of one's life, and by any outside forces (churches, parish overseers, corporations, customs inspectors, national governments, masters, proprietors). Interference, or oppression, is itself an extraordinarily extensive notion; Smith at times talks of inequality as a form of oppression, and of low wages as a form of inequity.[118] But it was just this multiplicity which was lost after his death. By the end of the 1790s, the freedom of noninterference had become something very much less, at least for political economy. It was little more now than the freedom not to be interfered with in one side of one's life (the economic), and by one outside force (national government). One of the objectives of this book is to look back, beyond the 1790s, at something closer to Smith's own conceptions.

3

Commerce and the State

The organization of commerce and the organization of government were intertwined, in late eighteenth-century Europe, in all the details of ordinary life.[1] The "commercial system of Great Britain," which is the principal subject of the *Wealth of Nations,* is a collection of regulations, bylaws, bounties, inspections, prejudices, rights, and statutes.[2] The "liberal system," or the "obvious and simple system of natural liberty," which is Smith's own idyll, as it is Turgot's and Condorcet's, is a principle of government; it is a generalization of the "ordinary laws of justice."[3] One of the responsibilities of the theorist of reform is therefore to identify the just duties of governments, or the goods which are justly public. It is to distinguish the dominion of commerce, and the dominion of government. But the theorists with whom this book is concerned were also preoccupied with the organization of ordinary political life. They were interested in policies for the immediate circumstances of commercial politics, and of unjust governments.

The political economy of food has been an emblem, at least since the 1760s, of the heartlessness of the liberal system. The introduction of free commerce in corn was a principal objective for Turgot and Condorcet, as for Smith. Free commerce, they argued, was the best protection against scarcity; government intervention in the supply of food would prevent the establishment of commerce, and could thereby lead to scarcity and even famine. Their arguments have been interpreted ever since as a simple prescription that commerce is good and government bad.[4]

The discussions with which this chapter is concerned suggest a different and more complex view. Turgot, Condorcet, and Smith proposed elaborate policies of government intervention, as will be seen. Their justification for such intervention was linked explicitly to their description of the operations and limitations of commercial processes. They put forward strikingly similar views of the corn trade, at virtually the same time. But Condorcet, unlike Smith, was obliged to defend himself against the charge of relentless support for free enterprise to which Smith was not subjected until after his death. Turgot, unlike Smith, studied the course of a real famine in painful detail in 1770. They went considerably beyond Smith to analyze the conditions—in the "markets" for labor and land as well as for corn—which lead to famine, and government policies in relation to these different markets.

Commitment to free commerce in corn was consistent, for Turgot and Condorcet, with support for government intervention in other markets. Turgot argued that conditions in different markets "are related to one another by a reciprocal dependence, and arrive at equilibrium themselves"; he even (in what was apparently the first use of a metaphor later used so widely in the analysis of markets) described the relations between buyers and sellers as "a sort of *tâtonnement*."[5] But he and Condorcet are also concerned with the slow emergence of markets, with persistent disequilibrium, and with government intervention to ensure minimum security in incipiently free economies. They described the dilemmas of public policy in the period following a major economic reform: the introduction of partially free commerce in corn in France in 1763–1769.

SCARCITIES, DEARTHS, AND FAMINES

In the *Wealth of Nations*, Smith described four different ways in which famines arise. The first is when wage income declines rapidly; Smith surmises that this was the situation of Bengal in 1770, under the oppression of the East India Company. The second is when the interruption of "all commerce and communication" causes wide variations in corn prices, and prevents movements of food between districts; this was the situation of England before the fifteenth century. The third is when total national income declines in a country which depends on food imports; this would be the situation of Holland if its real opulence were to fall. The fourth is when scarcity arises in a country with free commerce—usually because of war or bad weather—and improper government policies then contribute to "turn that dearth into a famine"; this is the situation which might arise in modern Europe.[6]

Smith was most concerned with the fourth case. He argued that free trade in corn is the best means to avoid famine: "The unlimited, unrestrained freedom of the corn trade, as it is the only effectual preventative of the miseries of a famine, so it is the best palliative of the inconveniencies of a dearth." Freedom of the corn trade is the best policy for the poor, as he repeats five times; it is "the best thing that can be done for the people." He is concerned with the "extensive corn countr[ies]" of modern Europe, and especially with Britain. He considers only those regulations which affect the inland (and to a lesser extent the international) trade in corn.[7]

Smith's views on scarcity are remarkably close to those of Turgot and Condorcet in their important works on the corn trade. Turgot's "Lettres sur le commerce des grains," published posthumously in 1788, were written while he was traveling as intendant through the remote Limousin province of France, during the scarcity of 1770. (John Morley later explained, for a Victorian audience, that Turgot's position could be compared to that of a "Chief Commissioner" in India, obliged "to deal with a famine, just as the English civilian has to do in Orissa or Behar.")[8] Condorcet's *Réflexions sur le commerce des blés* was published anonymously in 1776. Turgot and Condorcet were close friends, and discussed the two texts extensively; Condorcet continued to write about corn in his *Vie de M. Turgot* of 1786, and in his political works of the Revolutionary period.[9]

Turgot and Condorcet, like Smith, set out from the proposition that free trade in corn is the best means of preventing scarcity in European countries. "Freedom is the only possible preservative against scarcity," Turgot wrote in his "Lettres sur le commerce des grains." He pointed out that this was hardly a novel view: "It has been said a hundred times, and with good reason, that this freedom [of the corn trade] would be a sure remedy against the frequency of scarcities." He adds, however, that remedy is not immediate. "It has not been said, and should not have been said, that [freedom] should produce this effect starting in the first years when it is established."[10] Condorcet wrote in his *Réflexions sur le commerce des blés* that complete freedom of the corn trade is the "means of assuring the subsistence of the people."[11] He repeated, as late as 1792, that free commerce in corn is "the most sure means" of distributing grain equally over time.[12]

Like Smith, Turgot and Condorcet described the ways in which scarce commodities are divided under freedom of commerce. Smith said that free commerce tends to "divide the inconveniencies of [scarcity] as equally as possible" over time; Turgot said that free commerce would "divide, as rapidly and as equally as possible," the grain that already existed.[13] They dismissed fears of monopoly. Smith pointed to the "number of owners" and their "dispersed situation"; Condorcet mentioned the "number of sellers" and the "dispersed" location of harvested grain.[14]

Smith compared the popular fear of corn merchants to "suspicions of witchcraft" in earlier times; Condorcet said that in earlier times, "Jews and sorcerers" were accused of causing scarcities. Smith said of the corn trader that "it can never be his interest" to raise prices higher than is required by "real scarcity," even though he "discourages the consumption" of "the inferior ranks of people." Condorcet said that corn traders "have no interest in raising grains much above their natural price," but rather help to avert famine by bringing about a "diminution in the consumption of the poor."[15] Smith said in his unpublished lectures on jurisprudence of 1766 that the "police" (or regulation) of grain "is the cause of all that dearth it is intended to prevent"; Condorcet wrote in his *Vie de M. Turgot* that disorders and "famine are the fruit of the very laws which are intended to prevent them."[16]

Turgot's, Condorcet's, and Smith's arguments are similar up to this point. But Turgot and Condorcet go far beyond Smith in their accounts of actual scarcity. As Turgot says, he has been in a position "at every instant, to compare principles with facts." The crisis in the Limousin in 1770 showed that conditions in the corn trade were not a sufficient explanation for famine. Two things are necessary, Turgot says, if the consumer is to survive: "first, that the commodity exists; second, that it is within his reach or that he has sufficient means to acquire it."[17] For most of the crisis of 1770, it was the means that were missing, as Turgot showed in his official documents and unofficial letters of the period. The small proprietors could hardly feed themselves, and turned out their domestics and servants, who then had no food and no means of earning it. Prices were "prodigiously beyond the faculties of the people"; wages were fixed, and it was "absolutely impossible" for the people to pay; in the countryside, people were unemployed and had no wages; by late in the crisis, both commodities and the means to pay for them were missing.[18]

Turgot was concerned explicitly with failures in different "markets," including for labor and land rents as well as for corn.[19] People in the poorest, most remote parts of the province lived for much of the year on chestnuts, roots, and other foods which were not transported. Wages were fixed on the basis of "habitual prices," while corn prices rose freely. But "by a cruel linkage," prices were still not high enough to cover the costs of transport: "Despite the excess of need, grains could not rise to that price, because it was absolutely impossible for the people to pay."[20]

The habitual level of wages, more generally, was itself so low that even a modest diminution or discouragement of food consumption led to great suffering. The process by which commerce prevents scarcity requires "a lapse of time." Time is needed for the establishment of communications, and for commerce to "be born and to form." It is needed for an increase in "general wealth," to the point where even the very poor live on grain, and not on subsistence crops. General wealth is needed, in turn, so that wages are sufficiently above the level of subsistence—or contain sufficient super-fluity—that people can tolerate temporary reductions in consumption. The "superfluous" is indeed "very necessary"; if even the poorest laborers have some property which they can sell when prices rise, then competitive forces can eventually bring about a corresponding increase in wages.[21] "If commerce is to be able to prevent scarcities entirely," Turgot concluded in a letter to Dupont de Nemours, "the people would already have to be rich."[22]

POVERTY AND GENERAL EQUILIBRIUM

Turgot, far more than Smith, was a true visionary of general equilibrium. He argued in the "Lettres sur le commerce des grains" that the values of "commodities, revenue, wages, and population" tend toward equilibrium, in a proportion which would maintain itself so long as "commerce and competition are entirely free." The price of consumer goods in proportion to wages should approach "a point of equilibrium" such as to "procure for the entire society the greatest sum of production, enjoyment, wealth, and strength."[23] Smith imagines the division of scarcity as determined by a ju-dicious and foresighted corn merchant, "pretty much in the same manner as the prudent master of a vessel is sometimes obliged to treat his crew."[24] For Turgot, by contrast, the division of scarcity is by variations in price "of imperceptible degrees." "The debate between every buyer and every seller is a sort of *tâtonnement* which makes known to everyone, with certainty, the true price of everything." Under "entire freedom," this process of *tâtonnement* would reveal something close to true prices. Even the most enlightened public servants—whom Turgot called "angel" monopolists—could not hope to emulate, by "calculation," the "successive changes" which determine prices.[25]

But Turgot was primarily concerned in the "Lettres sur le commerce des grains" with conditions of disequilibrium. Both he and Condorcet moved beyond the explanation of scarcity toward an economic theory of disequilibrium. They distinguished three troublesome conditions in late eighteenth-century France. First, commerce and competition were not yet free. The freedom of the corn trade, Turgot wrote, would have to be "established without contradiction and without troubles," and for some considerable time, if its full effects were to be felt.[26] Second, people were not yet rich. They had few household assets—their "furniture and even their clothes"—which could be sold.[27] They were still so poor, in fact, that the process of convergence to competitive equilibrium would itself cause suffering of a sort which could not continue. "There must be some play in all machines," Turgot wrote, and some superfluous income for even the poorest people; "a clock all of whose wheels connected with one another with mathematical exactitude, without the slightest interval, would soon stop going."[28] Third, people were not yet thoroughly rational. For Condorcet, this was indeed "the only difficult question." People were not "led by reason," or by "the voice of their true interests." They remained prejudiced against "capitalists" and corn merchants, and believed that their interests could best be served by "bad laws." This condition, too, would change. But some lapse of time was again needed.[29]

In the *Réflexions sur le commerce des blés,* Condorcet put forward a theory of public policy for the period of transition to general wealth, general commerce, and general enlightenment. He answered the criticisms of free market policies which had been published since 1770, and defended himself against the charge of insufficient "respect for the misery of the people."[30] He favored private charity; in his *Vie de M. Turgot* he points out that Turgot personally borrowed money to pay for relief before requesting central government funds.[31] But he also sets out the proper role of government itself. He accepts that "equilibrium between those who have everything and those who have nothing" must be based on reciprocal need. But he argues that government must ensure security of subsistence for the poor, independent of trade: of the need "which the rich man has for the poor man's industry."[32]

In his later work on voting and constitutional reform, Condorcet was concerned with the difficulties of aggregating individual preferences into social decisions. In the *Réflexions sur le commerce des blés,* he identifies objectives which are the subject of extensive consensus. He considers that the "quantity of happiness" is not a proper object of government policy. But "welfare" *(bien-être)* is a necessary (although not sufficient) condition for happiness. Condorcet defines welfare in the minimal sense "of not being exposed to misery, to humiliation, to oppression." It is in this sense a proper government objective, or a "duty of justice"; "it is this welfare which governments owe to the people."[33]

"That all members of society should have an assured subsistence each season, each year, and wherever they live; that those who live on their wages, above all, should be able to buy the subsistence they need: this is the general interest of every nation, and it should be the objective of all legislation about subsistence foods." This is the first sentence of the *Réflexions sur le commerce des blés.* Condorcet goes on to say that the objective cannot be ensured by interfering with free commerce in corn. But other forms of intervention are more acceptable. Government "owes relief to those who suffer, and this is a duty of humanity." It should provide relief not by passing bad laws and expropriating corn, but by "assuring a salary and work to the poor."[34]

Condorcet considered that all government interference with commerce is unhelpful and indeed harmful. But there are circumstances, such as food shortages during the transition to completely free commerce, in which some intervention is needed "to avoid a greater evil." The problem for governments is then to choose policies which are not "unjust," and which have relatively minor harmful consequences. Like Turgot, Condorcet was concerned with the problems which arise when people do not have the means to buy corn at current prices. Merchants will not carry corn to places where they do not think they can sell it, and this can lead to scarcity. In such a case, the government must act. But it should not expropriate or subsidize grain, thereby harming the establishment of commerce. It should instead "assure the poor work and wages in proportion to the cost of commodities; and it will always be cheaper for the Treasury to put the poor in a position to buy corn, than to bring the price of corn down to within the reach of the poor."[35]

TURGOT'S POLICIES AGAINST FAMINE

The policies Condorcet describes are those which Turgot himself put into effect in the Limousin. Turgot's "Lettres sur le commerce des grains" were written in 1770 to the Controller-General of French finances. In the same period Turgot wrote another series of letters (only published in full in 1919), in which he described the course of the scarcity, his own actions, and the resources which the provincial authorities needed from the French government. He travels into the mountainous regions of the province. He receives letters from priests who have buried people who died of hunger.

He sends the Controller a piece of local adulterated bread. "Our misery," he writes to Dupont de Nemours, "takes all my time."[36]

Turgot is committed, throughout the crisis, to freedom of the corn trade. He assures Dupont, when his enemies in Paris accuse him of inconsistency, that he has not retreated ("No! No! I will never be a cowardly deserter"), and is more convinced than ever of the need for free commerce.[37] At the height of the scarcity, he insists on royal ordinances to reaffirm the freedom to transport and store corn.[38] But he meanwhile implements a remarkable series of public policies against famine. They include a program of public employment; support for food imports; selective reductions—and some increases—in taxes; and special regulations on land tenure relations.

Turgot's most important policy, from the outset of the crisis, is to provide work and salaries for the poor. He explains that in the countryside it is "wages [which are] in default." He therefore proposes to establish "Charity Offices and Workshops," and he asks for central government finance to supplement local resources. The poor who are able to work, he says, "need wages, and the best and most useful alms consist of providing them with the means of earning." Turgot insists in his local instructions that "real poverty" should be "not only relieved, but respected." He is concerned that public charity will "degrade" some of the poor, and he proposes special arrangements to meet the "justified delicacy" of people, especially in the big cities, who are only temporarily in need. He opposes bringing the poor together to distribute "soup or bread," which would be "a sort of authorized mendicity."[39]

The object of the charity workshops is "to spread money among the people." This is to be done through useful "public works," such as building roads and improving "public places"; Turgot solicits suggestions from small communities for works which could be useful to "the commerce of the Province," and which promote "the employment of women."[40] In his first response to Turgot, the Controller-General had offered 20,000 livres for public works, and 80,000 livres for buying rice for those who could not work; Turgot answered that this seemed to have been an error, and that he proposed to "invert" the proportions.[41]

Turgot's second policy was to increase "provisioning." As the crisis worsened, he used government resources, principally loans to grain merchants, to support imports into the province. The local trade had very little experience of long-distance commerce, and transport costs were prohibitively high even in prosperous years. Turgot therefore devoted about a tenth of the extra resources received from central government to bounties, indemnities, and interest payments for grain imports.[42] Once the grain was in the province, however, it went largely into the ordinary channels of trade. As Condorcet wrote in his *Vie de M. Turgot,* any other policy would have "the more lasting, the more general effect . . . of preventing the establishment of a regular commerce in grain."[43]

The third policy was to reduce taxes on the poor, and to set emergency impositions on the rich. Turgot asked that day laborers be exempted from national taxes, and also the poorest small proprietors, who had already "sold their furniture, their animals, their clothes in order to survive." He revoked all taxes on the Montagne region, where the scarcity was most terrible. But the charity workshops were to be supported in part by new compulsory contributions from rich proprietors. Turgot hoped that voluntary charity would suffice. Where it did not, "municipal officers of the community" were instructed to tax prosperous citizens according to "a roll of contributions." Payments would be in proportion to property income, and would be required of all proprietors, "without distinction."[44]

Turgot's fourth policy consisted of special restrictions on the rights of landowners. Early in the crisis, some proprietors had dismissed their *métayers,* or dependent tenant farmers. Turgot urged all proprietors to support such dependents, "less even on grounds of charity than on grounds of justice," and also out of their own interest. He later imposed a new ordinance in which all proprietors, under strict penalties, were required to maintain their *métayers* until the next harvest, and to bring back those they had sent away.[45] He also imposed restrictions on rents to be paid in kind. When grain prices rose to more than 150 percent of their ten-year average, rents could only be required in money, and at a level no higher than the 150 percent limit: "In times of scarcity, it is human and even just that the law should come to the aid of the tenant."[46]

The effect of Turgot's policies, by the end of 1770, was that the Limousin had been saved from widespread famine.[47] The 1769 harvest had been the worst of the century in the region, and the 1770 harvest was again bad, at a time of European scarcity. But by early 1771, the scarcity was only partial, despite continuing high prices. Mortality rates increased little in 1770 and 1771 (although more in 1772). In Condorcet's laconic summary, "This successful experiment had confirmed M. Turgot in the truth of his principles."[48]

In 1774 Turgot was summoned to Paris, and himself became Controller-General of Finances. His reform edicts of 1776, which were the subject of Louis XVI's *Lit de Justice,* were an attempt to extend throughout France the principles of policy developed in the Limousin. He proposed complete freedom of the corn trade, but insisted that the new policies would not "prevent the procurement of help for the indigent." If the price of grain rose so high that it was beyond the reach of ordinary wages, the government could "supply the needs of the poor . . . by facilitating for the people the means of earning adequate wages through their work." This would be "much more just and efficient aid" than expenditure on government trading, or than the system of regulation under which inquisitive magistrates could make "a parade of their paternal solicitude."[49] But the reforms proved too radical for Paris, and Turgot was removed from office only a few weeks after the registration of the reform edicts in March 1776; this was his final experience of economic policy.

INTERPRETATIONS OF SMITH AND TURGOT

For Turgot and Condorcet, as for Smith, government intervention in commerce is always to be regretted. "You know as well as I do," Turgot wrote to Hume, "what is the great objective of all governments on earth: submission and money."[50] But they also identify circumstances where only government policy can prevent the greater evil of unacceptable suffering. In countries where commerce is not yet fully established, some government intervention is necessary to ensure minimal welfare for all citizens. Turgot's and Condorcet's concern is to explain the conditions for such intervention, and thus for the transition to a fully commercial (and fully prosperous) society.

Turgot, Condorcet, and Smith were all resolutely opposed to government intervention in the corn trade, as has been seen. Turgot and Condorcet then went on to consider policies in other "markets" as well, and in conditions of incomplete commerce. Their analysis of policies against famine is in this respect much richer than Smith's. But Smith at no point rejected the more selective policies which Turgot implemented. He indeed indicated that he had not studied the "pretty exact accounts" of European famines.[51] His main concern was with the effects of corn laws in England and Scotland, where acute scarcity seemed to be a problem of the past.

It is unlikely that Smith read either Turgot's "Lettres sur le commerce des grains" or Condorcet's *Réflexions sur le commerce des blés,* neither of which was widely known in his lifetime. The extensive literature about Turgot's influence on Smith—beginning with Condorcet himself—is concerned to a great extent with theories of capital and investment, and only minimally with scarcity.[52] But Smith was certainly familiar with Turgot's later reform policies of 1774–1776. He owned a copy of the *Procès-Verbal* of the *Lit de Justice*.[53] He also owned a copy of Condorcet's *Vie de M. Turgot* (published after the last revised edition of the *Wealth of Nations*), in which Condorcet describes the Limousin policies, and praises the *Wealth of Nations* as "a work, unfortunately for the happiness of mankind, hitherto too little known in Europe."[54]

Smith frequently favored policies quite similar to those which Turgot and Condorcet proposed. He supported government intervention to oblige employers to pay their workmen in money, and not in kind (when prices were falling).[55] He favored progressive taxation: on rents, for example, such that "the rich should contribute to the public expence, not only in proportion to their revenue, but something more than in that proportion."[56] The reformer William Wilberforce relates that Smith reacted "with a certain characteristic coolness" to schemes for creating employment in remote districts (the Western Isles of Scotland).[57] But there are many other examples of what Siegmund Feilbogen, in his study of Smith and Turgot, describes as "the solidity of Smith's social policy"; Feilbogen lists nine grounds on which Smith justifies government intervention, and goes on to identify twelve instances of his support for "social equality."[58] Smith was even prepared to countenance exceptions to the freedom of the (foreign) corn trade "in cases of the most urgent necessity"; as Donald Winch points out, he is concerned with "second-best alternatives," at least in legislation on corn.[59]

Smith's discussion of scarcity has been of central importance to his posthumous reputation as a relentless proselytizer of free enterprise—as a theorist who promoted commerce, even in times of impending famine. Yet he was thought of during his lifetime as a friend of the poor. He was criticized by Malthus for an ill-judged concern with "the happiness and comfort of the lower orders of society."[60] His harsh reputation seems to have been founded on a novel interpretation of his views in the decade after his death in 1790, as has been seen: under conditions of war-induced scarcity of a sort which he had not experienced, and which he considered quite uncharacteristic of prosperous and civilized countries.[61] He favored complete freedom in one market, for corn; he was thought to have promoted "markets" in general, in the specific circumstances of widespread destitution. He opposed the regulation of the inland corn trade; he was thought to have rejected all forms of government interference, even to relieve the suffering of the poor. Yet his support for free commerce in corn was quite consistent with support of intervention in markets for labor, land rental, and public works: this is the implication of Turgot's and Condorcet's work.

THE LAPSE OF TIME

Turgot and Condorcet were concerned, explicitly, with circumstances in which commerce is not yet established, and in which the initial endowments of the poor are so low as to make destitution a continuing threat. They show that scarcities arise because of conditions in several different markets, and that governments must choose the best policy for each of these markets.[62] Their theory suggests a way of ordering policy choices during the often long lapse of time while markets emerge. Markets do not become established within a few months or a couple of years. Where wages and household endowments are low, scarcities can arise, quite suddenly, because of disruptions in several different markets. Governments cannot avert these crises simply by policies in relation to food. They must instead choose a combination of public interventions, appropriate to each market.

Condorcet's definition of minimal welfare—in terms of the responsibility of government to prevent misery, oppression, and humiliation—is open, evidently, to continuous revision. He himself included commodities other than subsistence food in the requirements of a life which was free of misery; he later included education and schoolbooks in the requirements of a life without humiliation. The most general importance of Turgot's and Condorcet's work on the corn trade is to be found, rather, in their analysis of the political limits to the operation of commerce. They use the metaphor of an economic system in the process of dynamic adjustment toward equilibrium. Government actions are both shocks to the machinery of society and conditions for its continued adjustment. Their analysis can be seen as suggesting criteria for choosing the least disruptive of these actions.

The first criterion is the organization of the market (or non-market arrangement) which will be affected. In Turgot's conception of general interdependence, interferences with freedom in any market can have systemic effects. But he also emphasizes differences across markets in the extent to which commerce and competition are complete. In respect to corn, for example, the long process of establishing freedom has begun, but is far from complete. It is therefore especially vulnerable to what Condorcet called "the more lasting, the more general effect" of government intervention. In respect to rural tenancies, by contrast, there are very few marketlike arrangements to be displaced. In respect to urban unskilled labor—the market affected by public works—commerce may be very solidly established, and will not be disrupted for long by public employment projects.

Turgot's and Condorcet's procedures imply that governments should interfere in those markets where the expected effects on the organization of commerce are smallest. The market for corn, where commerce is in the process of being established and where the long-term dynamic effects of government action are large, is particularly unsuitable. Turgot and Condorcet were indeed especially concerned with legal and psychological effects. The old, regulated corn trade attracted the sort of merchants whom Smith described as "wretched hucksters," and whose ill repute was for Condorcet "only too well founded."[63] A merchant could never know if the laws under which he has bought will be those under which he will sell; Condorcet pointed out that this uncertainty inhibited "real" merchants, and favored "men who know how to profit [from] prohibitive laws."[64] It was essential, under these conditions, to consider the long-term effects of government policies in different markets.

The second criterion is the distributional effect of the policy. Turgot, like Smith, recognized that government regulations tended to favor the rich over the poor, and the "master" over the "workman."[65] Laws were enforced to protect the rich, Condorcet showed, or according to the "interest or caprice" of the enforcers.[66] It was therefore important to evaluate the effects of policies on different groups. Employment policies, for Turgot, were more just and efficient than policies to reduce corn prices. Government expenditure would have to be financed by taxes, which fall on the poor as well as the rich. But the rich also buy corn; policies to subsidize the price of corn would be "alms for the rich at least as much as for the poor."[67] It will always be cheaper for the Treasury to provide employment for the poor, as Condorcet wrote, than to reduce corn prices for everyone.[68]

The third criterion is the nature of property rights. Government intervention is least bad, other things being equal, where the property rights to be violated by the intervention are least important. When Turgot proposed in his "Lettres sur le commerce des grains" to suppress certain privileges of bakers' and millers' guilds, he distinguished between the "superstitious respect" for property originally "founded on usurpations," and respect for the "most sacred of all property . . . the property of man in the fruit of his labor."[69] The rights of proprietors to impose rents in kind were similarly unrespectable; the rights of corn farmers were sacred. Condorcet distinguished property in the right to impose charges, for example, from "true property" in land or goods.[70] The classification of competing rights was a matter of considerable dispute; Diderot claimed, in opposition to Turgot's views, that no individual property rights are "sacred" in relation to "public concern" or "general utility."[71] The privileges of the mastership guilds, the advocate-general Séguier said in the *Lit de Justice,* were themselves a form of "real property."[72] Public perceptions of different rights could also be expected to change over time, as Condorcet showed. But government should try, as far as possible, to limit its interventions to those markets where property rights were considered, by public consensus, to be relatively unimportant.

The fourth criterion is the nature of the freedoms which are violated by different interventions. Turgot and Condorcet, like Smith, criticized government officials not only for violating property rights, but also for the "vexation," "oppression," and "visits" which accompanied such violations.[73] The Paris magistrates who paraded their paternal solicitude for the poor, Turgot wrote in his presentation to Louis XVI of the reform edicts, also prized their authority to "search the homes of laborers and traders," and to ruin merchants who had displeased them.[74] Such oppression was a reason to avoid intervention in the market for corn. The freedom of proprietors to send away their tenant farmers was by contrast based on injustice, or the denial of habitual obligations, and could therefore be violated with less regret.[75]

Government intervention in labor markets did violate personal freedom, especially when the poor were compelled to work in public projects which were thought of as degrading; Turgot's concern for the justified delicacy of poor people in the Limousin was an attempt to mitigate these effects. But to be dependent on the solicitude of the rich was also degrading. "Of all the words which console and reassure men," Condorcet wrote, "justice is the only one which the oppressor does not dare to pronounce, while humanity is on the lips of all tyrants."[76] Government interventions were least bad, in general, in those markets where only relatively unimportant freedoms are to be violated.

Condorcet's and Turgot's criteria amount to a quite complicated system for choosing between different policies. Governments could find themselves choosing between interventions in many different markets, on the basis of multiple criteria, and in circumstances where the criteria themselves are changing over time. But in the case of scarcity and famine, the criteria yield a clear ordering, where intervention in the markets for corn is worst, and intervention in rural tenancies, training, and labor markets is least bad. They provide a consistent method, more generally, for evaluating the consequences of government policies in different markets, in the course of the slow transition to complete commercial freedom.

4

Apprenticeship and Insecurity

A STRANGE ADVENTURE

Adam Smith was an unrelenting critic of apprenticeship, and his views were invoked by the opponents and supporters of apprenticeship schemes in the course of the eighteenth and nineteenth centuries. They were indeed the subject of the very earliest controversy over the *Wealth of Nations,* some weeks before it was first published in London in March 1776. "Here is a strange adventure," the abbé Morellet wrote to Turgot on February 26; he relates that as he was waiting, earlier in the day, for the proofs of his translation of "the piece by Mr. Smith"—a section of the early chapter of the *Wealth of Nations* dealing with corporations and apprenticeships—he received news that the manuscript had instead been seized by the police, and was deemed to be worthy of burning.[1] Morellet's translation, which had been commissioned by Turgot, was somewhat approximate; he speaks of various "transpositions," including bringing together Smith's remarks on the "difficulty of the art of agriculture" and on the "uselessness of apprenticeships."[2] But this "chapter of an English work on corporations," as the diarist Métra described it, was seen as a contribution to Turgot's criticism of established power; "one could never get permission" for its publication.[3]

My object, in this chapter, is to look at the arguments Smith put forward against apprenticeship, which took the entirely characteristic form, for Smith, of asserting that the institution of apprenticeship was both inefficient and unjust. Smith's criticism of apprenticeship regulations, together with his criticism of regulations on the corn trade, was at the heart of his view of economic reform. Like Turgot's reform edicts on the mastership guilds and on the regulation of corn, they together suggested an inclusive system of commercial freedom: for industry and for agriculture, and for the commerce in labor as well as for the commerce in commodities. Smith's observations on corporations—on the silk weavers of London, the cutlers of Sheffield, the "universities" of master smiths, the ancient corporations of bakers, and other partial associations of trades—have attracted much less attention, at least since the late nineteenth century, than his observations on food. This is a consequence, in part, of the conclusive success of efforts to reform the old apprenticeship corporations, both in England and in France. The historian, searching the past for the seeds of the present, has little interest in disputes over long-forgotten institutions and long-concluded controversies.[4] But the reception of Smith's views of apprenticeship played a critical role, as will be seen, in the remarkable transformation in his reputation in the decades following his death in 1790.

IT IS BUT EQUITY, BESIDES

Smith's arguments about apprenticeship were part of a much more general criticism of corporate, municipal, and parochial institutions, and in particular of the uncertain jurisprudence in which these institutions flourished. This more general criticism is in turn of substantial importance to understanding Smith's view of commerce and government, and of the sides of economic life—oppressive or vexatious, discursive or independent—which belong neither to commerce nor to the state.

Smith's arguments about apprenticeship can be grouped into four categories. The first, which is the closest to what would later have been thought of as an economic argument, is that exclusive apprenticeships tend to obstruct competition and to damage the public interest by keeping up wages and profits in particular industries, employments, or locations. The second argument is also, in part, about efficiency. Smith favored universal, obligatory education; he argues that apprenticeship is an unsatisfactory means of training workers either in particular skills or in habits of industry. The third argument is about both efficiency and equity; it is that apprenticeship, which is a restriction on personal liberty, is unjust to workers within apprenticeship relations and to other workers who are excluded from these regulated trades. The fourth argument is the closest to what would now be considered a purely political argument, although it is central, as will be seen, to Smith's account of economic change. It is that apprenticeships are unjust because they reflect an oppressive combination of public laws and corporate bylaws—a "corporation spirit"—in which laws are enacted for the benefit of the powerful, and enforced at the caprice of magistrates, masters, overseers, and churchwardens. They are themselves a source of insecurity.

Smith's four arguments were interpreted in strikingly different ways in the course of successive nineteenth-century debates over the reform and revival of apprenticeship, and I will look at each argument in turn. I will be concerned, principally, with the period preceding the reform of statutory apprenticeship in England in 1814. The four arguments provide an interesting illustration, it will be suggested, of Smith's capacity to appear as almost all things to almost all men; of the extent to which the *Wealth of Nations* has been (and is) an enormous mirror of changing economic times. Beatrice Webb wrote in her unpublished "History of English Economics" that subsequent critics "have forgotten that Adam Smith lived in an age of class oppression and that the 'Wealth of Nations' is a history book of social abuses." There was a profound change in his reputation, she said, which took place between 1776 and 1817, or between the publication of the *Wealth of Nations* and the publication of Ricardo's *Principles of Political Economy.* "What, then," she asks, "were the changes in events and ideas that transformed this crusade of the 18th century [into] the 'Employer's Gospel' of the 19th century?"[5] The debates over apprenticeship reform provide some insight, it will be suggested, into these events and these ideas.

There is a "double nature" or "twofold character" of Smith's work, Webb wrote, in which he is both a theorist who seeks to discover (and put to practical use) the laws of production, and at the same time a "reformer of social abuses." Each of Smith's four arguments against apprenticeship, as will be seen, is about economic theory (or efficiency) and also about social justice (or equity). Apprenticeship, for Smith, is *both* inefficient and unjust; it is *as* inefficient as it is unjust. The "affected anxiety of the lawgiver lest they should employ an improper person, is evidently as impertinent as it is oppressive," Smith said of the English statute of apprenticeships; the liberal reward of the laboring poor, he said earlier in the *Wealth of Nations,* will be of advantage to society, and "it is but equity, besides." The laws which prevented manufacturers from selling their goods in shops, and farmers from selling corn, "were evident violations of natural liberty, and therefore unjust; and they were both too as impolitic as they were unjust."[6]

It is this sense of the contiguity of economic and political reasons—of "equity, besides"—which makes the successive nineteenth-century disputes over apprenticeship such an intriguing illustration of the changing uses of political economy, and of the *Wealth of Nations* in particular. Apprenticeship is a "cultural institution," in K. D. M. Snell's description; it should be seen as embedded within "a wide range of social, legal, settlement, welfare and administrative considerations." There are evident changes, from this perspective, between the three phases of British apprenticeship that Snell distinguishes, from the "guild apprenticeship" before the Elizabethan statute of 1563, to the "statutory apprenticeship" of 1563–1814, and the "'voluntary' apprenticeship" of the period since 1814.[7] Yet one of the interesting characteristics of the nineteenth-century debates with which I will be concerned—of the history of economic thought about apprenticeship, in relation to its economic and political history—is the extent to which obsolete apprenticeship systems are themselves a subject of continuing dispute. History is put forward, in the debates, as a way to justify present policies. It is something which is either to be cherished (for opponents of reform) or to be overthrown. It is also, as it was for Smith, a way to discover laws or principles which persist over time. The pre-Elizabethan guilds are still present, in Smith's description, in the statutory apprenticeships; the corporation spirit, or the subordination of individual wills, is present in the new, voluntary apprenticeships of the later nineteenth century.

CORPORATIONS AND COMPETITION

Smith's first set of arguments is about competition. Statutes of apprenticeship, he says, are, like "the exclusive privileges of corporations," "a sort of enlarged monopolies." Their effect is to keep up both the wages of the workers and the profits of the masters. They obstruct "the free circulation of labour from one employment to another," just as the privileges of corporations "obstruct it from one place to another." "The intention of both regulations is to restrain the competition," and the effect of restraining that free competition is to keep prices high. If apprenticeships were ended, "the public would be a gainer, the work of all artificers coming in this way much cheaper to market." Smith's prescription was to "break down the exclusive privileges of corporations, and repeal the statute of apprenticeship, both which are real encroachments upon natural liberty, and add to these the repeal of the law of settlements."[8]

It is this set of arguments, about the economic inefficiency of apprenticeship, which was most conspicuous in the political discussions over the suspension and eventual partial repeal in 1814 of the Elizabethan stat-ute of apprenticeship.[9] The defenders of the old act, in particular, were at pains to refute Smith's arguments. William Playfair, the editor of the "eleventh edition" of the *Wealth of Nations,* was an ardent supporter of apprenticeship, and his edition is a compendium of counterarguments to Smith's criticisms. Smith's account of apprenticeship is annotated with ir-ritable footnotes: "In this particular assertion, Mr Smith is certainly en-tirely wrong"; "This seems to be founded on wrong information, having no sort of foundation in reality." Playfair also inserts a "Supplementary Chapter," "On Education," between chapters 1 and 2 of Book 5, in which he comments that "Dr Smith is an enemy to apprenticeships," asserts that "the control which the law gives a master over an apprentice, seems to be one of the most fortunate inventions in the present order of things," and recommends that "instead of suppressing, it would be well to encourage this species of bondage."[10]

Playfair, who was known for his theories of the decline of nations, and for his epigrammatic denunciations of French philosophy ("Prussia, the former headquarters of atheism," "Condorcet, a captain of assassins"), re-turned to the same theme in other works. Prejudice, he said, had in the case of apprenticeship led Smith astray, and his views should be "exam-ined, and refuted, if found wrong." Smith was even wrong, Playfair wrote, in denying that apprenticeships were truly ancient institutions, with their equivalent in Egypt and Rome: "Are we quite certain that the freed men, so often mentioned, were not people who had served apprenticeships?"[11] "It is very easy to trace the intimate connection between the theory of leaving trade free, and those levelling principles that ruined France for a long period," he wrote in a pamphlet of 1814; opposition to the statute of apprenticeship was "founded upon the same delusive theoretical principles which fostered the French revolution."[12]

For the early nineteenth-century opponents of the Elizabethan act, by contrast, Smith was a source both of true principles and of useful evidence. Smith's illustrations—the wheelwright who is permitted to make a coach, and the coach maker who is not permitted to make a wheel; the success of Manchester, Birmingham, and other manufacturing towns outside the scope of the act—recur in the reformers' arguments.[13] A committee of London Manufacturers formed in 1814 said of the act that it "strikes at the root of all our prosperity," by "the color it gives to the combination of workmen for the raising of wages."[14] The "least of the evils to be appre-hended" from such combination is "the progressive rise of Wages," say the members of a parliamentary committee of 1806 which recommended the repeal of the apprenticeship clauses of the act in respect of wool; this is in itself "abundantly sufficient to accomplish the ruin . . . of the whole commercial greatness of our Country." It is as though Smith's views scarcely needed to be repeated. "At this day," the committee observes, "the true principles of Commerce are so generally understood and acknowledged, it cannot be necessary for your Committee to do more than refer to them."[15]

Smith was the implicit hero, therefore, of the reformers. But what is striking in their arguments is the extent to which they picked and chose within his criticism of monopoly and restraint. Smith himself, to take one example, linked statutory apprenticeships repeatedly to the privileges of corporations. The early nineteenth-century opponents of apprenticeship were by contrast often at pains to distinguish between corporate and apprenticeship regulations. Sir Frederick Eden, for example, accepts Smith's criticism of apprenticeship, but objects to "his mistaken ideas respecting corporation laws," his attribution of removals of the poor "to corporation spirit," and his "much to be regretted" asseverations about the low quality of workmanship in incorporated towns.[16] It was hardly expedient in the decades following Smith's death, as Dugald Stewart commented in 1810, to think of "subjecting to the disputations of philosophers, the arcana of State Policy, and the unfathomable wisdom of the feudal ages."[17] Smith's criticism of arcane English corporations is notably absent, only a few years later, from the disputes over apprenticeship.

The parliamentary critics of apprenticeship are led into quite odd arguments in their efforts to avoid calling into question the corporate, English origins of the apprenticeship regulations. The system to be reformed is thus described, in a curious substitution of simile for history, as something which is more Indian than English. The intention of the apprenticeship act, said Serjeant Onslow, the leading parliamentary supporter of the 1814 amendment, was to introduce distinctions "as is created in India by the institution of castes." The Committee of London Manufacturers say that the apprentice is fixed in his trade "as if he belonged to one of the castes of India"; another parliamentary supporter of reform, George Phillips, said that "this principle went, in fact, to place the trading classes in this country on a level with the Indian castes."[18] Onslow's closing words, in moving the reform amendment, are a reminder that it is only apprenticeship, and not corporate privileges, which is in question: the amendment does not "affect, or alter the bye-laws, or privileges of any corporation, or company lawfully constituted: indeed, out of abundant caution, and to prevent any alarm that may have been industriously excited, I have inserted a clause to that effect."[19]

Smith's concern about the effects of apprenticeship on wages, profits, and prices, to take a different example, is decomposed in much the same way. Smith's presumption, as has been seen, is that high wages for "servants, labourers and workmen of different kinds" are an advantage to society, and "but equity, besides"; the liberal reward of labor, he says, is the "cause of the greatest public prosperity." He was much more disturbed by high profits than by high wages, and included in the second and subsequent editions of the *Wealth of Nations* a passage explaining that "in reality high profits tend much more to raise the price of work than high wages." It was also easier to restrict competition in the interest of profits than in the interest of wages: "We have no acts of parliament against combining to lower the price of work; but many against combining to raise it," and the "masters are always and everywhere in a sort of tacit, but constant and uniform combination, not to raise the wages of labour above their actual rate."[20]

In the debates of the 1810s, Smith's opinions are reduced, by the proponents of reform, to a concern only with the effects of apprenticeship privileges on wages. "Our merchants and master-manufacturers complain much of the bad effects of high wages," Smith observes, while "they say nothing concerning the bad effects of high profits. They are silent with regard to the pernicious effects of their own gains. They complain only of those of other people."[21] The masters of 1814 behaved very much as Smith described, as Lujo Brentano pointed out in his history of guilds.[22] George Phillips, who had been so concerned about Indian castes, felt it necessary to distance himself from Smith: "Adam Smith thought that combinations among workmen were not dangerous—because they were counteracted by combinations among the master manufacturers, which he believed to be more frequent. That able writer was mistaken in the fact." Masters did not frequently combine, Phillips went on; "on the other hand, the journeymen drove the reluctant into combination, through terror."[23]

There is yet another aspect of Smith's argument about apprenticeship and competition which is almost entirely missing in the debates of the 1810s. The apprentice and corporation laws were instituted and enforced, in Smith's description, for the security of relatively powerful people. The corporation laws obstruct both the free circulation of labor and that of stock, but "it is everywhere much easier for a wealthy merchant to obtain the privilege of trading in a town corporate, than for a poor artificer to obtain that of working in it." There is an inside and an outside community, in a quite literal sense. Within an incorporated town, Smith says, the different classes of traders and artificers thus buy from one another "somewhat dearer than they might otherwise have done"; "but in their dealings with the country they were all great gainers." The barriers to entry are barriers, quite literally, or at least inspections; they obstruct the farmers who set out for town to sell their corn, or the consumers, like Smith's customer "in the suburbs," who return home with smuggled work.[24]

Even within the class of artificers, in Smith's description, it is those who have least power—including apprentices who "cannot give money"—who do least well. Others are simply outside such protection as the regulations may provide. "Our spinners are poor people, women commonly, scattered about in all different parts of the country, without support or protection," Smith says. "In most parts of Scotland she is a good spinner who can earn twenty-pence a week."[25] The most oppressed of all, as so often for Smith, are the common laborers. Their understanding is generally much superior to that of mechanics in towns. But they are subject to the entire system of injustice constituted by the conjunction of the apprenticeship, corporation, and settlement acts. The exotic Orient appears here, for once, as an encouraging precedent: "In China and Indostan accordingly both the rank and the wages of country labourers are said to be superior to those of the greater part of artificers and manufacturers. They would probably be so every where, if corporation laws and the corporation spirit did not prevent it."[26]

Smith's description of insideness and outsideness—of the multiple identities of individuals, as people with privileges because they are members of apprenticed trades, or citizens settled in certain towns, or workers with certain skills—is missing, once again, in the invocations of political economy during the apprenticeship disputes of the 1810s. The London Committee of Manufacturers, who are more bold than their parliamentary allies in their references to "feudal times," do point out that the Elizabethan statute restricted apprenticeships to the children of prosperous families; the parents of woollen weavers were supposed (in a subsequently unenforced provision) to have sixty shillings a year in land, while laborers "were excluded and not permitted to quit husbandry."[27] The committee members appeal, even, to equity for illicit women workers: "Will you, by enforcing it at the peace, drive to the miserable and infamous resource of prostitution, the multitudes of women now employed in the fabrication of arms for the defence of the State?"[28] But the reformers' arguments about commerce and competition are close, in general, to the painfully contracted, lowly calculating political economy to which William Godwin objected in 1820, and which Francis Place defended.[29] Arnold Toynbee said of Smith's views on apprenticeship, in his lectures of 1881–82, that "it is the doctrine of free exchange of labour . . . that has brought political economists into collision with the feelings of the people." Yet Smith's own intention, he said, was to represent "the opinions of the workmen"; "we see that this doctrine was first popularised by a warm champion of the labourers as the true solution of all the evils of their state."[30]

EDUCATION AND APPRENTICESHIP

Smith's second set of concerns, about the inefficiency of apprenticeship as a way of teaching skills, is also ubiquitous in the debates over reform. He was unconvinced, in general, that extensive instruction or skill was needed in most manufacturing employments. He thought that country labor, in which people had to be able to work under widely varying conditions, required "much more skill and experience," and "much more judgment and discretion." Even watchmaking could be explained in the lessons of a few weeks, or perhaps of a few days, to be followed by "much practice and experience"; "long apprenticeships are altogether unnecessary." The effect of the statutory apprenticeship system was moreover to obstruct workers from moving from decaying to prosperous manufactures; the arts of plain linen and plain silk weaving, for example, were "almost entirely the same," and not very different from the art of weaving plain wool.[31]

The institution of long, bound apprenticeship was an unsatisfactory way of teaching even those skills and tastes which do turn out to be useful; it "has no tendency to form young people to industry." Journeymen and pieceworkers, Smith said, have an incentive to be industrious, and to conceive "a relish" for work; he indeed believed that they have a tendency rather to "over-work themselves, and to ruin their health and constitution."[32] But an "apprentice is likely to be idle, and almost always is so, because he has no immediate interest to be otherwise." He does not enjoy the "sweets" of work, and he may even conceive "an aversion to labour." Smith argues that apprenticeships can "give no security that insufficient workmanship" will not be put on public sale, a security which is much better provided by a system of marking plate or stamping cloth. The sale of shoddy goods, he says, "is generally the effect of fraud, and not of inability; and the longest apprenticeship can give no security against fraud." The risk of fraud is indeed greater in exclusive, privileged corporations. For the workman without privileges, it is the fear of losing customers "which restrains his frauds"; workers in the suburbs outside incorporated towns "have nothing but their character to depend upon."[33]

Smith's arguments reappear throughout the debates over reform. The London Committee points out that the Elizabethan Parliament was obliged to legislate again, thirty-eight years after passing the apprenticeship statute, over the true making of cloth: "The saddle was at last put on the right horse; the fraud of the master."[34] The 1806 Parliamentary Committee on the Woollen Manufacture, too, heard dire stories of shoddiness. One merchant was thus cross-questioned about the time, "perhaps forty years ago," when the cloth merchants of the West Riding "lost the clothing of the Russian guards":

A. I believe it was lost by regulations of the Russian government, it never returned back to Leeds after it was lost.
Q. Did you never hear it mentioned, as a leading cause of those regulations, that upon a grand review of the Russian guards, who turned out clad in coats, on a very rainy day, that the same coats the next morning were very much shrunk into jackets?

But the case of the Russian order was explained, in the end, by the iniquities of German trading houses and the protectionism of the Russians, and the committee concluded, with Smith, that apprenticeship was in no way essential for teaching skills. The committee indeed surmised, like Smith, that apprentices, who do not enjoy the immediate fruits of their industry, might instead learn lasting "habits of idleness and dissipation."[35]

The "true principles of Commerce," here too, are fairly contracted and calculating. But it is interesting that the wider scope of Smith's arguments—his view of the politics of education and apprenticeship—was virtually ignored, as in the case of his arguments about competition, by the parliamentary proponents of reform. It was the opponents of reform, and especially William Playfair, who pointed to the profound and even subversive scope of Smith's position. "To free youth from the shackles of apprenticeship, and subject infancy to the authority of schoolmasters, is the present bent of political economists," Playfair wrote in his supplementary chapter on education in his eleventh edition of the *Wealth of Nations*. He sees Smith's opposition to apprenticeship, quite generally, as the outcome of an imposing choice between two ways of life: between a society brought together by education, and a society brought together by training. "Whether or not it contributes to the comfort and happiness of the working man, to read and write, is a question not necessary to decide, and probably not very easy," he says. "Reading frequently leads to discontent, an ill-founded ambition, and a neglect of business . . . [I]t is at least clear that habits of industry, and a trade, are the most essential parts of the education of the lower order of people. But Dr. Smith is an enemy to apprenticeships."[36]

Playfair's supplement follows the chapter in the *Wealth of Nations* where Smith puts forward his plan for the universal, publicly funded education in local schools of the "children of the common people," and universal education, for Playfair, is in clear opposition to training and apprenticeship. "That portion of education, which appears to have got an exclusive title to the name, reading and writing, are, with the working classes, a very inferior object," he had written in his earlier work on the decline of nations. In 1813, describing the attentions of Smith's admirer Samuel Whitbread to the education of poor children, he concludes, "Perhaps we do not agree with him and many others, in regard to the advantage of men doomed to industry and privation being excited to read and write."[37]

Playfair is explicit, unlike Smith, in seeing education and training as two opposing systems. But the tension between the two projects constitutes the context in which Smith's arguments about apprenticeship should be understood. Smith is insistent, from the beginning of the *Wealth of Nations*, on the equality of natural talents. The difference between the philosopher and the common street porter, he says, "seems to arise not so much from nature, as from habit, custom and education. When they came into the world, and for the first six or eight years of their existence, they were, perhaps, very much alike."[38] Their "very different genius," as adults, is the consequence of the division of labor more than its cause. People are not born "stupid and ignorant" but are made so by their "ordinary employments"; by the simple, uniform nature of the work they can get; and by the circumstance that their parents, who "can scarce afford to maintain them even in infancy," send them out to work as soon as they can.[39] Smith's comments in his then unpublished lectures on jurisprudence would have confirmed Playfair's suspicions: "When a person's whole attention is bestowed on the 17th part of a pin," he says, it is hardly surprising that people are "exceedingly stupid," and England, where boys are set to work at "6 or 7 years of age," is to be contrasted most unfavorably with Scotland, where "even the meanest porter can read and write."[40]

The public "can facilitate, can encourage, and can even impose" a system of education on "almost the whole body of the people," Smith says. The "most essential parts of education" are "to read, write, and account," and even the poorest people should "have time to acquire them" before they begin their working life. It is interesting that education, here, is something that precedes, and is distinct from, training. The circumstances of commercial society impose the need for government expenditure on education. Smith's description of the genesis of stupidity and ignorance in commercial societies—of individuals "mutilated and deformed" in the "essential part of the character of human nature"—is indeed the most severe of all his criticisms of modern, civilized life.[41] But government-supported education is in no sense something which is itself needed in the interest of commercial prosperity. It is a consequence of economic advancement, and not a requirement of further advancement.

Smith is in fact resolute in identifying education as something which is good in itself, and not as the means to a distinct, commercial end. When he does talk of universal instruction as a means, it is in relation to the political ends of the society, or to the common interest in political security. People who are instructed "feel themselves, each individually, more respectable," and they "are more disposed to examine, and more capable of seeing through," political projects.[42] The ideal, that is to say, is of the disposition of enlightenment, or of universal public discussion, among thoughtful, reflecting, self-respecting individuals; the prospect of "political discussions among the multitude," which Dugald Stewart was obliged to repudiate in Edinburgh in 1794.[43]

Education is more generally, for Smith, something which is not only useful but also amusing. Even when he says, as a justification for teaching the principles of geometry and mechanics to the "children of the common people," that these principles are useful in common trades, he adds that they are also inspiring; the "introduction to the most sublime as well as to the most useful sciences." In the lectures on jurisprudence, he is once again more outspoken. The lack of education is, for "low people's children," "one of their greatest misfortunes." A boy who starts work when he is very young thus finds that "when he is grown up he has no ideas with which he can amuse himself." Even the poor need things to think or theorize about: "They learn to read, and this gives them the benefit of religion, which is a great advantage, not only considered in a pious sense, but as it affords them subject for thought and speculation."[44]

Apprenticeship, for Playfair, is a way for masters to "control" the young, and a source of "good moral conduct." To discourage apprenticeships, he wrote in 1814, would be "a great detriment to the moral order of society." They provide people in the "lower and middling ranks of society" with "the means of keeping their sons in due subjection during the first danger-ous years of manhood"; parents bind their children to be apprentices, "to keep them from becoming vagabonds and blackguards." Playfair com-pares "modern reformers," here too, to the "misled reformers" in France in 1793, "when the authority of husbands over wives and children, was represented as an infringement of natural rights, and a remain of the feudal system!"[45]

It is interesting that even the opponents of the Elizabethan statute made some sort of reference, before the 1814 repeal, to the beneficent conse-quences of apprenticeship for morality and subordination. The 1806 com-mittee thus regretted the decline in "opinions and feelings of subordina-tion," but concluded that apprenticeship in the woollen trade could do little to prevent it.[46] George Rose M.P., Serjeant Onslow's predecessor in investigating reform of the statute, explained in a debate of 1807 on Samuel Whitbread's Parochial Schools Bill—which was criticized on the grounds that it was likely to prejudice the morals of the poor "instead of teaching them subordination"—that "he had no doubt that the poor ought to be taught to read; as to writing he had some doubt."[47] Onslow himself repudiated, aghast, any notion that he might put "*national wealth* in competition with *national morals*." The London Committee suggested that even when apprenticeship was no longer itself compulsory, a parent might well wish to apprentice his child in the interest of the child's own in-terior life; of "that compulsory subordination, by which he is inured to habits of industry, which cannot be attained under a parent's roof, amidst the familiarity of relations."[48]

For Smith, by contrast, the prospect of instruction in subordination seems to have been a matter of the greatest indifference. It was unlikely to promote habits of industry, which were discouraged, rather, by long, sub-ordinate apprenticeships. It had almost nothing, in particular, to contrib-ute to the flourishing of moral sentiments. The habitual sympathy which is essential to virtue, Smith wrote in one of the last passages he added to the *Theory of Moral Sentiments,* is a matter of one's affection for one's relations and one's friends. He is strongly in favor of domestic education, or keep-ing one's children at home. He is in favor, even, of treating children with respect: "Respect for you must always impose a very useful restraint upon their conduct; and respect for them may frequently impose no useless re-straint upon your own."[49]

The apprenticeship debates prior to the 1814 repeal were imbued, like all other political discussion of the times, with the precedent of the French Revolution; with what the members of the 1806 Committee on the Woollen Manufacture described as the effects "so fatally exemplified not long since, in a Sister Kingdom."[50] Playfair spoke of Serjeant Onslow as the instrument of more resolute men, much as the opponents of slavery were duped in France in 1780. Onslow's bill would be "the first step to liberty and equality in this country, as the Society of the Friends of the Blacks, was in Paris, about twenty-five years ago," to be followed by "terrible revolution."[51] Smith had been widely described, as has been seen, as a friend of France, and his views on ignorance and universal education were indeed among his most popular in Revolutionary France. Condorcet observed in 1788, citing Smith, that true public instruction is the only remedy for the general stupidity that is a consequence of the division of labor. It is "workers who only know how to do one thing, or even one part of one thing," who are particularly likely to become unemployed, and to fall into poverty. In the system of public instruction proposed by Condorcet, children would not learn one trade; they would instead learn how to learn new trades.

For Condorcet, as for Smith, instruction is an end, far more than a means. If people were less ignorant, they would be better at buying things, and "less exposed to being victims of a thousand petty frauds, a thousand petty vexations." They would be better at leading "a common life"; they would have correct ideas of "their rights and their duties," and an understanding of "local jurisprudence." In Condorcet's last plan of public instruction during the Revolution, in which he also cites Smith, the system of education is extended to grown-ups, with classes on Sundays for mothers, fathers, and people of all ages. "In thus continuing instruction throughout life," it will become possible for people to keep their spirits active; to learn about new laws; to be instructed "in the art of instructing oneself."[52] Smith was one of the inspirations of the revolutionary projects of public instruction of 1788 and 1791; he was far closer to these projects, in his view of education, than to Playfair's system of moral subordination through occupational training.

A STATE OF NONAGE

Smith's third set of arguments against apprenticeship, about oppression and personal liberty, was the subject of virtually no interest in the parliamentary debates of the 1800s and 1810s. "The property which every man has in his own labour, as it is the original foundation of all other property, so it is the most sacred and inviolable," Smith says; the apprenticeship system, which prevents the poor man from using his labor as he thinks proper, "is a plain violation of this most sacred property," and thereby of "just liberty." The injustice, in turn, takes two distinct forms. In the first, which is closely related to the arguments about free circulation of labor considered earlier, workers are obstructed from moving from one occupation to another, or from one parish to another. "A thousand spinners and weavers" may be dependent, Smith says, on "half a dozen wool-combers"; the wool-combers, by refusing to take apprentices, can "reduce the whole manufacture into a sort of slavery to themselves."[53]

The apprenticeship system is closely connected, in Smith's description, to the law of settlements within the English Poor Laws. It is both complementary to and a component of the system of removals and certificates for the poor, which Smith described as "an evident violation of natural liberty and justice," and in which the common people, "so jealous of their liberty," are "most cruelly oppressed." The poor worker must thus provide "security"—the security of owning property in the parish, for example, or of having served an apprenticeship—before he can himself attain the "security" of being established or settled. He is scarcely free; he is subject to the will of "the churchwardens and overseers of the poor," and of "two justices of the peace." The skilled worker who has served an apprenticeship is prevented, even, from going abroad to exercise his trade: "The boasted liberty of the subject, of which we affect to be so very jealous . . . is so plainly sacrificed to the futile interests of our merchants and manufacturers."[54]

The other sort of injustice is internal to the apprenticeship relation itself. "The whole labour of the apprentice belongs to his master," Smith writes; he is a "servant bound to work at a particular trade for the benefit of a master." It is this relationship—this unfreedom—which makes apprentices indolent. The expectation that apprenticeship would provide training in skills, or education in morality, is doomed by the inequality of the relationship on which it depends. Smith thought it most improbable that people should work better "when they are disheartened than when they are in good spirits, when they are frequently sick than when they are generally in good health"; this was one of his many arguments in favor of high wages. Masters prefer periods of low real wages, in which their employees are "more humble and dependent." Smith's own view is that the "separate independent state" is far more conducive both to industry and to "morals."[55]

Smith's view of apprenticeship and natural liberty is close, once again, to the positions of reformers before and in the early years of the French Revolution. Turgot's edict for the suppression of the *jurandes* or guild wardenships, and their associated apprenticeships, was at the heart of the *Lit de Justice* of Louis XVI in March 1776. It was written a little before Turgot commissioned Morellet's first translation of the sections of the *Wealth of Nations*, as has been seen. Like Smith, Turgot was "in no way afraid that the suppression of apprenticeships" would expose the public to bad service. He spoke, like Smith, of the property one has in one's labor as "the first, the most sacred and the most imprescriptible of all"; he said of the apprenticeship system that it prevents the indigent worker from living by his work, that it rejects women, and that it forces the poor to submit to "the law of the rich."[56] In his *Vie de M. Turgot*, published in 1786, Condorcet described the suppression of the *jurandes* as a "great act of justice," by which "this odious and ridiculous slavery was abolished" (and which also led to reductions in prices). Only a few provisions remained, "like the ruins of ancient palaces"; one of the earliest Revolutionary acts in 1789 was indeed the repeal of these residual apprenticeship provisions, of which Brentano writes in his history of guilds that "in France the sovereign people finally swept the corporations away in the night of the 4th August, 1789."[57]

For Turgot's opponents, by contrast, the right to property in one's own labor was only one right of property among many others. It was not particularly imprescriptible; the proposed reforms would also "violate the property of the masters who make up corporations," for whom privileges are "a real property which they have bought, and which they enjoy on the faith of regulations." The reforms were also expected to exert a profound and sinister influence on social and economic relationships. If the *jurandes* are destroyed, the advocate-general Séguier said in the *Lit de Justice*, "all subordination will be destroyed; there will be no more weight or measure; the desire for gain will animate every workshop, and, since honesty is not always the best route to gaining a fortune, the entire public" would be at the mercy of secret enemies. One argument for apprenticeship is thus, as it was later for Playfair, that the "interior discipline" of the *jurandes* is needed to restrain "turbulent and licentious youth," and to prevent them from "believing themselves independent." Another, more subtle argument, is that commitment to a restricted group, or subordination to a community, is the necessary condition for prosperity. Séguier contrasts the "indefinite liberty" of "independence" with the "real liberty" of freedom under the "salutary fetters" of authority. The will of the individual, including his desire for gain, is regulated by the community: "Each member, in working for his personal utility, necessarily works, even without willing it, for the true utility of the entire community."[58]

In the English debates over apprenticeship reform a generation later, it was the arguments of Turgot's enemies, about property rights and also about subordination, which inspired both the proponents and the opponents of reform. The language of imprescriptible or natural rights seems to have been seen both as subversively foreign and—for Francis Place, the friend of Bentham and James Mill—as slightly ridiculous. Serjeant Onslow asserted, as has been seen, that he had no idea at all of interfering with "chartered rights." The artisans who supported apprenticeship asserted their "unquestionable right" to the "quiet and exclusive use and enjoyment of their several and respective arts and trades, which the law has already conferred upon them as a property."[59] The London Committee of Manufacturers even saw a violation, by artisans in apprenticed trades, of the rights of masters: "Are the masters to be the slaves of the journeymen?"[60]

The debates of the 1800s and 1810s reflect a painful conflict, nonetheless, between different sorts of rights, including the rights of different sorts of workers. The great promise of apprenticeship, for the artisans who opposed repeal, was the promise of "quiet." Even Smith conceded that the apprenticed trades provided a sort of security; journeymen who had served an apprenticeship in the common manufactures earned somewhat more than common laborers, and "their employment, indeed, is more steady and uniform."[61] It is this expectation which was overthrown, cataclysmically, in the expansion of manufacturing of the 1780s, 1790s, and 1800s. The 1806 investigation of the Committee on the Woollen Manufacture is a protracted exploration of the conflict between the "Domestic System" and the "Factory System," of the sentiments of masters and journeymen in the two systems, and of the transformation of individual lives as one system gave way to the other.[62] Apprenticeship, associated by tradition with the domestic system, seemed to offer the prospect of a return to security. Richard Sheridan, defending the petition of the calico printers (an occupation exempt from the Elizabethan statute) for "relief and protection" through enforced apprenticeship restrictions, describes the "monstrous" scene of an industry in transition. Children were taken into apprenticeship, served seven or more years in a "business confessedly injurious to their health," and were then replaced by new cohorts of children; one house, he said, employed fifty apprentices and only two journeymen. The expectation of steady and uniform employment was thus turned on its head, and it was only by restricting the employment of children as apprentices, Sheridan said, that the "matured" population could be protected; "he never was a proselyte to the doctrines of Adam Smith upon this subject."[63]

Apprenticeship, in these turbulent times, promises a return to the lost world in which, as one domestic master said to the 1806 committee, "men and masters are in general so joined together in sentiment, and, if I may be admitted to use the term, love to each other, that they do not wish to be separated if they can help it."[64] It was also a return, for some of the defenders of the apprenticeship system, to their own youth: to their own expectations of quiet, perhaps, or to the property rights they once earned with their indentured work. William Playfair himself had been apprenticed to a "very ingenious millwright," following the death of his clergyman father.[65] One of the most eloquent supporters of the domestic system in the 1806 inquiry, a journeyman called William Child, was asked by the committee if he had ever been bound: "I served sixteen years and a half as apprentice; I was put out by the parish in the year 1758, when I was seven years and six months old."[66]

The defense of apprenticeship in the 1800s and 1810s is far more poignant, in these circumstances, than the conflict between rights and privileges which Smith envisaged. It is a defense of the old industry against the new, and of the old against the young; of the old, even, against their own children. But what is entirely missing, in the debate about reform, is the defense of freedom within the apprenticeship relation—of the rights of the children themselves—which is at the heart of Smith's argument. The consequence of the repeal of the Elizabethan statute was to make apprenticeship voluntary, to allow freedom of movement between different industries and occupations. But for the apprentice himself or herself, to be an apprentice was to be unfree. It was to be, for a limited period, subject to the will of someone else.

The will of the person being bound was indeed of central importance to the jurisprudence of apprenticeship. In the statute defining parish apprenticeships—the system of pitiful bargains under which, in Dorothy Marshall's description, parish overseers disposed of children to other parishes for premiums of £7 10s for a little girl to a gingerbread maker, or £18 for a lame boy—churchwardens, overseers, and justices of the peace were thus given the right to bind pauper children "as if such Child were of full Age, and by Indenture of Covenant bound himself or herself."[67] But the counterfactual of consent—the "as if" they were free—was essential to the jurisprudence of other apprenticeships as well. The child bound by his or her parents would thus be required to covenant himself "of his own voluntary will"; to commit himself freely not to be free.[68] He was not fully free; if he were free, in the sense of being of full age, he could not be an apprentice. Like Mary Ann Davis, in one of the cases discussed by the 1806 committee, he or she must be "in a state of nonage."[69]

The apprentice was not fully unfree, either; he had to appear with his father and promise to learn how to be a responsible person. It was this no-man's-land of rights which Smith found so unpropitious to industry and to duty. But to the proponents of the apprenticeship reform of 1814, as to Playfair and to Turgot's opponents, the bondage of youth was something which was to be desired, and which would indeed persist in the new world of voluntary apprenticeship. Parents would still want their children to grow up in a severe and unfamiliar environment, as the London committee said. The people whose freedom was in question were only children, after all. As one member of Parliament, Alderman Atkins, concluded in the Commons debate on repeal, "The answer of the parents and masters is, 'We are afraid to trust you; we will have our bond, and then we have a security for your attendance to your duty.'"[70]

THE APPRENTICESHIP: A DIGRESSION ON THE SLAVE TRADE

Smith's arguments about apprenticeship and oppression were out of place, like his references to inviolable rights, in the prudent debates of the 1810s. But it is interesting that they were rediscovered when apprenticeship again became a subject of political importance in the course of the 1830s, in a startlingly different setting.[71] The discussions with which we have been concerned in the 1810s were a matter of only modest parliamentary interest. The House of Commons was even counted out at a crucial stage in the repeal of the Elizabethan statute: "there being only 27 members present, the House adjourned of course."[72] The debates of the 1830s over apprenticeship—or over "The Apprenticeship"—were by contrast one of the greatest parliamentary and political spectacles of the century.

The Abolition of Slavery Act of 1833 was introduced by the colonial secretary (Stanley, later Lord Derby) as a "mighty experiment," on which would depend the happiness and existence of "millions of men." But what it prescribed was something less than freedom. The concern of officials in the Colonial Office had been to identify what was described as "an intermediate state between slavery and freedom"—"a safer and a middle course," or a "transition state"—which would both protect the rights of the planters and train the slaves to be free.[73] The government had thus considered several proposals, including plans in which slaves would be free for two days a week, or in which they would be emancipated but required to pay taxes for the support of their former owners. The plan eventually adopted was "The Apprenticeship." The slaves were freed, but were to be "entitled to be registered as apprenticed labourers"; they were to be indentured to work without pay for their former owners for four and a half days a week, over a period of up to six years. In an inversion of the English system, it was only children under six—children who were too young to be apprenticed—who were actually set free.[74]

It was this "Apprenticeship," and its operation in the West Indies, which became the focus of reform in the later 1830s. The apprenticeship of the former slaves was profoundly different from the apprenticeship systems with which we have been concerned. But the debate over reform was a sort of grotesque reflection, nonetheless, of the disputes about English apprenticeship: about the conflict between different rights, or the oppressive decisions of magistrates, or the incentives to be industrious. Both the opponents and the supporters of the Apprenticeship thus argued in the language of earlier debates over apprenticeship in England. Admiral Sir Charles Rowley was reported to have "declared that, if born to a state of absolute labour, he would rather be a black man in Jamaica than a white labourer in England, it being his opinion, that in the former case he should sooner be his own master." Sir James Stephen, who drafted the scheme, believed that it was "evidently imprudent" to interfere with the "natural" operation of "incentives to Industry."[75] Joseph Sturge, the great Quaker reformer who traveled to the West Indies to document the horrors of the system, challenged Lord Brougham on the basis of the English law: "If when Lord Chancellor thou hadst a ward in chancery who was apprenticed, and his master was violating the terms of indenture, what wouldst thou do?"[76]

Daniel O'Connell, one of the powerful opponents of the scheme in Parliament, said that "it introduced a new state of society. There had been nations of hunters, and of shepherds, and of agriculturists, and of masters and slaves, but never before had they heard of a nation of masters and apprentices. An old woman of eighty was to become an apprentice, and she was to be told that if she lived till ninety-two, she would be out of her time, and might commence a life of gaiety and jollity on her own account."[77] The universal or axiomatic truths of political economy were invoked with reference to earlier debates. "The experiment of apprenticed labourers has been tried under circumstances infinitely more favourable, and has failed," another opponent said; it is a "truth so universally recognized, as to hold the rank of an axiom, that men can only be taught industry by having the fruits of their industry secured to them."[78]

The Apprenticeship was eventually repealed, two years ahead of time, in 1838. The debate by now engaged the young W. E. Gladstone, in one of his earliest major speeches (of which he wrote in his diary that "prayer earnest for the moment was wrung from me in my necessity: I hope it was not a blasphemous prayer, for support in pleading the cause of injustice"). Gladstone's cause, in the speech, was to defend apprenticeship in the interest of his own, planter, society. The Apprenticeship was, he said, an integral part of the compensation which was to be paid to the proprietors for the loss of their former slaves' time (and for "the freedom of the children"), along with the less indirect compensation of £20 million, also provided for by the act. It was a scheme by which "security was substituted for doubt, and estates became saleable."[79]

Gladstone also had recourse, as so often later, to high principles of law and commerce. He addressed himself, in his peroration, to the conscience of the English manufacturers: "Compare the child of nine years old—and some say, under—entering your factories to work eight hours a day—and some say, more." He compared the contract implicit in the 1833 act, in a remarkable simile, to the original or social contract: "We hear constantly, for example, of the original contract or compact between the ruler and the subject. Where is that contract written, or in what store of archives is it preserved? It is written in the nature of things . . . And so in this case." The right created in the act, he said—the right to six years of bound labor by one's former slaves—"was the nearest possible approach to the form of a contract."[80]

UNCERTAIN JURISPRUDENCE

Smith's fourth and final set of arguments is about the unjust and insecure jurisprudence of apprenticeship. I started by saying that this fourth argument was the closest to what would now be considered a purely political position. But each of Smith's arguments, as has been seen, turned out to be in some degree political; to be about efficiency and about "equity, besides." The characteristic of apprenticeship regulations, quite generally, is that they are both political (in the sense of being upheld by public law) and partial (in the sense of being enforced by private or parochial institutions). Apprenticeships in incorporated trades, Smith says, are regulated by the bylaws of the corporation; these bylaws are, however, "confirmed by a public law of the kingdom." The point of the Elizabethan statute of apprenticeship, in fact, was that "what before had been the bye-law of many particular corporations, became in England the general and public law" of market towns. The jurisprudence of the Elizabethan Poor Law, and the subsequent law of settlements within it, was in Smith's description similarly indirect. The relief of the poor was established by the public law of the kingdom (43 Eliz. c.2); its enforcement was then entrusted to the churchwardens, justices of the peace, and appointed overseers of each parish.[81]

The *Wealth of Nations* has been explained, since the early nineteenth century, as an extended, relentless criticism of government; in Smith's own phrase, as a "very violent attack . . . upon the whole commercial system of Great Britain."[82] What has been of less concern, in general, is how Smith himself understood the extent of government—what he took to be included within it. It was natural in nineteenth-century England to see government as coextensive, for the purposes of commercial policy, with the policies of the national state. But to limit the scope of Smith's attack in this way is to misdescribe it in an essential respect. For the objects of Smith's obloquy are not only the institutions of national government; they are also, and even especially, the oppressive government of parishes, guilds and corporations, religious institutions, incorporated towns, privileged companies. One of the most insidious roles of national government is indeed to enact, or to confirm, the oppressive powers of these intermediate institutions. The criticism of local institutions, with their hidden, not quite public, not quite private powers, is at the heart of Smith's politics; it is at the heart, too, of his criticism of the apprenticeship system.

Smith's description of bylaws and public laws was of very little interest to his opponents and followers in the nineteenth-century debates over apprenticeship. Sir Frederick Eden was critical, as has been seen, of Smith's frequent references to the corporation spirit in connection with apprenticeship.[83] He was also one of the earliest to object that Smith was far more concerned, in his account of apprenticeship and of the law of settlements, with the statutory basis of legislation than with the way it actually operated in eighteenth-century England: "In this instance, as in many others, the insensible progress of society has reduced chartered rights to a state of inactivity."[84] Eden's criticism of Smith's rather theoretical understanding of apprenticeship is undoubtedly justified, as Smith's modern editors show.[85] Smith relied to a great extent on reading statutes, and on Burn's *Justice of the Peace;* he may also have been concerned (as on other occasions) with corporate obstructions in France rather than in England, or with the same oppressive *jurandes* and *droits* that so preoccupied Turgot. As George Pryme, the first professor of political economy at Cambridge, wrote in his copy of Playfair's *Wealth of Nations,* next to Playfair's footnote about consumers smuggling commodities in from the suburbs, "Dr S. is speaking of Europe in general, not of Gr.Br. in particular."[86]

To confront Smith's prescriptions with the more complicated and in some respects more kindly history of eighteenth-century England is, however, to lose sight of the politics of his jurisprudence. For it is precisely the conditions which Eden describes, of imperfectly enforced, insensibly evolving laws, which Smith finds most insidious in English institutions. The laws are not enforced, but they are still there; they can be brought to life at any time, on the caprice of corporate or parish or church officials. Serjeant Onslow said in Parliament in 1814 that the statute of apprenticeship "has been frittered away," "unrepealed and unamended," leaving juries reluctant to convict under its provisions and causing "judges to act almost as legislators."[87] The crisis over reform in the 1810s was precipitated, in fact, by the transient success of certain "institutions" or "societies" of journeymen in bringing prosecutions against masters under these long-forgotten provisions. But the persistence of unenforced, untimely laws is in general, as Smith shows, of benefit to the powerful and the well informed: to the rich and not to the poor.

Smith's criticism of the jurisprudence of unenforced laws starts with the presumption that laws are in general devised in the interests, or with the counsel, of the powerful, and that they are enforced in the same spirit. There are several passages in Smith's chapters on wages in the *Wealth of Nations* which are often quoted by his more radical admirers, from William Godwin (in his attack on Malthus's *Essay on Population*) to Beatrice Webb, Lujo Brentano, and Arnold Toynbee.[88] Smith supported high wages, as has been seen, and he said that there are no acts of Parliament against combining to reduce wages; he also said that when the legislature attempts to regulate the differences between masters and their workmen, "its counsellors are always the masters. When the regulation, therefore, is in favour of the workmen, it is always just and equitable; but it is sometimes otherwise when in favour of the masters."[89] The masters were evidently the counsellors of Parliament in the reform of the apprenticeship statute, as Brentano points out.[90]

Laws are enforced, as well as written, in the interests of the powerful; the law does not deal impartially, Smith says, in treating the combinations of masters and workmen, and legislation concerning wages "enforces by law that very regulation which masters sometimes attempt to establish by such combinations."[91] Bylaws thus turn into laws, regulations into statutes, and parish ordinances into public principles. To Sir Frederick Eden, the insensible customs of English towns and parishes are something to be relied upon; to Smith they are to be treated with the utmost suspicion. For the point of his repeated references to the corporation spirit is just this: that corporations, like other restricted institutions, are societies held together not by rules but by a common spirit, insensible to outsiders. Their initiates, or their officials, are at one and the same time magistrates, masters, and members of "institutions." (There is much the same contrast, in the debate over the other, colonial "Apprenticeship," when Gladstone rebukes the Quaker Sturge for his lack of confidence in the special magistrates, sent from Britain to supervise both the punishment of the apprentices and their "valuation" for release. Sturge had said of the new magistrates that they were often "completely subservient" to the local magistrates, who were themselves "almost invariably planters and friends of the master," such that "Mr C. sat as a magistrate to value for Mr S., and Mr. S. for Mr. C." Gladstone, very much on his dignity, retorts that "these magistrates are a body of English gentlemen.")[92]

There is a further, even more insidious element in the oppression which Smith describes. This is the element, or opportunity, of personal vexation. Smith's account of the origin of regulations is in some respects highly abstract. It is interesting that Beatrice Webb, in summarizing Smith's "general principle" of government, turns suddenly to a sort of algebra: "If interest A be virtually the State, and if interest A be antagonistic to interest B, then any state regulation of the joint affairs of A and B will be disadvantageous to interest B."[93] Smith is opposed, in the specific case of English wage regulations, to the policies of masters and merchants; he also expects, quite generally, that the interests of powerful communities will be reflected in the policies of the institutions over which they exercise their power. But the specific form which this power takes is neither abstract nor impersonal. The state is, for Smith, composed of evolving, interdependent institutions, public, private, and semi-public. The interests and communities which he describes are composed of individuals, with evolving, personal objectives; they are subject to whim, or to jealousy, or to being disheartened.

The fluctuating jurisprudence of unenforced laws is thus especially propitious, in Smith's account, for the sort of highly personal oppression which he describes as vexation. The regulation which leaves room for individual discretion and local circumstance will leave room, too, for individual despotism. "The love of domination . . . I am afraid is natural to mankind," Smith says in the lectures on jurisprudence, and corporations, like the institutions of local revenue collection, are little republics of discretionary domination.[94] Vexation is a personal, as well as a political, condition; Smith refers often in the *Wealth of Nations,* as has been seen, to "mortifying and vexatious visits," "odious visits," the "certain hardness of character" contracted by excise officers.[95] It is highly unpredictable. It depends on the character of the officers, and on the characters of the people they dislike—in Serjeant Onslow's words, speaking of prosecutions under unenforced statutes, on "personal malignity."[96]

"Interests, prejudices, laws and customs" are Smith's principal concern in much of the *Wealth of Nations,* and their consequences are reasonably acceptable when the individuals who obey them, or enact them, are reasonably impartial.[97] The domestic system of manufacturing worked well in the enterprises, described to the 1806 committee, where men and masters were "joined together in sentiment." One's years as an indentured apprentice work well if one has a good master. One's trade works well if one can be sure that one's friends will be lenient if one infringes obscure ordinances. O. Jocelyn Dunlop says of the Hallamshire Cutlers, in the eighteenth century, that "heavy fines were inflicted upon those who were proved to have broken the gild rules. But in almost all cases the fines were remitted, so that bye-laws could really be broken with impunity . . . the fee [for apprenticeship infringements] was raised to £10, but the entries show that £9 19s was usually remitted."[98]

The difficulty with this system, in Smith's description, is that it is itself insecure. Smith tried to imagine what it would be like to be someone for whom the system does not work well: the child with the bad master, the calico printer whose work was no longer steady and uniform, the cutler whose fees were not in the end remitted. He saw, with his "melancholy and evil boding mind," that the system of bylaws and ordinances was never in fact sure, or secure.[99] It was especially insecure for people who were poor, or who were disliked. It was an unsure foundation, in any case, for the development of commerce. The opulence which depends on interests, prejudices, laws, and customs, Smith says, is "necessarily slow, uncertain, liable to be disturbed and interrupted by innumerable accidents."[100]

The liberty and security of individuals is for Smith the condition for the growth of commerce, and its most important consequence as well.[101] Like Turgot and like Condorcet, once more, he understands security in a personal, individual sense. One of Turgot's most profound economic writings is concerned, to illustrate, with the psychological and legal conditions for the development of credit. Turgot describes a credit crisis which unfolded in 1769 in the town of Angoulême, when an unscrupulous debtor initiated legal proceedings against his creditors under previously unenforced usury laws. He was convinced by the episode that usury laws must be repealed, if commerce were to become established. A "jurisprudence which was arbitrary, changing with public opinion," Turgot wrote, was both unjust and an insecure foundation for commerce.[102] Condorcet's commentary, in his life of Turgot, is strikingly reminiscent of the jurisprudence of apprenticeship in eighteenth-century England; it was thought, he said, "that one could let the law sleep, while reserving the possibility of awakening it at the will of prejudice, of public rumour, and of the whim of every judge."[103] This was not a setting in which commerce could flourish, or in which individual merchants could feel themselves secure.

William Playfair observed, in one of his supplementary chapters to the *Wealth of Nations,* that Smith, unlike the French economists, had no tendency "to hold human virtue in great esteem."[104] This is only partly true. For it is public virtue which was held by Smith in only limited esteem, or which he considered to be in only limited supply. He had very little confidence in the public spirit of merchants and manufacturers; one of his political projects, as has been seen, was to think of institutions which were independent of the discretion of judges, or the kindliness of parish overseers. This is the point, for example, of his celebrated "plan of ecclesiastical government, or more properly of no ecclesiastical government." "The clergy of every established church constitute a great incorporation," he said, and can be dangerous and troublesome when they are "under a regular discipline and subordination." His own prescription was therefore for free competition among religious sects, such that "no one could be considerable enough to disturb the public tranquillity."[105]

Smith's plan of universal public education, too, was the project of a society in which individuals are independent of institutions, and institutions are independent of individual virtue. Children do not learn subordination and the corporation spirit. They learn to see through projects, and to feel themselves to be respectable. They become the sort of people who can move from one employment to another, and from one parish to the next. They learn to have many different things to think about, hundreds of ideas which will jostle for their interest, just as there will be hundreds of sects to jostle for their souls. They learn to be virtuous, too. But it is a private or domestic virtue, quite unsuited to great public exertions. It is learned, above all, in the family, "amidst the familiarity of relations," as the London Committee of Manufacturers said so censoriously in 1814. For the virtue which Smith did esteem, greatly, was the virtue of ordinary sympathy, for one's family and one's friends. It was the virtue in which children are respected by their parents; "the wise security of friendship."[106]

HISTORY AND INSTITUTIONS

Smith's arguments about the apprenticeship system, and the uses of these arguments in the early part of the nineteenth century, provide some sort of answer to the question—Beatrice Webb's question—with which this chapter began. How was Adam Smith's crusade against oppression transformed, between 1776 and 1817, into the Employer's Gospel of the nineteenth century, she asked. It is as though we have seen the answer unfolding, week by week, in the Committees and Minutes of the agitation for apprenticeship reform. Each of Adam Smith's four arguments, about competition, education, exclusion, and the corporation spirit, turned out to be concerned with oppression and injustice, as much as or more than with efficiency. But each was presented, in the course of these early nineteenth-century disputes, as a question of incentives. The disputes may provide some insight, thereby, into the subsequent history of English political economy, and into the destiny of the eighteenth-century preoccupation with sentiments in economic and political life.

The debates over apprenticeship provide some insight, too, into the odd uses of history in economic policy. This chapter has been concerned with the intellectual history of economic ideas, in the setting of economic history. But history, like memory, is itself the subject of much of this history. The individuals with whom we have been concerned speak constantly about the past. They remember stories, as of the rainy day when the greatcoats of the Russian guards shrank into jackets, and they also remember ways of life. They describe the principles of commerce in great historical similes; they talk, as Playfair does, of the apprenticeship system of the ancient Egyptians. They turn the insensible evolution of corporate ordinances into a subject of controversy, and of political theory. They define the apprenticeship of the future by what it is not to be.

Adam Smith has been criticized, at least since Sir Frederick Eden's *State of the Poor*, for being a little out of date in his history of apprenticeship, and a little out of place. He died, in 1790, at the start of a period of prodigious turbulence in this history, and in the history of economic ideas about children and other laborers. But he did not himself present his description of English apprenticeships as being of principally historical (or principally English) interest. Walter Bagehot makes the interesting remark about Smith that he is less concrete, or historical, than he seems: "His writings are semi-concrete, seeming to be quite so."[107] Smith believed that he was uncovering eternal truths about social institutions. These truths took the form, quite often, of abstract principles about personal character and personal oppression. Smith's opinion, as has been seen, is that laws and regulations are influenced by powerful groups; that small institutions defend insiders and exclude outsiders under the protection of these laws; and that the fluctuating jurisprudence of public laws and small institutions provides opportunity for personal vexation, against insiders as well as outsiders. These are eternal or enduring historical truths, for which the evidence is to be found, in part, in the history of economic sentiments. Smith admired Thucydides, above all, for his demonstration that "nothing gives greater light into any train of actions than the characters of the actors." His own method is also that of Thucydides: to have a clear view of events which have happened, and of "those which will some day, in all human probability, happen again in the same or a similar way."[108]

Bagehot said of English political economy that it was a theory which was true only of a single kind of society: "a society of grown-up competitive commerce, such as we have in England."[109] The commerce was grown-up, in the sense of having been growing for some time, and also in the sense of being something which is carried on by grown-ups. There are difficulties, which are well known, in depicting children as being entirely without wills (as "consumption goods"), and there are also difficulties in depicting them as tiny little economic men. The difficulty posed by apprenticeship, in Smith's account, is that it is an institution which is concerned with the traverse from one of these conditions (and descriptions) to the other; with the no-man's-land into which children are inducted in a condition of "nonage," or semi-will, and in which they must learn to be decisive, to be rational, and to be good.

The debates over apprenticeship were concerned with people who were thought of as not entirely or not yet rational: children, or elderly slaves, or people who are very poor. It is within the apprenticeship relationship that they were supposed to learn how to be economic, or at least how to be industrious. But the interesting aspect of apprenticeship, in these debates, is that it instructs in so many other things as well. People learn about history (the history of their corporation, for example); they learn to be loyal; they learn to be subordinate; they learn the rules within which they are expected to pursue their own self-interest; they learn that the rules of their own corporation or institution are not the same as the rules of the public society. There is an odd moment, in the report of the 1806 Committee on the Woollen Manufacture, when the members turn to consider the psychological conditions of the domestic manufacturer. "Diligence, economy, and prudence are the requisites of his character, not invention, taste and enterprise," they conclude; "he walks in a sure road as long as he treads in the beaten track."[110] The requirements of being a good entrepreneur in the domestic system are not the same, that is to say, as the requirements in the factory system; the requirements may even, in certain circumstances, be inconsistent with one another. The good apprentice, too, may find herself expected to learn a long, conflicting, and inconsistent list of ways to be rational.

5

The Bloody and Invisible Hand

THE INVISIBLE HAND OF JUPITER

Adam Smith's ideas have had odd secular destinies, and the twentieth century was the epoch of the invisible hand.[1] "The profoundest observation of Smith," for Kenneth Arrow, is "that the system works behind the backs of the participants; the directing 'hand' is 'invisible.'" For Arrow and Frank Hahn, the invisible hand is "surely the most important contribution [of] economic thought" to the understanding of social processes; for James Tobin, it is "one of the great ideas of history and one of the most influential."[2] The object of this chapter is to look at the intellectual history of the invisible hand, and to put forward a view of what Adam Smith himself understood by it. What I will suggest is that Smith did not especially esteem the invisible hand. The image of the invisible hand is best interpreted as a mildly ironic joke. The evidence for this interpretation, as will be seen, raises interesting questions both about Smith and about the invisible hands of the twentieth century.

Smith used the words "invisible hand" on three quite dissimilar occasions.[3] The first use, in his "History of Astronomy" (which is thought to have been written in the 1750s, but was preserved by Smith for posthumous publication), is clearly sardonic. Smith is talking about the credulity of people in polytheistic societies, who ascribe "the irregular events of nature," such as thunder and storms, to "intelligent, though invisible beings—to gods, demons, witches, genii, fairies." They do not ascribe divine support to "the ordinary course of things": "Fire burns, and water refreshes; heavy bodies descend, and lighter substances fly upwards, by the necessity of their own nature; nor was the invisible hand of Jupiter ever apprehended to be employed in those matters."[4]

The second use is in the *Theory of Moral Sentiments,* in a passage pub-

116

lished in 1759, and retained unchanged throughout Smith's subsequent revisions of the work. It is here sardonic in a different way. Smith is describing some particularly unpleasant rich proprietors, who are unconcerned with humanity or justice, but who, in "their natural selfishness and rapacity," pursue only "their own vain and insatiable desires." They do, however, employ thousands of poor workers to produce luxury commodities: "They are led by an invisible hand to . . . without intending it, without knowing it, advance the interest of the society."[5]

Smith's third use of the invisible hand is in the *Wealth of Nations,* in a chapter concerned with international trade. He argues strongly against restrictions on imports, and against the merchants and manufacturers who support such restrictions, forming "an overgrown standing army" who "upon many occasions intimidate the legislature." Domestic monopolies, he says, are advantageous for specific industries, but not for the "general industry of the society." If there were no import restrictions, however, the merchant would still prefer to support domestic industry, in the interest of "his own security." He will thereby promote the interest "of the society": "He is in this, as in many other cases, led by an invisible hand to promote an end which was no part of his intention."[6]

The three uses of the invisible hand have posed problems for historians of economic thought. The hand is assumed to have an "altered role" between the first and the subsequent uses; for A. L. Macfie, "the function of the divine invisible hand appears to be exactly reversed," transformed from a "capricious" to a providential and "order-preserving" force. The change must be explained, in Macfie's view, as a matter of literary taste; Smith, who "enjoyed pithy, forceful phrases," simply remembered the invisible hand of Jupiter, but "reversed its relation to the natural order."[7]

My suggestion, instead, will be that Smith's attitude to the invisible hand was similar, and ironical, on each of the three occasions. He is amused by the polytheists who believe in the invisible hand of Jupiter in the "History of Astronomy"; in the *Theory of Moral Sentiments* and the *Wealth of Nations* he is amused by the individuals who are led by the invisible hand (the hand they cannot see, or the hand behind their backs). He is also amused by philosophers who believe in systems of divine order. There is even an element, in the latter case, of self-irony, or of self-recognition in the depiction of the philosopher, entranced by a beautiful and imaginary order.

The evidence for this interpretation is indirect. Smith himself does not seem to have attached great importance to the invisible hand, and his three references to it are all cursory.[8] Commentators on Smith, too, mentioned the invisible hand only infrequently prior to the twentieth century. It was not singled out, for example, in Dugald Stewart's memoir of Smith's life and work, or in Playfair's or McCulloch's editions of the *Wealth of Nations;* nor was it invoked in the major political celebrations of the centenary of the *Wealth of Nations* in 1876.[9] It was indeed to a great extent Smith's historicist critics, toward the end of the nineteenth century, who first made much of the invisible hand. For T. E. Cliffe Leslie, the assumption of a "beneficent constitution of nature," expressed in Smith's comments on the invisible hand, is a doctrine by which "the mischief done in political economy . . . has been incalculable"; for John Kells Ingram, following Cliffe Leslie, it is evidence of a "secret substratum" of doctrines in Smith's work, "half theological half metaphysical."[10] Carl Menger, by contrast, does not mention the invisible hand in his extensive defense of Smith in 1891; he in fact berates Smith repeatedly for his defective understanding of the unreflective social structures which were for later commentators a synonym for the invisible hand.[11] It is interesting that even the phrase "invisible hand" was hardly familiar at the beginning of the twentieth century; Alfred Marshall, defending Smith against his historicist critics, refers in 1923 to Smith's observations on "the unseen hand."[12]

It will be necessary, in these circumstances, to consider whether the invisible hand is the *sort* of idea that Smith would have taken entirely seriously. Smith is a famously troublesome subject of intellectual history (and biography), and his ideas of social order are especially elusive.[13] They are influenced, as will be seen, by his opinions of revealed and natural religion, and by his desire to avoid the unreasonable curiosity of others about these opinions. They are ironic in a Humean way. They reflect both his desire for "quiet," or the absence of public controversy, and his wish to convince the public of the value of his proposals. Like d'Alembert, excusing himself to Voltaire in 1757 for having published "bad articles about theology and metaphysics" in the *Encyclopédie,* Smith sought no conflict with official censorship; like d'Alembert, he seems to have believed that "time will make people distinguish what we thought from what we said."[14] But posterity, for Smith, has also been an enemy, or at least an untrustworthy friend.

TREMBLE, UNFORTUNATE KING!

The earlier intellectual history of invisible hands turns out to be generally grim. The most famous invisible hand in Anglo-Scottish literature is that of Macbeth's providence. "And with thy bloody and invisible hand," Macbeth apostrophizes the night in Act III, in the scene immediately before the banquet and Banquo's murder; he asks the darkness to cover up the crimes he is about to commit:

> Come, seeling night,
> Scarf up the tender eye of pitiful day,
> And with thy bloody and invisible hand
> Cancel and tear to pieces that great bond
> Which keeps me pale.[15]

Smith, who lectured on Shakespeare's use of metaphor, is likely to have known *Macbeth* well. He was certainly familiar with the Edinburgh theater of the 1750s, where West Digges in 1757 put on a celebrated performance of *Macbeth* with "the characters entirely new dressed, after the manner of the ancient Scots."[16]

Smith was a great admirer of Voltaire's tragedies, and Voltaire, too, invokes several invisible and disagreeable hands.[17] In his *Oedipe* of 1718—which is, in Voltaire's own description, free of the "coarseness" and multiple imperfections of Sophocles, and which begins with the arrival in Thebes of Jocasta's former lover—Oedipus is threatened twice by invisible hands. "Tremble, unfortunate King," the High Priest says in Act III; "an invisible hand suspends above your head" the menacing sword of vengeance. In Act IV, Oedipus recounts the memorable day in Corinth when, as he arrived at a temple with offerings to the gods, the altar began to shake, a terrifying voice was carried to him by the winds, and "an invisible hand pushed away my presents."[18]

There is an earlier invisible hand which is even more unpleasant, and which Smith probably also knew; it appears in one of Ovid's *Metamorphoses,* in which the hero (the warrior Caeneus, who is at the time surrounded by centaurs, one of whom is taunting him because he had been born a woman, Caenis) "twisted and plied his invisible hand, inflicting wound within wound."[19] The hand is invisible here because it is behind the victim's back; in the edition of Ovid which Smith owned there is an illustration, as a frontispiece to this particular book of the *Metamorphoses,* of a gloved hand stabbing a soldier between the shoulder blades with a long spear.[20]

The history of invisible hands does not improve when it is decomposed into its constituent ideas, or into ideas of invisibility and of large disembodied hands. The "exceeding mighty hand" of Zeus shoves Hector from behind in the *Iliad;* the Greek word *chirokratia,* or the rule of the hand, later meant government by force.[21] The hand of Jupiter, in Roman iconography as in the Latin writings familiar to Smith and his contemporaries, is an auxiliary of secular force: "The normal relationship in the Emperor's life is that illustrated by the coins, which show a gigantic Jupiter holding a protecting hand over the diminutive Emperor."[22]

In Christian writings, the hand of God was later a source of consolation for the devout. (The unfortunate Banquo announces, shortly before he is murdered on Macbeth's orders, "In the great hand of God I stand.")[23] But in the secular writings of Smith's contemporaries, large hands were generally oppressive. Condorcet accused Pascal—whom he greatly disliked, and whom Smith described as a "whining and melancholy moralist"—of wishing to make man feel that "he is under the hand of an all-powerful being," and, "feeling the weight of this all-powerful hand," to find Christian religion.[24] Turgot said that in large societies men could become "no more than a blind instrument in the hands of a leader"; in war, Kant said, men were "instruments in the hand of another (the state)."[25] Joseph de Maistre, in 1797, imagined an invisible hand even bloodier than Macbeth's. "The human species can be considered as a tree which is being pruned at all times by an invisible hand," he wrote in *Considérations sur la France;* the violent destruction in the aftermath of the French Revolution was to be considered salutary, in that the human soul, softened by incredulity and excessive civilization, could recover only by being "plunged again into blood."[26]

The word "invisible," too, was often disagreeable. It is an epithet which had been used of God, at least since Lactantius and Saint Augustine.[27] Smith, like Hume, uses it principally either of the objects of superstition or of the events which fill up the empty space in scientific systems. The first use is characteristic of Hume's *Natural History of Religion,* written at about the same time as Smith's essay on astronomy; Hume associates the invisible with "idolaters" and "absolute ignorance," and "invisible powers" with "fairies, goblins, elves, sprites."[28] In his lectures on rhetoric, Smith identifies "invisible" beings with "fairies, Nymphs, Fawns, Satyrs, Dryads and such divinities."[29] In the *Theory of Moral Sentiments,* as in his reference to the invisible hand of Jupiter in the "History of Astronomy," he invokes a "powerful and invisible being" when he is discussing "ancient heathen religion"; he also criticizes Socrates for "fancying that he had secret and frequent intimations from some invisible and divine Being."[30]

The second, scientific use seems to be associated for Smith with the first. He speaks on several occasions in the "History of Astronomy" of what he describes as the "chain of intermediate, though invisible events," by which philosophers and others connect the jarring or disjointed occurrences of nature.[31] The effort to organize events into an orderly, coherent, and continuous system—a system with no empty spaces in it, or no domains of ignorance—is indeed for Smith the "end of philosophy."[32] To describe these consoling intermediate events as invisible is evocative of ancient physical theories.[33] But the intermediate events which are invisible tend, even in this scientific use, to be those of which Smith is most suspicious: the "invisible effluvia" of Descartes, or Kepler's "invisible chain" of "immaterial virtue." The two uses in fact converge: in "civilized societies," Smith says, people are "less disposed to employ, for this connecting chain, those invisible beings whom the fear and ignorance of their rude forefathers had engendered."[34]

INTENTIONS AND INTERESTS

Adam Smith's exiguous published essays include a long discussion of the word "but," and he was in general a most circumspect writer.[35] He and Hume, in Macfie's description, were "careful, cool, patient, very wily thinkers," who "could laugh at themselves."[36] Smith's words are to be taken seriously, that is to say, as evidence of his ideas. They are chosen with extreme care, at least in his published and extensively revised writings. But he is also a great rhetorical writer; he chooses the words, or the style, that he thinks will persuade one audience or another. It is possible, therefore, that he used *words* which were to him slightly comical, or slightly unpleasant—the words "invisible hand"—to describe an *idea* which was of profound importance to his theoretical system. The words were a way of convincing the unconvinced.[37]

The idea of the invisible hand can thus be distinguished, as far as is possible, from the words in which it was described. It consists, in the *Wealth of Nations* and the *Theory of Moral Sentiments,* in three main notions: that the actions of individuals have unintended consequences, that there is order or coherence in events, and that the unintended consequences of individual actions sometimes promote the interests of societies. This idea (or set of ideas) recurs, in different forms, at several points in Smith's work. It corresponds, more or less, to the invisible hand of subsequent social thought; to the hand which is "one of the great ideas of history."[38] It is this multiple idea, therefore, which should be compared to the rest of Smith's thought, and about which one might reasonably ask whether it is the sort of idea with which Smith would have been pleased. The evidence is complex, as will be seen; there are some respects in which the ideas expressed in the image of the invisible hand were the sort of thing Smith liked, and others in which they were very much what he disliked.

The first sort of evidence is strongly in favor of the invisible hand, or in favor of the interpretation that Smith favored it. It is that the theory of the invisible hand is aesthetically delightful. "We take pleasure in beholding the perfection of so beautiful and grand a system," Smith says of public policy in the paragraph immediately following his reference to the invisible hand in the *Theory of Moral Sentiments;* political economy, as much as astronomy, is an exercise in soothing and pleasing the imagination. The passage in which the invisible hand occurs is indeed a digression between two descriptions of aesthetic sentiment, in a chapter of which the subject is beauty and utility: vistas of private opulence, Smith says, "strike the imagination as something grand and beautiful . . . The same principle, the same love of system, the same regard to the beauty of order" serves to recommend public policies as well.[39] It is interesting that Dugald Stewart, too, invokes sentiments of beauty when he speaks of an invisible hand, without reference to Smith: "So beautifully, indeed, do these passions and circumstances act in subserviency to [nature's] designs," that even when primitive man "follows blindly his instinctive principles of action, he is led by an invisible hand, and contributes his share to the execution of a plan, of the nature and advantages of which he has no conception."[40]

The "lovely quality" of invisible hand explanations, in Robert Nozick's description, consists in their capacity to yield an understanding of "some overall pattern or design," of a sort which is especially imposing because it does not include a reference to the pattern itself.[41] The contrast is between the explanation of, for example, a military march (that everyone is marching in step because they are trying to march in step), and the explanation of an at first sight jarring and discordant scene, which the theorist succeeds in depicting as an orderly and coherent progress. Smith's theory is "poetic," for Arrow and Hahn, because it shows that a social system moved by independent actions "is consistent with a final coherent state of balance."[42] These ideas of understanding are indeed distinctively Smithian. They correspond rather closely, in fact, to Smith's ordering of scientific systems in the "History of Astronomy": "how far each of them was fitted to soothe the imagination, and to render the theatre of nature a more coherent, and therefore a more magnificent spectacle, than otherwise it would have appeared to be."[43]

The second sort of evidence, to do with moral psychology and moral philosophy, is unfavorable. One reason to suspect that Smith was not entirely enthusiastic about theories of the invisible hand is that these theories are extremely condescending about the intentions of individual agents. Smith's three uses of the phrase have in common that the individuals concerned—the people who fail to see the invisible hand—are quite undignified; they are silly polytheists, rapacious proprietors, disingenuous merchants. The classical Latin word which is translated by "invisible" is *caecus,* which in its literal sense means "blind."[44] If *X* is invisible to me, then I am blind in respect of *X.* The association persists in modern theory. "An invisible hand explanation," Nozick says, shows that facts arise "from some blind mechanism," although "what arises via a blind process need not itself be blind."[45] It is interesting that Smith's contemporary Adam Ferguson comments, in a passage identified by Friedrich Hayek as the locus classicus of the doctrine of unintended consequences, that "every step and every movement of the multitude . . . are made with equal blindness to the future"; this is in a chapter of Ferguson's *Essay on the History of Civil Society* of which the title is "The History of Subordination."[46]

Smith is thought of, rightly, as a great defender of individual freedom. He is a defender of enlightenment, in the sense of the disposition of individuals to be independent and to see through projects; he sees the people as the best judges of their own interest (like Turgot), or as "a society of reasonable beings" (like Condorcet), and not (like Necker and like Ferguson) as a multitude who "in all this immense space which is called the *future* . . . never see more than tomorrow."[47] But the subjects of invisible hand explanations are blind, in that they cannot see the hand by which they are led. They are unenlightened. "General light, or general darkness; there is no middle course"; "lumière générale ou aveuglement général": this is Jeremy Bentham's eulogy to the enlightened public, in his defense of freedom of understanding and freedom of the press.[48] The enlightened disposition, for Smith as for Condorcet, is a more uncertain condition. But it is a disposition, at least, to reflect on one's own and other people's choices; to theorize; to think about the future.

The subjects of the invisible hand are also foolish, in that their intentions are puny and futile.[49] It is interesting that in his very last writing, Smith himself introduced a new, visible, disembodied hand. The systematic reformer, he says (a reformer much like Frederick the Great or the Emperor Joseph II), imagines that he can "arrange the different members of a great society with as much ease as the hand arranges the different pieces upon a chess-board"; he does not realize that in real societies every single piece has a principle of motion of its own.[50] This independence and idiosyncrasy of individuals is what Smith seems to be deriding in his account of the invisible hand; it is in this sense an un-Smithian idea.

The idea of the invisible hand has been associated, as will be seen, with Smith's purported "Stoicism." It is evocative, in some respects, of the comments of the Stoic Epictetus about the unintended social consequences of self-interested actions; Jupiter had so ordered human reason, Epictetus said, that "it can no longer be regarded as unsocial for a man to do everything for his own sake."[51] But Epictetus, Smith says, feels "the most sovereign contempt of human life. He never exults so much, accordingly his eloquence is never so animated as when he represents the futility and nothingness of all its pleasures and all its pains." Smith is himself anything but contemptuous of human pains and human intentions. The great tension at the heart of the *Theory of Moral Sentiments* is indeed over the morality of intentions and the morality of consequences (or "tendencies"): over the "irregularity of sentiments" in which we judge both the consequences of actions and the "sentiments, thoughts, intentions" which are their causes; over our interest in the "distress of Oedipus and Jocasta."[52] To be contemptuous of individual intentions, to see them as futile and blind, is to take a distinctively un-Smithian view of human life.

The invisible hand is un-Smithian, thirdly, in that it is founded on a notion of privileged universal knowledge. It presupposes the existence of a theorist (if not of a reformer) who sees more than any ordinary individual can. "Men are fond of paradoxes, and of appearing to understand what surpasses the comprehension of ordinary people," Smith says of the Physiocrats or Economists; the arrogance of the man of system, as of the Stoic philosopher in Lucian's "Philosophies for Sale," "is to fancy himself the only wise and worthy man in the commonwealth."[53] The disembodied hand is invisible to its millions of petty subjects, but it is visible to "us": to theorists. The sequence is in fact an inverted version of the story of the Emperor's new clothes, with the Emperor as the hero: the subjects in the streets think that the Emperor has no clothes, and that there is indeed no Emperor; but the Emperor himself, or his economic advisers, knows that he is actually there, invigilating their wills.

This knowingness of the theorist is characteristic of eighteenth- and nineteenth-century doctrines of unintended consequences. It is the complicity, characteristic of the sect of enlightenment, of which Condorcet said that Voltaire had been disabused when he visited England: he saw that "truth is not made to remain a secret in the hands of a few philosophers, and of a small number of men of the world instructed, or rather indoctrinated by the philosophers; laughing with them at the errors of which the people are the victim."[54] It was the spirit of Kant, too, especially in his earlier writings. The characteristic of individual actions, for Kant in his "Universal History," is "folly and childish vanity," in which individuals "are unconsciously promoting an end which, even if they knew what it was, would scarcely arouse their interest"; the role of the philosopher, by contrast, is to discover the "purpose in nature" which is hidden from individual agents.[55] The philosopher is enlightened, here, and the objects of his observation are blind. When Hegel talks of the cunning of reason—which "lets the passions work for it," and for which individuals are the means to an end—he is also talking of his own cunning; *die List der Vernunft* is *die List Hegels*.[56]

Smith's cunning is different. The *Wealth of Nations* is full of anecdotes of secret self-interest, in which the pursuit of material gain is uncovered, behind the "mysterious veil of self-delusion."[57] But the anecdotes are directed, above all, against the wise and the great; against emperors and theorists (including the theorist who whispers in the ear of the reforming emperor) far more than against the individuals who are their objects and subjects. Kant distinguished, in one of his early works, between finer, conscious souls and the self-interested multitude who pursue the common good without intending to do so:

> Most men are among those who have their best-loved selves fixed before their eyes as the only point of reference for their exertions, and who seek to turn everything around *self-interest* as around the great axis. Nothing can be more advantageous than this, for these are the most diligent, orderly and prudent; they give support and solidity to the whole, while without intending to do so they serve the common good, provide the necessary requirements, and supply the foundation over which finer souls can spread beauty and harmony.[58]

Smith's rhetoric is virtually the opposite. His principal examples of self-interested behavior, in the *Wealth of Nations,* include manufacturers in incorporated towns, parish worthies, dukes of Cornwall, medieval kings, proud ministers, established clergy, and university teachers.[59] His principal example of the unintended, undesirable consequences of public policy was the depression brought about in France by the regulations of Colbert ("instead of allowing every man to pursue his own interest his own way, upon the liberal plan of equality, liberty and justice.")[60] It is the wisdom of authority which Smith seeks to unveil, or the wisdom of finer souls.

The notion of a true or universal interest, unintended by individual agents, was indeed invoked as much by the eighteenth-century opponents of liberal reform as by its supporters. One modern claim made for the invisible hand is that it suggests ways to devise institutions and policies "which harness self-interest" for the social good; that its "relatively simple motivational precepts" are such as to "leave agents open to manipulation by authority."[61] Much the same claims were made by Smith's and Turgot's opponents. Smith, like Turgot, was criticized for his touching faith in the wisdom (or the heroism) of individual millers and bakers. It was Smith's opponents, rather, who had faith in the wisdom of authority, including the ability to harness individual exertions.

In the *Lit de Justice* held in Versailles for the registration of Turgot's ill-fated economic reform edicts, the unintended consequences of individual exertions were invoked in support of established and corporate institutions.[62] Turgot's main opponent in the proceeding, the advocate-general Séguier, defended the regulations of the apprenticeship guilds, and the policies of Colbert ("so wise, so hardworking, so foresighted"), against the dangerous freedom in which every worker and every artisan would be free to pursue "the thirst for gain" and "the discrepancies of an often disordered imagination." To "abolish regulations," Séguier said, is to threaten commerce itself, since all subordination would be destroyed. But in support of regulation he used the very language of unintended and unwilled effects. It is only within restrictive corporations and guilds or communities, he said, that the interests of individuals coincide with those of the society: "Each member, in working for his personal utility, necessarily works, even without willing it, for the true utility of the entire community."[63]

POLITICAL INFLUENCE

A fourth sort of evidence, which again suggests that Smith did not take the invisible hand entirely seriously, is that the theory of useful self-interest abstracts from several of the problems with which he was most preoccupied in his political economy. These problems, of political influence on commerce, are indeed the principal subject of the chapter in Book 4 of the *Wealth of Nations* where the invisible hand makes its fleeting appearance: they include the errors of merchants about their own interests, the influence of merchants over political regulations, and the particular difficulties of periods of transition from one regulatory regime to another. The invisible hand appears, in fact, in the middle of a powerful description of the propensity of merchants to pursue their objectives, successfully, by influencing restrictions on imports.

The main rhetorical force of the invisible hand, in the *Wealth of Nations,* is to persuade legislators that they will best achieve their own objectives— the objectives "of the society," or of the "public interest"—if they permit individual merchants to employ their capital as they themselves (the merchants) think most advantageous. But Smith explains in the same chapter that merchants not only consider themselves to derive advantage from monopolies and other regulations, but also do in fact derive such advantage. Merchants and manufacturers, he says, "are always demanding a monopoly against their countrymen," and they "are the people who derive the greatest advantage" from it. "In the mercantile regulations," Smith says at the very end of Book 4 of the *Wealth of Nations,* "the interest of our manufacturers has been most peculiarly attended to"; "the boasted liberty of the subject," in restrictions on exports, is "sacrificed to the futile interests of our merchants and manufacturers." The peroration of Book 1 is similar: the interest of the order of merchants and manufacturers, Smith says, "is always in some respects different from, and even opposite to, that of the public."[64]

The success of the invisible hand will depend, in these circumstances, on whether individual merchants choose to pursue their own interests by political influence, by the use of force, or in other ways. As Séguier pointed out, in his criticism of Turgot, "honesty is not always the most secure means to fortune."[65] William Playfair comments that Smith is indeed inconsistent in describing the restrictive interests of merchants as futile: "Dr. Smith, who, in so many instances, is for confiding in the sagacity of individuals, ought not in this case to set it entirely for nothing."[66] The invisible hand, that is to say, requires both good institutions and good norms, whereby individuals pursue their interests within the rules of well-defined games, and not by seeking to influence institutions and rules. On one view, these good institutions are the outcome of policy: the invisible hand, for Lionel Robbins, "is the hand of the lawgiver, the hand which withdraws from the sphere of the pursuit of self-interest those possibilities which do not harmonize with the public good."[67] On another view, as will be seen, they are the outcome of custom: institutions are good if they are themselves the unintended consequence of individual self-interest.

There is indeed something oddly ingenuous in Smith's sudden invocation of the timid, virtuous merchant, led by the invisible hand to pursue only harmonious interests. The merchant or manufacturer in the invisible hand passage is continually studying his own advantage. But he does not, for example, seek to collect together with other merchants to obtain special privileges for home production. He simply prefers home production because he has a comparative advantage in it: "He can know better the character and situation of the persons whom he trusts"; he knows the laws; he is averse to the "uneasiness" which he would otherwise feel "at being separated so far from his capital." It is interesting, too, that in a chapter mainly concerned with British restrictions on imports, Smith's ingenuous merchant is described as a resident of Amsterdam, trading in corn from Königsberg and fruit from Lisbon; he is a cosmopolitan figure, far less tempted than any English merchant to pursue his own advantage through political influence.[68]

Smith is ingenuous, too, in his counsel to statesmen as invigilators of the public interest. He was preoccupied, throughout the *Wealth of Nations*, with what he described as "the clamour and sophistry of merchants and manufacturers," and with their influence on the commercial system. The "invisible hand" chapter itself begins with a chronicle of existing restraints on imports, and ends with Smith's famous description of the intimidating standing army of monopolists. The prospect of a legislature "directed, not by the clamourous importunity of partial interests, but by an extensive view of the general good" appears as a remote, unlikely possibility. In disputes over commerce, as in disputes over the regulation of wages, when the legislature seeks to determine policy, "its counsellors are always the masters."[69] Yet it is this prospect—of government in the public interest, or of unimportune merchants, or both—to which the invisible hand is directed in the *Wealth of Nations*.

The idea of a commercial system, with its complex, changing relations between merchants and statesmen, is central to Smith's political economy, as it was to policies of economic reform in the 1770s and 1780s. Statesmen pursue their own self-interest, and merchants make the error of pursuing their self-interest through political influence. "To narrow the competition, is always the interest of the dealers," as Smith himself said of merchants and manufacturers, and it "must always be against" the interest of the public.[70] Smith's criticisms of government and of established institutions are essential to his economic thought; it is most unlikely that he would simply forget them in a grand theory of the social good.

CLERICAL SYSTEMS

The fifth kind of evidence is about Smith's religion. The invisible hand has been understood by historians of economic thought, at least since Cliffe Leslie's denunciation of "the clerical system of deductive reasoning," as the expression of Smith's religious, or deistic, or Stoic-inspired beliefs. It is for Jacob Viner one of the "teleological elements," or "religious ingredients," in Smith's system; for Macfie it is the hand "of the Christian Deity." This view poses evident problems for modern exponents of the invisible hand, whom Viner chides for considering Smith's religious opinions to "have only nuisance value."[71] The suggestion here will be that the theology of the invisible hand would have posed very serious problems for Smith as well.

Smith's religious opinions were the subject of public controversy from the time of his famous letter of 1776 about Hume's death. "You would persuade us, by the example of DAVID HUME Esq," George Horne wrote in his anonymous response to Smith, "that atheism is the only cordial for low spirits, and the proper antidote against the fear of death."[72] Comments on Smith's irreligious views, and on his friendship with Hume, were conspicuous in the English obituaries after his death in 1790, as has been seen. One of the concerns of his supporters, in the 1790s, indeed seems to have been to divert attention from discussion of his religious opinions. Dugald Stewart in his "Account" of Smith's life thus presented a prudently edited version of a letter from Hume to Smith, in which Hume congratulates Smith on the number of bishops who had bought copies of the *Theory of Moral Sentiments;* the deleted passages include Hume's description of the bishops as "these Retainers to Superstition," and of *Candide* as a sprightly "Satyre upon Providence."[73]

The most plausible understanding of Smith's Christianity is that he became, in the course of his life, "considerably more sceptical (or considerably less discreet)."[74] Of his three major undertakings in preparing work for publication, the first edition of the *Theory of Moral Sentiments* is fairly full of references to a deity of a Christian sort, although attended with circumlocutions, indirect speech, and frequent use of the verb "to seem."[75] The *Wealth of Nations* is almost entirely free of explicitly religious thought, and is frequently critical of established Christian religion.[76] The extensive additions and revisions which Smith incorporated in the sixth edition of the *Theory of Moral Sentiments* form a work which is strikingly less Christian than the parts of the book remaining from earlier editions.[77]

In several well-known passages, Smith is apparently marking his differences with Christian doctrines.[78] In other passages, he seems to be proposing a subtle and profound description of the psychological difficulties of disbelief. His account is similar to Hume's, in the *Dialogues concerning Natural Religion*, and in some respects more understanding, or more sympathetic. He describes the tragic choice of the person who is without faith: to believe in something (some providence) which one knows to be unbelievable, or to believe in the frightening eternity of "a fatherless world."[79]

It seems quite unlikely, in these circumstances, that Smith thought of the invisible hand as a device of Christian theology in any straightforward sense. The Christian connotation of the word "invisible" is a reason, rather, to suppose that Smith did not take it entirely seriously. If it had indeed been serious, it would have been close to unique, as a theological element, in Smith's writings on commerce.[80] It would also have been in striking conflict with the secularization of natural philosophy which was at the center of Hume's and Smith's understanding of natural law. For Smith's empirical and psychological version of natural jurisprudence, as much as Hume's, was in opposition to eighteenth-century "Newtonianism"; to experimental science in which the principles of motion could be deduced from nature, because they had been placed in nature by God.[81]

The friendship of Smith and Hume was conspicuous in the contemporary debate over Smith's religious opinions, and it is of interest, too, in trying to understand Smith's use of theological expressions.[82] "Various circumstances have brought suspicion on the religious principles of Dr Adam Smith," the devout son of Smith's acquaintance Sir John Sinclair wrote in 1837, and prominent among them was his relationship to Hume: "His intimacy with Hume was not only greater than ordinary courtesy, Christian charity, or literary friendship required; but was of that fraternal character which seemed to intimate coincidence of opinion and identity of sentiment."[83] My own view is that Sinclair's intuition was right, and that Smith's and Hume's religious opinions were indeed quite close.[84] What is more important, for our present purposes, is that Smith's expressions, in his correspondence with Hume and in much of his published (and posthumously published) writing on religion, are extremely close to Hume's celebrated irony.

Smith was evidently interested in irony as a literary form. He praises Swift, with "his severe ironical manner," and says of Swift and Lucian that they together form a "complete system of ridicule." Of Lucian, the great ironic critic of providence, and Hume's "favourite author," Smith says that "there is no author from whom more real instruction and good sense can be found."[85] "For Hume, irony is pervasive, virtually a way of life," Ernest Mossner writes.[86] Smith's own literary system was far more diverse. He was more "sensitive" than Hume (to use Turgot's expression), and he wrote, of the use of irony, that the role of sentiment is to judge "how far an agreeable irony may be carried, and at what precise point it begins to degenerate into a detestable lie."[87] But he was certainly ironical from time to time, and especially, following Lucian, in his descriptions of "grave" or "solemn and respectable characters, as Gods, Goddesses, Heroes, Senators."[88] If Hume (or Lucian) had spoken of an "invisible hand," one would be entirely confident that one was in the presence of irony. It seems to me to be difficult, in the case of Smith, to be confident that one is not.

SMITH'S "STOICISM"

There is one remaining, and more important point to be made about Smith's "natural religion." The invisible hand has been seen, even by those who are skeptical of Smith's Christianity, as the expression of Smith's faith in a Stoic providence. Toward the end of his life, it is suggested, Smith "was coming nearer to natural religion—the Stoic Nature—than to the personal God of revelation."[89] "Adam Smith's ethics and natural theology are predominantly Stoic," Raphael and Macfie write in their introduction to the *Theory of Moral Sentiments,* and Stoic doctrines correspond to Smith's "own views" and "own opinions." Smith accepted the "broad outline" of the Stoic system, Macfie says; the invisible hand can be seen, thereby, as one expression of a great philosophical and theological system which was indeed Smith's "own."[90]

Smith's moral and metaphysical writings, like Hume's, are an extended colloquium with Roman philosophy, and especially with Cicero.[91] This makes the pursuit of Smith's own opinions often difficult. He himself did what he could to obstruct the pursuit; he seems to have thought, like Cicero in *De natura deorum,* that "those however who seek to learn my personal opinion on the various questions show an unreasonable degree of curiosity."[92] The historian of ideas must look for these views in the reflections of Smith's prudence (his desire for a quiet life); of his decency (his belief that to live a quiet or tranquil life was itself virtuous, and that one of its requirements is to desist from disturbing the tranquillity of others); and also of a collective or childhood understanding of classical texts—

a common knowledge—which are understood now in quite different ways.[93]

There are good reasons, all the same, to suppose that Smith was quite skeptical about a great deal of the Stoic system. He was influenced by different Stoic doctrines; he was not himself, in some sense, an eighteenth-century Stoic. Within the overall Stoic system, moreover, or the conjunction of Stoic doctrines, it is the idea of a providential order—the idea of which the invisible hand is supposed to be the expression—to which Smith was most opposed. He was eclectic in his use of Stoic ideas; the leading modern scholar of classical influences on Smith, Gloria Vivenza, speaks of his "'alchemist's' use" of ancient ideas (the sympathy of the Peripatetics, the propriety of the Stoics, the prudence of the Epicureans, Aristotle's moderate virtues).[94] He was in evident sympathy with much of the Stoic view of virtue, as he presented it; with the view of Zeno (shared by Plato and Aristotle) that virtue, including the virtue of self-command, is something to be valued in itself.[95] But he disliked the Stoic's indifference to consequences and circumstances, and the Stoic's concern "not about the event, but about the propriety of his own endeavours."[96] He rejected Stoic views of evil (as part of a universal order), of suicide, of astronomy, of paradoxes of truth and honor, and of the happiness of the wise man. The Stoic wise man is for Smith a prig and a "coxcomb," who consoles himself with the "complete enjoyment of his own self-applause."[97]

The "stoical apathy and indifference," above all, is odious to Smith, and especially so when it impinges on the "private and domestic affections." Richardson, Marivaux, and Riccoboni, he says, are here "much better instructors than Zeno, Chrysippus, or Epictetus."[98] "Submission to the order of providence" is the "fundamental doctrine" of Stoic morality, in Smith's description.[99] But it is "altogether different" to the "plan and system" of nature. The "indifference" of the Stoic to the consequences of his actions, including the consequences for himself and his friends, is contrary to nature.[100] His submission to the cosmic direction of his conduct—to the direction of Jupiter, Smith says—is contrary to duty, and thus to morality.[101]

Smith's ethics is founded on his description of moral sentiments; on the emotions we feel for our friends and "our nearest connections," but which are in turn the sentiments by which entire societies are united. The virtuous individual, he suggests, will strive to do what is proper and what is kind, in the circumstances in which he finds himself. He is not directed by the great superintendent of the universe; he tries to direct his own conduct, in his own department of life. This is the opposite, in Smith's description, of Stoic positions. The sentiments which the Stoics seek to repress become for Smith the foundation of ethics (and even of politics); the Stoic concern with the "greatest possible quantity of happiness" of the universe is seen as a delusion, altogether different to the plan or system of nature.[102]

Smith's descriptions of Stoic doctrine should be read, it seems to me, with much the same discrimination as his descriptions of Christian religion. He uses the same language of psychological explanation: the Stoic providence is an object of "contemplation," and a source of "consolation." His periphrases—"the director of this spectacle of human life," "the Superintendent of the universe," the "great Physician of nature," the "all-wise Architect and Conductor"—have the same overheroic sound.[103] His Stoicism has the same prudential utility as his theology; it identifies him with a set of beliefs sanctioned by the devout Samuel Clarke, and it precludes suspicions of infidelity, or licentiousness, or Epicurean influence.[104]

Smith's Stoicism, like his Christianity, is revised and modified in the sixth edition of the *Theory of Moral Sentiments*. The passages he adds about Stoic doctrines are critical; the passages he deletes, much like the description of the doctrine of atonement which he also removes, are solemn expositions of Stoic convictions, in the Stoics' own words.[105] There may in fact be a tone of irony, or of gentle mockery, even in the first edition of the *Theory*. This was at least the impression of Edmund Burke, who was then still unknown to Smith; he congratulated Smith on the varied style of the book, and particularly on the "fine Picture of the Stoic Philosophy towards the end of your first part which is dressed out in all the grandeur and Pomp that becomes that magnificent delusion."[106]

The Stoic origins of the invisible hand, in these circumstances, provide little evidence for the view that Smith took the invisible hand seriously. The Stoic Jupiter, in particular—the Jupiter of the first invisible hand, in the "History of Astronomy"—is indeed for Smith the sign of a joke. Smith liked Lucian for his "gaiety" as well as for his irony, and Jupiter is Lucian's essential comic device: Jupiter trying to explain providence; Jupiter complaining of his thunderbolts; Jupiter looking for a Stoic who is intelligent enough to dispute with the followers of Epicurus; Jupiter worrying about being turned into a bracelet.[107] For Smith, too, Jupiter is a ridiculous figure; "the thunder bolt falling from his hand," or wrapping everything up "in a universal conflagration."[108] But the Stoic doctrine of providence is also, for Smith, a tragic delusion. It was suggested earlier that the idea of the invisible hand is un-Smithian in that it is condescending about the intentions of individuals, and in that it presumes the existence of an all-knowing, all-seeing superintendent. These are in fact Smith's most serious charges against Stoic doctrines; against the Stoic wise man, both self-absorbed and impossibly, irresponsibly self-denying, and against Epictetus himself, exulting in the futility of human life.[109]

ORDER AND DESIGN

The orderliness of the universe was a subject of inexhaustible interest in the disputes over natural religion of the eighteenth century. Like the character of human nature—as in disputes over whether all sentiments are to be derived from self-love—it was a condition so well examined as to have become a sort of mnemonic. Hume uses the same, slightly etiolated language in speaking of both sets of quarrels. "There is much of a dispute of words in all this controversy," he wrote of the discussions among philosophers about whether public spirit and private friendship are the expression of self-interest or self-love.[110] "There enters somewhat of a dispute of words into this controversy," he wrote of the discussions about cosmic order, in the voice of Philo in the *Dialogues concerning Natural Religion*.[111]

The condition of orderliness, in these discussions, is of importance, above all, because of its consequences for religious belief. It provides incontrovertible evidence, for the religious and Stoic philosophers with whom Hume took issue, of the existence of God. If we see a beautiful house, the Stoic Balbus says in *De natura deorum*, we do not think that it could have been built by mice and weasels.[112] "An orderly world, as well as a coherent, articulate speech," Cleanthes says in Hume's *Dialogues,* will "be received as an incontestable proof of design and intention."[113] These disputes provide the overall setting for Smith's observations on natural order and invisible design. His first invisible hand of the polytheists, in the "History of Astronomy," is described in words which are close to those of Balbus. In the *Theory of Moral Sentiments*, the invisible hand is evoked in the course of a description of "the beauty of order," in the accommodation of the rich and in public institutions.[114] In the *Wealth of Nations,* the invisible hand of "society" is the occasion for one of Smith's two references—the other is in his discussion of the French Economists, with their metaphysical paradoxes—to the "greatest possible" outcomes which are so characteristic, in his description, of Stoic delusions of universal order.

The refutation of the inference from the orderliness of the universe to the existence of God was for Hume a matter of deep and continuing conviction. There is less evidence, in what remains of his philosophical writings, to suppose that Smith took a great interest in this particular religious question. It is most unlikely that he believed, like Balbus and Cleanthes and Lucian's Timocles, in the existence of an all-ordering providence, whose invisible hand was visible only in the orderliness of the cosmos. It is more likely that he believed, like Hume, that the universe could be orderly without having been ordered. But the possibility of orderliness without order, or without the existence of superior intention, was also of political importance, and this was for Smith a matter of much greater interest.

There was a resemblance, in particular, between arguments about divine design and arguments about the designs of sovereigns. This resemblance was recognized by Samuel Clarke in his correspondence with Leibniz; those who contend that the world proceeds without divine direction, Clarke said, will tend "to exclude God out of the world," just as those who think that "in an earthly government things may go on perfectly well without the king himself ordering or disposing of any thing, may reasonably be suspected they would very well like to set the king aside."[115] Smith had no interest in doing without kings. But he was convinced—it was one of his deepest convictions—that things go along encouragingly well without the disposition, by the king, of the industry of individuals.

Smith's use of the metaphor of the invisible hand is ironic, in these circumstances, in its intimation of the existence of an all-ordering providence. It is serious, and unironic, in its intimation that there can be order without design; that a society can be prosperous without being conducted by an all-seeing sovereign, just as the universe can be orderly without being conducted by an "all-wise Architect and Conductor." But in a different and deeper sense, Smith is once more ironic. For the intimation of the invisible hand is that society will in fact turn out to be prosperous, or orderly, in the absence of government direction. It is this promise, as will be seen, which was at the heart of the invisible hand's twentieth-century renown. It is not a promise that Smith expresses in any explicit way. It is little more, in an important sense, than a hope, or a hint.

The existence of order does not imply the existence of design, Smith can be seen as asserting. This is the serious and unironic use of the invisible hand: the efforts of individuals can be successful, and can successfully promote the interests of the society, without being subject to the direction of sovereigns and legislators. Smith suggests, even, that such direction is likely to be unsuccessful. The existence of design, in the sense of government direction of industry, is likely to impede economic order. But Smith does not suggest, in the *Wealth of Nations* or elsewhere, that the nonexistence of design is in itself sufficient to ensure order, or prosperity. The nonexistence of design does not imply the nonexistence of order. But nor does it imply the existence of order: that there will in fact be order; that laissez-faire will ensure prosperity. This is Smith's deeper irony. It is the irony of a Stoic orderliness, as the outcome of an unordered cosmos.

A PERSUASIVE DEVICE

There is one reason, to summarize, for supposing that Adam Smith liked the invisible hand: on grounds of its loveliness. There are three reasons for supposing that he found it either uninteresting or uncongenial: on grounds of the disregard it implied for the futility of individual lives, the reverence it implied for all-wise theorists, and the conflict it suggested with his own description of the political pursuit of self-interest. The religious connotations of the invisible hand—its evocation of the Christian God, or of the Stoic providence, or of the existence of divine order—provided a further reason, it was suggested, for skepticism as to Smith's intentions.

The difficulty which remains, in these circumstances, is of how to understand Smith's own, to some extent conflicting, views. We have been concerned with evidence for a negative proposition: that the invisible hand, like the conception of providential order of which it seems to be the expression, is not particularly important in Smith's thought.[116] On the one hand, there is reason to suppose that Smith would not have spoken of the invisible hand in an entirely serious way. On the other hand, the conception of the invisible hand, if it were intended seriously, would have been in conflict with several of Smith's most profound convictions about individual sentiments, individual responsibility, and the intentions of individual merchants.

The conclusion is that the invisible hand was an unimportant constituent of Smith's thought. The idea of the invisible hand, like the words in which it is described, is un-Smithian, and unimportant to his theory. Several modern scholars of Smith's ideas, from Jacob Viner onward, have expressed disquiet of one sort or another about the invisible hand; about what Macfie calls the "strange contrast, if not conflict," between the invisible hand and other parts of Smith's work.[117] The invisible hand is of energizing power in Smith's system, Macfie says, but it is also in conflict with this system. The objective of historians of economic thought has been to question the second premise, or to try to reconcile the invisible hand with Smith's other ideas (of individual responsibility, or of empirical investigation). The objective here is complementary; it is to question the first premise, of the seriousness and importance of the invisible hand in Smith's overall scheme.

Smith's view of the invisible hand is on this interpretation one of mildly ironical (and self-ironical) condescension. He saw it as the expression of a system which soothes the imagination, and which might or might not correspond to relations in society. "It is very indifferent," Hume says, where we locate the "original inherent principle of order," whether "in thought or in matter." It is difficult, Smith himself says in the "History of Astronomy," to speak of scientific systems as "mere inventions of the imagination," and not to "make use of language . . . as if they were the real chains [of] Nature."[118] This ontological nonchalance was indeed a familiar position in the later eighteenth century. Kant locates order in thought when he speaks of the understanding as "itself the lawgiver of nature": "The order and regularity in the appearances, which we entitle *nature*, we ourselves introduce. We could never find them in appearances, had not we ourselves, or the nature of our mind, originally set them there."[119] Smith's language, in the invisible hand passage, is even more than usually cautious, as Richard Schüller, one of the critics of Smith's nineteenth-century historicist critics, pointed out. The individual "generally" does not intend to promote the public interest, Smith says; he "frequently" promotes the interest of the public more efficiently by pursuing his own interest.[120]

The invisible hand is a sort of trinket, for Smith; it is not a discovery of inherent order. But its very beauty—its loveliness to the imagination—is thereby of political importance. Smith is preoccupied, throughout his work, with the idea of persuasion, and the invisible hand is a way of persuading people, of appealing to their love of system.[121] The passage in which Smith introduces the invisible hand in the *Theory of Moral Sentiments* is a digression, as has been seen, between two passages about the love of system and the beauty of order, at the end of which Smith returns to his interrupted argument: "the same principle, the same love of system." In the first passage, the imagination is charmed by the orderliness of consumption goods (trinkets, houses, and other contrivances), and in the second passage, by the beauty and orderliness of political systems. "You will be more likely to persuade" public men, Smith says, if you appeal to their love of beautiful and smoothly functioning political schemes; to their "love of art and contrivance."[122]

The system of general economic order is such a scheme. It may or may not yield the "greatest possible" value of the industry of the country, or the most equitable distribution of the country's wealth. But it will at least work better than the visible hand of universal regulation. Its political importance consists, in fact, in its public loveliness, or in its potential to dissuade statesmen from the use of other, more oppressive hands. Smith's concern, at the point where he introduces the invisible hand in the *Wealth of Nations,* is to persuade legislators that they should desist from imposing restrictions on imports. It is not particularly easy, as Condorcet observed, to convince officials of the attractions of doing nothing.[123] It is easier, perhaps, to convince them that to do nothing is to cooperate in a great system of public order. The invisible hand is thereby a contrivance, and also a sort of obviating device; it crowds out weightier, mightier hands.

Smith is gently ironical, it seems to me, in his description of the susceptibility of public men; of their propensity to be led by the imagination, or by the love of beauty and order. But his irony is also *Selbstironie.* People "give up the evidence of their senses to preserve the coherence of the ideas of their imagination," he says; "even we" are delighted by our systems, and are "drawn in" to seeing them as "important and sublime truths."[124] It is in this sense, at least, that the invisible hand is a thoroughly Smithian idea. It is an ironic joke, and it is also a joke on himself. It is a joke, in any case, on his immense posterity as well.

EXPLANATION AND UNDERSTANDING

There is one remaining difficulty, if the proposed interpretation is convincing. It is to understand why the invisible hand has been so overestimated; why this one "great idea" has seemed, so often, to express all that is most important in Smith's work. There have been imposing changes of intellectual taste in the study of Smith's economic thought, and Smith is perhaps peculiarly susceptible to the history which consists of *idées-clé,* or of single principles which are thought to epitomize his entire theory. But the taste for the invisible hand has over the past century been both obdurate and resilient. It is of some interest, therefore, to see what it is—in the modern invisible hand, if not in Smith's—which has been of such moment, to so many economists, and so much economic policy.

Of the three conditions which together constitute the modern conception of the invisible hand—to do with the unintended consequences of actions, the orderliness of the ensuing events, and the beneficence of the unintended order—it is the third which has been of the greatest public importance. The first condition, as Karen Vaughn says in her entry for "invisible hand" in the *New Palgrave,* "must have been obvious" for a very long time.[125] (It was obvious to Telemachus in the *Odyssey,* in Bernard Williams's account.)[126] It is present, certainly, in Smith's idea of the invisible hand; one of his preoccupations in the *Theory of Moral Sentiments* is with what he describes as the "good or bad consequences of actions upon the sentiments both of the person who performs them, and of others." It is interesting, however, that Smith's most forceful illustration is of unintended consequences which are not good but frightful; this is the discussion of the "piacular guilt" of Oedipus, Jocasta, and others, who "without design"—or in "undesigned violation"—do things which would, if intended, have justly been seen as deeply wrong.[127]

The second condition, of orderliness—of orders which could have been designed, in Vaughn's description, or which are "understandable"—is more obscure. The question of whether a cosmic order could have been designed was of intense religious interest in the eighteenth century, as has been seen. But there is little reason to expect that it would have been of similar importance in twentieth-century economics. The modern interest, if any, is of a different sort. The theological argument takes the modal form of asserting that if a set of events is orderly, then it is not possible that these events are *not* the product of design. It is this argument with which Hume and other eighteenth-century opponents of natural religion took issue. The modern, secular assertion seems to be that if the set of events is orderly, then it is possible that they *are* the product of design.[128] This proposition is in itself as crushingly uninteresting as the assertion of unintended consequences. It is possible that the events were designed, or that they were not designed, or that they were chosen by mice, and so forth. What was of greater interest, apparently, in the twentieth century as in the eighteenth century, was the implicit politics of the modal proposition.

In its modern version, the argument about design thus takes the form of suggesting that if the world, or the economy, is so orderly that it could have been designed by a sovereign (or a planning commission), then there is no need for actual designs (or commissions). The outcome could have been planned; as it happens it was not; why therefore should we have a planner? Like Samuel Clarke's suspect philosophers, the enthusiasts of the invisible hand might very well like to set aside the sovereign. The suggestion in this form is reminiscent of Smith's own efforts to persuade statesmen that the outcome of doing nothing would be a contrivance as beautiful and systematic as the outcome of regulation. But it is thereby a variation of the third condition, about beneficence; the proponent of the invisible hand must show that the order which is not the result of design is also an order which is either beneficial or beautiful or both.

The other element in the order argument, that the unintended order is "understandable," is of more general interest. Vaughn, following Hayek, says that "without some notion of an invisible hand in human actions, social science would be impossible," and Arrow and Hahn, too, see the invisible hand as the principal contribution of economic thought "to the general understanding of social processes."[129] All phenomena, for Hayek, should be divided into three classes: the natural, the artificial (or those that are the "product of human design"), and the "distinct middle category comprising all those unintended patterns and regularities which we find to exist in human society." It is this third class of phenomena which constitutes the subject matter of social science, and "which it is the task of social theory to explain."[130] P.-J. Proudhon, in his *Système des contradictions économiques* of 1846, said that a quasi-theological orderliness is the condition for the scientific study of society; that the "preamble of any political constitution" must be "*There is a God;* which means: society is governed with counsel, premeditation, intelligence. This judgment, which excludes chance, is thus the foundation of the possibility of a social science."[131]

The interest of social science in independent, individual actions begins, in Vaughn's description, with the discovery that these actions give rise to "an understandable and orderly social process." But to suggest that events must be orderly or coherent—that they must exhibit "patterns or regularities"—if they are to be understandable is to reject Smith's own view of science. In Smith's and Hume's (and Kant's) conception of the understanding as the lawgiver of nature, the point of scientific enterprise is to impose a coherent order on otherwise jarring events; it is to imagine a system (or one system after another) which makes sense of the world, and not to discover that the world in fact makes sense. Orderliness is for Smith a quality which is "bestowed" upon phenomena.[132] Our ideas are (or can be) coherent in much the same way as statements are coherent or consistent; the coherence of individual acts, like the consistency of individual choices, is less like the coherence or consistency of statements.[133] Their order is one that "we ourselves introduce," in a Kantian fashion.

The more profound question of social understanding, or understandability, has to do with tastes in explanation. There is an evident sense in which intended outcomes are not particularly interesting as the subject of social investigation. If I am watching a game of cards, to extend one of

Smith's own examples, I can feel quite giddy if I look at "every single stroke"; I am not greatly interested, however, when all is explained to me in terms of "the nature and rules of the game."[134] If individuals do only what is ordained by God, or what they have been ordered to do by the national planning commission, then the search for social understanding is limited and uninviting. The consequences of their actions can be understood, or explained, but the explanation is of little or no interest to the social theorist.

One claim on behalf of "invisible hand explanations," made by Robert Nozick, is essentially aesthetic, as has been seen, and very much in Smith's spirit; it is that they are "lovely" or "satisfying."[135] But there is a different, and stronger, claim made by Hayek, in which the analysis of unintended actions is not only a contribution to but a condition for social understanding. The doctrine of constructivism associated with the Continental enlightenment, Hayek says, "has no room for anything which is 'the result of human action but not of human design' and therefore no place for social theory."[136] Spontaneous ordered structures not only are "superior to conscious action," but also are coextensive with social life, or with the realm of social theory; "indeed, any social processes which deserve to be called 'social,' in distinction to the action of individuals are almost *ex definitione* not conscious."[137]

The difficulty here is that the Hayekian social theorist is at risk of finding herself in much the same position as was taken, earlier, to be distinctively un-Smithian: a position of disregard for individual and futile intentions, and of reverence for the all-seeing theorist. Actions are attended, in general, by intentions, and by consciousness. The theorist, in invisible hand explanations, simply discards most of these intentions. The individual participant in social processes is depicted as someone who thinks. But she thinks about her own petty interests and not about the process of which she is a part; she thinks locally and not universally; she does not think theoretically.

This posture of the theorist, looking down like the Stoic emperor on the "feasts and mournings and markets" of the world, on its particular intentions and particular ways of thinking, is in conflict with much of Hayek's thought, as well as with Smith's.[138] For Hayek was himself critical of the objectivist position which tries to look at other men from the perspective of "somebody who was not himself a man," or "as we observe an ant-heap or a bee-hive."[139] Even Condorcet, at the dizziest moment of his faith in the limitlessness of enlightenment, in his "Discours de Réception" of

1782 at the Académie Française, insisted on the difference between the moral and the physical sciences: "Everything would be equal between them for a being who, a stranger to our species, would study human society as we study that of beavers or ants. But here, the observer is himself part of the society he observes, and truth can only have judges who are either prejudiced or seduced."[140] It is just this distant view which is characteristic of invisible hand theories. The people, Necker wrote in his *Sur la législation et le commerce des grains*, are like children, who act "without reflecting, but enlightened by their instinct."[141] For Dugald Stewart, in the observation quoted earlier, to be the subject of the invisible hand is to be unenlightened, to act out of instinct and not out of intention, to be like a bee:

> When, like the lower animals, he follows blindly his instinctive principles of action, he is led by an invisible hand, and contributes his share to the execution of a plan, of the nature and advantages of which he has no conception. The operations of the bee, when it begins, for the first time, to form its cell, convey to us a striking image of the efforts of unenlightened Man, in conducting the operations of an infant government.[142]

Invisible hand explanations, in Nozick's description, tend to work less well to the extent that the realms or patterns to be explained are associated with "reflective thinking." They are not notably successful, in particular, in providing an explanation of ethics; they encounter the "substantial stumbling block" of "consciousness, language, and self-consciousness." They work best when the activities in question (such as bartering one sort of commodity for another) are relatively unreflective, and relatively unencumbered with social theorizing (such as thinking about the emergence of money). They work least well when the activities are reflective, self-conscious, and concerned with universal theories; activities, for example, such as deciding whether to pursue one's interests by buying and selling commodities, or by influencing the political rules under which commodities are bought and sold.[143]

The difficulty, for invisible hand explanations of economic life, is that economic activities are often highly reflective. If buying and selling is a debate (as in Turgot's description), or a form of rhetoric (as in Smith's), then it is a cognitive, self-conscious sort of activity. It may involve thinking or talking about economic theories and rules, as well as about economic interests. Deciding how to pursue one's self-interest, or discussing one's decisions with other people, is a part of economic life, and it is also similar to much that happens in political life, or in moral life. There are occasions, that is to say, when it is a characteristic of economic agents, as of Nozick's moral agents, to "notice how we are behaving, decide to have our behavior conform to general principles of behavior, produce reasons for and against our beliefs and critically discuss them."[144] There are other occasions when it is reasonable to disregard all this reflectiveness, as being of only minimal importance in the lives of economic agents, no more than "futility and nothingness." The social (or economic) theorist needs different kinds of explanations for these different occasions; the invisible hand is a style of explanation, and not a condition of social understanding.

GREATEST POSSIBLE VALUES

It is the third condition of the invisible hand, whereby the unintended order turns out to be beneficial for the people whom it orders, which has contributed most to the modern renown of the invisible hand. Vaughn distinguishes two ways of thinking about spontaneous orders and their desirable consequences. In one, the system is "self-organizing in some way within the context of a set of social rules"; the rules or constraints in the system, as in Lionel Robbins's description of the invisible hand as the hand of the lawgiver, "could well be set by human design and can work for good or ill." In the other, the spontaneous orders are seen as "evolved orders where the rules themselves are the unintended products of human actions"; the "economic institutions of a society," like the beneficial consequences of these institutions, are the "unintended by-products of self-interested economic behaviour."[145] The two conceptions—the equilibrium and the evolutionary versions of the invisible hand—correspond to different economic theories, and to different views of economic policy; both have been of very significant importance in modern economics.

The invisible hand in the first conception is Arrow's and Hahn's "poetic device" of the general competitive equilibrium of twentieth-century economic theory.[146] There is a general sense in which this body of theory is indeed Smithian. It corresponds to the criterion of loveliness; it is as close as anything in modern economics to Smith's idyll of "a more coherent, and therefore a more magnificent spectacle." It is reasonable to assert, counterfactually, that Smith would have been pleased (or soothed) by the modern theory of general economic equilibrium. But it was not a theory that he knew, or of which he was in any precise sense the precursor. Smith was in fact quite reticent in using the metaphors of celestial and fluid mechanics. He avoids the Stoic-Epicurean word "equilibrium," which was by the 1770s a well-known figure of speech in political economy, and with which he was almost certainly familiar in its economic uses.[147] (The word appears only once in the *Wealth of Nations*, in an account of doctrines of the exact balance of trade, than which, Smith says, "nothing, however, can be more absurd.")[148]

Smith is similarly cautious in his references to maximization, at least with respect to aggregate or social quantities. In the *Theory of Moral Sentiments*, the idea of an order, or an "immense machine of the universe" such as to sustain "the greatest possible quantity of happiness," is a sublime object of contemplation, but one which should not serve as a distraction from humbler and more domestic duties.[149] It is only in the passage about the invisible hand, in the *Wealth of Nations*, that he refers in any sustained way to "greatest possible" quantities; he speaks four times in a few lines of "the greatest value" of production, and also mentions the "greatest possible value" of production, and the "greatest quantity" of money or goods. But the production to be maximized is in each case the product of the individual's own industry or his own capital. The maximand is an objective of individuals; it is what "may" or "is likely to" result from the individual's efforts.[150]

The invisible hand was for Smith an obviating device, as has been suggested. To rely on the self-interest of individuals was simply less bad for national prosperity (and less unjust) than to regulate their activities. But this was an extremely general prescription, consistent with Smith's skepticism about "exact regimens." The difficulty begins—the disparity between the poetic, logical invisible hand and the invisible hand which was of public importance or influence in the twentieth century—with the application of the prescription to economic policy. For the conditions of real commercial societies are strikingly different, as Smith and many others recognized, from conditions of perfect economic competition. The theorist can set up the conditions of his system in whatever way he likes, much as Smith's merchant in the invisible hand passage is identified as a cosmopolitan citizen of Amsterdam, with very little power to influence policy in Portugal or the Baltic. The statesman, advised by the theorist, has the additional possibility of trying to improve the conditions of real societies, and to make them more like conditions of free and perfect competition.

Smith's account of the invisible hand is oddly ingenuous, as has been seen, with respect to the propensity of entrepreneurs to pursue their own interests by influencing the political regulation of industry and commerce. "Every individual, it is evident, can, in his local situation, judge much better than any statesman or lawgiver can do for him," Smith says in the passage in the *Wealth of Nations* about the invisible hand. But the local situation is often a political situation. The local knowledge which is characteristic, in Smith's and Turgot's slightly condescending descriptions, of individual entrepreneurs is among other things a knowledge of local regulations, local vexation, and local lawgivers.[151] Smith describes the interests of merchants as futile, as Playfair observes. As Playfair also points out, he objects to the spirit of monopoly: Smith, "who thinks that trade should be left to itself, because individuals understand best their own interests, complains in unusually bitter terms of that desire of monopoly which is, and which must be, the concomitant of a desire to accumulate and become rich."[152]

The difficulty, for the modern theorist of the invisible hand, consists in the deduction, from the theory of general economic equilibrium, of principles of economic policy.[153] Smith's ontological modesty (his unconcern with whether orderliness is a condition of the mind or of the world) corresponds to a modesty with respect to policy, in which he simply averts his gaze from the great public objectives of improving entire societies. This is a possibility for the modern theorist, as well: to insist that the system of general competitive efficiency is no more than a set of definitions, without explanatory or normative consequence. But the invisible hand is in these circumstances of little public importance. Once it is seen as a guide to policy, then it becomes much less modest. Policy must be concerned, for example, to restrict monopoly (and perhaps also, eventually, to restrict or restrain the desire for monopoly). The pursuit of the public interest must consist not only in desisting from regulation, but also in establishing (and maintaining) an environment of free competition. Even Hayek spoke, in *The Road to Serfdom*, of "planning for competition," such that the role of the state was "to create conditions in which competition will be as effective as possible."[154]

Equilibrium is in these circumstances an ideal. There is even (as Necker wrote) an "art of equilibrium."[155] The "system of economic freedom" will only work, in Lionel Robbins's words, "if a conscious effort is made to create the highly artificial environment which is necessary if it is to function properly . . . [N]ot only the good society, but the market itself is an artifact."[156] As in Frank Hahn's account, quoted earlier, the central claim for the invisible hand is that "the market system operates on relatively simple motivational precepts which, in principle, leave agents open to manipulation by authority . . . [I]t suggests ways in which institutions and policies might be devised, which harness self-interest and render it socially acceptable."[157]

The hand which manipulates individual agents, here, is heteronomous, in Kant's sense. It treats individuals as means and not as ends. It is the hand of the sovereign; the individuals are something like horses, to be harnessed in the interest of their own happiness. In Necker's description of the art of administration, "the hand which encourages, which restrains, which restores, is no longer noticed, and one forgets its services."[158] The utility of every individual is an end, but it is not an end which the individual has himself devised or explained. For the effort of "the hand of the lawgiver" in restricting "the sphere of the pursuit of self-interest" is itself a political project. The government is not concerned, as in the mercantilist or regulatory regimes opposed by Smith, to enact laws directing citizens as to what they should sell, or import, or who they should employ. Its responsibility, rather, is to enact and to enforce laws about laws; about the circumstances in which citizens seek to influence laws and the enforcement of laws. It is concerned with corruption, intimidation, and political contributions, or with the transformation of money into political power. It influences the norms of political influence: the choice, for example, of how to distinguish the ingenuously from the disingenuously public interest, and the licit from the illicit exercise of political power.

EVOLVED ORDERS

The other way of thinking about the invisible hand—about desirable orders in which "the rules themselves are the unintended products of human actions," in Vaughn's description—is at first sight strikingly different. Hayek explicitly denies, on behalf of the theory of the "spontaneous order of the market," any objective of "maximising aggregate real social income."[159] The equilibrium version of the modern invisible hand corresponds to the utilitarian political objective of seeking to contribute, through the consequences of one's policies, to the greatest possible happiness of individuals. This utilitarianism, for Hayek, is a variation of the "false 'constructivist' rationalism" which was characteristic of the Continental European as distinct from the English enlightenment: a "constructivist particularist utilitarianism [which] rests on the belief that reason is capable of directly manipulating all the details of a complex society."[160]

It is the rules and institutions of an evolved order, more than its economic outcomes, which are in Hayek's view subject to the invisible hand. The English view of a liberal social order is founded, he writes, on "an evolutionary interpretation of all phenomena of culture and mind." The disposition of opportunities in the economy is ordered by an invisible hand. But so too are the rules which order the dispositions. So, in turn, are the rules which order the rules. (So, even, is the theory of rules and of rules about rules; the liberalism which Hayek favors "is itself not the result of a theoretical construction.")[161] The life of individuals, with its mournings and markets, is overseen by an imposing sequence of invisible hands, stacked up, one above the other, like airplanes waiting to land. The planes never land; they are not so much like airliners as like AWACS surveillance planes, suspended in a limitless holding position.

The outcome of all this surveillance, in Hayek's description, consists in "institutions which are necessary conditions for the achievement of men's conscious purposes," rather than in institutions which contribute to "social welfare."[162] But the criterion of necessity is established after the event; institutions are necessary if they turn out to have been needed. The criterion of success is to have succeeded, or to have survived. The rules which prevail do so, Hayek writes, because "the groups who observed them were more successful." "Grown institutions," together with "tradition and custom," are the proper subject of esteem. They have grown (as distinct from being planted, presumably when they were already large), and they have also been growing for some time. "It is this submission to undesigned rules and conventions whose significance and importance we largely do not understand, this reverence for the traditional," Hayek says, that "is indispensable for the working of a free society."[163]

The evolutionary version of the invisible hand is very far, here, from Adam Smith. Dugald Stewart was concerned, as has been seen, to defend Smith against the charge of trying "to unhinge established institutions," or of disputing "the unfathomable wisdom of the feudal ages."[164] But Stewart, too, had written of Smith that he "calls into question the utility of institutions"; Stewart himself was dubious as to "exaggerated conceptions of the wisdom of long experience."[165] Smith's description of traditional institutions in the *Wealth of Nations*—of the "barbarous institutions" of inheritance, or of "all the violence of the feudal institutions"—is strikingly lacking in reverence. The respect of "ancient sages for the institutions of their ancestors" led them, Smith says, to "find much political wisdom in what was, perhaps, merely an ancient custom."[166]

Smith's definition of jurisprudence, at the outset of his unpublished lectures, is similarly rationalist, in Hayek's terms: jurisprudence is "the theory of the rules by which civil government ought to be directed. It attempts to show the foundation of the different systems of government in different countries and to show how far they are founded in reason."[167] In the *Theory of Moral Sentiments*, too, custom is the subject of very little esteem. One of Smith's most coruscating passages is indeed concerned with the authorization in ancient Greece, by "uninterrupted custom," of the "exposition, that is the murder of new-born infants." Even philosophers, Smith says, were "led away by the established custom": "When custom can give sanction to so dreadful a violation of humanity, we may well imagine that there is scarce any particular practice so gross which it cannot authorise. Such a thing, we hear men every day saying, is commonly done, and they seem to think this a sufficient apology for what, in itself, is the most unjust and unreasonable conduct."[168]

Carl Menger, whom Hayek identifies as the most important nineteenth-century source of the theory of spontaneous orders, said of Smith and his followers, as was seen earlier, that "the broad domain of unreflectively created social structures remains closed to their theoretical understanding"; that they can justly be charged with a "pragmatism, which in the main had only an understanding for positive creations of public authorities."[169] Menger has been criticized, on the basis of these comments, for an "unsympathetic interpretation if not monumental misunderstanding of Smith," which is difficult to account for.[170] But even Hayek concedes that other eighteenth-century thinkers expressed the notion of evolutionary institutions "much more clearly than Smith himself ever did"; he surmises, oddly, that Smith "may have seemed to treat it as too obvious that the order which formed itself spontaneously was also the best order possible."[171] This is unlikely, at least if Smith shared Hume's and Voltaire's sprightly view of best possible worlds. As James Buchanan concludes, Smith's view was that "there is nothing sacrosanct about those laws and institutions that emerge in what may be called the natural process of social evolution." "Smith differs from the position that seems to be taken by F. A. Hayek, who holds Smith up as one of the discoverers of the notion that efficient results need not be willed or planned," Buchanan writes; but "Hayek extends this notion too far when he applies it to the emergence of law itself."[172]

Smith's theory and Hayek's have in common a profound dislike of the official knowledge of the state. The evolutionary version of the invisible hand is in this respect, at least, far closer to Smith than the equilibrium version. Hayek's distinction between the rule of law and arbitrary government—between "*formal rules* which do not aim at the wants and needs of particular people" and substantive rules which "provide for the actual needs of people as they arise and then choose deliberately between them"—has an evident affinity to Smith's political thought (as indeed to the "Continental" thought of Turgot or Condorcet).[173] The duty of the sovereign, for Smith, consists in "protecting, as far as possible, every member of the society from the injustice or oppression of every other member of it."[174] The fluctuating regulation of people's lives is itself a form of oppression. The vexation and personal injustice which Smith describes are such as to flourish in an arbitrary regime of regulation; Hayek speaks of "oppression by means of economic policy."[175] For Smith, as for Hayek, the misuse of knowledge by the state is the most frightening of despotisms.

The deepest difference between Smith and Hayek has to do, by contrast, with the knowledge of individuals (or with the idyll of universal enlightenment). There is very little in Smith which corresponds to Hayek's esteem for the unconscious, the blind, the untheoretical, the imperfectly understood. The most significant fact about the price system, Hayek writes, consists in its economy of knowledge, or "how little the individual participants need to know in order to be able to take the right action."[176] They might even make better choices if they knew less, or at least if they had less knowledge of a reflective, theoretical sort. Burke, more than Smith, is for Hayek the father of the "genetic" understanding of human institutions, and Hayek follows Burke in celebrating the littleness of individual reason. Like Burke, he is unimpressed by the empire of light: "We are afraid to put men to live and trade each on his own private stock of reason; because we suspect that this stock in each man is small." Like Burke, too, he sees in the cumulative or evolved knowledge of institutions a capital which is itself unknowable: a "latent wisdom," a "wisdom without reflection, and above it" a "great mysterious incorporation."[177] Max Weber described the disenchantment of the world associated with the scientific mind—"the knowledge or the belief that . . . there are in principle no *mysterious, incalculable powers at work*"—as a victory over something very close to Smith's invisible hand of Jupiter: "One need no longer have recourse to magic in order to control or implore the spirits, as did the savage for whom such powers existed."[178] For Hayek, the invisibility or incalculability of economic order is itself an object of reverence.

The knowledge of individuals is often estimable, for Hayek. But it is knowledge of the local (and not the universal), of the fleeting (and not the persistent), of the untheoretical. He is full of disdain for the "speculative or explanatory views which people have formed about . . . such collectives as 'society' or the 'economic system'"; the role of social science, in his description, is to start "from the concepts which guide individuals in their actions and not from the results of their theorising about their actions."[179] There is something of this disdain in Turgot's eulogy to the knowing local entrepreneur, who "alone has that experience which is the more sure because it is limited to a single object."[180] But for Smith, to know only a single thing is to be "mutilated and deformed" in an "essential part of the character of human nature." The "intellectual faculties" in every individual, for Smith, can be exercised in "rational conversation," in sentiments, in "the ordinary duties of private life," and in judging "the great and extensive interests of his country."[181]

Reason, for Smith, as for Philo in Hume's *Dialogues concerning Natural Religion*, is "so bounded a principle."[182] But the reason so limited, or so misprised, is in general the reason of the great. It is the reason of the pretentious; of the state, of established theory, of powerful merchants. The projects of universal religious explanation tend to be disconcerted, like those of established science (even of Newton's system, "the most universal empire that was ever established in philosophy").[183] So do the projects of the commercial or political statesman, in Hume's description; when a man forms schemes in politics or economy, something is sure to happen "that will disconcert his reasoning, and produce an event different from what he expected."[184]

The ordinary reason of individuals is more often the object of esteem, both for Smith and for Hume. "The qualities most useful to ourselves are, first of all, superior reason and understanding," Smith says in the *Theory of Moral Sentiments*.[185] In Hume's description of civilized society, "profound ignorance is totally banished, and men enjoy the privilege of rational creatures, to think as well as to act."[186] Even the propensity to barter and exchange, the foundation of commercial society, is for Smith a consequence of the faculties of reason and speech. The psychological inequality which is characteristic of the division of labor, in which the few have "an almost infinite variety of objects" while the lives of the "great body of the people" are "simple and uniform," is for Smith the "great public evil" of civilized society. But it can be prevented by universal public instruction, and by the "study of science and philosophy." The great body of the people can have multiple objects, or ideas with which to amuse themselves. They can become more disposed to examine political projects; they can be "instructed and intelligent."[187]

This is the disposition of enlightenment, once more. It is the heroism of the millers, carters, and bakers, so admired by the French exponents of economic reform, and so derided by Galiani. The "new conquering empire of light and reason" is in Burke's description a purgatory of universal reflectiveness; a "monstrous fiction" of "inspiring false ideas and vain expectations" in men destined to obscurity. It promises a tumult of multiple, competing theories, in which individuals are "hesitating in the moment of decision, sceptical, puzzled, and unresolved."[188] But Smith, unlike Burke, was a friend of enlightenment in this sense, as has been seen. His views of instruction and ignorance were invoked repeatedly in the early years of the French Revolution. He was unenticed by what Coleridge, writing against Burke, described as the "absurd opposition of Theory to Practice"; his view, like Coleridge's, is that "the meanest of men has his Theory: and to think at all is to theorize."[189]

Hayek's rejection of "theorizing"—his lyricism of the unconscious and the imperfectly understood—is in this respect quite un-Smithian. It also poses serious problems for the evolutionary version of the invisible hand. The evolved order is considered to be beneficial, as has been seen, because it permits individuals to achieve their own purposes. But to have conscious purposes, or to be guided in one's actions by concepts, is to be conscious of one's ends, and also of the means to these ends. It is to be in a position to choose one's means (as the subjects of the invisible hand choose between pursuing their ends by political and economic means). It is also, and above all, to be in a position to evaluate, oneself, whether one is or is not achieving one's ends. To be this sort of person is to be unsubmissive to great mysterious incorporations. It is to be in a position, at least, to call into question the wisdom of established institutions.

The difficulty, in general, is that there are different criteria for ordering "orders," and that the different criteria may induce the theorist of the invisible hand to support different policies. On one criterion, orders are good if they have become established over time. On a second, they are good if they correspond to what the individuals who constitute the order (who are ordered by it) themselves think to be good. On a third, orders are good if they can be shown to increase the possibilities for individuals to do what they wish to do (even when the individuals do not themselves have wishes, or opinions, about social orders). On a fourth criterion, orders are good if they correspond to certain principles, such as the security of individual rights and the non-recourse to force. But the four criteria do not always coincide. It is quite conceivable, and indeed familiar, that they will identify different orders, or policies. Benjamin Constant, for example, turned the evolutionary rhetoric of reverence for established institutions against Burke's own followers as early as the mid-1790s, when he argued that to overthrow the institutions established during the period of revolutionary reform would be to emulate the impetuousness of the Jacobin revolutionaries themselves. The appropriate policy, rather, was to rely on a "system of principles"; to preserve those revolutionary institutions which were just, and which had popular support; which corresponded to people's "ideas," and to "principles" as distinct from "prejudices."[190]

"The attitude of the liberal toward society," Hayek wrote in *The Road to Serfdom,* "is like that of the gardener who tends a plant and, in order to create the conditions most favorable to its growth, must know as much as possible about its structure and the way it functions."[191] This is one of the more charming metaphors of political power. To potter among the rosebushes is to be more enlightened and respectful, as a sovereign, than to keep sheep; than to be the sort of sovereign who thinks of one's subjects, in Kant's words, as "docile sheep, well fed, powerfully protected and led by a kind and understanding master, and [with] no lack of welfare to complain of."[192] But in the metaphor of the flower beds, too, there is an asymmetry of consciousness between the ruler and the ruled (the rosebushes of society, or the sheep). It is the gardener, or the shepherd, who thinks, or who theorizes. It is he, alone, who understands the "structure" of the invisible order, and whether it permits individuals to do what they wish to do. In a liberal order, Hayek writes, "justice [is] conceived as something to be discovered by the efforts of judges and scholars."[193] The liberal is a scholar, a judge, a theorist who gives enlightened and respectful advice to the ruler; he is the only wise and worthy man, or the only man, in a bower of flowers.

The evolutionary version of the invisible hand, in these circumstances, is no more reverent with respect to individual wills than the equilibrium version. The theorist is reluctant to provide advice on how to set the rules of economic institutions; he understands, nonetheless, how to make use of the wills of individual participants. Society requires that "the inclinations of men should frequently be thwarted, their will controlled, and their passions brought into subjection," Burke wrote in the *Reflections,* and there is something of this authoritarianism in theories of the invisible hand.[194] The liberal order, Hayek says, is "a method of social control"; it is "deemed superior because of our ignorance of its precise results." It can "utilise the knowledge and skill of all members of society"; it resolves the problem of "how to provide inducements which will make the individuals do the desirable things without anyone having to tell them what to do."[195] The hand of the liberal sovereign, like the hand of Necker's virtuous minister of finance, is no longer noticed.

The evolved order is even more heteronomous, here, than the equilibrium order. It controls the wills of individuals, and the individuals do not know that they are being controlled. They are not conscious of the social order; they cannot see it. But they are subject, all the same, to its invisible authority. They are even subject to its moral authority. For the individual has a duty, Hayek writes, to "submit to the adjustments which the market forces" upon him. His income is the "outcome of a mixed game of skill and chance," and "once we have agreed to play the game and profited from its results, it is a moral obligation on us to abide by the results even if they turn against us."[196]

The order of the market is thus something of which individuals are conscious (it is a moral order), and at the same time something of which they are unconscious (it is an invisible order). In his lectures on jurisprudence, Smith argued against the theory of an original contract, following Hume, that individuals cannot be bound by duties with which they are "unacquainted," or of which they do not have at least "some idea." The contract is not really a contract, at least for the posterity of the original persons; "they are not conscious of it, and therefore cannot be bound by it." It may be said, Smith adds, "that by remaining in the country you tacitly consent to the contract and are bound by it. But how can you avoid staying in it? . . . And how can you get out of it?"[197] This is the question for the subjects of the invisible hand as well. They must submit, in Hayek's theory, to something they do not, and could not, understand; they must give themselves up to the heteronomy of the elective will.[198]

TWO SHORTCOMINGS OF LIBERAL THOUGHT

Smith's ideas have had long and turbulent lives in what Kant described as the universal exchange of thought.[199] The invisible hand, in particular, was transposed, in the course of the twentieth century, into two enormous and opposing bodies of political and economic theory. These theories are not Smith's; all he did, it has been suggested, was to make a mild and ironic joke. But the difficulties of the equilibrium and the evolutionary versions of the invisible hand correspond to conflicts in Smith's own thought, and indeed in all subsequent thought about liberal economic orders. For Smith was being ironic, as on other occasions, about a deadly serious subject. His ontological (and political) nonchalance is itself jarring; it has something of what he describes, in Stoic doctrine, as "apathy and indifference."

The first conflict, or shortcoming of economic thought, is over the transformation of money into political power. In Smith's description of the invisible hand in the *Wealth of Nations*, the circumstance that individuals pursue their economic objectives by political means is largely ignored. In the modern theory of general competitive equilibrium, as in the theory of evolved orders, these circumstances (or the existence of market power) were also ignored, or assumed to be absent. The role of public policy, to the extent that policy consequences are associated with equilibrium theory, was to design efficient market institutions. In evolutionary theory, existing institutions were the subject of greater esteem; the role of the theorist, if not of public policy, was to remind individuals of their moral obligations in respect of market games.

The difficulty, in all these positions, is that the liberal economic order— the system ordered by the invisible hand—is inefficient in the presence of extensive market power. Individual participants in a market economy set out with different initial endowments; their endowments change over time; and they sometimes seek to use these endowments (of money, or of power) to influence the rules of the economy itself. If they do so, on any substantial scale or with any substantial success, the invisible hand of economic freedom will be of little use. But to prevent individuals from using their own endowments is itself a violation of freedom. To prevent individuals from trying to influence public policy is to subvert political freedom.

The incidence of economic and political competition is thus of decisive importance for the liberal economic order. Individuals have opinions about social orders, they have opinions about the means of achieving their objectives within a given social order, and they have opinions about how changes in social orders could help them to achieve these objectives. Smith is a subtle observer of the condition which he describes as "the mysterious veil of self-delusion," or which Condorcet called *fausse conscience:* of the process by which individuals come to believe that the outcomes which are best for them are also best for the society, or for other people. To try to distinguish between false and civic consciousness—between the subversive and the innocent pursuit of self-interest, or between the petty- and the public-spirited exercise of political rights—is to impinge, through economic policy, on the foundations of political power.

Economic activity was for Smith a highly discursive and reflective way of life. This is one reason, as has been seen, that it is an often unpropitious subject for "invisible hand explanations." Hayek's classification—into the natural, the unintended, and the artificial—is indeed profoundly un-Smithian. Even the natural and the artificial are interrelated, in the philosophical thought with which Smith (and Hume) were most familiar; nature, Balbus says in *De natura deorum,* quoting the Stoic Zeno, is an *ignis artificiosus,* a "craftsmanlike fire."[200] The relationship between the artificial and the unintended, above all, is for Smith at the heart of moral and social investigation. If there were to be a task, or a subject of social theory, it would consist, for Smith as for Hume, in the investigation of the coexistence of intended and unintended effects, of the self-conscious and the unself-conscious activities of individuals, of the relatively reflective (the political and the moral) and the relatively unreflective. These are among Smith's most persistent preoccupations, in the *Theory of Moral Sentiments* and in most of the *Wealth of Nations;* they are oddly absent in his description of the invisible hand, and of the policies about money and power which are (or should be) its complement.

The other shortcoming of liberal economic thought has to do with faith. All versions of the invisible hand, those of modern economic theory as well as Smith's, are the expression of optimism about the system of economic freedom. The equilibrium version is the less dependent on faith or hope. It is a deduction of consequences from conditions; its optimism, if any, is about the efficiency of economic policy in establishing the rules or conditions of economic institutions. The "evolved order" version of the invisible hand, by contrast, has all the faith of evolutionary theory. Institutions succeed if they survive, and the existent (or the surviving) is for that reason deserving of reverence. Even the defects of institutions are the expression of unseen purposes which individuals, including theorists, are too ignorant to understand. But all is in general for the best, "over a large number of individuals or over a long period of time."[201] The "new philosophy" of social science of the nineteenth century, in Proudhon's description, with its exclusion of chance and its submission to "evidence," "makes everything converge toward the theological hypothesis, as though toward the last of its problems," and its "humanitarian atheism" leads, in turn, toward "the reconstruction or scientific verification of all the demolished doctrines."[202]

Smith's optimism, or the foundation for his belief in the liberal economic order, is different, and more profound. There is little justification, as has been seen, for considering the invisible hand to be a theological element in his thought, or the representation of "a theory of ultimate natural harmony," to be set, in turn, "in the wider context of [his] ultimate faith."[203] He has little or no confidence in the wisdom of economic policy (especially in respect of the transformation of money into power), and even less confidence in the timeless wisdom of institutions. But he does have two reasons for confidence in the system ordered by the invisible hand. One reason is not economic, in the terms of modern thought (or not to do with efficiency); it is that a system in which individuals make their own choices about how to live, or where to work, or how to use their money, is more just than a system in which these choices are the objects of government regulation. The other reason—the argument about the obviating device, or the second worst outcome—is to do with efficiency, although it is less than resounding. It is that the liberal system is not the worst of all systems; it is less inefficient, at least, than the system of regulation.

Smith, like Hume, lived in an imaginative universe of profound uncertainty. Like Hume, he had come to tolerate a way of life, or a way of thinking, in which almost all judgments were incomplete, provisional, propositions to be discussed, and not to be convinced of. His engagement with the question of disbelief—the tragic choice, described in the *Theory of Moral Sentiments*, between an impossible optimism and the "very suspicion of a fatherless world," infinite and incomprehensible—left him relatively comfortable with the incomplete and the unresounding. His indifference or nonchalance is in this respect quite unlike the indifference of the Stoics, secure in the paternity of providence; it is more like the security of the Epicureans, in Cicero's description, endlessly discussing the meaning of terms in natural philosophy, and the pleasures of friendship.[204]

Smith was in a secular sense a man of faith. As Macfie writes, "He was an essentially pious man."[205] But his faith, like Hume's and Condorcet's, is in the mildness and thoughtfulness of most individual men and women. He is induced, thereby, to believe that they will usually not pursue their interests in grossly oppressive ways, and that they will usually wish to live in a society in which other people are not grossly oppressed or deprived. They will wish to be decorous. This, and little more, is the foundation of the system of economic freedom. It is a pious hope, as well as a shortcoming of liberal economic thought.

6

Economic and Political Choice

RATON WAS QUITE ASTONISHED . . .

The disposition of enlightenment is a condition of the liberal economic order described by Smith and Condorcet. Individuals are the best judges of their own interests, and they have the best knowledge of their own local circumstances. They are independent and unprejudiced; they are civilized, in the sense that they wish to resolve conflicts by negotiation and not by violence. They are unfrightened of portents, or of feudal injustice. Their predilection, as in Smith's description at the beginning of the *Wealth of Nations,* is for "fair and deliberate exchange."[1] But this discursive and deliberative disposition is also, under certain circumstances, subversive of the economic or market order. For to be enlightened is to be disposed to make political as well as economic judgments. It is to make judgments about judgments, including about the relationship between economic and political choices, and between economic and political interests.

One shortcoming of the liberal economic order, as was seen in Chapter 5, is that individuals seek, on occasion, to pursue their own (economic) interests by political means. They seek regulation, political influence, and protected monopoly. They have money, and they use it to buy power. A second, related shortcoming is that the invisible order is very unlike a divine providence, or an established system of institutions, in which individuals should have confidence, or which they should revere. It is the outcome of innumerable, unruly judgments. It may or may not be good. A social theory of the individuals who make these judgments must be concerned with intended (or "artificial") as well as with unintended events, and with self-conscious, reflective choices. It must be a theory of people with theories.

The best resolution of the difficulties of the liberal economic order, for its late eighteenth-century exponents, was to be found in even more en-lightenment. The most conspicuous object of reverence, in their theories, is the fair, kind, and enlightened individual. Their prospect seems to be of a universe of small proprietors, most of whom are sufficiently foresighted to understand that their own lasting self-interest, which coincides with the interest of the society, consists in competing by economic means (such as being industrious and well informed), and not through political influence. Regulations will dwindle away, or be repealed, and will not be reintroduced. Even the richest proprietors will be unconcerned to buy political power. There will be exceptions, of course. But the reason to have confidence in such a system is that individuals are usually and increasingly peaceable and reasonable.

For Condorcet, more than for Smith, the conflicting, shifting relationship between economic and political judgments is at the heart of economic thought. Condorcet and Turgot were even more bitter critics than Smith, in the 1770s, of the way of life and way of thinking of economic regulation. They were less willing to make the ingenuous assumption (as Smith does from time to time, including in the account of the invisible hand in the *Wealth of Nations*) that merchants are concerned with their own security, or with the character and situation of the persons whom they trust, rather than with the privileges to be obtained through political influence. But Condorcet was also closely involved, at a later period of his life, before and during the French Revolution, with the reform of economic policy. He wrote extremely detailed proposals for the constitution of a competitive economic order, and for the procedures by which economic and political disputes could be conducted. He was preoccupied, in his last writings on public instruction, with the prospects for an eternity of individual enlightenment, in which individuals would live by the norms of prudent and peaceable competition.

Condorcet's economic writings have been the subject of only modest interest to historians of economic (or political) thought. Joseph Schumpeter's account is fairly typical: he describes Condorcet as a mathematician whose "contributions to economics are not worth mentioning," and who "propagated 'natural rights,' popular sovereignty, and equal rights for women, and was a great hater of Christianity—in all of which, ardor completely extinguished his critical faculty."[2] Condorcet's economic writings are to be found in pamphlets and one extended study (the *Réflexions sur le commerce des blés* of 1776) on the corn trade; in his largely mathematical

Essai on voting of 1785; in a long and detailed work on the constitution of provincial assemblies, published in 1788; in articles and pamphlets of the Revolutionary period on fiscal and monetary reform; and in the posthumous *Esquisse d'un tableau historique des progrès de l'esprit humain*, especially in the "fragments" of the "Tenth Epoch," which were published in the 1840s. His concern, in these writings, is either with the immediate preoccupations of late eighteenth-century policy (the reform of indirect taxation, the regulation of the corn trade, the circulation of paper money), or with extremely long-term conditions (the norms of competition, or the nature of self-interest). He wrote very little, that is to say, about the theory of value, the theory of rent, the theory of capital, or the other landmarks of the history of economic thought. The only part of his work which has been of interest to subsequent economists is indeed his description of social choice and voting, a theory which has been seen as concerned with political rather than economic decisions. His own, idiosyncratic politics—his "ardor" both for political reform and for economic competition—is an anomaly in terms of the nineteenth- and twentieth-century reception of enlightenment thought, of the twin opposing processions which culminate in the cold universalism of the state, and the cold isolation of markets.

"Raton was quite astonished to find himself interested in this work, which all turns on human impoverishments," Voltaire wrote in 1776 of Condorcet's most sustained work on political economy, the *Réflexions sur le commerce des blés*, published earlier that year. ("Raton," or the little rat, with his aging "paws," was Voltaire's name for himself, in the mawkish code he uses in his correspondence with friends.) "It is so human," Voltaire said of the book; "Raton immediately got into it with extreme pleasure," he was "charmed" by the description of the man who would rather be ruined by a hailstorm than by an injustice, and he "laughed" at the jokes against Necker.[3] But Voltaire also turned out to be one of the very few admirers of the *Réflexions*, which was seen, even by Condorcet's early twentieth-century commentators, as a minor polemic.[4] Condorcet was writing during a period of unprecedented turbulence in economic policy; and in the relationship between theory and policy, between mathematical and literary writing, between political, metaphysical, and economic reflection. His own views, especially of the foundations (or metaphysics) of political economy, changed considerably, in these fluctuating, turbulent times. This indistinctness—this sense of openness to all possibilities—is itself part of the charm of Condorcet's economic thought.

GENERAL ECONOMIC INTERDEPENDENCE

Condorcet's *Réflexions sur le commerce des blés* is a sequel to Turgot's "Lettres sur le commerce des grains" of 1770. Both are concerned with public policy in relation to scarcity; in both, detailed descriptions of market conditions are combined with the outlines of a highly abstract theory of general economic interdependence. In the "Lettres sur le commerce des grains," as was seen in Chapter 3, Turgot provides a precise account of the equilibrium of commercial relations. He is concerned, he explains, with the "well-being" *(bien-être)* of consumers "from a general point of view." Prices and quantities in different markets "are related to one another by a reciprocal dependence, and arrive at equilibrium themselves." When "commerce and competition are entirely free," this "point of equilibrium" is also the point of greatest "production, enjoyment, wealth, and strength."[5]

Turgot's system is the foundation of Condorcet's own work. In his earlier "Valeurs et monnaies," Turgot had outlined a subjective theory of value in which two or more contracting parties *(contractants)* arrive, by a process of "learning," at equality of exchangeable value. Subjective valuations are "different for each individual," in Turgot's description; they depend, for each contracting party, on his needs and on "the order of utility which he assigns to them among his other needs."[6] In Condorcet's description, some years later, the things which meet an individual's needs, or which seem to him to have utility, "have a value for him, of which the importance of this need, the degree of this utility, the intensity of this pleasure or this pain, are the natural measure."[7] In the course of exchange procedures, individuals change what they are prepared to offer as they get more information about other individuals' offers. Prices change "by imperceptible degrees," Turgot writes; "the debate between every buyer and every seller is a sort of *tâtonnement* which makes known to everyone, with certainty, the true price of everything."[8]

Turgot seems to have made a considered choice not to use mathematical notation in his economic work. "I did not want any algebra in it at all," he wrote of an earlier study.[9] But "true prices," in his sense, are the prices which correspond to maximal well-being; they are equivalent to what Condorcet's friend Lagrange a few years later called multipliers. The word *tâtonnement* itself had a distinctive mathematical connotation in the 1770s, but one which was largely pejorative. Lagrange's objective (in his work on methods of solving equations) was thus "to avoid all *tâtonne-*

ment"; not to be "reduced to simple *tâtonnement*, a means which is not only long and tedious, but almost impracticable." Condorcet, too, described *tâtonnement* methods as "long and tedious," and contrasted Lagrange's method with previous efforts which were "no more than a form of *tâtonnement* and of what might be called divination."[10] Yet this undistinguished technique is transposed, in Turgot's system, into a prodigious social procedure: the depiction, some years before the *Wealth of Nations*, of decentralized decision making as an exercise in social maximization.

True prices, for Turgot and Condorcet, can never be arrived at by administrative decision. Even the best-informed and most enlightened officials—a monopoly "composed of angels," in Turgot's description—will find it impossible to emulate the multiple causes which determine prices in individual exchanges. Turgot imagines a state trading company which has no objective "other than the good of the state," and which combines an "angelic probity" with "a more than angelic intelligence"; such a company, he says, will never be able to calculate the "multitude of obscure facts, the mass of unknown causes, acting slowly and by degrees" which "combine and change the price of tradeable things." The administrator who believes that he can "direct the course of prices by means of this sort of calculation" would be like Quesnay's opponent Doctor Silva, seeking to resolve, with a stroke of his pen, problems which would have caused "Newtons and Bernoullis to turn pale throughout their lives." Turgot's advice to the controller-general, in the resounding last words of his "Lettres sur le commerce des grains," is to have confidence in the consequences "of complete freedom, that is to say of the observation of exact justice."[11]

Condorcet's prospect is much the same. The consequence of freedom, he says in the *Réflexions sur le commerce des blés*, will be "to procure the greatest possible competition between buyers . . . the greatest possible competition between sellers," and thereby the "equalization of prices." "Remove the fetters" from industry, he says, and it might become possible to establish an "equilibrium" between the needs of the rich and the poor.[12] His hopes, in this respect, change very little in the course of the 1770s, the 1780s, and the Revolution itself. There is only one "true commercial interest, the same for all nations; it is the restoration of the most complete freedom," he writes in 1790.[13] He calls, as late as June 1793, for policies to make investment attractive for "even the richest capitalists": "It is not a question here of maintaining extreme inequality; it is simply a matter of abandoning everything to the free will of individuals."[14] "The competition to buy and to sell, the balance which is established between the buyer and the seller," constitutes the "natural course of commerce," he says in one of his very last writings, the posthumously published fragment of the history of the Tenth Epoch (in the *Esquisse des progrès*). His prospect, in the depths of the Revolutionary Terror, is as resounding as Turgot's:

> If society imposed no chains on industry, if it leveled the obstacles which industry confronts . . . all the efforts of free industry, encouraged, directed by each toward his own interest, would be united for the common interest of all; they would produce that growing prosperity without which any society languishes and declines.[15]

GIVING THE IMPRESSION OF DOING NOTHING

Condorcet's and Turgot's conception of general economic equilibrium is more elaborate than Smith's; it is more of a system (in Smith's own sense of the pleasure to be derived "in beholding the perfection of so beautiful and grand a system").[16] But Condorcet is also, like Turgot, preoccupied with the inexactness and incompleteness of existing economic systems. He describes the propensity of merchants, and indeed of farmers, to pursue their own interest through political intrigue, rather than through industry or industriousness. He observes the self-interest of officials. He concludes that the interests of all individuals are complicated, difficult to depict, and unstable over time. He goes beyond Turgot, above all, to a theory of economic policy, for imperfect political and economic institutions.

The normal behavior of merchants, in Condorcet's description of the "ordinary course of events in the regime of prohibition," is to seek advantage through political influence. They must "buy the preference of subaltern officials." Even the small cultivator "falls into dependence on all the subaltern officials who are employed to enforce the laws on subsistence food." He is subject to "inspections, prohibitions, condemnations, vexations." He must "learn to uncover the ruses of these subalterns, and must become instructed in the art of seducing them." There are "true merchants exercising a free commerce." But there are also "men who know how to make a profit from the restrictions imposed by prohibitive laws."[17]

The regime of regulation has cumulative effects, of an insidious and persistent sort. For it is only under the regime of freedom that commerce can be constant, or a condition in which one can have confidence. All other legislation must be changeable, and "prohibitive laws, even according to their apologists, must vary with circumstances": "A merchant will never know, under their empire, if the laws under which he has bought, will be those under which he will sell. In this situation, too, all the resources of commerce will be reduced to the extraordinary enterprises which one risks when there are great profits, and which are undertaken only by merchants who know how to ensure the indulgence of the law."[18] The merchant, in Condorcet's description, is continually occupied in calculating the "probability that, if he refuses to sell at a particular price, a part of his grain will be left unsold"; he must fear the competition of other merchants, increases in supply ("the arrival of foreign grain"), and reductions in demand. This is the ordinary course of commercial life. But under the empire of prohibition, the merchant must also concern himself with quite other risks: with the probability of changes in the law, or of changes in the "arbitrary tolerance" under which officials "can either close their eyes, or enforce the law, according to their interest or their caprice."[19]

The way of thinking of merchants, their spirit or mentality, is itself influenced by regulation. The "protection accorded to a particular form of commerce harms commerce in general," Condorcet wrote in his *Vie de M. Turgot,* and "every privilege for buying, or selling, or manufacturing, far from encouraging industry, transforms it into a spirit of intrigue in those who have privileges, and stifles it in others." The opposition to freedom of commerce corresponds to "the prejudices of traders themselves, or rather to the interest of accredited traders. For it is they alone who love regulations, for the reason that these regulations make new or important operations dependent on government, and thereby set aside the competition of traders who are not rich enough to have protectors."[20] The sort of people who become merchants or traders, in such a setting, are those who have a taste, or a talent, for political intrigue. They are disliked by public opinion, and they are not the sort of people ("honest men," Condorcet says) who would be discouraged, by public dislike, from going into commerce.[21]

Condorcet's description of the normal way of thinking of officials is even more somber. The computation and information required of an official monopoly—even of the monopoly composed of angels—would be beyond mortal (or immortal) powers. Ordinary mortal officials have their own fears, and their own interests. These fears are unlikely to be alleviated by the policy of laissez-faire, Condorcet says in his pamphlet of 1775, "Monopole et Monopoleur." "How can it be that a wise government should place its confidence in the different interests of men, that it should suppose that the avarice of buyers and the greed of merchants will counterbalance each other without anyone interfering, and that it should let individuals be [*qu'il laisse faire*]?" he asks ironically. "Can that be called governing? Is it not much finer to interfere in everything, to want to take account of everything, to direct everything? And this is the course that has been adopted almost everywhere. It gives administrators a great deal of importance." "These regulations, these laws, this anxious administration" never fail to attract the admiration of the foolish, Condorcet writes; "thus, in the prohibitive regime, there is glory for the leader, and profit for the subalterns; and those are fairly good reasons."[22]

One of the arguments made against liberal policies of laissez-faire, by Necker and others, was that they tend to imbue officials with a sense of tranquillity, such that "in the embrace of exaggerated principles, one enjoys a profound repose; with a single principle, that of perfect freedom, one governs the world without the slightest difficulty." (The great principles of political economy are, for Necker, above "analysis" and "argument," and must be understood, by the statesman, as undivided wholes. "It is necessary to envelope them in one's thought," he said, and Condorcet used to refer to Necker thereafter as "M. Enveloppe.")[23] Dugald Stewart, who quotes this passage from Necker's "Éloge de Colbert" in his biography of Smith, suggests that Smith's prescription of "the unlimited freedom of trade" is likely to have the effect of "flattering the indolence of the statesman."[24] But indolence was one of the lesser failings of the administrative mind, in Condorcet's description. "How many men are there who do not prefer their vanity to their repose?" he asks.[25] The position "in favor of freedom" was almost always at a disadvantage in relation to the "position in favor of doing something." Doing something was not, in general, the most sure position. "It is simply the most sure for the administrator, who, whatever mistakes he makes, has nothing to fear from the people, provided only that he takes action."[26]

The desire for esteem was a characteristic, in Condorcet's description, of even the pettiest officials. "There is nothing to be gained by protecting absolute freedom, and no one ever made a reputation for himself by giving the impression of doing nothing," he writes. The interest in reputation is not entirely to be despised, and "the objective of every honest alderman is the love and esteem of the people of his town." But there is a different sort of alderman, who is more likely to resort to the "abuse of municipal authority" in order "to make himself admired by his people." "The officials who are in charge of police regulations, the mayors of towns, can find that they have an interest in maintaining a regime that gives them greater importance," where they have the advantage of exercising absolute power, at least in times of scarcity, and "where they have the pleasure of hearing it said that they have provided food for the people, that their paternal cares have preserved them from famine and death."[27]

"Vexations on the part of minor magistrates are an almost universal evil," Condorcet says, and they are made far worse by national policies. "The counsellor to the king sees nothing of all this," but the laws he recommends have as their consequence "the exactions of subaltern officials, seizures, amends, legal procedures," the "discouragements, embarrassments, abuses, vexations" of the prohibitive regime. The bourgeois in the towns becomes "a sort of petty tyrant" in relation to the countryside around him, and he is in turn dependent on the magistrate who protects his power.[28] This is the world that Turgot described in his "Éloge de Gournay," of "interminable litigation," of "obscurity and impenetrable mystery, resulting from a multiplicity of local rights and laws published at different times," of "offices without number" and the "multiplication of visitations."[29] It is also the world in which Tocqueville, whose journey into the sentiments and customs of the ancien régime was based, in part, on Turgot's writings, found the origins of the first or administrative French revolution of the 1750s and 1760s: the "universal passion for positions"; the endless uncertainty of fiscal administration, under which "no cultivator can predict one year in advance what he will have to pay the following year"; the "immense arbitrary power" of the local collector of the *taille,* "almost as much a tyrant as a martyr," for whom the roll of contributions is the record of "his fears, his weaknesses, or his vices."[30]

THE SOUL DISCOURAGED

Condorcet's expectation, in all these descriptions of economic sentiments, is of an extremely protracted transition to the system of complete freedom. The transition is made more difficult because of the extent to which the ways of thinking of merchants (or cultivators) and officials have been influenced by years, even by centuries, of regulation. Political power is a means of economic success, and economic power is a means of political success. The mentalities of officials influence the merchants, and the merchants influence the officials. The cultivator learns how to seduce officials, in the towns in which people live "by ruses and oppression," but his "soul is wasted and discouraged."[31] People want money, but they also want esteem, and repose. The transition will never in fact be complete, because people's ways of thinking, like their objectives, change continuously over time. The new universe of commercial freedom will itself be uncertain, or unfinished. It will be a world of custom, in which people are contented with reasonable probabilities. Condorcet is admirably explicit in addressing one shortcoming of liberal economic orders, to do with the transformation of money into political power, and of political power into the power to influence markets. He is also explicit in addressing the other shortcoming, of the inconstancy of the invisible order (the order of complete freedom and exact justice). His prospect is indeed very close to the scene of interminable discussion, of wisdom with reflection, of continuous evaluation of consequences and probabilities, which was Burke's purgatory of the politics of enlightenment. "I am conscious of everything that circumstances require, in the way of slowness, circumspection, even of timidity," Turgot wrote in his memoir on freedom of lending at interest, and Condorcet, too, saw the progress toward commercial freedom as a process of long-drawn-out, faltering reform.[32] The new order, when it came, would still falter. It would be the object of only the most reserved and circumspect confidence.

Condorcet, like Turgot, founded his hopes for the new system on the passage of time, on the increase in the number of people employed in commerce, and on the repetition of exchange transactions. The "prejudices of the people" against commerce constituted "the only difficult question" for the defenders of the system of freedom, he wrote in the *Réflexions sur le commerce des blés*. "Public opinion," or at least "popular opinion," was not yet in favor of freedom, and people still felt hatred for grain merchants. "The only remedy for this evil is habit, and a commerce which is public, and carried on by a large number of people," Condorcet concluded; "people will see the operations [of commerce] with less fear; and as each merchant will employ a certain number of ordinary people, the effect will be that, even among the people, there will be many who come to the defense of this commerce." But the prospect with which he sought to "reassure the capitalists" was distinctly somber: "the hatred of the people" will be diminished, and "this hatred will be forced to divide itself among a larger number of men."[33] His final view of a just commercial order is similarly muted. The effect of better laws, he wrote at the end of his life, will be that "the interest in acquiring things by illegitimate means will present itself less often, to a smaller number of individuals, and in less diverse and less seductive forms."[34]

The effect of "the general freedom of buying and selling," in Turgot's description, will be to ensure efficient prices and to protect natural freedom. But it will not prevent corruption, or the sale of shoddy cloth. "This is not to say that there will not be merchants who are scoundrels, or consumers who are dupes; but the consumer who is tricked will learn, and will stop going to the merchant; the latter will be discredited and thereby punished for his fraud; and all this will never happen very often."[35] One must have confidence, in these circumstances, in the effects of repeated exchanges, and on the learning which is their consequence. There is even a process of moral learning, as the sort of people who are likely to become merchants are less likely to be scoundrels. Turgot says, of the "demeaning constraints" placed on the grain trade, that they will hardly encourage people to become grain merchants, and "if there were people who were still prepared to take on this trade, they would no doubt count these new risks, and their shame, as among their expenses of doing business, and pass them on to consumers."[36] In the slow transition to the regime of freedom—the revolution in opinions—there will be a different process of change, as merchants are more likely to be the sort of people who do not enjoy inveigling subaltern officials, or passing on the costs of shame.

The system in which Condorcet and Turgot have confidence is one in which individuals are influenced by custom, and also by reflection. They have become used to commerce. They are also used to estimating whether they are likely to be duped, whether they should inveigle aldermen, or whether the system of freedom is one in which they should have confidence. It is a changing, unheroic sort of society. But it is the only sort of society which is suited to the changing circumstances of economic life. For economic choices, in Condorcet's description, are always intertwined with choices about politics and about moral sentiments. People in their economic lives (their lives as merchants) pursue their objectives through political means, and in their political lives (their lives as officials) they pursue economic objectives. They have many different, sometimes conflicting objectives. They desire esteem, like the honest alderman, and they also desire importance. They choose between luxury and political influence.[37] They choose, too, between luxury and peace of mind. The cultivator whose soul is discouraged by the deviousness of towns is unlikely, in Condorcet's description, to invest in order "to procure superfluities which he must buy at the price of his repose."[38]

It is difficult, in these cases, as in the "cases of conscience" of the Doctors of the Sorbonne, even to know one's own mind.[39] One reason is the persistence of unjust laws and uncertain jurisprudence: "Establish that it is forbidden to rent money like any other commodity, and you will not be able to know, without a legal expert or a priest, whether you are an honest man or a scoundrel," Condorcet wrote.[40] Another reason is inner uncertainty, and self-delusion. Condorcet says of the European slave owners, "honored by public esteem," men of public morality, that they are "led by a false conscience" which serves their own interests.[41] Individuals have preferences for social systems, as well as for ways of life. Many merchants thus condemn exclusive privileges, and favor the principles of commercial freedom, as Turgot wrote in his account of Gournay's reforms. But almost all of them have some reason to support exceptions to these general principles; "each one, whether out of interest, or routine, or seduction, always wished for some small modifications or exceptions."[42] It is difficult, often, to distinguish one's self-interest (of various sorts) and one's interest in social principles. Why is there so little legislation against commercial dishonesty (other than in the grain trade)? Condorcet asked during the Revolution. "It is because people have understood the difficulty of distinguishing the innocent from the guilty; because they have been afraid to punish industriousness, in the belief of only punishing bad faith."[43]

Political reform is in these circumstances, for Condorcet, a precondition of economic prosperity. "It is perhaps through the improvement of the political condition of the cultivator that freedom will do most" to increase food production, he wrote in the *Réflexions sur le commerce des blés*.[44] The cultivator, like the trader, will be more independent, more industrious, more secure, and more eager to invest. He will be more willing to support the system of commercial freedom. He will have lost his distrust or "defiance" of government, "which the long habit of being counted for nothing has made so quick to flare up."[45] But economic reform is at the same time an end in itself. It is not only a condition of economic prosperity; it is itself a political objective. As Condorcet wrote of Turgot, his zeal was for "the freedom of commerce, or rather for the justice which prescribes that everyone should be allowed the free exercise of their legitimate property (for there is a more noble justification for the freedom of commerce than its utility, however extensive that may be)."[46]

Individuals have political interests, and in particular they have an interest in their own "political condition"; the interest, Condorcet says, "which every individual has in protecting his rights."[47] But these political interests, or objectives, are intimately involved with the events of economic life. It is indeed in the course of their economic activities—carting grain to market, buying salt, paying taxes, building highways—that the cultivators described by Condorcet (and later by Tocqueville) come into closest contact with the unjust and fluctuating jurisprudence characteristic of the ancien régime. Their interest in political and legal rights is not thereby an economic interest, in the sense that they want an improvement in their political condition only (or principally) in order to improve their economic condition. The reform of criminal and civil law is one of Condorcet's principal concerns in the *Réflexions sur le commerce des blés*, and it is a political as much as an economic ideal: "A civil jurisprudence, such that every citizen can understand the laws which determine his fate, that one no longer needs to be rich in order to defend one's property, that the poor man should no longer see his modest possessions as belonging to him only in a precarious way, because he is in the power of every rich man, every prosecutor, every bailiff."[48]

Individuals also have an interest in the political condition of other people. They have opinions about societies—about systems, or theories of systems—as well as about the influence of society on their own interests. They are interested in the political interests of others. They are spectators, as well as participants, in the great drama of political change. Condorcet indeed uses the word "spectacle" repeatedly of political interests, in the *Réflexions sur le commerce des blés* and in later writings. There are those, in his description, who will prefer "not to be humiliated by the spectacle of the oppression of their fellow men."[49] "Joachim Schwartz," the Protestant pastor whom Condorcet takes as one of his pseudonymous personalities, tells the slaves to whom he dedicates his abolitionist pamphlet that one of his objectives is to satisfy his own heart, "torn apart by the spectacle of your ills."[50] "The spectacle of the equality which reigns in the United States, and which assures its peace and prosperity," will be "useful to Europe," Condorcet writes in a different pseudonymous self; "the love of Americans for equality" will surely prevent the prohibitions, protected monopolies, visitations, and restrictive corporations which have produced such "absurd vexations in Europe."[51] "It is not," he says in the *Réflexions sur le commerce des blés*, "as though there were no ills other than those which directly hurt our own individual person. Is the spectacle of the oppression of the poor, of the unhappiness of an entire nation, not an unbearable torment from which one longs to be free?"[52]

POVERTY, TAXES, AND UNSALUBRIOUS FACTORIES

The interdependence of government and commerce will be an eternal characteristic, in Condorcet's description, of the liberal economic order.

The system of exact freedom will never be complete, and even if it were complete, individuals would still have political as well as economic objectives. Condorcet looked forward to the "virtual nonexistence" ("cette presque nullité") of government, and he wrote, in 1792, that people who wish to be free and peaceful need "laws and institutions which reduce to the smallest possible quantity the action of government." But he contrasted this view with the position of "the anarchists," who glimpsed the principle of minimal government only "out of a vague sentiment of defiance," and who sought "that nonexistence of government which is born of disorder, suspicions, struggles between different powers." The outcome he prefers is rather the result "of a system of laws, profoundly combined."[53] His most consistent economic interest—and the principal respect in which he added to Turgot's system—is indeed in the theory of public policy. As he wrote in the *Réflexions sur le commerce des blés,* interference with free commerce is sometimes unjust, sometimes useless, and sometimes harmful to trade. Government should never adopt policies which are unjust. But "it may be obliged, in order to avoid a greater evil, to use means which are harmful without being unjust."[54]

Governments are continually confronted, in Condorcet's description, with the choice of lesser evils. The theory of public policy, or of a profoundly combined system of minimal government, is thus a matter of intense practical consequence. Condorcet was indeed concerned, in virtually all his economic writings, with particular and practical circumstances in which government is obliged to interfere with commerce. His earliest illustration of efficient, just, and minimal government, as was seen in Chapter 3, is in relation to policies to prevent famine. He asserts that it is in the general interest of every nation that "all members of society should have assured subsistence"; even absolute governments seek to ensure "that people die of hunger only in the long term."[55] This objective could not be achieved, in the conditions of eighteenth-century France, without government action. Commerce was not yet complete, in the sense that physical communications, like relationships of trust in long-distance trade, were still underdeveloped. People were not yet enlightened, and they were not yet rich. They were indeed so poor, at least in certain regions, that they sometimes fell into utter destitution before equilibrium could be reestablished. The point of Turgot's policies in the Limousin, as was seen earlier, was to intervene in markets for labor (through public employment schemes), but not for corn, and certainly not to determine corn prices. Such intervention would be temporary, it would benefit the people most in need, and it would interfere with only relatively unimportant rights.

Condorcet's account of policies against poverty provides a second illustration. He anticipated that the eventual effect of freedom of commerce would be to reduce poverty. But he devotes a long discussion to the "causes of poverty" in his *Essai sur les assemblées provinciales* of 1788, the second of the substantial works in which he writes at length about economic policy. (The setting, in keeping with Condorcet's concern with the theory of public policy, is an extended reflection on the constitution and functions of municipal and provincial assemblies, published soon after the convocation of the estates-general for 1789.)[56] The first cause he describes is the unequal distribution of wealth, which is itself the consequence of "bad civil or fiscal laws." The second cause is "the lack of sufficient wages"; this Condorcet attributes in part to the fact that "in place of general competition" between workers and the employers who need their labor, there is competition only on the basis of guild and master-apprentice relationships. Condorcet is more troubled by a third and different cause of poverty, namely, that industries "substitute machines" for human labor. But even this cause of poverty would be only transitory. Technical change, like changes in "taste" or "customs," could lead to loss of employment for workers who "only know how to do one thing." "But is it really true that that the invention of machines will be a continuing cause of poverty for different classes of individuals?" Condorcet asks, in a remarkable evocation of economic interdependence:

> Does the invention of a machine make some technical product less expensive? There is thereby more money to use for new commodities; what people save on one kind of consumption is transferred to other enjoyments. There are hands who need new employment, but at the same time there are resources in reserve to pay their wages. A certain amount of time is needed, no doubt, to reestablish equilibrium, and this period of time will be shorter to the extent that there is more freedom.[57]

Condorcet's immediate concern was with the period of disequilibrium. He recognized that virtually all governments, as in the case of famine, would implement policies to prevent members of society from falling below a certain minimum level of subsistence. To live in any other sort of society would indeed be excruciating, and the spectacle of the extreme poverty of others is itself a source of torment. But policies against poverty should nonetheless be chosen so as to interfere as little as possible with individual freedom. The most efficient policies are those whose effect is to prevent people from becoming poor, as distinct from supporting them in "public establishments" (as under the English poor laws, Condorcet pointed out later).[58]

Condorcet's proposal, in his pre-Revolutionary work on provincial assemblies and in the *Esquisse des progrès*, was for a system of social insurance funds and savings associations whereby even the poor could be protected against sudden losses in income. One of the main causes of poverty was that many poor families have no assets, and are liable "to fall into misery at the least accident." With social insurance, they would become independent, and full participants in the process of economic change. They could survive illness, accidents, reductions in wages, and temporary unemployment without falling into extreme poverty. Establishments for social insurance, set up by government or by associations of individuals, would to a great extent reduce these causes of "inequality, dependence, and even misery"; they would be "using chance itself to oppose chance."[59]

Condorcet also, as has been seen, supported policies for universal instruction, which would have the effect, among others, that workers would be more likely to be able to adjust to changes in production.[60] It is interesting, however, that he distinguished between public institutions which should be provided directly by public funds (such as courts and police), those where competition is possible but unlikely (such as city lighting and streetcleaning), and those "where competition must be respected." He put public instruction, together with the services of doctors and midwives, in the last category, and insisted that public funds should not be spent to "make competition impossible." One reason was "to preserve for parents a real freedom of choice in the education they owe their children"; another reason, as will be seen in Chapter 7, was to prevent the "exclusive influence" of government on instruction.[61]

Government policy was essential, to take a third illustration, in relation to conflicts between different rights, and in particular to environmental harm, a subject to which Condorcet returned repeatedly in his economic writings. "There is only one case in which the law can legitimately restrain property rights," he wrote in the *Réflexions sur le commerce des blés;* it is when the exercise of the right violates security, or the antecedent rights of others. The example he gives is of the use of land for an agricultural practice which, "by corrupting the air, causes illnesses in neighboring homes." In this case, government is justified in forbidding certain uses of land, and in undertaking public works to "restore the salubriousness of the air," without the consent of (but with compensation for) the property owner.[62] In his *Vie de M. Turgot,* Condorcet turned to the misuse of the property rights of "owners of rivers, proprietors of ponds," especially in constructing dams and causing flooding. He favored "the purchase of these rights, whose exercise is so dangerous, of these properties which, by their nature, harm everything in their environment." But economic arrangements of this sort required such detailed knowledge, and were so conducive to "abuse of power," that they should be decided on and undertaken only by freely elected assemblies.[63]

It is interesting that Condorcet justifies these interventions on grounds not of economic efficiency but of justice. People want to preserve the value of their homes, and they also want not to be oppressed by their neighbors. Government regulations ("police") must not be justified on weak grounds of "utility or prudence," Condorcet writes in his *Essai sur les assemblées provinciales*. They should be concerned, rather, with those exercises of the property rights of one person which can be shown to result in harm for others, and where the "wrong" (the "tort") can be established "with a very great probability." Laws which regulate the conflicts between different rights are not "in themselves dangerous for the maintenance of political liberty, or of civil liberty," he says, because they are not "necessarily arbitrary." The arbitrariness disappears when the harm to others is demonstrated clearly and openly. Condorcet gives the example, once again, of air pollution: "If a factory is unsalubrious for neighboring houses, then one can, without violating the proprietor's rights, forbid it from being established in towns."[64]

The conflict between legitimate interests will eventually be very rare, Condorcet concludes in his description of the Tenth Epoch in the *Esquisse des progrès*. An individual may try, in the interest of his own conservation, to prevent another individual from using his property in a way that seems advantageous to him. But the interest is in many cases "less that of conservation, than of not changing one's location, which is a matter of rather different interests." Even when the conflict of interests and rights is genuine, it may have been exacerbated by misconceived public policies. The role of government is to prevent such conflicts, both by establishing rules such that "the use of the property of an individual, the exercise of his industry, should not damage the health of his neighbors," and by encouraging research, including on ways "to overcome or destroy the dangers of these sorts of industry or agriculture."[65]

Condorcet's last economic interest, and the one where he moved furthest beyond Turgot, was in trying to bring together different principles of government policy into a theory of public finance and public expenditure. He wrote extensively about tax policy, both before and during the Revolution. In his work on fiscal reform, he attempted to evaluate the transition from indirect to direct taxation, from the perspective both of equity—as between those who gain and those "who lose by the tax reform"—and of whether particular reform schemes will "reestablish equilibrium"; a description of this transition—a single long footnote in his *Vie de M. Turgot*—is one of the very few places in which he uses mathematical notation in his economic writings.[66] He was later concerned with such details of progressive tax schemes as the appropriate size of tax brackets (the increment should be "gradual" and "almost imperceptible"). He was particularly disturbed by marginal disincentives: it was necessary to "regulate progressive taxation in such a manner that it should not become useless, for an individual, to acquire a new piece of land, or to invest a new capital sum."[67]

Condorcet's theory of public expenditure is founded, like Turgot's theory of general economic equilibrium, on a conception of individual evaluations of marginal utility. There are certain public objectives—such as ensuring that no one dies of starvation or extreme deprivation—which are the subject of extensive consensus. But public expenditure which is no more than useful should in general be undertaken only with the consent of all those affected. Such "unanimity of consent" could be forgone only when the project was clearly proved to be useful, and when it was "impossible or very difficult" to prevent those who did not consent from profiting from it. Each individual should thus consent to the project on the basis of having compared the costs and benefits which he will himself expect to incur. Subsidies for public services, for example, "should stop precisely at the point where it is in general more useful for each individual to pay this subsidy than not to pay it." Some public expenditures, more generally, are not strictly necessary; "in this case, they have as their limit the point where the utility of the expenditure becomes equal to the evil produced by the taxation."[68]

"Work on public expenditure," Condorcet wrote, should not be undertaken in the spirit of "parsimony," or of the effort to reduce expenditure. It should rather be founded on "economy," or on the effort to "do the best possible at the least cost." The object should be to "compare, for each component, for each degree of this expenditure," the benefits and costs to individual citizens. Even in relation to expenditure for the most important purposes, "there is a point where it ceases to be equivalent to the wrong which it produces . . . True economy consists of identifying, for each object, the precise point where the utility ceases to be real."[69] Condorcet was aware, all the same, that the ideal procedure of evaluation posed substantial political and practical problems. There were instances, such as the operation of polluting factories, in which individual rights and interests were strongly in conflict. The process of public choice—a sort of political *tâtonnement,* in which every benefit of a project is compared to every cost—was dauntingly complex. "We are today very far removed," he wrote, "from that exact equilibrium" in which government expenditures and receipts are equal, and determined annually by the appropriate political powers.[70]

FORMAL METHODS

The world which Condorcet depicts in his economic writings is a turbulent and disorderly scene. It is unpropitious, at first sight, for the procedures of scientific investigation. The theory of economic policy, which is Condorcet's principal concern, must be practical as well as theoretical. It must be a political as well as an economic science, and an art as well as a science. The individuals who are its subjects are full of fears and whims. They are in conflict with one another, and within themselves. They are also people who have opinions about economic policy. They are the subjects of economic theory in the sense that they are what the theory is about. But they are its subjects, as distinct from its objects, in the sense that they themselves have economic theories, including theories of economic policy. They influence economic policy. This is the case even in Condorcet's writings about the ancien régime; in his writings of the Revolutionary period, individual economic subjects actually decide on policies.

The equilibrium of perfect commercial freedom, or of perfect public policy, is in these circumstances little more than a political objective, of a fairly general sort. Condorcet was indeed critical of the overenthusiastic use of formal or scientific terms in the economic, political, and moral sciences. In his very first economic writing, he comments, in two long letters to the Milanese philosopher Pietro Verri, on the "use of the language of geometry" in "the economic sciences." Verri had put forward the somewhat eccentric suggestion that "the price of things is in direct proportion to the number of buyers, and in inverse proportion to the number of sellers." Condorcet observes ("if a geometer may be so bold") that mathematical language is in this case "very far from leading to more precise ideas." He explains, more generally, that the "quantity of the universal commodity" (i.e., money), or of some particular commodity, can be considered as numbers. The economic sciences are indeed quantitative in this sense. But "the desire to buy and the desire to sell are not susceptible to any calculation, and yet variations in price depend on this moral quantity, which itself depends on opinions and on passions."[71]

Condorcet goes on to compare economic problems of price with the famous three-body problem in celestial mechanics which then preoccupied d'Alembert and Lagrange. The great mathematicians considered bodies in space as "masses without extension" (point masses), and limited the problem by "a hundred simplifying conditions." Yet even this restricted problem was still unresolved. "The effect of the forces which act upon the mind of the narrowest merchant is far more difficult to calculate," Condorcet concluded.[72] D'Alembert had earlier complained, in an essay on the application of one science to another, about the "abuse" of geometric methods in metaphysical or moral sciences which "cannot be subjected to any calculation"; "on every page one sees such big words as *axiom, theorem, corollary,* and so forth." Condorcet is more permissive. He does not exclude the application of mathematics to political economy, but he points to the difficulty, and possible indeterminacy, of economic problems.[73]

Like Turgot, Condorcet did not want any algebra in his economic writings, and seems to have regretted (in his work on tax reform) that he "had availed himself of algebraic signs" in calculations which were "not very complicated."[74] Equilibrium, in economic life as in fiscal policy, is an objective which one "should not even hope to ever be able to attain," at least in a "rigorous manner."[75] The Economists or Physiocrats, he wrote at the end of his life, had presented parts of their system in "too absolute and magisterial a manner," had affected "an obscure and dogmatic language," and had alarmed people with the "generality of their maxims, the inflexibility of their principles"; it was wrong to interpret principles which are true only "in general" as though they were "absolute and precise truths."[76] Theorists of "public and private economy," he said, were often impeded or misled, despite their great political insights, by their lack of mathematical knowledge. But the opposite problem also arose: "Is it not the case that the technique of calculation has been lavished uselessly, because those who used it either disdained to concern themselves with moral and political considerations, or did not even think of doing so?"[77]

Every object is "deprived of all its perceptible qualities, all its individual properties . . . [T]he object itself is then forgotten; it ceases to exist." This is Condorcet's description of the mathematical approach, in an address to

Lycée students in 1786, and it exemplifies the axiomatic reasoning which he found so disturbing in contemporary political economy. It was a way of thinking to which he was himself attracted, at all times. "Numbers, lines speak more than is generally believed, to their growing imaginations," he said of the mathematical instruction of very young children, in the same address.[78] But he was also concerned, at many periods of his life, by the misuse of techniques of calculation in the moral and political sciences. He was disturbed, above all, by the loss of individual properties, in the aggregation of quantities of happiness or utility, in the generalization of moral or mental characteristics, and in the derivation of general and natural laws.

The understanding of individual diversity was of the greatest importance even in natural history, Condorcet suggested in his *Éloge de M. Buffon*. He said of Buffon, whom he disliked, that "he seems to have taken note, in each species, of no more than a uniformity of proceedings and habits, which give the idea of beings obeying a blind and mechanical force, while by observing more closely, he would have been able to perceive very noticeable differences between individuals." These differences, between different beavers, for example, or different parrots, or between individual beavers at different times or in different settings, might indeed suggest something similar to the processes of reasoning. Only long and continuous observation, Condorcet said, would make it possible to understand how beavers live, "emancipated from the fear by which they are struck in the presence of man."[79]

Condorcet was preoccupied, throughout his life, with the more or less useful applications of formal methods in economic, political, and empirical sciences.[80] He was tolerant of diverse formal techniques, and of diverse views of knowledge. Even d'Alembert, he wrote, had adopted a too narrow view of metaphysics and the political sciences: "He may seem, perhaps, not to have been sufficiently aware that in the sciences whose object is to teach how one should act, man can, as in the conduct of his life, be content with probabilities which are more or less strong." In these cases, Condorcet says, "the true method consists less in searching for rigorously proved truths, than in choosing between probable propositions."[81] It is not difficult, he says, to demonstrate the impossibility, in the natural and the moral sciences, of achieving "the rigorous certainty of propositions of geometry." But people who attack the certainty of human knowledge have gone further, and thus gone astray: "They have wished to conclude that man has no reliable rules for settling his opinion on these matters, and in this they have deceived themselves."[82]

Condorcet's view of scientific truth changed continually, and confusingly, throughout the course of his life. In the *Réflexions sur le commerce des blés,* he looked forward to a change in public opinion in respect of the freedom of the corn trade, similar to the change in respect of the circulation of the blood, of inoculation, and of universal gravitation.[83] One objective of the social mathematics with which he was concerned in the 1780s and 1790s was to protect the "truths" of society, amidst a "mass of uncertain and changing opinions."[84] But he was also intensely conscious of the seductiveness of the mathematical imagination. He was conscious, especially in his efforts to describe a universal public instruction, of the uncertainty of empirical truth. "I have always loved mathematics and philosophy almost equally," he wrote of his mathematical essay on voting, and he seemed at times to be divided, like Faust, between two souls; between the philosopher's interest in the world of individual, diverse lives and the mathematician's interest in the bright and glittering world of numbers and lines.

It is a "general truth," he wrote in the *Esquisse,* that "the truths of theory are necessarily modified in practice." The method of philosophy consists in "savoir ignorer," in "knowing how not to know, in the end, what it is still, what it always will be impossible to understand."[85] This procedural and probabilistic view of knowledge was Condorcet's eventual prescription for the sciences of society, and it was closer to Hume's view than to d'Alembert's. Condorcet's theory of probability is likely to have been influenced by Hume's *Treatise,* as Keith Baker has shown, and his "truths" are also distinctively Humean. "Can I be sure, that in leaving all established opinions I am following truth; and by what criterion shall I distinguish her?" Hume asks in the *Treatise.* Our objective, he says, should be "a degree of belief, which is sufficient for our purpose," and reasoning which is convincing in one subject (such as history or politics) is insufficient in others (such as metaphysics); his own "only hope" is to point out to philosophers "those subjects, where alone they can expect assurance and conviction."[86] This was Condorcet's hope, as well, at least in the last years of his life. Truth was a matter, in part, of recognizing the sort of truthfulness which is appropriate for each sort of knowledge; in "recognizing the different degrees of certainty to which we may hope to attain," or in "appreciating the degree of certainty or likelihood" of each science.[87]

Political economy, on such a view, must have recourse to an eclectic collection of techniques, of greater or lesser certainty. The imposing system of general economic equilibrium is convincing as an objective, but one can expect it to be disconcerted or modified in practice. The objective of an optimal policy for public expenditure, where each individual has compared the costs and benefits of public subsidies, is remote from political practice. There are other objectives where the economic theorist needs quite other techniques. He or she might be concerned, for example, to describe well-being in a particular society, in the sense of the extent to which poverty, or extreme deprivation, is a condition of only a very few individuals. It should be possible, Condorcet says, to identify measures of simple necessity, given that most individuals within a society would "have more or less the same needs," and "in general the same tastes, the same ideas of utility." Such measures could provide the statistical foundation for describing constant and important economic relations; they would be based, however, on information about population and social conditions as well as about prices, and they would make no attempt to sum individual utilities.[88]

Even the empirical foundations of quantitative research were to be the subject of continual discussion and revision. Condorcet was one of the pioneers of the collection of economic, demographic, and health statistics. But he was insistent that statistical series should be prepared in such a way as to be useful to future investigators, whose concerns were as yet unknown; that public statistical registers should be designed in advance "even for the results of research which people have not yet begun to think about."[89] Tables of births, marriages, and deaths, for example, should provide the investigators with "all the general facts which emerge from this mass of facts, and not only with those which one might have had the intention of looking for when the tables were drawn up."[90]

The choice of economic techniques must itself be subject to revision. The theorist of political or economic relations, like the public official, and like the individual who makes choices in his or her own life, must continually evaluate the degree of probability appropriate to a particular set of circumstances. He or she must also choose between different techniques of choice, for different sets of circumstances. In the case of conflicts over the use of property rights, the wrong or "tort" must be established "with a very great probability." Individuals must make collective decisions on public subsidies, based on each person's evaluation of his own expected utility. They must decide on the utility of economic policies, and on the constitutional procedures for deciding on subsequent decisions about economic policy; Condorcet envisaged, for example, that elected assemblies would pronounce (on the basis of two-thirds or three-quarters majorities) on the "utility" of financing expenditure by selling the assets of public establishments.[91] These are all techniques of aggregation across individuals. But they are not like the operations of Necker's administrative genius, summing the utility of individuals, and enveloping all in his thought. They are techniques, above all, of self-aggregation.

SOCIAL CHOICE AND ECONOMIC PROCEDURES

Condorcet's theory of voting and social decisions, which is the most sustained of his work, is a response to these difficulties of economic and constitutional thought. His *Essai sur l'application de l'analyse* of 1785 was the only substantial book he published during his lifetime and under his own name, and it was followed by several later and less well known writings. (In his last paper on voting, published just before he went into hiding in Paris in 1793, he notes that he has presented various new views since 1785, and adds, "I believe that I am still very far from coming to the end" of these investigations.)[92] The *Essai* is an effort, in part, to resolve some of the problems with which he was concerned in political economy: in particular, the problems of public policy in an imperfectly competitive economy, and of the formal depiction of imperfectly regular or orderly individuals.

The theory of political decisions was mathematical, for Condorcet, in a way that political economy was not (or not yet). He presented the *Essai* as a contribution to confirming Turgot's hypothesis that the "moral and political sciences" are suited, just as much as the physical sciences, to mathematical reasoning; it is dedicated to Turgot, and Condorcet also sent a presentation copy to Adam Smith.[93] Condorcet was unsatisfied, as has been seen, with the crude uses of mathematical methods in political economy. His work on voting can be seen as an attempt to identify a different region of the social sciences, more promising for social mathematics. Condorcet looked forward, in his last paper on social choice, to a "general theory of elections." "In this type of study," he wrote, "moral observations [and] the results of experience" both can and must be supported by mathematical method; even practical voting methods must be subjected to "what are, in some respect, artificial means of simplifying and shortening procedures."[94]

Condorcet's work on social choice and on economic policy are connected, in the first place, because economic policy is itself one of the subjects of social decisions. Condorcet was concerned, in his work on corn, poverty, and environmental conflict, with the political conditions for economic equilibrium. Political decisions were needed to remove obstructions to free commerce, to reduce ignorance, and to find fair procedures for resolving conflicts. But such decisions were not always the subject of consensus. Decisions about taxes—in the light, for example, of Condorcet's principle that subsidies should stop precisely at the point where it is in general more useful for each individual to pay the subsidy than not to pay it—were particularly cumbersome. The theory of economic policy required a further theory, of decisions about policy.

Condorcet's *Essai* is generally seen as being concerned especially with the choice of candidates in elections. It is interesting that Condorcet's first extended illustration of what was subsequently described as the impossibility of finding a "Condorcet winner"—the circumstance that, under certain distributions of preferences, every candidate in a majority election will be defeated by some other candidate—is instead taken from voting on economic policy. The three positions (which later became candidates A, B, and C) are thus that:

1. "Any restriction placed on commerce is an injustice."
2. "Only those restrictions placed through general laws can be just."
3. "Restrictions placed by particular orders can be just."

It was these questions which Condorcet proposed to reduce "to a system of propositions which are contradictory pairwise." Elsewhere in the *Essai*, he emphasizes the solemn nature of the legal and constitutional questions under consideration. He frequently uses the metaphor of individuals as "players" in "games," and of "society" as playing a game "repeated an indefinite number of times" (in criminal procedures, for example); he adds that "we apologize for using the word 'game' of such a serious matter . . . [I]t was Pascal who gave us the example."[95]

Turgot had commented, much earlier, on the difficulties of making collective decisions about economic policy in the presence of shifting majorities: when the majority which opposes laissez-faire reforms, that is to say, is composed of individuals each of whom favors only one exception to the reforms.[96] In his later work on voting, Condorcet continued to emphasize economic and constitutional decisions. Some of his studies on social choice thus appear as appendices to his work on the constitution of provincial assemblies; the principal functions of the assemblies would include deciding on taxation, public works, government property, and "the repayment of public debt." He particularly recommended pairwise voting for decisions about changes in the form of taxation. The form of elections should be suited, more generally, to the subject of the voting; decisions which would result in "some inequality among the citizens, some restriction placed on the exercise of their liberty or their property," should be adopted only with a "very great" majority (or on the basis of a "very great probability").[97]

There is a second and more profound connection between Condorcet's work on economic interdependence and on social choice. His skepticism about the use of excessively exact or precise methods in political economy is founded, as has been seen, on the conviction that individual opinions and desires are diverse, uncertain, changing, and often erroneous. This is also the presupposition of his work on social decisions. In a letter to Frederick the Great, Condorcet presented what he described as the principal results of his *Essai sur l'analyse* in stark terms. One was to show that "the death penalty [was] absolutely unjust," because one can have no "absolute certainty of not condemning an innocent person." The other was to show the "impossibility of succeeding, by means of the forms to which the decisions might be subjected, in fulfilling the conditions which one should require" of majority decisions. This implied that the possibility of correct decisions depended on the distribution of individual opinions; in Condorcet's words, on whether people are "very enlightened."[98]

Condorcet's "impossibility" result is not a proposition about the consistency of axioms in the modern sense. But the idea of the impossibility of formal solutions to social problems—to the problem, in particular, of grouping together diverse individual opinions and interests—is central to Condorcet's theory of social choice, as it is to his political economy. He returns, in his proposals for education in mathematics and the social sciences, to the prospect of shifting majorities, in which the summing of opinions which are individually rational (or where each individual has "reasoned correctly") leads to an "evident contradiction"; "it is therefore necessary to look for what one should substitute for the majority decision, when it is impossible that such a decision exists."[99]

Condorcet's inclination—in social choice and in the theory of economic equilibrium—is to look for these eventual substitutes in probabilistic judgments. The difficulties of aggregation which he describes arise, in general, from the diversity of individual preferences: across different individuals, across the same individual over time, and even within a given individual in a given decision procedure. One method of coping with diversity, or heterogeneity, is to assume it away: to impose restrictive conditions on the distribution of individual preferences (in the theory of social decisions), or on the rationality of individual behavior (in the theory of market equilibrium). The other method, to which Condorcet inclined, is to incorporate diversity into political and economic theory: to put forward propositions which are true under conditions of behavioral heterogeneity.

Condorcet's view of decision theory as probabilistic has been of relatively little interest to subsequent theorists, and it is true that his famous results do not depend on probabilistic reasoning.[100] But his description of voting as a search for truth, which yields propositions of greater or lesser probability, is consistent with his emphasis on the imperfections of social and economic procedures. The problem of voting is to collect individual opinions—which are uncertain, changing, and dissimilar—into a social decision. The problem of the theory of general economic equilibrium is to describe economic interdependence without depicting individuals as machines who calculate, or as components of a "huge hydraulic machine." The problem of economic policy is that the circumstances of individuals are dissimilar, and also different from those which would obtain under conditions of "complete freedom" (or complete competition). Some people are too poor to survive during the period of time while food prices fall, or while employment slowly increases; some have an interest in specific restrictions on commerce; some have opinions, or preferences, about the sort of society in which they wish to live: it is the sum of these different interests which is supposed to be expressed in economic policy.

It is interesting that Turgot and Condorcet use virtually identical language in speaking of the determination of true prices in perfectly competitive markets, and of the determination of true judgments in fair elections. In his evocation of *tâtonnement,* Turgot says that the debate between "every buyer and every seller" makes known ("fait connaître") to everyone, with certainty, the true price ("le vrai prix") of everything. Condorcet says, in his account of pairwise voting, that the object of an electoral procedure is to make known ("faire connaître") the true opinion of the majority ("le voeu véritable"). But it is not always possible to identify a true majority decision. Prices do not always make known important relations of value; relations which are constant, in Condorcet's phrase, and also "important for the general order of societies."[101]

Condorcet makes clear, in his late work on inconclusive elections, that the object of voting procedures is not to uncover some elusive general will. It is rather to identify a social opinion which corresponds, to a sufficiently reliable extent, to the opinions of individuals.[102] He makes no suggestion, therefore, that the truth of political judgments is the expression of an "ideal" or "general" will.[103] A true decision is rather one which is the outcome of a fair procedure, in which the participants are themselves at least reasonably enlightened; when they are instructed, and unfrightened. When the form of elections is erroneous, the procedure is unfair; when individual opinions are especially dissimilar, then even a fair procedure cannot identify a true judgment.

Condorcet's insistence on the truth of decisions is on this view constitutional as well as metaphysical. A fair procedure yields judgments which are true, in the sense that they are politically legitimate. They may not be the judgments which a given individual would choose. But they are judgments which all individuals should accept. "The grounds for submitting to laws is the probability that they will conform to the truth," Condorcet writes; laws are likely to be true if they have been adopted by a suitable majority in a fair procedure.[104] This is the most that can be expected, too, in the theory of economic interdependence. When the preferences and endowments of individuals are especially dissimilar, then the procedures of complete freedom will not determine "true prices." But there are policies which express true judgments, in Condorcet's view of truth; there are true descriptions of economic conditions.

Rousseau's observations on elections in *Du contrat social* provided the setting, in a general sense, for Condorcet's theory of social choice. The "general will is always right, but the judgment which guides it is not always enlightened," Rousseau wrote; it was for this reason that all individuals "are in need of guides," and that the extraordinary role of the legislator is to "institute a people . . . to change, so to speak, the nature of man." Individuals in voting are expressing their opinion as to what to the general will might be; they are not expressing their own opinions, or their opinions about truth.[105] Much of Condorcet's political writing can be seen as an extended objection to this view of political life. The obligation of the individual to the majority is in Condorcet's view binding only to the extent that the majority respects his or her individual rights. It is possible that the decision of a legitimate and democratic government will turn out to be unjust; the right to contribute to the making of laws, which "zealous republicans" have regarded as the most important of all rights, is the least essential of the basic rights of man, and can in a society of ignorance and injustice become a source of tyranny. A nation is an "abstract being," and as such it can be neither happy nor unhappy; to calculate "a sort of median value" of individual happiness would be to "adopt the maxim, too prevalent among ancient and modern republicans, that the few can legitimately be sacrificed to the many."[106]

The condition of the state, for Rousseau, is to be an "association," and not an "aggregation."[107] For Condorcet, the procedures of political life are much closer to the physical scientists' conception of an aggregate, or an assemblage of previously independent and unconnected entities.[108] Lycurgus, the hero of *Du contrat social,* was for Condorcet a monster of injustice and inhumanity, with his system of education in patriotic songs, his society of collective property and collective, republican mealtimes.[109] There is no particular or individual will in Rousseau's perfect legislation; Condorcet's legislation, which is never perfect, is an expression of the interests and opinions of individuals. For Rousseau, commerce and private interest and domestic occupations are a corruption of public life, and the *corvée* impositions are less contrary to liberty than taxes; for Condorcet, following Turgot's *Lit de Justice* of 1776, the abolition of the *corvée* brought an end to the "most odious yoke that has ever weighed upon free men." For Rousseau, "long debates, dissensions, tumult" were the sign of the impending decline of the state; for Condorcet, "long discussions" in which "all proofs are developed, all doubts discussed," were the condition of civilized society, and the only reliable basis for truth.[110]

Condorcet's view of political truth was even more inconstant than his view of truth in science. His early enthusiasm for the theories of the Economists and Physiocrats, as implemented in Turgot's policies, was succeeded by a more circumspect view of economic reform. His enthusiasm for the formal theory of political decisions, in his *Essai sur l'analyse,* was succeeded by a period of extended and detailed constitutional negotiation. His enthusiasm for the new reign of truth, in the early years of the Revolution, was succeeded by an effort, which lasted until his death, to imagine a kind of public instruction which consisted, above all, in the long, slow investigation of different kinds of truth. He was intensely conscious, both before and during the Revolution, of the falseness of the language of politics; he spoke of "plunder in the name of justice, tyranny in the name of liberty or equality, barbarism in the name of humanity." But he gave himself up, for a time, to frightening political rhetoric. "Germans," he exclaimed in 1792, "dare only to speak to your tyrants in the severe language of truth, and Europe will within a few months be free, peaceful, and prosperous.[111] His last political position, and his last view of truth, was nonetheless one of unrelenting modesty. He looked forward, in the *Esquisse,* to a future of sufficient enlightenment; a future in which the "model" of the physical sciences would help individuals to be free of "submission even to the authority of enlightenment."[112]

DISCUSSIONS AND CONSTITUTIONS

The relationship between individual choices and social outcomes is for Condorcet the central problem of political economy. The difficulty which he identifies in his work on voting—that it is impossible, under certain distributions of preferences, to derive a true majority decision—recurs, in different forms, throughout his writings on economic policy and economic method. The angelic monopolist who tries to sum individual expectations by substituting enumeration for decentralized market procedures is doomed to futility. So is the despot who sums the happiness of his subjects. So too is the theorist who sums individual decisions—on the basis, at least, of a simple model in which all individuals are considered to be more or less the same, and more or less like "machines who calculate, and who decide for the outcome where there is most to be won"—into a huge machine of economic society.

Condorcet's concern with procedures is under these conditions at the heart of his political theory. The interdependence of economic choices can itself be thought of as a sort of procedure. Condorcet's conception of true political decisions was associated, it has been suggested, with the presumption that a judgment is likely to be true if it is the outcome of a fair procedure. Something very similar can be said of economic decisions. Turgot's and Condorcet's idyll of perfect commercial freedom can indeed be understood in a procedural sense. The true price of a commodity is the price that would be revealed under entirely fair procedures. The conception of value is counterfactual; true prices are the prices which would obtain if all the relevant procedures were to be fair.

The problem, in relation to markets as well as to voting, is that real procedures are not entirely perfect or fair; this is the point of Condorcet's work on incomplete market organization, inconsistent information, insufficient initial endowments, and inequitable enforcement of rules. One conclusion, therefore, is that it will sometimes be impossible—given distributions of individual preferences—to arrive at true or equilibrium prices. Governments can exclude certain outcomes, such as that any member of society should become utterly destitute. But the object of public policy, subject to these constraints, should be to influence procedures rather than outcomes.

A related conclusion is that the rules which are supposed to influence economic procedures should be chosen through political procedures which are themselves fair. The counterfactual conception would thus be political as well as economic; true prices are the prices which would obtain if the relevant market procedures were to be augmented, where necessary, on the basis of fair procedures for social decisions. The reforms decided on might well be minimal; Condorcet's own preference for quasi-unanimous decisions on all policies that affect individual rights suggests that he anticipated very minor improvements to market procedures. But the important point is that the improvements—and the procedure itself—would have been chosen by the people who participate in the procedure.

Individuals' preferences, in Condorcet's description, include preferences for social outcomes, for the "spectacle" of a certain sort of society. They are thereby the sorts of preferences which are both interdependent and influenced by cognitive events, in the form of public and private discussion. Discussion is indeed at the heart of Condorcet's political thought; the greatest need in the post-Revolutionary period, he wrote at the very end of his life, and the greatest service of social mathematics, is to enable people to become accustomed to the "slow and peaceful course of discussion."[113] It is this prospect of limitless and endless discussion, in turn, which most provoked Condorcet's contemporary critics. The condition that "everything is to be discussed," Edmund Burke wrote, will make people indifferent to the constitution of their own state: governments will feel "the pernicious consequence of destroying all docility in the minds of those who are not formed for finding their own way in the labyrinths of political theory."[114] "What is this trembling light which we call *reason*," Joseph de Maistre asked, this "deceiving cloud" which is all we have left when we have added up "all probabilities" and "discussed all doubts and all interests?"[115] Condorcet was for de Maistre a proselytizer of doubt, indecisiveness, and indocility; he was "perhaps the most odious of the French revolutionaries."[116]

Discussion, for Condorcet, must precede decision; the moment of decision itself can be considered as a point in time, and thus as a period so (infinitely) short that it can be depicted, "with method and precision," as one in which values do not change.[117] But changes in values or preferences are nonetheless an important characteristic of the world which Condorcet describes, in economic as in political procedures. Political decisions follow a "reasoned discussion" of "all the opinions and all the grounds on which these opinions could be based."[118] The committee room, like the market, is for Condorcet a place in which people speak and dispute. Turgot described the process of *tâtonnement* as a sequence of dialogues or discussions between pairs of exchangers: a "debate between every buyer and every seller," which makes known the true price of everything. The difference from later conceptions of economic interdependence—in which *tâtonnement* is silent, and also blind—is striking. Prices are "cried out," in a Walrasian *tâtonnement*, but by a central, disembodied crier. The exchangers listen and do not speak. They determine their demand and supply silently, "after reflection, without calculation, but exactly as would be done by calculation."[119]

Condorcet's universe is much more like John Stuart Mill's than like Walras's. Mill takes a long passage from Condorcet—in which Condorcet says that "opinions formed on the basis of past experience" should be able to serve as a foundation for social knowledge—as the epigram to Book 6 of his *Logic*, on the moral sciences.[120] But reasoned discussion, too, is important to Mill, as to Condorcet: the "free and equal discussion" which is at the heart of *On Liberty*, the discussion which can alone "show how experience is to be interpreted," the capacity to rectify one's mistakes "by discussion and experience," which is for Mill "the source of everything respectable in man."[121] Good economic theories, like true elections, should correspond to what happens when a person chooses on his own, as Condorcet wrote in his last paper on social choice; to the procedures of "an individual who wished to make a choice scrupulously, by following a method which was general, regular, and uniform in all cases."[122]

PELION AND OSSA

Condorcet's prospect is of two gigantic systems of interdependent choice. In one, individuals choose what to sell or to buy or to invest, and they also choose how to compete; they choose, in particular, whether to compete by economic means (such as reducing prices), or by political means (such as influencing regulation). In the other, they choose economic policies, and they also choose how to choose economic policies; they make decisions as to which sorts of policies should be the subject of political choice, and which should be decided on only in the course of extended and constitutional procedures. The system of economic freedom is juxtaposed to and completed by a similarly monumental system of political freedom. There are many inadequacies of the liberal economic order, or respects in which it falls short of perfect competition. But these failings are themselves among the concerns of a liberal political order. Individuals will decide, in a scrupulous manner, and after extensive discussion, on the constitution of political and economic freedom. They will then decide, in the setting of the appropriate constitutional procedures, on such problems as may be posed by the occasional failings of the system of economic freedom. They will vote, interminably, on social security, on marginal taxes, or on environmental conflicts.

Condorcet's liberal idyll, his Pelion of economic competition and his Ossa of constitutional choice, has been the subject of continuing derision. One objection is that it is impossibly dull. People would die of boredom in Condorcet's future society, Sainte-Beuve wrote in 1851: everyone would live in a condition of "universal mediocrity"; each individual would turn imperceptibly into a "reasonable and rational philosopher"; there would be no place "for great virtues, for acts of heroism."[123] This heroism of the unheroic is something to which Condorcet himself looked forward. He imagined small farmers who live surrounded by "a thermometer, a barometer, a hygrometer," who are instructed in the "means of instructing themselves," and who keep registers in which they write down their own observations of the weather. The man of enlightenment, in Condorcet's description, is "taken up with the education of his family, with the details of domestic administration." He goes to courses for the education of adults, while "industry multiplies its efforts." He studies "new laws which are proposed or promulgated," and "operations which are being undertaken or prepared in the diverse branches of administration." It is not a "useless and almost shameful life," Condorcet says, to "remain quietly in the bosom of one's family, preparing the happiness of one's children, cultivating friendship, exercising benevolence," and thinking about one's duties and one's sentiments.[124]

The other and more grave objection to Condorcet's idyll is that it is unrealistic, and thereby unreliable. It assumes that individuals are generally, or at least potentially, reasonable; that they are mild, thoughtful, and peaceable. Their disposition, usually, is to improve themselves by discussion and experience. They compete assiduously in selling and investing. But they do not only compete. "While it may be natural to wish to win when one is put in the situation of being compared with someone else, is it also natural to place oneself, endlessly, in such situations?" Condorcet asks in the "fragment" of the history of the Tenth Epoch.[125] They prefer, or they eventually learn to prefer, to compete by socially undestructive means; on the basis of industry and not of intimidation or influence. They support policies—legislation and administrative regulations—which further their own economic interests. But they recognize that there are other political choices—choices of a constitutional sort—in which their long-term interests coincide with the constructive interests of the society.

This view of the enlightened disposition was for Condorcet's opponents no more than a childish delusion. Individuals were not naturally mild, in the opinion of Bonald or Robespierre, Burke or de Maistre. They did not become civilized, or sociable, in the course of the slow, discursive experience of secular virtue. They were subjugated only by reverence, or submission, or fear. If they were to become thoughtful, or virtuous, they would have to be educated in virtue. Robespierre's prospect, of moral instruction or moral education, was indeed Condorcet's final preoccupation, his final dread.

John Morley wrote that of the philosophers who had been "scattering the seeds of revolution in France, only Condorcet survived to behold the first bitter ingathering of the harvest"; "he only was left to see the reaping of the whirlwind."[126] Condorcet lived, and contributed to the discussion of policy, in a period of extraordinary change. His earliest writings on political economy and economic policy are from the *fin de régime* of a sovereign, Louis XV, whose reign began in 1715. He wrote in support of freedom of commerce during Turgot's experiment in economic reform in 1774–1776, and again in the period of constitutional reforms of the late 1780s. He continued to argue for economic freedom in the last writings he published before going into hiding from the Revolutionary Terror in 1793, and in his final, posthumously published writings. He was concerned, throughout this prodigious epoch of political turbulence, with the relationship between economic and political choices, and with the grounds on which individuals might have confidence in economic freedom. But his own opinions also changed profoundly over the period. "There is no one who has not observed, in himself, that he has changed his opinion about certain objects, according to the period of time, to circumstances, to events," he wrote in his *Essai sur l'analyse*.[127] He believed, above all, in reasoned discussion; how would his own views not change?

Condorcet's last preoccupation, in the midst of the whirlwind of revolution, was with the disposition of enlightenment. He recognized, as has been seen, that the liberal economic and political order imposes strong conditions with respect to individual dispositions or ways of thinking. He also recognized that the effort to realize these conditions—to encourage or to induce change in ways of thinking—poses continuing political problems. One important change in his opinions, over the period from the 1770s to the 1790s, thus consisted in an increasing propensity for probabilistic reasoning; an increasing willingness to live with uncertainty. The other change was in his view of public education, or public instruction.

The French Revolution itself, for Condorcet, was above all a change in ways of thinking. "A happy event has suddenly opened up an immense scope to the hopes of humanity . . . [T]his revolution is not in a government, it is in opinions and wills," he wrote at the end of his work on public instruction.[128] This was a familiar view among the friends of enlightenment. "An event in our times," Kant wrote in 1798, has revealed powers "in human nature" such that "a view opens up into the unbounded future." The event was a disposition; it was the sympathy of disinterested spectators for the French Revolution, in which "their reaction (because of its universality) proves that mankind as a whole shares a certain character in common."[129] But the events of the 1790s were also, for Condorcet, as for Kant, a frightening revelation of the power of interested passions.

Condorcet's description of the liberal disposition, in these circumstances, is poignantly uncertain. The perfection to which he looked forward, in the long "fragment of the history of the Tenth Epoch," was no more than an evaluation of probabilities: "The normal condition of man, in an entire people, should be to be led by truth, although subject to error; subject in his conduct to the rules of morality, although sometimes led into crime; . . . happy, as much as is possible in the midst of the pain, need, and loss which are for him the necessary consequence of the general laws of the universe." His description of the prospect for inducing improvement in these normal conditions is similarly somber. His writings on public instruction, as will be seen in the next chapter, are scrupulously tentative with respect to moral and political education. In the "fragment," he rejects even the prospect of instruction in truth. The advantage of reason, he writes, is to protect one from "the false calculations of one's interest, the sophisms of passion," and the "ruses of charlatans"; it can be encouraged only if "in place of teaching truths, one limits oneself to direction in how to find them."[130]

Condorcet's view of instruction in how to think—in the reform of the soul—changed profoundly in the course of the 1770s and 1780s, and especially during the Revolution. In the *Réflexions sur le commerce des blés*, he argues for a reform of civil and criminal jurisprudence ("such that every citizen can understand the laws which determine his fate"), and also for "a public education, truly worthy of the name," which will "teach every man to love his country and its laws, to feel the need for public esteem and the price of good conscience."[131] This is fairly close to the public education of the Economists or Physiocrats, to their "tutelary authority," formed on the model of Chinese despotism, whose objective is to "extinguish all dissent" with respect to the "natural and fundamental laws" which make themselves manifest to men "by the enlightenment of reason, cultivated by education."[132] It is close, too, to Turgot's notorious promise to Louis XVI, drafted by Dupont de Nemours and commented on by Tocqueville, that with the introduction of public education, "within ten years, your nation will be unrecognizable [in] its good morals, its enlightened zeal for your service and that of the country . . . [A]t the end of some years, Your Majesty will have a new people."[133]

By the time of his *Vie de M. Turgot*, in 1786, Condorcet was less than zealous in his support for education in public morality. Turgot himself wrote to Dupont de Nemours, some years before his proposals for a secular public education, that the Economists seemed incapable of ridding themselves of "their tic with respect to tutelary authority," which was a "stupidity," and "dishonored" their doctrine.[134] Moral instruction, as described in Condorcet's *Vie de M. Turgot*, is distinctly minimal; it begins with the "analysis and development of moral ideas," and it relies, above all, on the "justness of disposition" which is a condition of almost all individuals.[135] In his writings on public instruction after 1790, Condorcet had become resolutely opposed to all instruction in civic duty, or in conscience. Little children should not be made "to admire a constitution, and to recite by heart the political rights of man"; there should be "no sort of catechism." The example of England, here, was a warning for other countries, in that "a superstitious respect for the constitution or for certain laws to which people persist in attributing national prosperity" had become "part of education," a "sort of political religion" of which the effect was to prevent improvements in the constitution itself. The new French constitution was something which should be taught in public schools only as a matter of information, or "if one speaks about it as of a fact."[136]

The disposition of individuals is "the only difficult question" for the system of economic freedom, Condorcet wrote in 1776, and he was preoccupied, until the very end of his life, with the history and prospects of the human spirit. Oppression made individuals less enlightened, in his description; this is the process of what he described as the soul discouraged, or, as he said in his *Vie de M. Turgot*, "the soul of people degraded by fiscal tyranny."[137] But enlightenment is also, as has been seen, the condition of economic improvement. Individuals must wish, in general, to increase their wealth by legitimate as distinct from "illegitimate means," such as fraud, theft, or "buying other people." Their interest in wealth must be sufficiently well understood that they can estimate the extent to which "the uncertainty of success, the dangers to which one is exposed, the reduction of legitimate resources, occasioned by the loss of the confidence of others," will more than compensate, on even the "crudest calculation of interest," for "the advantage of an injustice."[138]

Individuals, in the system of economic freedom, must be disposed to make enlightened choices, in the sense of adding up all probabilities and discussing all doubts. They must be sufficiently dispassionate to see that their own, enlightened self-interest coincides, often, with the general interest in social tranquillity and social justice. They must occasionally—as when they are reflecting on lasting and constitutional choices—see that social tranquillity actually constitutes one of their interests, as well as coinciding with or furthering these interests. Necker said of the people, in the study to which Condorcet's *Réflexions sur le commerce des blés* was a response, that in the immense space of the future, they never see more than tomorrow. Condorcet believed that the people will be able to imagine a future which is so remote that they do not even know who they will be, or in what their interests will consist.

The psychological requirements of economic freedom are in this sense a particular case of the quite general problem of liberal orders: of the disposition of enlightenment, or of the circumstance, described in Mill's introduction to *On Liberty,* that "liberty, as a principle, has no application to any state of things anterior to the time when mankind have become capable of being improved by free and equal discussion."[139] Condorcet's "fragment of the history of the Tenth Epoch" begins with a related and disturbing problem: with "the analysis of the means of shaping the morality and the reason of an entire people," or of "creating a public morality."[140] His answer consists in a moral laissez-faire, in which the liberal political constitution protects individuals from all public intervention in the freedom of understanding. He wishes people, in John Morley's description, to exercise their individual reason "methodically and independently, not without cooperation, but without anything like official or other subordination."[141]

Condorcet's most extended illustration is taken, in the "fragment," from the circumstances of economic freedom, or of legitimate and illegitimate competition. He has confidence in the reform of unjust laws (which multiply conflicts of interest); in the freedom of the press; in social equality; in public information. If laws are simple, just, and well executed, if there is equality of rights and less inequality of wealth, if "indirect taxes, privileges, and regulations of commerce" do not create "the means of oppression" and the "means of fraud," if misery is no more than "a misfortune, an accident for a few families," then the interest in acquiring things by illegitimate means will present itself "less often, to a smaller number of people, and in less varied and seductive forms." "When commerce and industry are free," there will be only a constructive "competition to buy and to sell," with less conflict or opposition of interests.[142] The disposition of enlightenment will become more resilient, and will flourish. But it will not be a disposition that can be the subject of instruction, or that can be given to the people. It will be likely, and it will not be certain.

7

Condorcet and the Conflict of Values

COLD, DESCRIPTIVE CARTESIAN REASON

Condorcet has been seen, since his death in 1794, as the embodiment of the cold, oppressive enlightenment.[1] He was for Sainte-Beuve "the extreme product and as it were the monstrous brain" of the "final school of the eighteenth century," with its "orgies of rationalism"; he denied the diversity of human life; "he believed that he held the key to the happiness of men and of future races."[2] Condorcet's conception of the connectedness or universality of values, in particular, has seemed to epitomize the illusions of enlightenment thought. The celebrated chain of virtues in the *Esquisse d'un tableau historique des progrès de l'esprit humain*—"that nature links together truth, happiness, and virtue by an indissoluble chain" —has been seen as a pitiful, ominous error.[3]

These illusions were a counterpoint, in the twentieth century, to some of the most influential ideas in modern political philosophy. The assertion of universal and unalterable principles was for Isaiah Berlin "the central dogma of the entire Enlightenment," and its denial was the central insight of the "counter-Enlightenment."[4] It was similarly central, thereby, to the tragic destiny of enlightenment ideas. Goods conflict by their very nature, for Bernard Williams; for Berlin, "these collisions of values are of the essence of what they are and what we are."[5] Condorcet's idyll, in Berlin's description—the idyll of "one of the best men who ever lived"—was transformed, in the course of the nineteenth century, into an emblem of terror; a "deep, serene, unshakeable conviction in the minds of some of the most merciless tyrants and persecutors in history."[6]

The conception of essential conflict, or the denial of universal virtues, was even of modern political importance, in the East European revolutions at the end of the twentieth century. "Lately, it has become a habit to speak ill of the eighteenth century," the novelist Milan Kundera wrote in 1986, of "the atheist rationalism of the Enlightenment," of "Leibniz's famous declaration: *Nihil est sine ratione,*" and of the "Russian totalitarianism" that is their outcome.[7] The long eighteenth century began with Leibniz, on this view, or with what Václav Havel called "cold, descriptive Cartesian reason"; it reached its extreme product in the French Revolution, and its slow decline was only recently complete. Skepticism about "the slightest suggestion of Utopianism," for Havel, was the distinctive characteristic of the dissident movement in Central Europe. There was in fact too much skepticism, he wrote; too much suspicion of "even a very timid, hesitant, tactful attempt to appeal to justice." But Havel, too, believed that he had been tempted by an impatience that "had something almost communist in it; or, more generally, something rationalist": the conviction "that the world is nothing but a crossword puzzle in which there is only a single correct solution to the problem."[8]

I will be concerned, in this chapter, with Condorcet's idea of the connectedness of values, and its relation to the supposed universalism—the belief in universal and eternal principles of human existence—of the enlightenment. Condorcet was concerned, as will be seen, with the conflict as well as with the connectedness of values: with the diversity of individual opinions; with the shortcomings of proto-utilitarian theories of happiness; with individual rights and individual independence; and with trying to show that the imposition of universal and eternal principles is the most sinister of despotisms. The effort to reconcile conceptions of conflict and of uniformity was itself of central importance in Condorcet's political ideas.

Condorcet's writings on the conflict of values provide an odd and illuminating view of the sect of enlightenment. Condorcet sounds at times like Herder, as will be seen, or like Hölderlin; like Smith or like Hutcheson. He sounds close, too, to the ideas of the liberal critics of enlightenment in the post-Napoleonic Restoration. As in Tocqueville's famous hypothesis in *L'ancien régime et la Révolution,* there is a continuity, across the frontier of the French Revolution, between the philosophical (and administrative) ideas of the ancien régime and the politics of the nineteenth century. But where Tocqueville sees the origins of regulatory oppression in the first revolution of the 1750s and 1760s, Condorcet's writings suggest a different continuity. There is a sort of counterenlightenment within the enlightenment, that is to say, in response to the proto-revolution; a proto-history of the nineteenth-century liberalism of Constant, of Mill, and of Tocqueville himself.

Condorcet is an interstitial figure, on this view, rather than a *ne plus ultra* of eighteenth-century philosophy. But his political ideas are thereby of some modern interest. He belongs to neither side, entirely, in the philosophical dichotomy of uniformity versus diversity, or of universal connectedness versus the endlessness of conflict. His concerns are quite subversive, in fact, of the dichotomy itself: of Constant's diptych, in which "variety is organization; uniformity is mechanism. Variety is life; uniformity is death."[9] The philosophy of enlightenment, in Condorcet's political writings, is not entirely cold and not entirely oppressive; it is not even entirely unfamiliar, in the dissident liberalism of the late twentieth century.

DIVERSITY AND UNIFORMITY

Condorcet was a monument of his times well before his death in the Terror. Burke wrote of him in the plural—"the Jourdans and the Condorcets and the whole of that sect of Philosophic Robbers and Assassins," or "the Condorcets [who] have stirred up" religious oppression. For Bonald in 1796, as for Sainte-Beuve later, the *Esquisse* was the "final *production*" of destructive philosophy, or a text which could explain the phenomenon of Revolutionary France. De Maistre, in 1797, spoke of Condorcet as the token both of his times and of timeless dogmas: of the "enemy sect" which has been roaring against Christianity like a lion, "from Celsus to Condorcet."[10] Malthus presented his *Essay on Population,* in 1798, as a criticism of "such men as Godwin and Condorcet"; the *Esquisse,* Malthus said, should be considered as a sketch not only of Condorcet's opinions, but also of those "of many of the literary men in France, at the beginning of the Revolution."[11] Condorcet is still, in modern philosophy, a figure weighted with representativeness: for Charles Taylor, a constituent of the "mechanistic, atomistic, homogenizing" science of "a Helvétius, a Holbach, a Condorcet, a Bentham," or of "materialist and utilitarian writers like Bentham, Holbach, Helvétius and Condorcet."[12]

For his political friends, too, Condorcet was an icon of enlightenment. Destutt de Tracy described him as "the greatest philosopher in modern times."[13] Yet he is known, to a striking extent, through the renown of a single great book (the *Esquisse*), which is itself known only through posthumously collected fragments, edited in the 1790s with the explicit intention of presenting a source of "useful regrets," and a "monument" to "the most useful truths."[14] His writings on individual and collective values, like his writings on political economy, are to be found in anonymous pamphlets, mathematical essays, eulogies, reflections on Epicurus, projects for primary school instruction, and polemics about monopoly. They are buried, like the political ideas into which Tocqueville inquired, in the tomb of the ancien régime, in disputes over long-obscure economic regulations.[15]

My principal concern in what follows, as in the previous chapter, will be with Condorcet's economic writings, mostly of the early and middle 1770s; with his writings on voting and political decisions in the middle and late 1780s; and with his writings on public instruction during the Revolution. Condorcet's political and philosophical opinions changed substantially in the course of his public life, as has been seen. He became considerably more skeptical, in particular, about the Economists' or Physiocrats' prescriptions of freedom of commerce without political freedom; about the prospects for education in enlightenment; and about the application, to societies of individuals, of the determinist ideas of the mechanical sciences. It is reasonable, he wrote in his "Éloge de M. d'Alembert" of 1783, "to be content with more or less great probabilities."[16] But the idea of civilized conflict is a continuing theme in all the writings with which I will be concerned. To change one's mind—to question the eternal truth of even one's own opinions—is itself, for Condorcet, of political importance.

Condorcet was preoccupied, in the first place, with individual diversity. Political economy must not, he wrote, emulate the simple application of mechanical principles, as though to a "huge hydraulic machine"; it must not presume a spurious order or regularity in "the mass of operations carried out, in an independent manner, by a large number of men, and directed by the interest, the opinion, by the instinct, so to speak, of each of them."[17] A world in which everyone has the same opinions is for Condorcet a true horror. One of the worst consequences of a society divided into different estates is thus that men tend to conform to received opinion: one can "guess a man's opinion by the uniform he wears." Such a man is likely to be incapable of "existing or thinking on his own"; to support only "that which his order or his company has prescribed that he will think and believe."[18]

The diversity of opinions is of central importance, in the 1780s, to Condorcet's work on the application of mathematical reasoning to political choice. Condorcet was best known, before the Revolution, as the permanent secretary of the Academy of Sciences. His *Essai sur l'application de l'analyse* of 1785 takes as one of its principal themes the difficulty or impossibility of choice under conditions of widely differing individual preferences.[19] Procedures for making collective decisions lead to contradictory results, Condorcet showed, when different groups of voters rank candidates, or economic policies, according to different orderings. Individuals disagree, for "good or bad reasons," over even the most general political orderings of constitutional proposals.[20] They also find it difficult to decide on their own preferences; the procedures of a deliberative assembly should indeed be as close as possible to those that a single individual follows in examining a question, and making a choice.[21]

In his last major published work, on principles of education, Condorcet again identified the diversity of opinions as a preeminent good. Public instruction should not extend to political and moral education, which would be contrary to the "independence of opinions." Children would still, perhaps, "receive opinions" from their families. But these opinions would not then be "the same for all citizens." They would not have the character of a "received truth," or a "universal belief." Even if religious or political opinions were, at first, "more or less the same in all families," they would soon become dispersed, if they were not supported by public power. The word "uniformity," which Condorcet uses in a positive sense in speaking of the convergence of laws, is here used of a sinister conformity of opinions: "All the danger would then disappear with the uniformity."[22]

Condorcet was profoundly opposed, secondly, to the proto-utilitarian theory of Helvétius and Necker: as an account of human behavior, as a principle of virtue, and as a principle of public policy. "Men are not machines who calculate and who always decide on the outcome where there is most to be won," he wrote in his *Réflexions sur le commerce des blés* of 1776.[23] People do not act only out of self-interest, and their self-interest is itself influenced by their moral sentiments: "The idea that there exist a hundred thousand unhappy people around us is a painful experience just as real as an attack of gout."[24] "I am not of the opinion of Helvétius," he wrote to Turgot, "because I admit, in man, a sentiment whose force and influence he does not seem to me to have suspected." His view, like Turgot's, seems to have been that Helvétius's theory was slightly ludicrous: "Whatever he may say, he will not prevent me from loving my friends; he will not condemn me to the mortal boredom of thinking endlessly about my own merit or glory."[25]

Turgot, in the same correspondence with Condorcet, criticized Helvétius for his superficial understanding of human sentiments. The proposition that men act only out of their own interest is either childish (equivalent, trivially, to saying that "men desire only that which they desire") or false. The proof is that people feel remorse, and that they have to make an effort to overcome their feelings when the feelings are in opposition to their interests; "that they are touched by novels and tragedies, and that a novel whose hero acted in accordance with the principles of Helvétius . . . would be most displeasing to them."[26] Condorcet wrote later that Turgot "considered novels as being books of morality, and even, he said, the only ones in which he had seen morality."[27] This seems to have been his own opinion as well. He was opposed, as has been seen, to public instruction in morality (giving children "principles of conduct," or "teaching them truths"). By reading "short moral stories," children would instead become disposed "to reflect on their sentiments."[28]

To read novels, Condorcet wrote, is the best way to understand how our actions influence "the people who surround us," and this is in turn "the most important and the most neglected part of morality"; it is "the domestic virtues, those which are suited to all men, those by which each person influences the welfare of the people who have particular relations with him" which have the greatest influence on the general happiness of society.[29] The prescription of early utilitarian theory—that public utility, or the calculation of public interest, is the foundation of virtue—was thus for Condorcet profoundly deluded.[30] He insisted, especially in his writings on public instruction, on the importance of emotions. Morality was founded on moral sentiments and on domestic virtues. Simple, "almost organic" feelings were the basis of a sensibility which is "the first active principle of all morality, as of all virtue, and without which it is no more than a calculation of interest, a cold combination of reason." Sensibility and rationality were indeed substitutes, in some circumstances: "The man of compassion has no need to be enlightened in order to be good," while "in the unfeeling man, on the contrary, a small amount of goodness requires very great enlightenment."[31]

Condorcet was even more strongly opposed to the proto-utilitarian presumption that it was possible, or desirable, for governments to sum the happiness of different individuals. The object of policy should be to promote the enjoyment of the natural rights of individuals, he wrote, and not "the greatest utility of society, a vague principle and a fertile source of bad laws."[32] He was fiercely critical of contemporary efforts to compare the "quantity of happiness" induced by different government policies (as in Necker's calculations of the total quantity of happiness of two thousand people living at the level of subsistence, versus one thousand people who were "a little better" clothed). Happiness was not the same thing as welfare, Condorcet wrote, and it was not a proper object of government policy. It is welfare, and not happiness, which is "a duty of justice" for governments. Welfare "consists in not being exposed to misery, to humiliation, to oppression. It is this welfare which governments owe to the people. It is necessary to happiness, and it may not be sufficient. But it is up to nature to do the rest."[33]

"Motives of utility," Condorcet wrote in his pamphlet on the admission of women to rights to citizenship, cannot "counterbalance a true right"; "it is in the name of public utility that people have filled the Bastille, and instituted the censorship of books."[34] To speak of the collective happiness (or unhappiness) of individuals—as distinct from the collective means of individual happiness—is to violate justice; it is to be willing to sacrifice the "few" to the "many."[35] In his writings against slavery, Condorcet rejected the cold discussion of interests: "I do not think that a man should speak coldly of revolting excesses." The prosperity of commerce, he said, should not be "put in the balance" against justice; "the interest of power and of the wealth of a nation must disappear before the right of a single man."[36]

Condorcet's conception of individual independence, thirdly, is central to his political ideas. Politics, like morality, is a matter of sentiments and emotions. People's motives, in his writings on political economy, are complex and conflicting, as has been seen. A farmer might decide to remain in agriculture, rather than choosing a supposedly more honorable position elsewhere: "Man prefers to depend on nature than on other men; he suffers less if he is ruined by a hailstorm than by an injustice." Tax reform, Condorcet said, would "relieve the sentiment of oppression, a thousand times more painful than the sentiment of misery." Freedom of commerce would reduce, for the poor, the horror of being ignored: "the idea of being counted for nothing."[37]

Freedom is itself a sentiment; an end and not an instrument. "Feeling the sweetness of liberty," Condorcet wrote, is quite different from knowing "how to calculate its advantages."[38] He was horrified, early in the Revolution, by the prospect that "liberty will be no more, in the eyes of an avid nation, than a necessary condition for the security of financial operations"; he criticized the Economists or Physiocrats for seeming "too much to forget the interests of political freedom for those of freedom of commerce."[39] But freedom, too, takes diverse forms. In his "Réflexions sur l'esclavage des nègres" of 1781, Condorcet described two different "sorts of liberty." One is close to Rousseau's conception of political liberty, and it is not, Condorcet says, something that is felt by everybody; it is the liberty "to be subject only to laws which emanate from the general will of the citizens." "But there is another liberty," Condorcet goes on: the liberty "of disposing freely of one's own person, of not being dependent, for one's food, for one's sentiments, for one's tastes, on the whims of a man. There is no one who does not feel the loss of this liberty, who does not have a horror of this sort of servitude."[40]

Condorcet's other liberty—the liberty of "not being dependent," on a man or on men—is a condition of the inner self. It is private: "A man is called free if he is not subject in any of his private actions to the arbitrary will of an individual."[41] It is freedom in relation to the will of other individuals, and also to the will of society. The liberty of political, moral, and religious opinions, Condorcet says, is "one of the most precious parts of natural liberty." But it would be only illusory if "society were to take hold of new generations, to dictate to them what they should believe." The person who brings with him into society the opinions which his education has given to him "is no longer a free man." He is "the slave of his masters"; his chains are the more difficult to break "because he does not feel them himself, and he believes that he is obeying his own reason, when he is doing no more than submitting to that of another."[42]

It is interesting that Condorcet went on to describe the liberty and diversity of opinions as a characteristically modern good. He contrasted it to the liberty of the ancients: "The ancients had no conception at all of this sort of liberty; they seem in fact to have had no object, in their institutions, except to destroy it. They would have liked to leave men with nothing but the ideas, the sentiments, which entered into the system of the lawmaker. Nature, for them, had created no more than machines, of which the law alone was to regulate the springs and direct the action." Condorcet was indeed the inspiration, here, for Benjamin Constant, as Constant says in his famous essay on ancient and modern liberty. Constant takes individual rights as the synonym of Condorcet's "sort of liberty"; he writes that "the ancients, as Condorcet said, had no conception of individual rights. Men were no more, so to speak, than machines of which the law regulated the springs and directed the wheels."[43]

To impose universal and eternal principles, finally, was for Condorcet the most dismal tyranny. The legislators of antiquity, he wrote, sought to establish eternal constitutions. But to teach the constitution "as a doctrine in conformity with the principles of universal reason" was a despotism of public power. It is to "violate liberty in its most sacred rights, under the pretext of teaching people how to cherish it." The object of instruction should be not to consecrate an "eternal empire" of established opinions, but to "submit them to the free examination of successive generations." It should set out, for men and women, "the discussions which are of interest to their rights or their happiness, and should offer them the means necessary to decide for themselves." People should be informed of new political principles, and also of "the conflicts of opinion which are raised about these principles."[44]

To see other individuals as children was for Condorcet the opposite of enlightenment. This was the point of his criticism of proto-utilitarian calculations in political economy; of the despots who offer happiness to their subjects.[45] The project was even more sinister in public education. The "supposed philosophers" of eternal political truths, Condorcet wrote, wish to impose their influence on young children, who will then love the laws and the constitution "by a blind sentiment." They wish to guide the people, to induce an "obedience which would be truly passive, because it would be blind"; the people would then be no more than "docile instruments to be disputed over by adroit hands, to reject or break or use at their will."[46]

Wisdom and reason are not the privilege of a few people, who deceive everyone else and "take hold of their imagination," "charged with thinking for them, and directing their eternal childhood." "How can they be so sure that what they believe is or always will be the truth," Condorcet asked. "Who gave them the right to judge where it is to be found?" This is not enlightenment but fanaticism: "dazzling men instead of enlightening them, seducing them for the truth, presenting it to them like a prejudice."[47]

THE INDISSOLUBLE CHAIN

This Condorcet—Constant's Condorcet, or the Condorcet of endless, discursive conflicts of opinions—is a quite incongruous figure. He believes in the diversity of sentiments and in the uniformity of rules. He thinks that there are universal political truths, and that these truths are endlessly to be called into question. Condorcet's celebrated remark in the *Esquisse* is made almost in passing, and it is concerned particularly with moral conditions: will not our later work prove, Condorcet asks, that "the moral goodness of man . . . is susceptible of indefinite improvement, and that nature links together truth, happiness, and virtue by an indissoluble chain?"[48] But he refers on many other occasions to the lack of conflict between superficially different political objectives or interests.[49] He even suggests that the "link" or "chain" could provide some sort of foundation for politics. The ancients, he wrote in his mathematical essay on voting, were concerned in their constitutions with counterbalancing different interests: "The words 'liberty' and 'utility' occupied them more than 'truth' and 'justice'; and the link which connects these objects to one another, although it was perceived, perhaps, by some of their philosophers, was not understood sufficiently distinctly to serve as the foundation for politics."[50]

On the one hand, Condorcet says that different people have diverse conceptions of the political good, as they must, in fact, in a free society. Political words have different meanings at different times, and for different people.[51] On the other hand, he identifies political "objects"—objects such as truth and justice—to which the words refer; he even sees in the connectedness of these underlying objects the foundation of politics. Is it convincing, therefore, to protest, as he does, that individuals must be free, for all eternity, to make their own decisions about their own interests? Is it reasonable, if one believes in unique political truth, to confide this truth, or this prospect of future improvement, to the doubt, error, and delay of political discussion?

Condorcet's difficulties, here, are imposing. He is a figure who belongs to the enlightenment and also to the world of its critics. This makes his thought elusive in a peculiar respect; it becomes necessary, if one is to try to understand his philosophical and political difficulties, to think oneself into two different philosophical worlds, and into the turbulent times in which one coexisted with the other. But to understand Condorcet's dilemma—to think oneself into his own politics of conflict, or into the choices of individual conduct with which he was concerned, or into the distinctive universalism of moral sentiments of the late enlightenment— is to understand something of the modern *Nachlass* of enlightenment thought.

CIVILIZED CONFLICT

Condorcet's continuing idyll, in the first place, was of civilized or constitutional conflict. His own effort to reconcile uniformity and diversity consists, that is to say, of trying to influence the forms that conflict takes. His principal innovation in political theory is to have outlined a constitutional setting for political conflict. He observes the diversity of opinions and interests; he seeks to institutionalize political dissonance. The premise of his famous work on social decisions was the heterogeneity of preferences. The difficulties of voting with which he was concerned arise when individuals have preferences which are not merely diverse, but diverse in a particular way.[52] The point of his constitutional recommendations, under these circumstances, is to introduce deliberation, delay, and the prospect of reversibility.

Condorcet's favored method of pairwise elections can, as he pointed out, require long, slow, and tedious exercises in consecutive voting.[53] He was opposed to strong executive power; "a divided executive," in Lord Acton's words, "which, through the advocacy of Condorcet, took root in France, has proved to be weakness itself."[54] He thought that countries should have a second chamber composed of wise men—it would have consisted, in the case of England, of men such as "Locke, Hume, Smith, Price"—whose principal duty would be to introduce delay into controversial constitutional procedures.[55] Even when he was most engaged in the politics of Revolutionary foreign policy, his prescription was for discussion. To the Spanish, in 1792, he proposed a republican constitution: "But if the reasonings on which I rely do not seem like demonstrations to the Spaniards, what right would I have to wish them to prefer my reason to their own? I will therefore not say to them: Adopt what I regard as necessary to the existence of a free people; but I will say to them: Seize hold at least of what you today think of as liberty; and . . . you will then at least be allowed to examine, to discuss all opinions."[56]

The best decision procedures—or the ones that are "in some sense natural"—are for Condorcet those that correspond to the decision making of a single individual. The individual weighs up different grounds for choice, he discovers new grounds, he changes his mind, he tries to be as scrupulous as he can.[57] It is this conception of indecisive choice which Condorcet sought to generalize in political life. He favored the "smallest possible" or "virtually nonexistent" government.[58] He thought that decisions which would restrict any individual's rights should be adopted only with a very great majority; in difficult cases, it is always best, when possible, to "put off the decision."[59] This is not a very glorious political society. But it is not a despotic society either, or one in which individuals are sacrificed to universal truth.

Condorcet suggests, quite frequently, that he has a privileged insight into the common interests of individuals and groups; that he can see, more clearly than the individuals themselves, their common interest in enlightened policies. This is very much in the spirit of the times; of the invisible hand, visible to the philosopher and invisible only to the individuals concerned. But like Smith, Condorcet makes no suggestion that this hidden order should be imposed on unenlightened citizens, that they should be persuaded or even encouraged to see it. What he presents, instead, is an outline of the politics of a society in which conflicts are recognized and respected.

Condorcet's belief in the connectedness of values has oddly little effect on his constitutional principles, or indeed on his own political actions. He believes in the universality of political objects, but he does not believe in doing much to impose them. He engages in long and tedious discussions, including with himself; his vision of the future, or of the foundation of politics, turns out to have very little to do with his own political life.

INCONSISTENT UNIVERSALISM

A second element in Condorcet's dilemma was thus of political inconsistency, or of the relations between principles and policies. He is open, it seems, to the charge either of hypocrisy or of having some sort of double personality. His contemporaries were indeed drawn in their descriptions of him to the oxymoronic: he was placid and turbulent, an "enraged sheep," for Turgot; hot and cold, a "snow-covered volcano," for d'Alembert; or, for his bitter enemy Robespierre, a "timid conspirator."[60] For Antoine Diannyère, the author, in 1797, of the first extended account of the *Esquisse,* Condorcet's openness to discussion was a political virtue: "Let us never more forget, alas! That the truths of theory are necessarily modified in practice and that it is Condorcet who established this in his last work!"[61]

The question of political inconsistency is related to a very serious charge against all utopian thought. The belief in future perfectibility, it is suggested, is either ignored (by the utopian) in his own politics, or used as a justification for present oppression. Bonald thought that the *Esquisse* could explain the phenomenon of Revolutionary France, in which men coldly commanded desolation and death "out of pure love of posterity," justifying present horrors "by the advantage of ensuring for future generations enlightenment, virtues, happiness."[62] This is unjust in relation to Condorcet's own Revolutionary life (of which John Morley wrote that he "faced the storm with a heroism of spirit that has never been surpassed").[63] But the milder question, of whether the utopian ignores his beliefs or predictions in his present politics, is still troublesome; the question, that is to say, of the role of universalist beliefs in political life.

This difficulty—of individual consistency, or of the relationship between one's beliefs and the way one lives one's life—was a subject of intense discussion before the Revolution, and it provides some insight into Condorcet's dilemma. Condorcet's most prolific writing was as a eulogist and biographer, and he had a continuing interest in the idea of "a life." His *Vie de Voltaire* was an effort, mostly unsuccessful, to defend Voltaire against the charge of political insincerity.[64] His *Vie de Turgot* was the history of a good political life; in John Stuart Mill's description, "one of the wisest and noblest of lives, delineated by one of the wisest and noblest of men."[65]

The difficulty for Condorcet, as for Turgot, was to believe in the universality of at least some political truths, and at the same time to esteem the different, conflicting beliefs of others. The contraposition in modern political philosophy of universalism and what might be called "conflictism"—the view that conflict is an essential constituent of moral and political life—was not a characteristic of eighteenth-century thought.[66] But Condorcet was clearly something close to a universalist in Berlin's (and A. O. Lovejoy's) sense. He believed all men and women to possess in common certain uniform, constant characteristics; he thought that these characteristics were of political importance, and that they pointed, in particular, to the prospect of legislation which would be just for all individuals, and in all societies.[67]

It is this universalism which seems to be in conflict with Condorcet's politics, or with the way in which he led his political life. Condorcet was quite familiar, in his philosophical writings, with the difficulties of reconciling one's opinions and one's way of life. He wrote in the *Esquisse*—in his project of a history of ancient philosophy—that the skeptics, who believed that "one should doubt even the necessity of doubting everything," were refuted only by their own actions: "If they were fairly solidly refuted by the instinct of other men, by the instinct which they themselves were directed by in the conduct of their lives, they were never well understood, or well refuted by philosophers." The conduct of one's life, for Condorcet, as a Humean and an opponent of determinism, is the sort of thing that can stand in the relation of refutation to philosophical opinions.[68]

Condorcet's problem of political consistency can be seen as the obverse of the skeptic's, and also as a variant of it. It is known to be difficult for the skeptic to live his skepticism; the problem for Condorcet, as a timid universalist, was of how not to live his universalism. The skeptic, for whom his own impressions (or political principles) are no more plausible than the impressions (or principles) of anyone else, retreats into a denial of himself.

"So thoroughgoing a detachment from oneself is not easy to understand," as Myles Burnyeat says, and indeed constitutes the "ultimate incoherence of the skeptic philosophy."[69] Condorcet's problem was to be a dogmatist—to believe, at least, in the universal truth of his own political principles—without living his dogmatism. The thoroughgoing universalist is so attached to his own principles that he wishes to impose them (to impose himself) on the world. This is something that Condorcet could not bring himself to do; it is not a way in which he could conduct his life. For the universal truth in which he believed was a truth about respect for rights. His dogma, that is to say, was that one should never impose one's dogmas on other people.[70]

The prospect for the pluralist of values, in Bernard Williams's description, is to end up "as a rueful spectator of political change," induced by his theory of values into an inaction which he dislikes (and which may even impinge on his claim to have political principles).[71] The prospect for the universalist, which is more sinister, is to be induced by his belief in eternal political truth into overaction, into Bonald's immolation of the present. Condorcet, with his conception of the life of a public and private man, was intensely conscious of this peril. He is here, too, an interstitial figure: someone who was still (like Voltaire) a part of the old régime of a public life written in letters to foreign sovereigns, and incipiently (like Turgot, or like Goethe) part of the new world in which one's life is something to be constructed, something consistent and sincere, in the light of political and public opinion. Sainte-Beuve was not unjust when he said of Condorcet that he believed he held the key to the happiness of men. Condorcet's difficulty, thereby, was to hold the key in his hands and not to use it (or to use it only meekly). In Havel's (and Berlin's) metaphor of the puzzle, it was to know the correct solution and not to write it in, on present institutions conceived as a blank political page.

One of Robespierre's most frightening speeches, in 1794, was a denunciation of men of indecision, and in particular of Condorcet, the timid conspirator; of men who hesitate, even, between Epicurus and Zeno. The duty of society, for Robespierre, was to create, as its "chef d'oeuvre," "a rapid instinct which, without the belated support of reason," will determine the moral behavior of ignorant men.[72] Robespierre was strikingly close to Burke, here: to the little ode to prejudice, in Burke's *Reflections on the Revolution in France,* as a condition which "does not leave the man hesitating in the moment of decision, sceptical, puzzled, and unresolved." He was close, too, to Bonald: to Bonald's strictures against the governments of Europe for ignoring their duty in respect of "the morality of society" or "the direction of men."[73] These were Condorcet's enemies, during and after the Revolution. His own universal principle was to oppose the official principles of society, and to promote doubt and irresolution. It was not a particularly coherent position, but it was not ignoble either.

DOMESTIC VIRTUES

Condorcet's universalism was founded, thirdly, in a quite modest conception of moral uniformity. All men and women are in some minimal sense the same, and this is why truth and justice are the same for everyone. They have equal and individual rights, and "we call these rights *natural*, because they derive from the nature of man."[74] These were familiar thoughts in the 1780s. But Condorcet was idiosyncratic in the extent to which he identifies the nature of man with moral sentiments and moral reflection. He set a view of universal sentiments which is close to Hume's, or Smith's, in the politics of constitutional rights. In his pamphlet on women's political rights, he wrote that "the rights of men follow uniquely from the fact that they are feeling beings, susceptible of acquiring moral ideas, and of reasoning about these ideas. Thus women, who have these same qualities, necessarily have equal rights. Either no individual of the human species has true rights, or all have the same."[75] The order of qualities, in this definition, is notable: the definition proceeds from sentiments, to the subsequent acquisition of moral ideas (especially by children), and then to reasoning about the ideas.[76]

It is the universality of simple moral sentiments, on this account, which is the foundation of natural uniformity. Everyone, in Condorcet's view— women and men, slaves and masters, children and parents, foreigners and citizens—has experienced similar, simple sentiments of pity and affection. The sentiments he describes in his work on instruction, and in his criticism of early utilitarianism—the sensibility of young children, their propensity "to reflect on their sentiments," the "domestic virtues" which are suited to all men and their influence on "particular relationships"—were of central importance to his view of human nature. He said that "justness is, of all qualities, the one which has most influence on the details of conduct, and the one which nature has distributed most universally and most equally."[77] Domestic inequality was especially insidious: "Equality is everywhere, but above all within families, the prime element of happiness, peace, and virtue."[78]

Condorcet's conception of moral sentiments, like Turgot's, was strongly influenced by Scottish moral philosophy, and especially by Adam Smith. It was a view of sentiments, and not of sensations.[79] His correspondence with Turgot about Helvétius and the prospect of utilitarian novels was very much in Smith's spirit; Victor Cousin said of the passages quoted earlier, about novels and tragedies, that they "could be considered as a resumé of the entire moral philosophy of Hutcheson and Smith."[80] The idea of the universal distribution of moral qualities was considerably older: Zeus is said in Plato's *Protagoras* to have instructed Hermes to deal out justice and shame equally to all, and Protagoras comments to Socrates that everyone who is human must have some sense of justice.[81]

What is striking, in Condorcet's conception, is that he takes these simple and domestic sentiments as the foundation of a theory of justice.[82] The propensity to moral reflection is what all individuals have in common. But it is also the basis on which they make political judgments. Moral conceptions extend outward, as it were, from sentiments to reasons, and from the family to the universe. Condorcet's idea seems to have been that children tend to experience moral sentiments as soon as they form the "distinct idea of an individual," and that these feelings of sympathy—of imagining what it is like to be someone else—lead them to recognize and be distressed by the oppression of other individuals. Their feelings of pity can be distorted by a bad upbringing and cruel customs. But the recognition of others as being like oneself, as people with whom one has "moral relations," is the core of a universal sense of justice.[83]

This core sense of justice is the basis for one's judgments of other societies. Condorcet, like Turgot, wanted to find some universal political truth: some sense in which it was reasonable to say, even of practices which have the excuse of "the invincible error of a universal custom" (like slavery at the time of Epaminondas), that they are wrong. He wanted to be able to deny "that every law which is made by a legitimate power is just," even when the power is democratic: "What? When the people of Athens passed a law which decreed the death penalty for those who broke statues of Mercury, can such a law be just?"[84] His suggestion seems to have been that this universal truth is founded on pity and fellow feeling. One should judge a political figure—the emperor Theodosius, for example, or Aureng-Zeb—not for his opinions (which are those of his times) but for his moral character: "on the basis of his character, and, if one may put it this way, of his moral constitution."[85]

It is interesting that Condorcet's inspiration, here, seems to be Epicurus. Epicurus imagined a world without gods, Condorcet wrote in the *Esquisse,* and a morality without religion. (His gods, Condorcet says, were "indifferent to the actions of men, strangers to the order of the universe"; "in some sense an hors d'oeuvre of this system.")[86] But Epicurus also imagined what it is that is to take the place of religion, and what was to be the foundation of Condorcet's own system. "It is in the moral constitution of man that one must seek the basis of his duties, and the origin of his ideas of justice and of virtue," Condorcet wrote; this is a "truth from which the Epicurean sect was less remote than any other."[87]

Condorcet's universal political truths—or the values which do not conflict—are on this interpretation quite minimal. The requirement of justice is to recognize the rights of other individuals; to treat them as though they were people with whom one has moral relations. Condorcet's idyll, in the *Esquisse,* was of universal domesticity. He had in fact been talking, just before his famous comment on indefinite perfectibility, about increased understanding of "moral sentiments" and "our moral constitution," and about the "habit of reflecting on one's own conduct." If one is respectful of the people around one, then one will be more likely to respect the rights of others. Condorcet went on, immediately, to look forward to "the entire destruction of the prejudices which have established an inequality of rights between the two sexes, fatal even to the one whom it favors." Such a change would promote "the domestic virtues, which are the first foundation of all others," and should thereby remove a fertile source of "injustices, cruelties, and crimes." The private virtues, Condorcet had written in his *Vie de Turgot,* are incompatible with domestic slavery and with the "barbaric contempt for foreign nations"; "national hatreds" will eventually disappear, he said in the *Esquisse,* with the progress of domestic enlightenment.[88]

Sainte-Beuve mocked Condorcet for his "credulity" in believing in the equal, universal distribution of "justness of spirit," and the *Esquisse* is a deeply credulous book.[89] It is as though Condorcet had given himself up, hidden from the Terror in his room in the rue Servandoni, to a suspension of skepticism or disbelief. He believed that simple moral sentiments are what all men and women have (or have once had) in common. They are the foundation of virtue. They are also the foundation of rights, and thereby of justice and liberty. This is a utopian conception. But it is not thereby false, and it is not a sinister utopia.

THE IMAGINARY ENLIGHTENMENT

Condorcet's principles, in these writings, are strikingly different from the cold, unfeeling, all-summing "mechanical philosophy" which is supposed to be characteristic of the French enlightenment. The French scholar Max Rouché wrote of Herder that his political originality consisted in serving "simultaneously as a precursor of the Revolution and of the counter-Revolution," and Condorcet can be seen as a visionary of the enlightenment and also of the counter-enlightenment.[90] Herder's conquest of the enlightenment, Ernst Cassirer wrote, was a true "self-conquest," or a defeat which is really a victory.[91] Condorcet's victories and defeats, too, are within and of the enlightenment.

Condorcet was horrified, like Herder, that society should be seen as a huge "machine," that people are "docile instruments," that their opinions should be determined by the "uniform" they wear.[92] Like Schiller, he rejected the happiness that is imposed by despots: "The crown has its own conceptions / Of what a human's happiness should be."[93] Like Hölderlin, he saw the most insidious oppression in the virtuous state, or the state as a "school of morality."[94] Like Kant in *What is Enlightenment?* he imagined a dire world in which men and women will be eternally children, while others "think for them"; like Kant in the "Contest of Faculties," he set the rights of men "above all price (of utility)," including the happiness which is bestowed by government, as though by a kind master to his "docile sheep."[95]

There is something oddly similar to ideas that are thought to be idiosyncratically German, in fact, in Condorcet's descriptions of individual freedom. For Bonald (and for Sainte-Beuve), the *Esquisse* was the monstrous apogee of enlightenment thought, of a French philosophy which since the middle of the eighteenth century had been marching, inexorably, toward the Jacobin Terror. The writings with which we have been concerned suggest, instead, that Condorcet should be seen as an early figure in the liberal criticism of deterministic and utilitarian ideas. If there are two sides in the great intellectual divisions of the 1790s—the French enlightenment versus its critics, or uniformity versus diversity, or scientific knowledge versus the expression of sentiments—then he belongs, in some sense, to both.

Condorcet's work suggests, indeed, that the frontier between the two sides is quite difficult to find. Condorcet's "German-ness" is little more than the reflection of common sources (including Smith, Hume, and Rousseau), and common opponents. One of Turgot's more improbable works, in this cosmopolitan time, was a long study of the "character of German prosody," with particular reference to Klopstock's use of spondees and trochees.[96] Condorcet's objects of obloquy are also Herder's and Kant's: Helvétius, for example; or Quesnay, as in Kant's "Transcendental *Physiocracy*."[97] But this common discourse is itself of philosophical interest. Condorcet, the quasi-Scottish theorist of domestic emotions, and the quasi-German theorist of the sovereign individual, turns out to be a disruptive figure in the orderly division of eighteenth-century intellectual territory.[98] Leopardi spoke in one of his satires of French civilization of the "common voices" of European philosophy at the beginning of the nineteenth century: "a sort of little language, or a strictly universal vocabulary," in which people can speak of "things which belong to an intimate universal nature," in "Europeanisms" such as "despotism," or "sentimental," or "analysis."[99] There were common European voices of critical enlightenment before the Revolution as well; voices, like Condorcet's or Kant's, for whom the intimate universal nature is to be protected, above all, against the virtuous, calculating, and happiness-dispensing state.

The frontier in time is even more elusive. The object of the leaders of the French Revolution, in Tocqueville's famous phrase, was to "cut in two their destiny," or to separate "by an abyss" what they were to become from what they once had been.[100] It is difficult, under these circumstances, to see the continuity between the old and the new. But it is also difficult to see lesser abysses: discontinuities within the enlightenment and before the Revolution. Condorcet's own place, on the basis of the works we have been considering, is as a dissident philosophe. Like Turgot, in Tocqueville's description, he is a philosopher and economist with a "taste for political freedoms."[101] Like Diderot, he is a encyclopedist who is interested in emotions.[102] But his work suggests a more general point as well, about the sect of enlightenment and its political heritage.

Tocqueville's hypothesis is that the truly revolutionary transformation of eighteenth-century France took place between the 1750s and the mid-1770s. It was in that period that the sentiments, opinions, and ideas of millions of people in France were transformed, in part by the theories of men of letters, the "principal politicians of the time."[103] It was then, too, that the reorganization of French government—in the first, administrative revolution, and under the posthumous influence of Quesnay—established the basis for the all-controlling and all-transforming modern state.[104] "Tocqueville introduces doubt at the most profound level: and what if there was no more, in this language of discontinuity, than the illusion of change?" François Furet writes. The Revolution was a transformation, above all, in values and sentiments; it was made possible by the centralization of the French state, and "everything begins around 1750."[105]

Tocqueville's thesis—his journey into the tomb of the France which is no more—is a work of prodigious historical intuition. But it suggests a rather obvious question, of what happened to the ideas of the philosophes between 1776 and 1789. One answer—Bonald's, or Burke's, or Sainte-Beuve's—is that the ideas were simply produced on a larger scale. This is consistent, for example, with the conception of Condorcet's *Esquisse* as the final production of philosophical rationalism. The historian Cochin uses a more subtle metaphor; the decades before the Revolution were a period of "incubation," in which ideas of destructive individualism were nurtured in hundreds of clubs and societies.[106] (For Tocqueville himself, the ideas were already quite well disseminated in the middle of the century, to the point where they had inflamed "even the imagination of women and peasants.")[107]

Condorcet's difficulties suggest a different answer, which is also obvious. It is that ideas about enlightenment in fact changed in very important respects in France in the period before the Revolution, and that these changes (in what Condorcet called the "disposition of minds") were a response, in part, to the events of the first revolution. The counter-Revolutionary criticism of the Économistes, of cold utilitarian calculation, of the virtuous and education-dispensing state, is present, that is to say, within the enlightenment itself. Condorcet was a critic of Helvétius and Quesnay, even of his much-admired Voltaire, well before their secular apotheosis in the Revolution.[108] The abyss of the early 1790s hides what came before, or the extent to which the origins of revolutionary (and socialist) ideas are to be found in the ancien régime; this is Tocqueville's thesis.[109] But it also hides what came after, or the extent to which the origins of nineteenth-century liberal ideas are to be found in the French enlightenment, and especially in the enlightenment critique—including Condorcet's critique—of the enlightened despotism of the 1760s.[110]

THE LIBERTY OF THOUGHT AND DISCUSSION

The great early nineteenth-century liberals are themselves witnesses for this interpretation. Constant, as has been seen, invoked Condorcet as the source of the distinction between ancient and modern freedom. In his first major political works, of 1797, he defended Condorcet repeatedly against the opponents of the Republic, indulgent of the principles of the Terror, who used the "memory of Robespierre" to insult the shades of Condorcet and Vergniaud: "Eternal contempt to whoever does not respect these names, dear to enlightenment."[111] There are "certain positive and un-changeable principles," Constant said, which are "true in all climates," are "uncontestable," and "can never vary"; they are the principles which iden-tify the "fundamental rights of individuals."[112] Constant used words which are close to Condorcet's, again, in his famous challenge to the happiness-producing state: "Let it limit itself to being just; we will take it upon our-selves to be happy."[113]

Tocqueville himself, in his criticism of the first, philosophical revolu-tionaries of the 1760s, sounds at times strikingly like Condorcet. The Économistes were favorable to the free exchange of commodities, without favoring political freedom, he wrote; for Condorcet, as has been seen, they forgot the interests of political freedom for those of freedom of com-merce.[114] Diversity itself was odious to them, Tocqueville said, and they set "public utility" in the place of "private rights"; for Condorcet, public util-ity must cede before the private rights of individuals. Tocqueville was horrified, like Condorcet, by the aspiration of the state to "form the spirit of citizens," and by the depiction of a "mechanical regularity" in the acts of individual citizens. He contrasted the "benefits" of freedom and "the pleasure of being able to speak, act, breathe without constraint"; Condor-cet had distinguished, as early as 1776, between "the advantages of free-dom" and "the pleasure which one feels in being free."[115]

John Stuart Mill, too, spoke in Condorcet's words when he said that the truth must not abide in the mind "as a prejudice," or that the "liberty of thought and discussion" requires instruction in conflicts of opinion ("if opponents of all-important truths do not exist, it is indispensable to imagine them"); when he said that "all attempts by the State to bias the conclusions of its citizens on disputed subjects are evil." In the famous peroration of *On Liberty,* he spoke, as Condorcet did, of men as docile in-struments: of the "State which dwarfs its men, in order that they may be more docile instruments in its hands."[116]

Mill told John Morley "that in his younger days, when he was inclined to fall into low spirits, he turned to Condorcet's life of Turgot; it infallibly restored his possession of himself."[117] Morley's own conclusion, in 1870, was to identify Condorcet clearly as a visionary of liberal individualism. Condorcet would have been most profoundly opposed, he said, to "any final and settled and universally accepted solution of belief and order."

The main political distinction which he drew, in fact, was between Condorcet on the one hand, and "De Maistre and Comte" on the other, with their "organised and systematic reconstruction" of society. Condorcet's conception of future perfection was entirely different; in Morley's words, a "religious scrupulosity, which made him abhor all interference with the freedom and openness of the understanding as the worst kind of sacrilege, was Condorcet's eminent distinction."[118]

Condorcet is often defensive, in his political writings; he responds to events, and to the ideas of the early opponents of enlightenment ideas. He defends Turgot, in the 1770s, against the criticism of having sought to impose cold, abstract principles of political economy; he looks, in the 1780s, for defensible uses of mathematical methods in the social sciences (in the theory of voting and constitutions); he defends the freedom of instruction and understanding, in the 1790s, against Marat and Robespierre. His writings are thereby a mirror of prodigiously turbulent times. But they are a mirror, too, of the continuity of enlightenment ideas before and after the Revolution.

"Her political sentiments were very different from mine; she belonged, with passion and *all the same,* to the eighteenth century and to the Revolution," Guizot wrote of Sophie Condorcet, in whose house he lived when he retired into opposition in 1820; she was also, he adds, a person of high and generous character.[119] The project of discontinuity which Tocqueville described in the men and women of the Revolution—the effort to cut time in two—was a project, of a different sort, for the liberals of the nineteenth century. They too wished to divide their destiny from what had come before; to show, like Guizot, that the political sentiments of the eighteenth century were very different from their own. This was a counsel of evident prudence. The French Revolution (and the "Bankrupt Century") had furnished a boundless supply of "appalling parallels," John Morley observed in 1888; having written about Voltaire and Turgot, he found that even his views of the Disestablishment of the Welsh Church were subject to the criticism of French influence, or of tending "to the disintegration of comprehensive political organisations."[120] Yet this Victorian sense of a dissected destiny, this ordering of sentiments by centuries, is itself the setting, still, for the recollection of the eighteenth century.

Sainte-Beuve, Condorcet's nemesis, wrote of the French philologist (and collector of Serbian folk songs) Claude Fauriel that he represented "the eighteenth century turning itself naturally into the nineteenth." In the period of discontinuity of "these two intellectual régimes," Sainte-

Beuve said, Fauriel epitomized in a "peaceful, silent progression," the "interior work" by which the end of one era was transposed into the origin of the other. He was one of the "hidden intermediaries," in whom "two epochs, divorced and ruptured on the surface, cling to each other as though by the entrails."[121] My suggestion has been that Condorcet, too, is an intermediate figure, the intersection of two universes of thought. Fauriel, the private secretary of Fouché at the Ministry of Police, the companion of Sophie Condorcet for twenty years until her death in 1822, the friend of Schlegel and Manzoni, is no more than a minor, mildly sinister passer-by. Condorcet's interior choices—his conception, above all, of the endless freedom of discussion—are part of the origin of all subsequent liberal thought.

8

A Fatherless World

A DIFFERENT ENLIGHTENMENT

The disposition of enlightenment, in Condorcet's description, is a discursive, disorderly condition. It is a characteristic of individuals who are skeptical, puzzled, and unresolved; who have long conversations with their children; who are disposed to reflect on their own sentiments and their own conduct. Their lives are somber. Condorcet's prospect, in the "fragment" of the Tenth Epoch of his *Esquisse d'un tableau historique des progrès de l'esprit humain,* in which he looks forward to an eternity of civilized competition, is of a normal condition in which men and women are happy, in the midst of "pain, need, and loss."[1] But life is not without its mild, reflective pleasures. Like Hume, Condorcet sees introspection as the most agreeable of domestic activities. What can compare, Hume asks in the *Enquiry concerning Morals,* with "the unbought satisfaction of conversation, society, study, even health and the common beauties of nature, but above all the peaceful reflection on one's own conduct?"[2]

The economic thought which has been the subject of this book is part of political (or philosophical) thought, and the economic life which it depicts is part of political, emotional, and moral life. John Stuart Mill, in his essay of 1836 on the definition of political economy, used the image of the "wall of a city," constructed in the "more advanced stage of the progress of knowledge" around the territory or the settlements of economic life. Political economy, in his description, had in the nineteenth century become a science with its own territory, its own definition, and its own method of investigation.[3] The concern of this book, by contrast, has been with an earlier and less bounded scene, in which the territory of economic life extends in all directions. It is within this panorama that I have tried to depict a different political economy (a political economy less concerned with utility, with uniformity, with universal commercial interest), and a different enlightenment. I have looked, like Adam Smith in the *Philoctetes* of Sophocles, for a "romantic wildness."[4]

Eighteenth-century political thought, as it is expressed in Smith's and Condorcet's economic writings, is concerned with individual diversity, with conflicts of interest and conflicts between different principles, with vexation, with history, with personal and public oppression. The economic disputes of the 1770s and 1780s were the occasion, as has been suggested, for important changes within the thought of the French enlightenment (of the "sect" of enlightenment, in the most restricted sense). Diderot's and Galiani's criticism of the Economists or Physiocrats for the "smiling colors" of their imagined universe, Condorcet's criticism of the Economists for forgetting political freedom, Turgot's criticism of their "laws of order" and their "tutelary authority," Smith's criticism of their "exact regimen," Condorcet's criticism of Necker's efforts to sum the quantity of happiness, Turgot's criticism of Helvétius for disregarding remorse, friendship, and the taste for novels; all these, it has been suggested, were the expressions of a different, more liberal, and more romantic enlightenment. Smith, Carl Menger wrote, was the Aristotle to Quesnay's Plato; he was "a splendid speculative thinker," and he was in addition "an indefatigable observer [who] had given his system a broad supporting basis of knowledge based on experience and had tried to establish his philosophical theses by an all-round consideration of actual data."[5]

The idyll of economic enlightenment is itself, in these circumstances, an inexact and uncertain condition. It has lost the determined orderliness of exact regimens, or of laws of order. Its uncertainty is in turn closely intertwined with the elusive condition of the disposition of enlightenment. One of the shortcomings of the liberal economic order, as has been seen, is that individuals seek to pursue their own economic interests by political means. They seek regulation, political influence, and protected monopoly; they buy power with money, and money with power. They also pursue their interests by what Condorcet described as "illegitimate means."[6] They use the ruses of fraud, and the ruthlessness of force. They cannot be relied on to act always, or even usually, as prudent and well-informed judges of their own interests. They do not reflect enough on their own conduct; they are not the sort of enlightened individuals in whose lives the system of free competition is secure.

The other shortcoming of the liberal order—which is its inconstancy— is also a matter of enlightenment. Condorcet's continuing political preoccupation, as has been seen, is with the conditions for civilized conflict. He imagines elaborate constitutional procedures for conducting disputes over everything from property rights in ponds to the future constitution of representative government. But these procedures, too, are insecure if too many individuals are frightened, or mutilated by ignorance, or dependent on powerful neighbors. They are insecure if the individuals who constitute the political society are themselves insecure.

The disposition of enlightenment, or the mildness of the human spirit and the improvement of the human mind, is thereby the condition of political security. Condorcet's indissoluble chain, which links together truth, happiness, and virtue, is a version of an older idyll, described in Hume's essay of 1752, "Of Luxury." Education and industry, Hume says, are "favourable to human happiness," and favorable, too, to intellectual development, as "profound ignorance is totally banished." There are advantages for political society, as people become more free of "superstition, which throws the government off its bias," and as "knowledge in the arts of government naturally begets mildness and moderation." People become more sociable, they have more conversations; "both sexes meet in an easy and sociable manner," and "it is impossible but they must feel an increase of humanity, from the very habit of conversing together, and contributing to each other's pleasure and entertainment. Thus industry, knowledge, and humanity are linked together by an indissoluble chain."[7]

There is a related, and more insidious shortcoming of the liberal orders. It is that they do not contain within themselves the sources of their own improved orderliness. They require the disposition of enlightenment, and there is very little that they can do to invoke it. Like sovereigns, in Hume's description in his essay "Of Commerce," the men and women of the new political society "must take mankind as they find them, and cannot pretend to introduce any violent change in their principles and ways of thinking. A long course of time, with a variety of accidents and circumstances, are requisite to produce those great revolutions, which so much diversify the face of human affairs."[8] Even the lawlike regularities of political economy, or of political science, are subject to endless doubt and endless discussion; they are theories of people with theories. The liberal orders can provide for public instruction, including, as Smith imagined, for instruction in "thought and speculation," and in the condition of being "more disposed to examine, and more capable of seeing through" political projects.[9] They cannot, without ceasing to be liberal, or without becoming Robespierre's sort of order more than Condorcet's, educate people to be enlightened. Like Hume, in "Of Luxury," Condorcet and Smith have very

little interest in a "miraculous transformation of mankind, as would en-
dow them with every species of virtue, and free them from every species of
vice; this concerns not the magistrate, who aims only at possibilities."[10]

SMITH AND CONDORCET

The two figures with whom this book has been principally concerned,
Smith and Condorcet, are in a number of respects profoundly dissimilar.
They are different, above all, in their own dispositions or constitutions.
Condorcet, as has been seen, was disposed to be credulous, especially in
his *Esquisse des progrès.* Credulity, for Smith, is a shortcoming of young
children, "and it requires long and much experience of the falsehood of
mankind to reduce them to a reasonable degree of diffidence and distrust
. . . The natural disposition is always to believe. It is acquired wisdom
and experience only that teach incredulity, and they very seldom teach it
enough."[11] Condorcet was impetuous; he was disposed to rashness, and to
volcanic tempests. He wrote fairly often, including in his polemics of
the 1770s in favor of freedom of commerce, in a tone of sustained and
haphazard indignation. Smith was, by contrast, extraordinarily cautious
and circumspect. The writings he published during his lifetime are replete
with qualifications ("it seems," "frequently," "no doubt"); Dugald Stewart speaks of "those qualified conclusions that we admire in his writings."
Smith's strictures with respect to bellicose tradesmen, Stewart says, "are
expressed in a tone of indignation, which he seldom assumes in his political writings."[12]

Smith's and Condorcet's experiences of the world were also profoundly
different. Smith lived for much of his life in the deepest retirement, mostly
in the small seaside town of Kirkcaldy. His experience of public or political
life consisted of a single extended journey to France and Switzerland in
1764–1766—which provided a great deal of the material for the *Wealth of
Nations*—and of a period, at the end of his life, as one of George III's
commissioners of customs in Edinburgh.[13] Condorcet, while he left Paris
only infrequently, lived for more than a quarter of a century at or close to
the center of French (and European) politics. He was deeply engaged in
the events of the French Revolution, as an elected politician, a daily parliamentary reporter (for the *Chronique de Paris*), a member of government
commissions (on the rights of Jews, the decimalization of weights and
measures, the reform of the currency, the organization of public instruction), and, eventually, as a victim of Robespierre's Terror.[14]

Smith died in Edinburgh in July 1790, just a year after the fall of the

Bastille, and there is very little evidence, as was seen in Chapter 2, as to his view of French events. He seems to have owned four of Condorcet's pamphlets on constitutional reform, written as late as September 1789; the paragraphs in his last additions to the *Theory of Moral Sentiments,* prepared for publication in the winter of 1789–90, which have been interpreted as an indirect commentary on French politics, take the entirely characteristic form of a commentary on conflicts of values. There are two different principles of public life, Smith says, which consist in "a certain respect and reverence" for established institutions, and in a desire to improve "the welfare of the whole society"; "in times of public discontent, faction, and disorder, those two different principles may draw different ways."[15] Condorcet, who survived Smith by less than four years, lived during that period through a lifetime of political disorder. The most powerful of his political writings, about individual rights, about public instruction, and about the freedom of thought and discussion, reflect an explicit and poignant response to the destruction of Revolutionary principles under the despotism of 1791–1793.

In several matters of economic policy, Smith and Condorcet, confronted with similar questions, provided different answers. Fiscal reform was one such matter, and Condorcet's only serious criticism of Smith was over his support in the *Wealth of Nations* for the indirect taxation (on carriages and other luxuries) which Condorcet, Turgot, and Dupont de Nemours regarded as a purgatory of vexation.[16] Smith was in general far less impetuous than Condorcet with respect to commercial, fiscal, and legal reform. Like Condorcet, Smith regarded Turgot and his reform edicts of 1776 with veneration.[17] But he was skeptical of many projects of institutional reform, especially toward the end of his life. The competition to invent a new, simple legal form for the transfer of property rights established in the 1780s by Joseph Windisch-Grätz—the Austrian count who translated *Aufklärung* as "populorum cultura"—provides a good illustration. Condorcet was an enthusiastic supporter of the project, which combined the late eighteenth-century passions for universal (or at least for European) reform, for rational jurisprudence, for the security of property rights, and for literary competitions. Smith's eventual suggestion, after a protracted and inconclusive correspondence, was that Windisch-Grätz should confine his efforts to improving the "style books" used by lawyers in various countries, and in Austria in particular: "These collections, which are the produce of the wisdom and experience of many successive generations, I believe to be, with all their faults (and the best that I have seen are not without many faults) much more perfect than anything which, either any single man or any single Society of men are capable of inventing."[18]

UNCERTAINTY AND IRRESOLUTION

There are other respects in which Smith's and Condorcet's economic and philosophical thought is far more similar; they have been the principal subject of this book. The most evident of these similar inquiries—these similar ways of thinking—has to do with the freedom of commerce. Freedom in one's economic life is an end in itself, for Smith as for Condorcet. It may well be good as a means to the end of increasing general (or individual) welfare; it is also good in itself. "It is but equity, besides," as Smith said of the liberal reward of labor which is the consequence of freedom from regulation of the price of work.[19] Or as Condorcet said, more portentously, in his *Vie de M. Turgot*, "there is a more noble justification for the freedom of commerce than its utility, however extensive that may be."[20] Economic life is difficult or impossible to distinguish from the rest of life, and one's freedom to buy or sell or lend or travel or work is difficult to distinguish from the rest of one's freedom. Smith's and Condorcet's descriptions of interference with the freedom of commerce are sometimes extraordinarily concrete. The laborer or the artisan wishes to carry something along a certain road, and he finds it blocked by subaltern officials; he wishes to enter a certain room, and he finds it closed to him, because he is not a member of a certain guild; he wishes to live in a certain village, and he is seized by the servants of churchwardens and removed to the village in which he was born; he wishes to live quietly in his own home, and the servants of customs and excise officers enter to search his house.

Smith, like Condorcet, refers frequently to "freedom of trade," "liberty of trade," "natural liberty." But the distinctness of "economic freedom"— the sense in which there is a special, innocuous kind of freedom, a freedom which, in the words of the friends of Coleridge's shipowner, was "necessary to the prosperity of Trade and Commerce, a *necessary Evil* in the process of moneygetting"—was an innovation of the 1790s, as was seen in Chapter 2.[21] So too was the abstractness of economic freedom; its distinctness from all the concrete details of political and personal oppression. Both Smith and Condorcet were exceptional, even in the setting of the pre-Revolutionary world, in their preoccupation with the personal details of freedom of commerce. There is very little about the sentiments of brewers and seamstresses in the writings of Quesnay, for example, or of

Dupont de Nemours. In the later setting of the post-Revolutionary reconstruction, Smith's and Condorcet's sense of freedom was seen as confusing, and subversive. Condorcet's writings on the freedom of commerce were of virtually no interest in the period of Say's or George Pryme's redefinition of political economy as the "science concerned with wealth"; Smith was seen as the last theorist of an earlier, confused time, in which it was not yet understood that the scientific principles of political economy were "applicable alike to a despotism and to a democracy."[22]

The second preoccupation which is common to Smith and to Condorcet is with economic sentiments. Economic life is full of vexations, of visitations, of the concrete details of oppression. It is also full of emotions. Individuals decide to become common sailors, in Smith's description, because they are disposed to like adventure, and because they are influenced by the sight of the ships and the conversation of seaport towns: "The distant prospect of hazards . . . is not disagreeable to us." Dealers in malt and hops dislike "trouble, vexation, and oppression," and "though vexation is not, strictly speaking, expence, it is certainly equivalent to the expence at which every man would be willing to redeem himself from it."[23] Condorcet, writing to Necker in the pseudonymous person of a laborer of Picardy, says that the obligation to make declarations to a judicial tribunal about the destination of one's corn "will be enough to make one disgusted with this commerce." "Do you think we will risk [our] savings," he asks, in order to be "exposed to having quarrels with the petty officials of your legislation, to be held to ransom by your secret agents?"[24] The popular odium attached to corn dealers, in both Condorcet's and Smith's description, is such as to attract only men without "character," or for whom the prospect of public dislike is only a modest disincentive.[25]

Smith's system of moral sentiments exercised a profound influence on Condorcet's moral thought, both in his early exchanges with Turgot about Helvétius, and, most directly, in his last writings of the 1790s about public instruction and the future society of the "Tenth Epoch." As the nineteenth-century scholar Mathurin Gillet wrote, in a study of Condorcet's "utopia," Condorcet "is the servile disciple of no master, although his inclination of preference is to the sentimentalism of Adam Smith."[26] Economic relationships, like moral relationships, are for Condorcet suffused with sentiments. The essential disposition of moral life, for Condorcet as for Smith, is to think oneself into the feelings of other people; to feel sympathy. This is similar, in its reflexiveness, to the disposition of economic life. To think about economic decisions is to think about how other people think.

All individuals (the philosopher and the street porter, the philosopher and the common sailor) have much the same universal disposition, in Smith's and Condorcet's relentless evocation of natural equality. The way to understand the decisions of individuals in their economic lives, of dealers in malt and proprietors of ponds, of seamstresses and flower sellers, is to think of them as people like ourselves; to think oneself into their lives. Smith "introduced into his theory of the motives to exertion and sacrifice various desires and sentiments besides those which have wealth for their object," T. E. Cliffe Leslie wrote in 1879, and he examined their operation in "many of the ordinary employments of life . . . the butcher's, the jeweller's, the soldier's, the sailor's, the barrister's, the author's." Smith's examination was based on observation, and it was unjust, Cliffe Leslie concluded, to charge him with "evolving from his own consciousness the circumstances and motives that diversify the employments of a nation."[27] But to think of others as though their consciousness were like our own, or as though our sentiments were the reflection of theirs, was also a question of justice, for Smith, as for Condorcet; a question of sympathy.

A third preoccupation which is similar in Smith's thought and in Condorcet's has to do with public instruction and public enlightenment. Smith's denunciation of civilized society, in the chapter on public instruction in the *Wealth of Nations,* is a description of the process by which the division of labor tends, unless prevented by a system of public instruction, to bring about an epidemic of "gross ignorance and stupidity." The individual "whose whole life is spent in performing a few simple operations" cannot exert his understanding, or use his intellectual faculties, and he is thereby "mutilated and deformed." He has the capability of understanding, which is universal, and it is torn from him: "The torpor of his mind renders him, not only incapable of relishing or bearing a part in any rational conversation, but of conceiving any generous, noble, or tender sentiment, and consequently of forming any just judgment concerning many even of the ordinary duties of private life. Of the great and extensive interests of his country, he is altogether incapable of judging."[28]

Condorcet refers to Smith in his first proposal for "a true public instruction," shortly before the Revolution; he concludes that universal public instruction is the "only effective remedy" for the ills of modern commercial societies.[29] In his memoirs on public instruction of 1791–92, he again invokes Smith: "Instruction is the only remedy for this ill . . . The laws proclaim an equality of rights, and only institutions for public instruction can make this equality real."[30] Universal instruction was identified, for much of the eighteenth century, as a source of economic prosperity. The advice of Mentor or Minerva, in Fénelon's *Télémaque*, much like Quesnay's advice to Louis XV, is that the sovereign should "establish public schools, to teach fear of the gods, love of country, respect for the laws," and should also ensure that young men are trained to be good carpenters or oarsmen, "industrious, patient, hardworking, clean, sober, and cautious."[31] But Smith's view of education, like Condorcet's, was strikingly different. Public instruction, like the freedom of commerce, is an end in itself, as much as or more than it is a means to the end of national (or individual) prosperity.

All children, in Smith's description at the outset of the *Wealth of Nations*, have the capability to become philosophers; the difference between philosophers and porters is a matter of habit, custom, and education rather than of genius and disposition, and they were "perhaps, very much alike" until they were six or eight years old. All children also share the natural disposition to curiosity, to wonder, and to conversation. The lack of education is thus for the children of the poor "one of their greatest misfortunes." They are deprived of "subject for thought and speculation," Smith said in his lectures on jurisprudence; a boy who starts work when he is very young finds that "when he is grown up he has no ideas with which he can amuse himself."[32] Instruction in science, Condorcet writes, should be seen "as much as a means of happiness for individuals as of useful resources for society"; it should encourage a use of time which, "although limited, even, to simple amusement," is not thereby "a frivolous occupation." Instruction, or the development of the intellectual faculties, is a source of "reflective pleasure," and at the same time a protection against "that painful disquiet which is associated with being aware of one's own ignorance, and which produces the vague fear of not really being in a position to defend oneself against the ills by which one is threatened."[33]

The great benefit, for society, of public instruction is indeed political more than economic. It consists, above all, in political security. People who are instructed, Smith says, are less liable to "the delusions of enthusiasm and superstition." An "instructed and intelligent people" are "always more decent and orderly than an ignorant and stupid one." "They feel themselves, each individually, more respectable":

They are more disposed to examine, and more capable of seeing through, the interested complaints of faction and sedition . . . In free countries, where the safety of government depends very much upon the favourable judgment which the people may form of its conduct, it must surely be of the highest importance that they should not be disposed to judge rashly or capriciously concerning it.

Science is the "great antidote to the poison of enthusiasm and superstition," Smith says; public diversions induce a "gaiety and good humour," a "temper of mind," a disposition to see the ridiculous in political projects, which wards off "that melancholy and gloomy humour which is almost always the nurse of popular superstition and enthusiasm."[34] This is Hume's idyll of enlightenment, once again; his indissoluble chain. In Hume's easy and sociable age, "men enjoy the privilege of rational creatures, to think as well as to act"; science, conversation, and good humor vanquish superstition, and knowledge begets mildness and moderation.[35] It is Condorcet's idyll, too. Even the constitution of one's own country, in Condorcet's project of public instruction, is something which should be taught in public schools only as a matter of information, or as if one is speaking about a fact. Children should not be made "to admire a constitution, and to recite by heart the political rights of man." The object of the new public instruction should rather be to set out for individuals "the discussions which are of interest to their rights or their happiness," and to "offer them the means necessary to decide for themselves."[36]

The fourth preoccupation which is similar in Smith's and Condorcet's economic thought is with uncertainty. Natural philosophy and moral philosophy, Smith says in his account of education in the *Wealth of Nations,* correspond to two universal dispositions of individuals. One is the disposition to wonder and curiosity; to think about and try to connect the apparently disjointed phenomena of nature (or of human contrivance). The other is the disposition to moral reflection: "In every age and country of the world men must have attended to the characters, designs, and actions of one another," and they must also have tried to connect their observations into general maxims, principles, or rules.[37] The course of ordinary life, that is to say, is to be surrounded by disconnected and often disorderly events: thunder and storms, the pulleys and wheels of dye workshops, the sentiments of other people.[38] It is to imagine that these events make sense; that they constitute a system, or an order.

This universe of imaginative uncertainty is also the universe of commerce. The individuals Smith describes in the *Wealth of Nations,* like Condorcet's merchant, calculating the "probability that, if he refuses to sell at a particular price, a part of his grain will be left" unsold, are continually judging, and misjudging, their prospects of success.[39] They are like the "leading men of America," who choose between "piddling for the little prizes which are to be found in what may be called the paltry raffle of colony faction," and seeking "the great prizes which sometimes come from the wheel of the great state lottery of British politics."[40] They try to make sense of their own prospects, and of the lotteries under which they live. But they are confronted, like the angelic administrator described in Turgot's "Lettres sur le commerce des grains," with a "multitude of obscure facts, the action of a mass of unknown causes, acting slowly and by degrees," which "combine and change the price of tradeable things."[41] They should understand, like the man of practical or particular reason, in Hume's essay "Of Commerce," that they ought never to draw their "arguments too fine, or connect too long a chain of consequences together": "Something is sure to happen, that will disconcert his reasoning, and produce an event different from what he expected."[42]

Even reason is uncertain. Reason, for Smith as for Hume, is a condition which is continuously disconcerted. It is to be revered, and it is also to be ridiculed. It is diverse, as was seen in Chapter 5, in the discussion of the invisible hand. It is different in different circumstances, in different individuals (the reason of domestic life, and the pretentious reason of the great), and at different times. Condorcet's procedural and probabilistic view of political economy, too, was influenced by Hume, as was seen in Chapter 6. In the political and moral sciences, Condorcet wrote, "man can, as in the conduct of his life, be content with probabilities which are more or less strong."[43] His universe, like Smith's, is a place of uncertainty and irresolution. It is the universe described by Hume in his essay "The Platonist":

> To some philosophers it appears matter of surprise, that all mankind, possessing of the same nature, and being endowed with the same faculties, should yet differ so widely in their pursuits and inclinations, and that one should utterly condemn what is fondly sought by another. To some it appears matter of still more surprise, that a man should differ so widely from himself at different times; and, after possession, reject with disdain what, before, was the object of all his vows and wishes. To me this feverish uncertainty and irresolution, in human conduct, seems altogether unavoidable.[44]

A SYSTEM OF SENTIMENTS

Smith's philosophical universe, like Hume's, is one of profound insecurity. To be a philosopher, in his description, is to be surrounded by a swirling, swerving disorder of impressions, and to imagine that the impressions, or the phenomena, constitute a single, beautiful, orderly system. The universe is made up of "events which appear solitary and incoherent," he writes in his "History of Astronomy," and the endeavor of philosophy is "to introduce order into this chaos of jarring and discordant appearances." It is the "science of the connecting principles of nature."[45] To think philosophically is to find tranquillity. But it is also to be conscious that the order one has introduced is the product of one's own imagination; that all philosophical systems, as Smith says in his description of Newton's cosmology, are "mere inventions of the imagination."[46] It is to find oneself, suddenly and frighteningly, plunged again into the universe of disconnected impressions. The aesthetic experience of philosophy indeed consists in an endless, recursive journey, from the perception of a multitude of individual, incoherent events, to the perception of a sufficiently orderly universe, and back once more to the perception of incoherence.

"The universe is nothing but a *heap* of perceptions without a substance," James Beattie wrote in his *Essay on Truth*, of Hume's metaphysics; the soul is for Hume, in Beattie's description, "nothing but a mass, collection, heap, or bundle, of different perceptions, or objects, that fleet away in succession, with inconceivable rapidity, perpetually changing, and perpetually in motion."[47] This is the universe of Lucretius, or of a multitude of obscure events, veering and swerving in an immeasurable infinity.[48] It is the universe of Lucretius, too, in the sense that it is the expression of a metaphysical uncertainty, of what Smith described as "the very suspicion of a fatherless world." Who could be powerful enough to rule "the sum of the immeasurable," the philosopher asks, in the words of Lucretius which Philo quotes in Hume's *Dialogues concerning Natural Religion;* and who could hold in his hand the "mighty bridle of the unfathomable"?[49] It is a source of consolation, Smith says, to believe in the powers of a "great, benevolent, and all-wise Being, who directs all the movements of nature." It is a source of melancholy to think that "all the unknown regions of infinite and incomprehensible space may be filled with nothing but endless misery and wretchedness."[50] The destiny of the philosopher is to oscillate, endlessly, between one condition and the other, or between the perception of orderliness, and the perception of a heap.

"All knowledge resolves itself into probability," Hume wrote in Book 1 of the *Treatise,* and it is an extended, recursive procedure of the correction of judgments and sentiments. There is in every probabilistic judgment, "beside the original uncertainty inherent in the subject, a new uncertainty derived from the weakness of that faculty, which judges." But the process is similar, in general, to the reasoning of common life; to the confidence of the merchant, for example, in the experience of the accountant and in the "artificial structure of the accounts." Even the philosopher, who is plunged, from time to time, into the deepest darkness, is restored by living and talking like other people, "in the common affairs of life" ("I dine, I play a game of backgammon, I converse, and am merry with my friends . . .").[51] In one view of science, the life of the philosopher is like Newton's, in Wordsworth's *Prelude:* "The marble index of a mind for ever / Voyaging through strange seas of Thought, alone."[52] Smith and Hume's view is very different. They live and talk in the midst of a multitude of impressions and sentiments. They try to make a system, or successive systems, out of all these sentiments. They are sometimes confident, and sometimes uncertain. They are in this respect, as in other respects, like everyone else; their own sentiments, like everyone else's, are part of the sentiments to be corrected, or part of the multitude.

The image of a system of individual impressions, or sentiments, is omnipresent in Smith's philosophical thought, as in Hume's, and as also in Condorcet's. It is the aesthetic, in particular, of Smith's moral philosophy, or of the "sentimentalism" which in Gillet's description was common to Hume, Smith, and Condorcet. Morality itself, in this theory, is the outcome of innumerable individual judgments, reflections, sentiments, and conversations. It is a collection of relationships, including relationships between individuals and their own past and future selves. It is a system of domestic virtues. It is without "substance," or foundation, in the sense that it is uncertain; it is not the sort of order which is directed, like the "movements of nature," by an "all-wise Being," or by a single, unified theory.

Dugald Stewart, in his "Account" of Smith's life, describes Smith's theory of moral sentiments as the outcome of a successive rejection of earlier explanations of the principle of moral judgment. Smith, like Hobbes (in his controversy with Ralph Cudworth), thus rejects the view that moral distinctions are founded on reason. Like Hume (in his controversy with Francis Hutcheson), he rejects the view that moral distinctions are founded on feeling, or on moral sense.[53] Both Smith and Hume then propose systems of sympathy, in which moral judgments are the result of a discursive and sociable process of reflection, in the course of which people think about their own and other people's feelings, and correct their sentiments. In Hume's system, it is our judgment of and pleasure in the useful consequences of actions which are at the heart of the convergence of moral sentiments. Utility, or the "pleasure of utility," is the principle of moral judgment. But at this point, Smith rejects even Hume's system. In his own system of sympathy, the convergence of sentiments depends on judgments about motives, as well as about consequences; on judgments about the judgments of others (their gratitude); and on the "general rules" of sympathy with motives and with gratitude.[54]

The fundamental principle of Smith's theory, in Stewart's description, is that the objects of moral judgments are the actions (and judgments) of other people. The principle of moral judgment, that is to say, is that there is no fundamental principle of moral judgment. There is no foundation; all there is, is the correction and convergence of sentiments. Smith is more concerned than Hume with the general rules which Hume described as an "unphilosophical species of probability," and which provide a sort of mnemonic in moral reflection; as Hume himself says, our situation is in "continual fluctuation," and it would be impossible that we could "ever converse together on any reasonable terms" without some general points of view, or general rules.[55] But Smith is also more concerned than Hume with people's motives, or with the stories of why people act in the way that they do. Reasonable conversations, in his view, are concerned with the character and moral choices of individuals, as much as or more than with the consequences or utility of the individuals' actions.[56] They are conversations, often, about "our nearest connections," and about the "private and domestic affections."[57] As in Condorcet's morality of domestic virtues, they are conversations about one's own moral constitution, and about the moral constitution of one's friends, one's sisters, one's children. As in Turgot's morality of indulgence, they are the conversations of people who are "touched by novels and tragedies," and who are interested in "the circumstances which excuse the individual."[58]

Hume's and Smith's systems of moral sentiments are scrupulously cleansed of everything, or almost everything, which is a matter of revelation.[59] They are systems of secular virtue. Cudworth's morality founded on reason, which Hume and Smith rejected, was a morality founded on divine order; moral distinctions were like the discovery of truth and falsehood because there are laws of duty which are also God's laws. Hutcheson's moral sense, too, was a condition of nature, implanted in nature by God. It was ineffable, or beyond the power of rational understanding. The procedures of a continuing, conversational morality—of the system of moral sentiments—are far more insecure. For the general rules of morality of which Smith makes so much are derived exclusively, in Dugald Stewart's account, from the sentiments and experience of the world. "Still he

insists," Stewart writes, that "our moral sentiments have always some secret reference, either to what are, or to what we imagine ought to be, the
sentiments of others"; "still, he contends" that the jurisdiction of even the
innermost conscience "is, in a great measure, derived from the authority"
of the turbulent outside world.[60]

The substance of the system of moral sentiments, in these circumstances, is to be found in the sentiments themselves, or in the individuals
whose sentiments they are. "These beings, feeling, thinking, and willing,
proposing ends to themselves, and choosing means, constitute an order of
things at least as real and at least as certain as the supposedly purely material beings, moved to action by purely mechanical causes," Turgot wrote
to Condorcet in 1774, against the "irreligious philosophers" who sought
to found morality on pleasure and pain.[61] Condorcet's indissoluble chain
of truth, happiness, and virtue is in this setting no more than a provisional,
fluctuating source of security. It is the expression of a probabilistic judgment that most people, most of the time, will be "subject in their conduct to the rules of morality, although sometime led into crime."[62] Like
Hume's other indissoluble chain, of industry, knowledge, and humanity, it
is the expression of confidence in the disposition of individuals to discuss
and to live by principles of morality; to be mild and moderate, and to feel
an increase of humanity, from the very habit of conversing together.

CIVILIZED POLITICAL DISCUSSION

The aesthetic of Smith's political philosophy is very similar. Smith's
"philosophical politics," like Hume's, is in large part a theory of political
sentiments. It is a description of a world without violent conflicts over political principles, without revolutions, and without certainty. "The good
temper and moderation of contending factions seems to be the most essential circumstance in the public morals of a free people," Smith wrote in
his account of education in the *Wealth of Nations*, and it is this idyll, of innumerable, decorous political conversations, which is at the heart of his
political thought.[63] The most essential part of education, Smith said in his
lectures on jurisprudence, or at least of education within families, is that
the child should learn "to bring down its passions" and to accommodate
to others. Even philosophical education in universities, he says in the
Wealth of Nations, should tend "to improve the understanding, or to
mend the heart."[64] The disposition to mild-humored political discussion,
or to seeing through political projects, is itself the foundation of political

security. As in Hume's easy and sociable age, "factions are then less invet-
erate, revolutions less tragical, authority less severe, and seditions less frequent."[65]

There is no divine right, in this political universe, and no divine order.
"Hume's political philosophy is wholly and unambiguously secular," Duncan Forbes writes in *Hume's Philosophical Politics;* in the political philosophy of the *Treatise,* there is "no mention of God," and an "uncanny silence with respect to anything to do with religion, natural or revealed."[66]
Sovereign princes, in the *Wealth of Nations,* are in no respect the representatives of political principles, or of political wisdom. They, together with
their ministers, serve rather as a depiction of the universal interest of all
individuals in bettering their own conditions; they include princes who
imagine that they have an interest in adulterating the coinage, dukes of
Cornwall who pursue their interest in public revenue by selling rights in
tin mines, the "proud minister of an ostentatious court" who builds great
highways to be "seen by the principal nobility," the medieval king who
grants privileges to wealthy burghers as to the "enemies of his enemies."[67]
The purpose of political history, Hume wrote in the peroration to his *History of England,* is to instruct in "the great mixture of accident, which
commonly concurs with a small ingredient of wisdom and foresight, in
erecting the complicated fabric of the most perfect government."[68]

The foundation, or principle, or "substance" of politics is thus to be
found, like the foundation of moral judgment, in the sentiments of millions of individuals, or in their disposition to civilized political discussion.[69]
Politics is for Smith and Hume a matter of "legal and constitutional machinery," as Donald Winch has written, more than a matter of political virtues (the "specifically political qualities" of men in public settings).[70] This
machinery requires very little in the way of civic virtue. The corporations
which Turgot's opponent Séguier described as "little republics" within the
state, in which each worked for the good of all, and without which no artisan would be more than "an isolated being," were for Smith a locus of
endless oppression. The independence which Séguier described as "a vice
in the political constitution" was for Smith a condition of political freedom.[71] It is just, in Hume's view, to take, as a maxim of political constitutions, the false proposition "that every man must be supposed a knave."
But it is also the case, he adds, that "men are generally more honest in
their private than in their public capacity."[72]

The virtue which contributes to legal and constitutional security is for
Smith and Hume a very modest condition. Like the domestic virtues, or

the conversations about gratitude and remorse, which constitute the system of moral sentiments, it is an unheroic sort of heroism. It is a condition of the "middle station" of life, with its characteristic virtue of friendship ("among equals"), and of which Hume wrote that it is the "middling rank of men, who are the best and firmest basis of public liberty."[73] Turgot, too, wrote to Condorcet that "it is in the middle station [*l'état mitoyen*] that are to be found sentiments which are honest, directed, and fortified by education, by reflection, by the need for public esteem."[74]

These political virtues are the virtues of humanity, and they are even, in some circumstances, the virtues of women. "Humanity is the virtue of a woman," Smith wrote in the *Theory of Moral Sentiments*, and it consists in the "exquisite fellow-feeling which the spectator entertains with the sentiments" of others; it requires "no self-denial, no self-command, no great exertion of the sense of propriety." But the man of humanity, in the last passages that Smith added before his death, is also the hero of Smith's political philosophy. He is the opposite, in any case, of the man of system, or of the sovereign prince, with his "general, and even systematical, idea of the perfection of policy and law."[75]

Condorcet's political philosophy is in several respects very different. He was more credulous than either Smith or Hume; he was less immune, by constitution, to the disorder of enthusiasm.[76] He was more ingenuous, before the Revolution, about the heroism of ministers, and even of sovereigns (there was an "indissoluble chain," he said in 1782, describing the future enlightenment of the young son of Louis XVI, which in the case of sovereign princes connected "personal interest and justice, their own happiness, and that of their fellow citizens").[77] He was far more interested and involved than either Smith or Hume in the philosophy and the politics of democracy, before as well as during the Revolution.[78] But the aesthetic of Condorcet's politics, too, is of a system of sentiments. Political life is a scene of innumerable interests, opinions, preferences, and decisions, jarring and swerving. The role of the political philosopher is to imagine that the scene is in fact orderly. It is also to imagine systems of political order, including constitutions, and rules for making political decisions. It is to invent ways in which individuals can cooperate to order their own preferences and political sentiments.

There is no certainty, in this liberal political order; there is no *paternoster*. Public instruction, Condorcet wrote at the end of his life, should not have as its object "philosophical or political dogmas"; there should be no sort of catechism.[79] For Talleyrand, who, like Condorcet, wrote extensively on public instruction, the French constitution of 1791 would not exist "if it did not spread its roots in the soul of all citizens, if it did not imprint, for ever, new sentiments, new morals, new habits": "The declaration of rights and the principles of the constitution should in future make up a new catechism for childhood, which will be taught in even the smallest schools of the kingdom."[80] But for Condorcet, children should not be taught to revere even true political opinions; to adore those principles which "it will one day be their right and their duty to judge with impartiality."[81] It will be their right, that is to say, to be like the "political Pyrrhonists" of the Revolution, in Benjamin Constant's description of 1796, who go here and there, "collecting doubts, weighing probabilities, and endlessly asking of the majority whether they still prefer present forms."[82]

In Condorcet's new, discursive political society, as in Hume's, there is very little political virtue. The sovereign is in no respect a wise and far-sighted father. But neither is the sovereign people. The error of supposing "that every law which is made by a legitimate power is just," Condorcet wrote in his *Vie de M. Turgot,* could have arisen only "in republics, in those, even, which have the appearance of democracy. Anywhere else, they would have seemed the expression of the most abject flattery."[83] The only source of certainty, in such a society, is to be found, once again, in domestic virtues and domestic conversations. Hume looks forward to an improvement in the "tempers of men," as a consequence of having conversations with women, and meeting them in an easy and sociable manner.[84] Condorcet, too, is prepared to defend the softness or sweetness of modern life; to look forward to the "easy virtues" of a world in which improvements in education and laws would have made "the courage of virtue almost useless."[85] He also recognizes the frightening insecurity of such a world, in which there is no foundation of political order, either in reverence for divine right, or in fear, or in political virtue.

There is a moving passage at the end of Condorcet's first Memoir on Public Instruction, of 1791, when he asks his readers to "suppose, for example," that in the capital of a country with a free constitution, there should arise a small group of dangerous men, that they should form further groups in five hundred other cities, that they should gain docile supporters, that they should eventually seize hold of all powers, governing "the people by seduction, and public men by terror." By what means, he asks the "friends of equality, of liberty," could "your laws, which respect the rights of men, prevent the progress of such a conspiracy?" Condorcet finds his own answer, and the possibility of "public virtues," in public instruction.[86] But even this possibility, he came to believe, was no more than the distant expectation of an almost universal habit. Sainte-Beuve said that people would die of boredom in Condorcet's future society, and that everyone would live in a condition of "universal mediocrity."[87] This was indeed Condorcet's prospect: of a country whose history is without "acts of heroism," where the great virtues are ever less necessary, and in which the object of policy, in respect of these public virtues, is "to make them useless, and not to make them usual."[88]

ECONOMIC SENTIMENTS

Economic life, too, is a system of sentiments. It is in Turgot's description a "multitude of obscure facts," a "mass of unknown causes," a "multitude of causes which combine with one another and change the prices of things which can be bought and sold."[89] It is an unpromising territory for the spirit of system, which is "dazzled by an idea or a principle," and which "wishes to know everything, explain everything, arrange everything," Turgot also wrote, in his "Éloge de Vincent de Gournay"; it is a "multitude of operations, the knowledge of which is prevented by their very immensity, and which moreover depend continuously on a mass of circumstances which are always changing, and which one can neither control nor predict."[90] For Condorcet, too, economic relationships are not susceptible of the order or regularity of "absolute and precise truths," or of "general principles of mechanics." Economic life is rather a "mass of operations carried out, in an independent manner, by a large number of men, and directed by the interest, the opinion, by the instinct, so to speak, of each of them."[91]

The objective of the "new science" of political economy, in these circumstances, is to depict an irregular order. It is suited, in Condorcet's description, to the new, modest philosophical thought of the seventeenth and eighteenth centuries. John Locke, Condorcet wrote in the *Esquisse des progrès*, "fixed the limits of human understanding"; he understood that the method of philosophy consists in "savoir ignorer," or in "knowing how not to know, in the end, what it is still, what it always will be impossible to understand." Unlike Leibniz, Locke was content with "a modest philosophy," and with the persistence of doubt in respect of the great questions of spirituality and liberty. He showed, Condorcet wrote, that the analysis of individual ideas was the only way "not to lose oneself in this chaos of incomplete notions, incoherent and indeterminate, which chance has presented to us without order, and which we have received without reflection." Locke's new philosophical method was suited, in Condorcet's description, to the new political economy of the eighteenth century. For the object of political economy was to seek a general law in "this apparent chaos," this "external shock of opposing interests,"

> this astonishing variety of works and products, of needs and resources; in this frightening complexity of interests, which links to the general system of societies, the subsistence, the well-being of an isolated individual; which makes him dependent on all the accidents of nature, on all the events of politics; which extends, in some respects, to the entire globe his capacity to experience either enjoyments or deprivations.

Political economy must also, however, be concerned to recognize the limits of general laws. Even when the principle of entire freedom had been recognized, Condorcet wrote, there would still be duties of "public power"; they would consist, above all, in preventing or moderating the "inevitable ills of nature," or "unforeseen accidents."[92]

The depiction of economic life as a heap or mass or multitude was omnipresent in the period with which this book has been concerned. The development of political economy, Hegel wrote a little condescendingly in the *Philosophy of Right,* "affords the interesting spectacle (as in Smith, Say and Ricardo) of thought working upon the endless mass of details which confront it at the outset and extracting therefrom the simple principles of the thing."[93] One of the criticisms of Smith, in the period of reconstruction of political economy in the 1790s and 1800s, was indeed that he was too little concerned with the simple principles of the thing, or too much concerned with all the details of economic life. The *Wealth of Nations* is a "confused assemblage," "a vast chaos of good ideas, pell-mell with pieces of positive knowledge," Jean-Baptiste Say wrote in the "Discours préliminaire" to his *Traité d'Économie Politique.* But it is "not a complete treatise," and it is quite inadequate as an exposition of general or fundamental principles. "Smith is lacking in clarity in many places, and in method almost everywhere," Say writes; his book is a "depository of facts," full of "long digressions," and overfull of "so many details."[94]

The *Wealth of Nations* is unsystematic, in this sense; in the philosophical sense of the spirit of system, which Turgot described as an enthusiasm for "explaining all phenomena" and for the "general principle" as distinct from the "particular fact," as a misunderstanding of "the inexhaustible variety of nature." But it is also unsystematic in the popular sense of the spirit of system, as a political disposition, or a commitment to principle in public life. The merchant Gournay, for Turgot, was a man of system in this second sense (and, in fact, "every man who thinks has a system").[95] Smith is again less systematic, in his own description. In his elaborate, extended comparison between the man of system and the man of humanity—between the public spirit which is inspired by the love of system, and the public spirit which is inspired by the love of humanity—he sees a certain charm in both principles. He describes the circumstances (in times of "turbulence and disorder") under which the two principles tend to mix together. But he takes a position, in general, in favor of the man of humanity; of moderation, accommodation, "fellow-feeling," and respect for other individuals, including for their privileges and prejudices.[96]

Smith's use of the phrase "the invisible hand," it was suggested in Chapter 5, is the expression of these conflicting inclinations with respect to the spirit of system. On the one hand, the invisible hand is the depiction of "something grand and beautiful," or of "the beauty of order." On the other hand, it is slightly ridiculous. It is a toy, much like the "trinkets" and "toys" of the rich; it corresponds to the beauty "of art and contrivance." It is the sort of thing which is attractive to the man of system, enamored with the beauty of his own ideal plans.[97] It is attractive, too, to the systematical philosopher, or to the philosopher who does not yet "know how not to know." Smith's use of the familiar, unsecular image of the invisible hand is the expression of this ambivalence; of his own uncertainty about whether his system is "an attempt to connect in the imagination the phenomena" of economic life, or "the discovery of an immense chain of the most important and sublime truths."[98] It is also the expression of doubt about the immense superiority of his own judgment, and about the consequences of his own plans, or principles.

The difficulty, at its most general, is of how to live with insecurity. For the system of economic sentiments, or of economic relationships, is one of profound insecurity. It is insecure in the metaphysical sense that has just been described; it is an imaginary order, and not an eternal truth of nature. But it is also insecure in the sense that it is an order, and it is at the same time a plan, or a policy. It is the description of a principle which makes sense out of the chaos of economic life; it is the description of a principle of policy, or of politics; and it is also the description of the limits of this policy, or of the circumstances in which the principle of entire freedom must be supplemented by the principle of public power. There are "institutions which are useful for the general society, which society should establish, direct, or oversee, and which are a supplement to what the will of private persons, or the competition of individual interests might not be able to do immediately," Condorcet wrote in the *Esquisse des progrès*.[99] There are certain public institutions, in Smith's description in the *Wealth of Nations*, which are highly advantageous to a "great society," and of which "the profit could never repay the expense to any individual or small number of individuals."[100]

The system of economic relationships is insecure, too, because it is subject to continuous reexamination. It is a system of order, and it is also a system of policy, or a system which is supposed to have good consequences for what Smith, in his account of the man of system and the man of humanity, described as "the welfare of the whole society."[101] It suggests policies (including policies for public institutions) which are supposed to supplement the will, or the calculations of profit, of individuals. But the "whole society" is constituted by a mass or multitude of individuals, who have opinions about their own interests, about the interests of the society, and about the policies which are likely to promote these interests. It is a system of people with systems; it is the sort of society in which no party, as in Hume's description of eighteenth-century England, "can well support itself, without a philosophical or speculative system of principles, annexed to its political or practical one."[102]

The individuals who are depicted in the eighteenth-century economic writings with which this book has been concerned are occupied in a discursive, uneasy, self-conscious way of life. They are contracting parties, and they are thereby the sort of people who form expectations, and have ideas about principles. The obligation in a contract, Smith says in his lectures on jurisprudence, is constituted by the "reasonable expectation" of the person to whom the promise was made. The doctrine of the original contract, he also says, following Hume, is unsound because the people who are supposed to have consented to it "are not conscious of it, and therefore cannot be bound by it . . . They must have some idea however confused of the principle upon which they act."[103] All these contracting parties have ideas, principles, and expectations. They are interested, like the commercial travelers who were James Anderson's correspondents in *The Bee*, in "the history of the human mind."[104] They are inquisitive, like the man of speculation who is disposed, in Smith's description, to "enter into many reasonings" about the effects of distant events (an earthquake in China) on "the commerce of Europe, and the trade and business of the world in general."[105]

The world of eighteenth-century commerce was insecure, or risky, in the sense that it was full of new investments and new economic relationships. The rise of commerce, for Turgot, was "a revolution which can only operate slowly and by degrees"; it required confidence, experience, relationships with correspondents, and the establishment of "means of communication of every sort."[106] Commerce and communication, together with the regular execution of justice, was the condition for the "great revolution" which Smith describes in early modern Europe. One means of communication was by the exchange of goods; another was by the circulation of money and credit ("the judicious operations of banking," Smith wrote, provide "a sort of waggon-way through the air"); yet another was by the exchange of news. The merchants whom Turgot encountered in Angoulême had opinions about public debt, about rumors of European war, about the solvency of the king of Spain, about bad weather in the Baltic, about the anxieties of Lyon silk traders. People who live in the capitals of great empires, in Smith's description, "enjoy, at their ease, the amusement of reading in the newspapers the exploits of their own fleets and armies." But they are also wracked by anxiety. The Amsterdam merchant, trading in corn from Königsberg and fruit from Lisbon, who is at the heart of the description of the invisible hand in the *Wealth of Nations*, likes to have at least some of his capital "always under his own view." He feels "uneasiness" at "being separated so far" from it. He likes the "home-trade," because "he can know better the character and situation of the persons whom he trusts," and the "laws of the country from which he must seek redress."[107]

The new world of commerce was insecure, too, because it was subject to frequent and often sudden changes in laws, regulations, and the jurisprudence of property. Napoleon, reflecting in St. Helena on the "universal agitation which torments us," the "furious oscillations" of modern times, identified their principal source in a "great revolution in property." The first sort of property, in land, had been augmented, he said—this was at the time when he was studying the *Wealth of Nations*—by a second sort of property, in industry; this was augmented, in turn, by a third sort of property, "derived from the enormous charges raised from taxpayers," and distributed by the government. The conflict among these three kinds of property, he said, was the "great struggle of our times."[108] Turgot's reform edicts of 1776, at the outset of the epoch of universal agitation, had also turned on the conflicts among different kinds of property, and different kinds of rights: the privileges of bakers' and millers' guilds, the right to impose charges, the "superstitious respect" for property originally "founded on usurpations," and respect for the "most sacred of all property . . . the property of man in the fruit of his labor."[109]

The world which Condorcet and Turgot describe in the provincial France of the last decades of the ancien régime is one in which "the rigidity of laws has given way to force of things," and an "arbitrary and fluctuating jurisprudence" has "moderated in practice its speculative principles." It is also a world of prohibitive laws, which vary with circumstances, and whereby "a merchant will never know, under their empire, if the laws under which he has bought will be those under which he will sell."[110] The whole commercial system of Great Britain, which is the object, Smith says, of his violent attack in the *Wealth of Nations,* is itself an immense, haphazard, changing organization of regulation and vexation.[111] Smith refers in his discussion of apprenticeship to fourteen consecutive statutes which obstruct the "free circulation of labour."[112] Richard Burn's *Justice of the Peace,* which was one of Smith's important sources, includes, in its 1758 edition, no fewer than forty-two paragraphs concerned with "starch and hair powder," and refers to well over one hundred statutes on the woollen manufacture, which it seeks simply to "reduce into some kind of order."[113]

The eighteenth-century system of commerce was insecure, above all, in an even more insidious way. For it was subject to continuing flux not only in events, and in rules, but also in the dispositions of the individuals (the *moleculae*) of whom the system is composed. "My intention is in no way to confound the conditions of men; I wish to reign only by justice and laws," Louis XVI said at the end of the *Lit de Justice* over Turgot's edicts.[114] But a flux in the condition of men is the essential circumstance of modern commerce, in Smith's, Turgot's, and Condorcet's description. The desire of bettering our condition, which Smith describes in the *Wealth of Nations* as "uniform, constant, and uninterrupted," or "universal, continual, and uninterrupted," is the "principle from which public and national, as well as private opulence is originally derived."[115] To better one's condition is, however, to change one's condition; it is also to change one's disposition, and to become a different sort of person.

The flux in conditions and dispositions is thus at the heart of late eighteenth-century commercial life. This was the opinion, at least, of the opponents of commercial reform. Séguier argued in the *Lit de Justice,* against Turgot and against the king, that the "indefinite freedom" of commerce would lead to a "default of security," and thereby to the destruction of all the activities of commerce, which was itself dependent on "the most blind confidence." It would lead to an influx of people into the large cities (where they would be able to live from "the smallest commerce"), and to a transformation in their ways of thinking. This indefinite freedom, he said, "knows no other laws than its caprices, and admits no other rules than those which it sets for itself; this sort of freedom is nothing other than a true independence." "As soon as the spirit of subordination will be lost, the love of independence will start to germinate in all hearts," Séguier foresaw; "the multitude, which nothing will be able to contain, will cause the greatest disorders."[116]

The love of independence is for Smith, by contrast, a cause of public prosperity. "Nobody but a beggar chooses to depend chiefly upon the benevolence of his fellow-citizens," he writes in his eulogy to the "fair and deliberate exchange" of civilized society, at the outset of the *Wealth of Nations*. ("Even a beggar does not depend upon it entirely," Smith goes on to say, with a characteristic taste for the exception and the observation; the beggar exchanges money for food, and old clothes "for other old clothes which suit him better.")[117] Seneca, whom Smith describes as "that great preacher of insensibility," pointed in *De beneficiis* to the folly of seeking benevolence, or the exchange of benefits, in commercial relations: "In an inn or hotel no one regards himself as the guest of the landlord."[118] This insubordinate, insensible independence of commercial relations was for Smith a sign of the universal disposition of men, or of what distinguishes the society of men from the society of dogs; of the independence of spirit which makes possible the interdependence of economic lives. "It is not from the benevolence of the butcher, the brewer, or the baker, that we expect our dinner," Smith says. It is rather from our relationship to them, as more or less equal participants in a rhetorical, cognitive exchange. We "address ourselves" to their self-love, we "talk to them" of their own advantages, we "interest" them in a transaction, we "show them that it is for their own advantage"; this is the "meaning" of commercial exchange.[119]

Séguier's foreboding, in respect of this universal discursiveness, was that it would turn out to be unlimited; that the freedom, or license, which admits no other rules than those which it sets for itself, and which is busily interested in the rules for making rules, will in the end destroy all rule. For one characteristic of eighteenth-century commerce, much observed then and subsequently, was that the rules which delineate the universe of commerce—the rules as to what it is that can be bought and sold—were themselves in a condition of continuous change. A commercial society, Turgot wrote in 1753, was one in which the participants "as it were, buy and sell happiness."[120] Everyone, that is to say, is buying and selling; individuals are buying and selling social condition, happiness, Indian cotton, political influence, defective goods, horses, places, consideration, the factitious benevolence of the innkeeper. It is "the true London maxim, that every thing is to be got with money," Jane Austen wrote in *Mansfield Park*.[121]

This universality of transactions was not in itself novel, in the history with which eighteenth-century observers were familiar. Like Seneca, Tacitus described the rise of "self-interest," or "own utility" *(sua cuique utilitas)*, in imperial Rome: "Everything was for sale [*venalia cuncta*]," "everywhere there were auctions and speculators, and the city was disturbed by lawsuits."[122] But the transactiveness of commercial society was particularly unsettling in the new circumstances of an incipiently indefinite freedom of commerce, or at least of a new interest in commercial freedom. For Smith's or Turgot's independent merchants were interested in buying and selling bread or visits to inns, and they were also interested in the rules which governed the sale of bread and visits to inns. They chose what sort of thing to sell (which branch of commerce to embrace) on the basis, in part, of their estimation of the riskiness of a particular sort of commerce, including the risk of incurring ill repute.[123] Once they were established in a particular branch, they were confronted, repeatedly, with the further choice of how to advance their own advantage. They had to choose, in particular, between the use of political and commercial (or "competitive") means to drive out their competitors. They had to choose what sort of people to be.

Smith says of the individual competitor in "the race for wealth, and honours, and preferments," in the *Theory of Moral Sentiments,* that "he may run as hard as he can, and strain every nerve and every muscle, in order to outstrip all his competitors. But if he should jostle, or throw down any of them, the indulgence of the spectators is entirely at an end."[124] The uneasy circumstance, in the real races of commerce, is that jostling is both difficult to define, and defined differently at different times. Conversation, in Smith's domestic, sociable morality, is one of the ways in which individuals correct their sentiments, and come to understand how other people think and feel. The man who is condemned to spend his life performing a few simple operations becomes incapable, Smith writes in the *Wealth of Nations,* of enjoying "any rational conversation," or conceiving "any generous, noble, or tender sentiment." But conversation can also lead one astray. In one kind of (bad) conversation, in the *Wealth of Nations,* the young boy in a seaport town is enticed, by "the sight of the ships and the conversation and adventures of the sailors," to underestimate the dangers of the "lottery of the sea," and to go to sea. In another bad conversation, it is "the great roads, the great communications" which become the "subjects of conversation at the court," to the detriment of "little works" of "extreme utility." In yet another, even worse conversation, merchants encourage one another to compete by unjust means, or at least by jostling merchants in other branches of trade: "People of the same trade seldom meet together, even for merriment and diversion, but the conversation ends in a conspiracy against the public."[125]

It is only the very immensity of commercial relationships, in these circumstances, which can provide the foundation of civilized competition. Smith seems to have been confident, like Turgot and like Condorcet, that the system of commercial freedom would provide very much less opportunity for conspiracy, or for the use of political (as opposed to commercial) means of competition, than the system of commercial regulation. He believed, like Turgot, and, later, like John Stuart Mill, that "the conditions of any exchange cannot be unjust, except to the extent that they have been influenced by violence or fraud."[126] He was confident that there would be very little opportunity for violence in a free, civilized, commercial society, and little advantage to be derived from fraud. Condorcet imagined that in the new world of the Tenth Epoch, "the interest in acquiring things by illegitimate means will present itself less often, to a smaller number of individuals," and that individuals will become better at estimating "the uncertainty of success, the dangers to which one is exposed, the reduction of legitimate resources, occasioned by the loss of the confidence of others."[127] This prospect, founded on what Condorcet described as the "crudest calculation of interest," is Smith's own best hope as well. The "influence of commerce on the manners of a people," Smith said in his lectures on jurisprudence, is that they turn to "probity and punctuality," as to the most "fashionable" of virtues:

> A dealer is afraid of losing his character, and is scrupulous in observing every engagement. When a person makes perhaps 20 contracts a day, he cannot gain so much by endeavouring to impose on his neighbours, as the very appearance of a cheat would make him lose. Where people seldom deal with one another, we find that they are somewhat disposed to cheat . . . Wherever dealings are frequent, a man does not expect to gain so much by any one contract as by probity and punctuality in the whole.[128]

The commercial society becomes more resilient, on this consoling view, as it becomes ever more enormous. But the opposite view is also possible;

it was the advocate-general Séguier's view, for example, thirteen years before the beginning of the French Revolution. The isolated individuals of the new, universal society would not, on this view, cluster into orderly neighborhoods of commerce, in which their dealings would be repeated frequently over time. They would have fleeting, instantaneous, distant relationships. Smith said of the speculative merchant that he is "a corn merchant this year, and a wine merchant the next, and a sugar, tobacco, or tea merchant the year after."[129] He may also be someone who speculates on changes in regulation this year, and who next year buys regulations, or the enforcement of regulations. The interest in "the general happiness of the society," Condorcet said in 1776, "ceases almost absolutely for the owner of money, who, by a banking operation, within an instant becomes English, Dutch, or Russian"; so, too, may the interest in conforming to the disposition, or the character, of the society.[130] On one view, that is to say, the swerving *moleculae* of the universe of commerce tend to become more orderly, or more well disposed, as the size of the universe increases. On the opposite, frightening view, they become less orderly. They make innumerable contracts each day, but with distant, different people. They are not, perhaps, disposed to cheat. But their circumstances are even more insecure, in that they are not even certain what it is like to be a cheat, and what it is like to be well disposed. They are buying and selling, buying and selling; in the end, they are buying and selling rules, and customs, and their own dispositions.

The theories of moral, political, and commercial enlightenment with which I have been concerned have a similar composition, or aesthetic; the composition of a system of sentiments, or of a swerving universe of individuals, which is at the same time a system. But the different systems are also the same system, in the sense that they depend on one another. The discursive political society, or the philosophical politics of good-tempered discussion, requires a society of good-tempered, prudent moral sentiments; this is the condition for civilized conflict. The system of commerce requires an orderly political constitution, in which the public power that defines the limits of commercial freedom is itself the subject of political discussion, and of orderly political reform; this is Condorcet's Pelion of economic competition and his Ossa of constitutional choice. The system of commerce, as has just been seen, requires a system of moral sentiments, or a good-tempered, prudent society; this is the condition of civilized competition.

The odds, in this lottery of civilized society, are cosmic; the probabilities of political, economic, and moral improvement are all founded upon one another, and they may all, eventually, turn out to be without foundation. Smith, when he uses the image of the invisible hand (which is also Macbeth's invisible hand, and Oedipus'), is expressing his own confidence in the system of indefinite freedom of commerce, and his judgment that it will have good consequences for the society. Condorcet, when he uses the similarly familiar, similarly unsecular image of the indissoluble chain (which is also the chain of the son of Louis XVI), is expressing his confidence in the system of secular, discursive virtue, and his judgment that it too will have good consequences for the society. But their judgments are not the expression of sublime and important truths. They are judgments about how people might live, in a world without sublime truths; judgments about other people's judgments.

A WORLD UNRESTORED

"The Emperor has left us in a prophetic agitation," François-René de Chateaubriand wrote in 1841, in his *Mémoires d'outre-tombe*. In the life of political society, "everything is transitory. Religion and morality are no longer admitted, or everyone interprets them in his own fashion." There is a "universal society," a "confusion of needs and images," an "anarchy of ideas," in which distances will disappear, and in which "it will not only be commodities which travel, but also ideas which will have wings."[131] The emperor's own prophecy was much the same, in his lugubrious reflections on the *Wealth of Nations,* surrounded in St. Helena by the vexatious authority of the British Indian Empire. It was the system of "freedom of commerce for all," Napoleon said to Las Cases, which "agitated all imaginations," which, with its revolution in property, "led naturally to independence," and which was "entirely identical with equality." "I have not forgotten the power of the sentiment of equality over the imagination," he also said; "it is the passion of the century, and I am, I wish to remain, the child of the century!"[132]

This view of the commercial imagination—Napoleon's view, or Chateaubriand's—was quite unseemly, in the new, orderly Europe of the post-Napoleonic restoration. Enlightenment was in Hegel's description of 1807 the dominion of pure insight and its diffusion, which seeps into society like a perfume, or like an infection. Its enemy was faith, and faith is conquered by consciousness; "it moves listlessly to and fro within itself. It has been expelled from its kingdom."[133] The political restoration of the 1810s was the return of faith to its kingdom, and kingdoms, all over Europe. It was the reinstatement of faith in religion, in political authority, in the security of thrones, in the subordination of dispositions, in the innocuousness of philosophy, in the orderliness of science, in a France restored, under the "paternal government of her kings."[134]

The reconstruction of political economy as an innocuous, unpolitical subject, in the generation following the French Revolution, was a part of the extended process of restoration. So was the First Empire itself. Napoleon said to the Conseil d'État, in 1800: "We have finished the novel of the Revolution: the time has come to begin its history, to see only that which is real and possible in the application of principles, and not that which is speculative and hypothetical. To follow any other path today, would be to philosophize and not to govern."[135] As J.-E.-M. Portalis, Napoleon's minister of religion and the principal author of the Civil Code, wrote in his eulogy of Turgot's opponent Séguier, the emperor (the "august liberator who has received into his arms a France torn apart by impiousness and anarchy") had sought to "reestablish the altars, in order to settle and confirm the first of empires." Séguier would have been happy, Portalis said, to see the "rebirth of France." He would have been pleased, in particular, with the reconstruction of guild organization, as "a great principle of order," in opposition to the "false speculations of avidity," and to the materialist and atheist spirit of the eighteenth century, in which philosophers "saw nothing, everywhere, but sad games of chance."[136]

One foundation of the long nineteenth-century restoration was the reconstituted political power of established religion; the reunion of eternal and secular reverence. "Is the Nineteenth Century to be a Contrast to the Eighteenth? Is it to extinguish all the Lights of its Predecessor? Are the Sorbonne, the Inquisition, the Index expurgatorius, and the Knights Errant of St Ignatius Loyola to be revived and restored?" John Adams wrote to Thomas Jefferson in November 1815, as they studied the news of the Congress of Vienna.[137] But the religion of the nineteenth century was founded on the revival of faith, as well as of power. "The official religion of the century both in England and France was lifeless and mechanical," John Morley wrote of the eighteenth century in his essay on Condorcet.[138] The established religion of the nineteenth century was concerned, by contrast, with the thoughts and feelings of men. The slow decline of incredulity, or the process by which "the respect for religion gradually recovered its empire," was in Tocqueville's description in *L'ancien régime et la révolution,* a matter of sentiments and memories more than of political institutions. It was "the fear of revolutions," Tocqueville wrote, which brought an end to the incredulity of the eighteenth century, or at least to its outward signs; it was a disorder of the mind, more than of the heart, or of morality, which had been the most extreme of all the effects of the irreligion of the Revolution.[139] The restoration was founded, too, on a new security of individual identities, in the world of Smith's and Condorcet's and Chateaubriand's cosmopolitan, stateless merchants. Condorcet wrote in 1792 that to require passports of those wishing to leave France was a "formal attainder against individual freedom," including the freedom of one's "interests" and one's "tastes"; it was a way to make the individual "hate the country which one can only make him love by the sentiment of his independence, and by the free exercise of his faculties."[140] But the 1790s were also a period of expansion for the new religion of national identity. For Napoleon's correspondent Joseph Fiévée, writing in 1802 from London, the sense of the "superiority" of one's own nation was an "instinct," and one which had been "cruelly betrayed by the French writers of the eighteenth century."[141] The instinct of national sentiment was reinforced, in turn, by a new security of racial identity, and of racial superiority; by what Benjamin Constant described in 1826 as "the new system which ingenious writers have established on the difference of races," and which for Constant was a "new pretext for inequality and oppression."[142]

The restored security of the early nineteenth century was founded, even more ubiquitously, on a religion of science, common to the men of the restoration and to their enemies, the votaries of new revolutions.[143] The new sect of "industry" in the 1820s, Constant wrote, takes as its foundation "the pretention of certain men who proclaim themselves to be the guides of everyone"; "the ideas of liberty have very little to do today, this sect says, because we are entering an epoch where it is much more urgent to coordinate than to dissolve, and where a positive theory must succeed critical theories."[144] This was the spirit of the scientific socialism of the middle of the nineteenth century; of the evolutionary view of class struggle, in the words of Engels, which was "destined to do for history what Darwin's theory has done for biology."[145] It was also the spirit of the scientific study of wealth. Political economy is an experimental science, Jean-Baptiste Say wrote; "our knowledge in political economy can be complete, that is to say, we can succeed in discovering all the general facts which together compose this science . . . [It] is established on unshakable foundations, from the moment when the principles which serve as its basis are rigorous deductions from unquestionable general facts."[146]

All these new religions were expected, eventually, to transform the dispositions of the multitude. For the reconstruction of order, in the post-Revolutionary world, was to be a restoration, above all, of unquestionable and unquestioned ways of thinking. The changes in sentiments with which so many nineteenth-century observers were concerned—Tocqueville's "sort of inner shuddering" of the last decades of the ancien régime, Southey's "great moral revolution" of the lower orders in England, the revolution "in the Minds of the People" of which John Adams reminisced to Thomas Jefferson, the decline in "opinions and feelings of subordination" which so preoccupied the Committee of 1806 on the English woollen manufacture—were the object, throughout Europe, of continuing wonder. They were juxtaposed, in different, shifting ways, to the changes which took place in the course of the French Revolution itself; to the "most important of all revolutions . . . I mean a revolution in sentiments, manners, and moral opinions" which could be dated, in Burke's description, to October 6, 1789.[147]

The principles of public instruction were in these circumstances of the highest political interest. The ultraconservatives of the restoration had some desires in common, as Constant suggested slyly in "De la liberté des anciens comparée à celle des modernes," with the eighteenth-century enthusiasts of Sparta; with Mably and with Rousseau. Like Mably, they wished to educate men to be virtuous, and to obey the law. They wished to prescribe belief; they wanted the law to exercise its authority not merely over the deeds of individuals, but "to extend into their thoughts, their most fleeting impressions."[148] They believed, like the men of the Revolution, who sought, in Condorcet's description, to "take hold of new generations, to dictate to them what they should believe," that government should "take hold of new generations, to fashion them as it wishes."[149]

The conservatives of the restoration were no longer frightened by the commercial disposition, Constant suggested. They understood that commerce had become "the ordinary condition, the single objective, the universal tendency, the true life of nations." But they wanted an obedient, a dependent, and for Constant a bizarre form of commerce. They wanted industrious subjects, whose only objective was happiness. They wanted to be free, themselves, to give happiness to their subjects. They wanted subjects who were prejudiced and frivolous; who were easily led, with the help of "positive knowledge and the exact sciences."[150]

There is "a hidden relation between these two words: *liberty* and *commerce*," Tocqueville wrote in 1835, in the journal of his voyage to England

and Ireland. For to be free one has to become accustomed to "an existence full of agitation, of movement, of danger; to be always watchful, and at every moment to look around one uneasily; this is the price of liberty. All these things are equally necessary to succeed in commerce."[151] But the disposition of commercial life could also, for Tocqueville, be a source of political oppression. In one outcome, which was characteristic of France in the late eighteenth century, the discontents of commerce went hand in hand with the disposition to revolution. In a different outcome, which was characteristic, in Tocqueville's later description, of France under the Second Empire, the effect of the commercial way of life was rather to distract individuals from public interests. It turned them, like the imaginary subjects of Constant's conservative statesmen of the 1810s and 1820s, into the obedient dupes of oppression. It filled their lives with "debilitating passions," with "the desire to become rich at any price, the taste for business, the love of gain, the quest for well-being and for material enjoyments." In an oppressive society of this sort, individuals are easy to govern. It encloses them in private life; "it isolates them; it makes them cold in relation to one another; it freezes them." It makes them "tremble at the very idea of revolutions."[152]

The relationship between the disposition of commerce and the disposition of political liberty was for Tocqueville the overwhelming question of nineteenth-century public life. The unquiet, independent mind—the *regard inquiet* of the English, or, for Constant in 1819, the *noble inquiétude* of modern individuals—was sometimes, as in Manchester in the 1830s, or in Hamburg and Lübeck in the 1780s, an adjunct of liberty.[153] But it was sometimes an adjunct of oppression; the oppression of incipient revolution, or of the orderly, frightened societies of post-restoration Europe. There is a good disposition of enlightenment, that is to say, in which commerce and liberty are interrelated in the sentiments and opinions of individuals. There is a bad disposition of enlightenment, in which individuals are imprisoned by their own discontent, or by their own cupidity, in a society of universal commerce.

SUITABLE EQUALITY

This book has been about an earlier and more unsuspecting world, in which the agitation of commerce—the unquiet imagination of ordinary life—was the subject of less fear. It was a time of bounded uncertainty; an uncertainty of which the consequences were expected to be no more than a slow revolution. But the disputes of this earlier time are also familiar, as I suggested at the beginning of the book, in the new society of universal commerce of the early twenty-first century.

The European revolutions of 1989–1991 have been taken to mark the eventual end, after two centuries, of the long epoch of revolutions. The twenty-first century, on this view, is to be the epoch of a new and less insecure political society; a universe of commerce. But there is also a different view, in which the early twenty-first century is rather the end of the epoch of the post-Revolutionary and post-Napoleonic restoration. It is the end, that is to say, of the epoch in which faith has been restored to her kingdom. The collective resolve to bring to an end the "novel" of the French Revolution, and to prevent all future revolutions, was itself a source of faith, or at least of security. It was the foundation of the two hundred–year-long coalition of laissez-faire and political conservatism, in which the system of commercial freedom was in alliance, against Napoleon's last instincts, with the "old system" of political order. It is this coalition which may now be insecure.

I have been concerned, in this book, with an economic thought in which uncertainty is the overwhelming condition of commercial society, and in which "interference with the freedom and openness of the understanding," in the words Morley used of Condorcet, is "the worst kind of sacrilege."[154] It is odd, at the moment of the most enthusiastic triumph of the system of "indefinite freedom of commerce," to remind oneself how important uncertainty was to the greatest theorists of this system; how much they disliked enthusiasm. But there is a new freedom that has come with the eventual defeat, after almost two centuries, of the opposing system, or of the positive theory of the coordination of economic life. It is a freedom, or an opportunity, to remember a different economic enlightenment.

I have talked often about the shortcomings of the liberal economic order. The most obvious shortcoming is the one to which Napoleon pointed, in St. Helena. The system of economic freedom is founded on the equality of all individuals, and it is at the same time subversive of equality.[155] This is the endless circle in which individuals become rich, and use their money to buy power, to buy other individuals, and to influence the ways in which other individuals think. The imaginary world of the enlightenment is one in which no one is enormously rich, and no one is enormously poor (or poor enough to be bought); as Hume wrote, in his essay "Of Commerce," "a too great disproportion among the citizens weakens any state. Every person, if possible, ought to enjoy the fruits of his labour, in a full possession of all the necessaries, and many of the conveniencies of life. No one can doubt, but such an equality is most suitable to human nature."[156] Smith seems to have assumed that equality in this sense was the condition of mid-eighteenth-century England, and Condorcet tried to ensure, with his elaborate projects of social insurance, or insurance against the inequality of security, that it would be the condition of late eighteenth-century France. But they also expected that the disproportion among the citizens would continue to ebb and flow, in all future systems of commerce. Equality, in Mona Ozouf's description, summarizing the debates over universal public instruction in which Condorcet was involved during the early years of the French Revolution, was "not a condition, but a process of becoming."[157]

The insidious shortcoming of the liberal economic system, in these circumstances, is the system's own insecurity. It is founded on the (minimal) security, or the (minimal) equality, of all individuals, and it is at the same time subversive of all security. Smith and Condorcet lived in an imaginative universe which was prodigiously uncertain by the orderly standards of the early twenty-first century; a fatherless world. They were each, in different ways, confident in the future of the human disposition. They had faith, of a sort, in the ordinary virtues of conversation, and in the ordinary exchanges of political discussion. They believed, like Constant, that individuals in commercial societies longed for individual independence, and not, like Tocqueville, that they were frozen in individual isolation. They believed in the odd condition of humanity, which was for Smith the characteristic virtue of women, and which for Condorcet was a word on the lips of all tyrants. They believed, even, in their own capacity, and in the capacity of others, to live without certainty. This is much more difficult in the twenty-first century. But our ordinary enjoyments are still a little like those that Adam Smith described in December 1762, in a lecture on the historical style of Thucydides: "It is these uneasy emotions that chiefly affect us and give us a certain pleasing anxiety."[158]

Notes
Acknowledgments
Index

NOTES

Abbreviations

Corr. *The Correspondence of Adam Smith.* 2nd ed. Ed. E. C. Mossner and I. S. Ross. Oxford: Clarendon Press, 1987.

EPS Adam Smith. *Essays on Philosophical Subjects.* Ed. W. P. D. Wightman and J. C. Bryce. Oxford: Clarendon Press, 1980.

LJ Adam Smith. *Lectures on Jurisprudence.* Ed. R. L. Meek, D. D. Raphael, and P. G. Stein. Oxford: Clarendon Press, 1978.

LRBL Adam Smith. *Lectures on Rhetoric and Belles Lettres.* Ed. J. C. Bryce. Oxford: Clarendon Press, 1983.

OC *Oeuvres de Condorcet.* Ed. A. Condorcet O'Connor and M. F. Arago. Paris: Firmin Didot, 1847–1849.

OT *Oeuvres de Turgot et documents le concernant.* Ed. Gustave Schelle. Paris: Alcan, 1913–1923.

TMS Adam Smith. *The Theory of Moral Sentiments.* Ed. D. D. Raphael and A. L. Macfie. Oxford: Clarendon Press, 1976.

WN Adam Smith. *An Inquiry into the Nature and Causes of the Wealth of Nations.* Ed. R. H. Campbell and A. S. Skinner. Oxford: Clarendon Press, 1976.

Introduction

1. *WN,* p. 664; Comte de Las Cases, *Le Mémorial de Sainte-Hélène,* ed. Joël Schmidt (Paris: Éditions du Seuil, 1968), 2:1441–42.

2. "Discours préliminaire," in Jean-Baptiste Say, *Traité d'Économie Politique, ou simple exposition de la manière dont se forment, se distribuent, et se consomment les richesses* (Paris: Deterville, 1803), pp. v–vi, xxv; Jane Marcet, *Conversations on Political Economy; in which the Elements of that Science are familiarly explained,* 2nd ed. (London: Longman, 1817), pp. 5–6.

3. "Sur le préjugé qui suppose une contrariété d'intérêts entre Paris et les provinces" (1790), in *OC,* 10:136.

4. Condorcet, letter of 1771 to Count Pietro Verri, in *OC*, 1:282–284; [J. B. de La Porte], *Le défenseur de l'usure confondu, ou réfutation de l'ouvrage intitulé: Théorie de l'intérêt d'argent* (Paris: Morin, 1782), pp. 1–3, 9.

5. "Discours préliminaire," in Say, *Traité d'Économie Politique*, p. vi.

6. George Pryme, *An Introductory Lecture and Syllabus, to a Course delivered in the University of Cambridge, on the Principles of Political Economy* (Cambridge: Smith, 1823), pp. 3, 6.

7. G. W. F. Hegel, *Phenomenology of Spirit* (1807), trans. A. V. Miller (Oxford: Oxford University Press, 1977), p. 31.

8. "Sur l'instruction publique" (1791–92), in *OC*, 7:536–537; on Condorcet's conception of social science, see Keith Baker, *Condorcet: From Natural Philosophy to Social Mathematics* (Chicago: University of Chicago Press, 1975).

9. "An Early Draft of Part of *The Wealth of Nations*," in *LJ*, p. 570.

10. Thomas Robert Malthus, *An Essay on the Principle of Population, as it affects the Future Improvement of Society, with Remarks on the Speculations of Mr. Godwin, M. Condorcet, and other Writers* (1798), in *The Works of Thomas Robert Malthus*, ed. E. A. Wrigley and David Souden (London: William Pickering, 1986), 1:5.

11. Immanuel Kant, *The Contest of Faculties*, in *Kant's Political Writings*, ed. Hans Reiss (Cambridge: Cambridge University Press, 1970), p. 183.

12. This is in a letter of February 27, 1799. See Robert Darnton, "Condorcet and the Craze for America in France," in *Franklin and Condorcet: Two Portraits from the American Philosophical Society* (Philadelphia: American Philosophical Society, 1997), p. 37.

13. "Avertissement" to the *Esquisse des progrès*, in *OC*, 6:282.

14. Arthur Condorcet O'Connor, *Le Monopole cause de tous les maux* (Paris: Firmin Didot, 1849), 1:51.

15. Condorcet was critical of the new society of the United States on several grounds, including the continuing regulation of commerce, the persistence of slavery, and certain remaining limitations on religious tolerance. "De l'influence de la révolution d'Amérique sur l'Europe" (1786), in *OC*, 8:13; "Sur l'instruction publique," in *OC*, 7:434–435.

1. Economic Dispositions

1. *LRBL*, pp. 112–113. These are students' transcriptions of lectures which Smith gave in 1762–63 at the University of Glasgow. Smith had no intention that the lectures should be published, and he indeed destroyed virtually all his manuscripts, including the text of earlier lectures on rhetoric, shortly before his death. See Dugald Stewart, "Account of the Life and Writings of Adam Smith, LL.D." (1793), *EPS*, p. 327.

2. Stewart, "Account," pp. 271, 291–292, 314–315.

3. Smith to Andreas Holt, October 26, 1780, in *Corr.*, p. 251.

4. *WN*, pp. 25, 30.

5. William Robertson, *The History of the Reign of the Emperor Charles V* (London: Strahan, 1769), 1:18–20; after Charlemagne, Robertson wrote, "the darkness returned, and settled over Europe more thick and heavy than formerly" (p. 20).

6. "Lettres sur le commerce des grains" (1770), in *OT*, 3:326; "Mémoire sur les prêts d'argent" (1770), in *OT*, 3:192.

7. "Monopole et monopoleur" (1775), in *OC*, 11:43; Laurence Sterne, *A Sentimental Journey* (1768) (London: Penguin Books, 1986), pp. 33, 38. Sterne's book was extraordinarily popular in France in the 1770s and 1780s. Two of its most notable admirers were Condorcet's friends Amélie Suard and Julie de Lespinasse, who indeed adopted the name "Eliza," after Sterne's beloved Anglo-Indian Eliza Draper (which was also the pet name given later to Condorcet's daughter). See Francis Brown Barton, *Étude sur l'influence de Laurence Sterne en France au dix-huitième siècle* (Paris: Hachette, 1911), pp. 25–37, and *Correspondance inédite de Condorcet et Mme. Suard, M. Suard, et Garat (1771–1791)*, ed. Elisabeth Badinter (Paris: Fayard, 1988), pp. 139, 180.

8. *WN*, pp. 25–26, 29.

9. *LJ*, p. 352.

10. *TMS*, p. 50.

11. *WN*, pp. 120, 768.

12. *Réflexions sur le commerce des blés* (1776), in *OC*, 11:161, 191.

13. "Reason and sentiment concur in almost all moral determinations and conclusions," David Hume wrote in the *Enquiry concerning the Principles of Morals*, and they also concur, or coexist, in the commercial relationships that Smith and Condorcet describe. David Hume, *Enquiries concerning the Human Understanding and concerning the Principles of Morals*, ed. L. A. Selby-Bigge (Oxford: Clarendon Press, 1962), p. 172.

14. Giacomo Leopardi, "Zibaldone di pensieri," in *Tutte le opere*, ed. Walter Binni (Milan: Sansoni, 1993), 2:1213–16, 1234–35.

15. "'Sentiments' and 'passions,' as Hume uses those terms, are far from excluding thought and judgment. They positively require them," Annette Baier has written. In Hume's theory of morality, based on "reflective passions and corrected sentiments," thought is as essential as it is to pure reasoning; both "reflection" and "correction," in turn, are essentially sociable activities. Annette Baier, *A Progress of Sentiments: Reflections on Hume's Treatise* (Cambridge, Mass.: Harvard University Press, 1991), pp. 180–181. See also Peter Jones, *Hume's Sentiments: Their Ciceronian and French Context* (Edinburgh: University Press, 1982); John Mullan, *Sentiment and Sociability: The Language of Feeling in the Eighteenth Century* (Oxford: Clarendon Press, 1988); and Chapters 5 and 8. On Smith's account of emotions and judgment, see Martha C. Nussbaum, *Poetic Justice: The Literary Imagination and Public Life* (Boston: Beacon Press, 1995).

16. "Letter to the *Edinburgh Review*" (1756), in *EPS*, p. 253.

17. *WN*, pp. 285, 376, 405, 412, 722–723. In Duncan Forbes's description,

Smith gave "the theme of commerce and liberty a philosophical foundation in the nature of man," and this is in turn related to "the most important psychological factor in social progress [which] is the fact that men are highly sensitive to the opinions and feelings of others." Duncan Forbes, "Sceptical Whiggism, Commerce, and Liberty," in *Essays on Adam Smith*, ed. Andrew S. Skinner and Thomas Wilson (Oxford: Clarendon Press, 1975), p. 194.

18. "Of Commerce," in David Hume, *Essays Moral, Political, and Literary*, ed. Eugene F. Miller (Indianapolis: Liberty Classics, 1987), p. 265.

19. *Réflexions sur le commerce des blés*, in *OC*, 11:197, 201, 207–208.

20. *WN*, p. 910.

21. *WN*, pp. 145, 376.

22. *WN*, p. 412.

23. *WN*, p. 96.

24. Hume, "Of Commerce," p. 265.

25. *WN*, pp. 96, 99–101.

26. Condorcet, *Esquisse d'un tableau historique des progrès de l'esprit humain*, in *OC*, 6:232–234, 248–249.

27. *WN*, pp. 782, 783, 788; *Essai sur la constitution et les fonctions des assemblées provinciales* (1788), in *OC*, 8:476–477; "Sur l'instruction publique" (1791–92), in *OC*, 7:192; and see Chapters 4 and 8. See also Emma Rothschild, "Condorcet and Adam Smith on Education and Instruction," in *Philosophers on Education: Historical Perspectives*, ed. Amélie Oksenberg Rorty (London: Routledge, 1998), pp. 209–226.

28. "The History of Astronomy," in *EPS*, p. 50; Smith also speaks in his history of ancient physics of the "pusillanimous superstition" which was characteristic of the "first ages of the world," and which consisted in the ascription of "almost every unexpected event, to the arbitrary will of some designing, though invisible beings." "The History of Ancient Physics," in *EPS*, p. 112.

29. "Of Superstition and Enthusiasm," in Hume, *Essays*, p. 78; "The History of Astronomy," in *EPS*, p. 50.

30. "Alexander the False Prophet," in *The Works of Lucian*, trans. A. M. Harmon (Cambridge, Mass.: Harvard University Press, 1992), 4:235. This is the work of Lucian's of which Smith says in his lectures on rhetoric that "few things are more entertaining," and which Hume describes at length in the *Enquiry Concerning Human Understanding: LRBL*, p. 52; Hume, *Enquiry*, pp. 120–121; and see Chapter 5.

31. David Hume, *A Treatise of Human Nature*, ed. L. A. Selby-Bigge (Oxford: Clarendon Press, 1978), p. 444; *TMS*, p. 30.

32. "Fragment de l'histoire de la Xe époque," in *OC*, 6:566–567.

33. *TMS*, pp. 32–33.

34. *TMS*, p. 164; *WN*, p. 797.

35. *WN*, pp. 285, 418, 610.

36. *WN*, pp. 729, 828; *Esquisse des progrès*, in *OC*, 6:171.

37. On anxiety and authority in sixteenth-century England, see Stephen Green-

blatt, *Shakespearean Negotiations: The Circulation of Social Energy in Renaissance England* (Berkeley: University of California Press, 1988), chap. 5.

38. *WN*, p. 798.

39. "Monopole et monopoleur," in *OC*, 11:45, 54; *Réflexions sur le commerce des blés*, in *OC*, 11:205, 223.

40. *WN*, pp. 664, 910.

41. *LJ*, pp. 50, 61, 120, 430, 480.

42. *Esquisse*, in *OC*, 6:14; "Fragment de l'histoire de la Xe époque," in *OC*, 6:594.

43. "Sur l'instruction publique," in *OC*, 7:259.

44. *Vie de Voltaire* (1789), in *OC*, 4:182.

45. A "Reform der Denkungsart," a change in the "Sinnesart des Volks." Immanuel Kant, "Beantwortung der Frage: Was ist Aufklarung?" (1784), in *Werkausgabe*, ed. Wilhelm Weischedel (Frankfurt: Suhrkamp, 1968), 11:55, 61; *What is Enlightenment?* in *Kant's Political Writings*, ed. Hans Reiss (Cambridge: Cambridge University Press, 1970), pp. 55, 59.

46. Ian Ross and David Raynor, "Adam Smith and Count Windisch-Grätz: New Letters," *Studies on Voltaire and the Eighteenth Century*, 358 (1998), 172.

47. G. W. F. Hegel, *Phenomenology of Spirit* (1807), trans. A. V. Miller (Oxford: Oxford University Press, 1977), pp. 329, 331.

48. Johann Gottfried Herder, *Journal meiner Reise im Jahr 1769* (Stuttgart: Reclam, 1976), p. 79; Robert Southey, "On the state of the Poor, the principle of Mr. Malthus's Essay on Population, and the Manufacturing System" (1812), in *Essays, Moral and Political* (London: John Murray, 1832), pp. 110–111. This new disposition or spirit of the times, Southey said, was associated with the "manufacturing system," of which "Adam Smith's book is the code, or confession of faith" (p. 111).

49. Tore Frängsmyr, *Sökandet efter Upplysningen: En essä om 1700-talets svenska kulturdebatt* (Uppsala: Wiken, 1993), pp. 13–32; Franco Venturi, *Europe des lumières: recherches sur le 18e siècle* (The Hague: Mouton, 1971), p. 3; Robert Darnton, "George Washington's False Teeth", *New York Review of Books*, March 27, 1997, p. 34; J. G. A. Pocock, *Barbarism and Religion*, vol. 1, *The Enlightenments of Edward Gibbon, 1737–1764* (Cambridge: Cambridge University Press, 1999), pp. 7, 9.

50. "It was an overall purpose of Enlightenment to discourage all forms of metaphysical certainty," Pocock writes; the disposition of enlightenment was a condition both of the writers (some of them philosophers or philosophes) of whom this was the intention, and of all the other, less philosophical individuals, who might come, eventually, to live without certainty. Pocock, *Barbarism and Religion*, 1:250.

51. "What Morellet did in France, why should I not do that elsewhere?" Herder, *Journal meiner Reise im Jahr 1769*, pp. 29, 80, 86–87.

52. "Apologie de l'abbé Galiani," in Denis Diderot, *Oeuvres*, ed. Laurent Versini

(Paris: Robert Laffont, 1995), 3:123–160; "Observations sur le Nakaz," ibid., 576–577.

53. Immanuel Kant, *Critique of Pure Reason*, trans. N. Kemp Smith (New York: St. Martin's Press, 1965), p. 412.

54. A quality relative to "universal human inclinations and needs" thus has a market price *(Marktpreis);* a quality relative to taste alone (such as "wit, lively imagination, and humour") has a luxury price *(Affektionspreis);* moral qualities based on "the maxims of the will" (such as "kindness based on principle") have "an unconditioned and incomparable worth." Immanuel Kant, *Groundwork of the Metaphysic of Morals*, trans. H. J. Paton (New York: Harper and Row, 1964), pp. 102–103. See also Kant's observations on the market price of talent, the luxury price of temperament, and the inner worth, beyond all price, of character. *Anthropologie in pragmatischer Hinsicht*, in Kant, *Werkausgabe*, 12:634.

55. D'Alembert, "Eléments de Philosophie" (1759), quoted in Ernst Cassirer, *The Philosophy of the Enlightenment*, trans. Fritz C. A. Koelln and James P. Pettegrove (Princeton: Princeton University Press, 1951), p. 4.

56. Edmund Burke, *Reflections on the Revolution in France* (1790), ed. Conor Cruise O'Brien (London: Penguin Books, 1982), pp. 170, 188.

57. Alexander Carlyle, *Autobiography of the Rev. Dr. Alexander Carlyle* (Edinburgh: William Blackwood and Sons, 1860), p. 547.

58. Kant, *What is Enlightenment?* pp. 55–56, 59.

59. Anderson proposed to publish reports from "gentlemen in foreign parts," which could be submitted either to "mercantile houses" with Edinburgh connections (from Venice to Elsinore), or to the editor (written, "if possible," on "one sheet *undivided;* for in Britain every slip of paper, however small, pays a separate postage"). James Anderson, "To Foreign Correspondents," *The Bee, or Literary Weekly Intelligencer*, 1 (1791), xvii–xxviii.

60. Burke, *Reflections on the Revolution in France*, pp. 171, 183, 213, 308, 359. Pocock, in his pluralist account of European "Enlightenments," argues that "Burke himself was an Enlightened figure, who saw himself defending Enlightened Europe against the *gens de lettres* and their revolutionary successors." Pocock, *Barbarism and Religion*, 1:7, 251. Burke's *Reflections*, with its observations on the changing use of metaphors of light—"if this gentleman means to confine the terms *enlightened and liberal* to one set of men in England," he says of Richard Price, and, of Talleyrand's views of enlightened usury, "if the word 'enlightened' be understood according to the new dictionary, as it always is in your new schools"—was of vast influence, undoubtedly, in the diffusion in English, in the course of the 1790s, of the political use of the word "enlightened," and of the conception of a sect of enlightenment. Burke, *Reflections*, pp. 182, 308–309.

61. Abbé Barruel, *Mémoires pour servir a l'histoire du Jacobinisme* (London: Le Boussonier, 1797), 1:27, 316, 382–383; 2:128.

62. William Playfair, "Introduction," in Adam Smith, *An Inquiry into the Nature*

and Causes of the Wealth of Nations, 11th ed., ed. Playfair (London: T. Cadell and W. Davies, 1805), 1:xvi–xvii, xxx; many of the meetings were supposed to have been concerned with subsidizing the price of irreligious books.

63. Alexis de Tocqueville, *L'ancien régime et la Révolution* (1856), ed. J.-P. Mayer (Paris: Gallimard, 1967), pp. 230–231, 238–240, 255–263, 283–286.

64. Ibid., p. 257.

65. On the crisis of "the movement of the Enlightenment" in the fifteen years which preceded the Revolution and the relationship between "social history and political economy," see Venturi, *Europe des lumières,* pp. 28–29; see also Steven L. Kaplan, *Bread, Politics, and Political Economy in the Reign of Louis XV,* vol. 2 (The Hague: Martinus Nijhoff, 1976).

66. *TMS,* p. 229.

67. "Sur l'instruction publique," in *OC,* 7:215; *Esquisse,* in *OC,* 7:224–225; and see Chapter 7.

68. *WN,* p. 456.

69. "Éloge de Vincent de Gournay" (1759), in *OT,* 1:602, 605, 620; "Fondations" (1757), in *OT,* 1:591.

70. Ferdinand Galiani, *Dialogues sur le commerce des blés* (1770) (Paris: Fayard, 1984), p. 175.

71. "Apologie de l'abbé Galiani," in Diderot, *Oeuvres,* 3:132, 138.

72. Note (p), in *The Wealth of Nations,* ed. Playfair, 2:253 (comment on Book 4, chap. 3, in *WN,* p. 493); note (f), 2:559 (comment on Book 4, chap. 8, in *WN,* p. 660).

73. Jean-Jacques Rousseau, *Discours sur les sciences et les arts,* ed. Jean Varloot (Paris: Gallimard, 1987), pp. 44, 61, 76; d'Alembert, "Lettre à J.-J. Rousseau, citoyen de Genève," in Rousseau, *Discours,* p. 373; "Droit Naturel," in Diderot, *Oeuvres,* 3:44, 47.

74. "Of Refinement in the Arts," in Hume, *Essays,* pp. 270–271, 277; and see Chapter 8.

75. "Essais sur la peinture pour faire suite au salon de 1765," in Diderot, *Oeuvres,* 4:506.

76. Salons of 1761 and 1763, ibid., 4:218, 278. See Pierre Rosenberg, "Un peintre subversif qui s'ignore," in *Chardin,* ed. Rosenberg (Paris: Éditions de la Réunion des musees nationaux, 1999), p. 33.

77. Letter of 1785, in *Corr.,* p. 286; *The Autobiography of Johann Wolfgang von Goethe,* trans. John Oxenford (Chicago: University of Chicago Press, 1974), 2:350.

78. *Procès-Verbal de ce qui s'est passé au Lit de Justice, Tenu par le Roi à Versailles, le Mardi douze Mars 1776* (Paris: Imprimerie Royale, 1776). The texts of the six edicts are printed in *OT,* 5:200–213, 218–229, 234–238, 238–255, 260–265, 267–269, and a long extract from the *Procès-Verbal* in *OT,* 5:273–295.

79. "Lit de Justice," in *OT,* 5:288.

80. Jean-Etienne-Marie Portalis, *Éloge d'Antoine-Louis Séguier, avocat-général*

au Parlement de Paris (Paris: Nicolle, 1806), pp. 66–67, 80, 82; see also, on Séguier, Kaplan, *Bread, Politics, and Political Economy,* vol. 2, chap. 9.

81. "Lit de Justice," in *OT,* 5:295.

82. Jacques Necker, *Sur la législation et le commerce des grains* (1775), in *Oeuvres complètes* (Paris: Treuttel and Würtz, 1820), 1:5, 126–128, 131.

83. "Lettre d'un laboureur de Picardie" (1775), in *OC,* 11:9, 15, 18.

84. Tocqueville, *L'ancien régime,* pp. 43–44, 47, 182, 270–271.

85. Ibid., pp. 271, 273, 276.

86. Alexis de Tocqueville, *L'Ancien Régime et la Révolution: Fragments et notes inédites sur la Révolution,* ed. André Jardin, in *Oeuvres complètes,* ed. J.-P. Mayer (Paris: Gallimard, 1952–1953), vol. 2, pt. 2, pp. 37–38, 44–47.

87. Tocqueville, *L'ancien régime,* pp. 72, 280, 291.

88. *WN,* pp. 341–345.

89. Tocqueville, *L'ancien régime,* p. 373, and *L'Ancien Régime et la Révolution: Fragments et notes,* p. 381.

90. "They acted by the ancient organized states in the shape of their old organization, and not by the organic *moleculae* of a disbanded people": this is Burke's description of the English during the Restoration and the Revolution. Burke, *Reflections,* p. 106.

91. Herder, *Journal meiner Reise im Jahr 1769,* pp. 94–95, 114–115.

92. Jean-Jacques Rousseau, *Émile* (1762), in *Oeuvres complètes* (Paris: Pléiade, 1969), 4:596, 633.

93. Johann Georg Hamann, *Briefwechsel,* ed. Arthur Henkel (Wiesbaden: Insel, 1965), 5:290–291; idem, *Sämtliche Werke,* ed. Josef Nadler (Vienna: Herder, 1951), 3:279. See also Jean Blum, *La vie et l'oeuvre de J.-G.Hamann, le "Mage du Nord," 1730–1788* (Paris: Felix Alcan, 1912), pp. 289, 515; Isaiah Berlin, *The Magus of the North: J. G. Hamann and the Origins of Modern Irrationalism,* ed. Henry Hardy (New York: Farrar, Straus and Giroux, 1994), pp. 107–108.

94. Hegel, *Phenomenology of Spirit,* pp. 339, 353, 359–360; idem, *Philosophy of Mind* (1830), trans. William Wallace (Oxford: Clarendon Press, 1971), p. 256.

95. Louis-Gabriel-Ambroise de Bonald, "Observations sur un ouvrage posthume de Condorcet," in *Oeuvres complètes,* ed. J.-P. Migne (Paris: Migne, 1864), 1:721–723.

96. "Sur l'Économie Politique," ibid., pp. 297, 299; "De la Richesse des Nations," ibid., p. 309.

97. *TMS,* p. 157.

98. *WN,* pp. 142, 310, 496, 563, 947.

99. *WN,* pp. 138, 157, 394, 405, 636, 639, 648, 734, 823, 853.

100. *WN,* pp. 827, 898–899, 927, 936. Vexation is also one of Laurence Sterne's preoccupations: "VEXATION upon VEXATION," as in the eventual wreck of the post-chaise. Laurence Sterne, *The Life and Opinions of Tristram Shandy* (1759–1767) (London: Penguin Books, 1985), p. 494.

101. "Mémoire sur les prêts d'argent," in *OT*, 3:161–164, 199; see also Emma Rothschild, "An Alarming Commercial Crisis in Eighteenth-Century Angoulême: Sentiments in Economic History," *Economic History Review*, 51, 2 (1998), 268–293.

102. *Réflexions sur le commerce des blés*, in *OC*, 11: 145–146, 191.

103. Thomas Paine, *The Rights of Man*, pt. 2 (1792) (London: J. M. Dent, 1956), pp. 153, 158, 238.

104. *Esquisse*, in *OC*, 6:190–191.

105. "De la nature des pouvoirs politiques dans une nation libre" (1792), in *OC*, 10:607; "Sur l'impôt progressif" (1793), in *OC*, 12:632.

106. "Lit de Justice," in *OT*, 5:288.

107. Burke, *Reflections*, pp. 194, 197, 351–352. Burke's eulogy to the fiscal state was the object of considerable merriment, even to his friends. Philip Francis wrote in his copy of the *Reflections* that "if I understand this stuff, he means to affirm that public virtue increases with the increase of the revenue . . . then the more the people are taxed below, the more virtue there will be above." Francis says that he himself comes to the "opposite conclusion, viz that money and virtue are not related . . . Mr B would have been of the same opinion, if it had suited his purpose." These are annotations in the copy of the *Reflections* that Burke sent to Francis in October 1790, now in the Houghton Library at Harvard University. Of Burke's famous peroration, in which he calls on the proponents of political reform to "make the reparation as nearly as possible in the style of the building," Francis asks, "In what style would you repair the government of Morocco?"

108. Samuel Taylor Coleridge, *The Friend*, in *The Collected Works of Samuel Taylor Coleridge* (Princeton: Princeton University Press, 1969), Vol. 4, pt. 1, p. 198.

109. Leo Tolstoy, *War and Peace*, trans. Rosemary Edmonds (London: Penguin Books, 1982), pp. 1188–91.

110. "Fragmente" (1810), in Adam Müller, *Ausgewählte Abhandlungen*, ed. Jakob Baxa (Vienna: Gustav Fischer, 1931), p. 86; "Der Staat, als nützliche Entreprise," in Adam Müller, *Vermischte Schriften über Staat, Philosophie und Kunst* (Vienna: Heubner, 1817), 1:228.

111. Comte de Las Cases, *Le Mémorial de Sainte-Hélène*, ed. Joël Schmidt (Paris: Éditions du Seuil, 1968), 2:1441.

112. Burke can be credited with one of the first great public uses of "market" in its most abstract sense, when he writes, in 1795, that "the moment that government appears at market, all the principles of market will be subverted." *Thoughts and Details on Scarcity*, in *The Works of the Right Honourable Edmund Burke* (Boston: Little, Brown, 1894), 5:154; see also Chapter 2.

113. Burke, *Reflections*, pp. 134, 194.

114. "Monopole et monopoleur," in *OC*, 11:41.

115. "Réflexions sur la jurisprudence criminelle" (1775), in *OC*, 7:8.

116. "Foire" (1757), in *OT*, 1:580.

117. *Procès-Verbal*, p. 39; "Déclaration Royale supprimant les règlements de police, ainsi que les droits et offices établis à Paris sur les grains," in *OT*, 5:221.

118. "Lettre d'un laboureur de Picardie," in *OC*, 11:21; *Réflexions sur le commerce des blés*, in *OC*, 11:235.

119. This is Gustav Schmoller's phrase, quoted in Anton Zottmann, *Die Wirtschaftspolitik Friedrichs des Grossen* (Leipzig: Franz Deuticke, 1937), p. 26.

120. *WN*, pp. 136–137, 141.

121. *WN*, p. 472, and fn. 60; *TMS*, p. 230.

122. Sir Lewis Namier, *The Structure of Politics at the Accession of George III* (1957) (London: Macmillan, 1961), p. 45.

123. *WN*, pp. 471–472.

124. Burke, *Reflections*, pp. 197–198.

125. *WN*, pp. 793, 797.

126. *WN*, pp. 157–158.

127. *Vie de M. Turgot*, in *OC*, 5:28, *Réflexions sur le commerce des blés*, in *OC*, 11:200; and see Chapter 6.

128. *Sur les assemblées provinciales*, in *OC*, 8:391.

129. *WN*, p. 797; *Esquisse*, in *OC*, 6:264.

130. "Lit de Justice," in *OT*, 5:279, 288, 291, 293.

131. *WN*, pp. 135–136.

132. Felicité de Lamennais, *Essai sur l'indifférence en matière de religion* (Paris: Tournachon-Molin, 1820), 1:88–89, 158. On criticisms of Voltaire's double religion, or irreligion, see Owen Chadwick, *The Secularization of the European Mind in the Nineteenth Century* (Cambridge: Cambridge University Press, 1975), pp. 10, 104.

133. Tocqueville, *L'ancien régime*, pp. 238–239, 259–260.

134. [Abbé Barruel], *Les Helviennes, ou Lettres Provinciales philosophiques*, 4th ed., (Paris: Briand, 1789), 1:5.

135. "Lit de Justice," in *OT*, 5:290, 293.

136. Lamennais, *Essai sur l'indifférence*, 1:52, 390.

137. *Rapport sur l'instruction publique, Fait au nom du Comité de Constitution, par M. Talleyrand-Périgord* (Paris: Assemblée Nationale, 1791), p. 4; and see Chapter 8.

138. *Vie de Voltaire*, in *OC*, 4:20.

139. Letters of December 26, 1769; February 2, 1770; March 23, 1770; and December 21, 1770, in *OT*, 3:77, 374, 384, 398–399. Tocqueville says of Turgot that "the taste for political freedoms" came to him only late in life, and Turgot's projects of public education of the early 1770s—his promise to Louis XVI, in a memorandum drafted by Dupont de Nemours, of a "new people"—are far less concerned with the rights of humanity, or of individuals, than Condorcet's later proposals. Tocqueville, *L'ancien régime*, p. 257; "Mémoire sur les municipalités" (1775), in *OT*, 4:580–581, 621; and see Chapter 6.

140. Letter of July 10, 1769, in *The Letters of David Hume*, ed. J. Y. T. Greig (Oxford: Clarendon Press, 1932), 2:205; see also n. 1, in *Corr.*, pp. 114–115.

141. *WN,* pp. 674, 678, 830.

142. *Esquisse,* in *OC,* 6:191; *Sur l'instruction publique,* in *OC,* 7:202.

143. François de Fénelon, *Les aventures de Télémaque* (Paris: Garnier, 1994), pp. 166, 524; "Critical Bibliography," in Fénelon, *Telemachus, son of Ulysses,* ed. and trans. Patrick Riley (Cambridge: Cambridge University Press, 1994), p. xxxii.

144. This is the description given in the oration of Lomosonov in 1755, quoted in Nicholas V. Riasanovsky, *The Image of Peter the Great in Russian History and Thought* (Oxford: Oxford University Press, 1985), p. 32.

145. "Instruction," in *Documents of Catherine the Great,* ed. W. F. Reddaway (Cambridge: Cambridge University Press, 1931), pp. 262–263.

146. Sir James Steuart, *An Inquiry into the Principles of Political Oeconomy,* ed. Andrew S. Skinner (Edinburgh: Scottish Economic Society, 1966), 1:16–17, 25.

147. Stewart, "Account," p. 322.

148. "Of Commerce," in Hume, *Essays,* p. 254.

149. Albert O. Hirschman, *The Passions and the Interests: Political Arguments for Capitalism before Its Triumph* (Princeton: Princeton University Press, 1977). See also Nannerl O. Keohane, *Philosophy and the State in France: The Renaissance to the Enlightenment* (Princeton: Princeton University Press, 1980), esp. chap. 5.

150. "Smith was concerned, far more than earlier writers, with the 'great mob of mankind,'" as Hirschman writes, and Smith also believed, more than Montesquieu or Steuart or Necker, that even the mob, or the "people," have complicated lives. Hirschman, *The Passions and the Interests,* pp. 109–112. Like Stephen Holmes, in his essay "The Secret History of Self-Interest," I would identify the "pitiful impoverishment" of nineteenth- and twentieth-century economists' "moral psychology"—or what Hirschman describes as the "reductionist step," the "narrowing of the field of inquiry" of social thought—as coming after, rather than as a consequence of, the *Wealth of Nations.* Smith's account of self-interest, Holmes writes, is one of "exceptional finesse"; it is also, in its insistence on the equal deviousness of the poor and the rich, both "subversive" and "profoundly egalitarian and democratic." Stephen Holmes, *Passions and Constraint: On the Theory of Liberal Democracy* (Chicago: University of Chicago Press, 1995), pp. 43–44, 63.

151. *WN,* pp. 663–664; and see Chapter 5.

152. *Réflexions sur le commerce des blés,* in *OC,* 11:105–106; Necker, "Éloge de Jean-Baptiste Colbert" (1773), in *Oeuvres complètes,* 15:42, 45–46; and see Chapter 6.

153. Lamennais, *Essai sur l'indifférence,* 1:63, 88, 373–374, 396, 517.

154. Lamennais, *Réflexions sur l'état de l'église en France pendant le dix-huitième siècle, et sur sa situation actuelle* (Paris: Tournachon-Molin, 1819), pp. 42–44.

155. See Lucretius, *De rerum natura,* for example, 2.55–61; "Alexander the False Prophet," 47, in *The Works of Lucian,* 4:235.

156. Letter of December 28, 1773, in *Correspondance inédite de Condorcet et de Turgot 1770–1779,* ed. Charles Henry (Paris: Didier, 1883), p. 155. "Your distinction between indifference in morality and indulgence seems to me to be infinitely just," Condorcet wrote in reply; see *Correspondance,* p. 156.

157. *Sur la législation et le commerce des grains,* in Necker, *Oeuvres complètes,* 1:4, 131, 254.

158. "Sur l'instruction publique," in *OC,* 7:211–215; and see Chapters 6 and 7.

159. Alexis de Tocqueville, *Souvenirs* (Paris: Gallimard, 1964), p. 87.

160. Woodrow Wilson, *An Old Master and Other Political Essays* (New York: Charles Scribner's Sons, 1893), pp. 25, 130.

161. Tocqueville, *L'ancien régime,* pp. 262–263.

162. Bernard Bailyn, *On the Teaching and Writing of History* (Hanover, N.H.: University Press of New England, 1994), p. 88.

163. Jean-Baptiste Say, *Cours complet d'économie politique pratique* (Paris: Guillaumin, 1840), 2:540.

164. *Réflexions philosophiques sur l'égalité* (1796), in Necker, *Oeuvres complètes,* 10:346, 371, 496.

165. Lucien Febvre, *Le problème de l'incroyance au 16e siècle: La religion de Rabelais* (1942) (Paris: Albin Michel, 1968), pp. 16, 424–425.

166. Baker, *Condorcet: From Natural Philosophy to Social Mathematics,* p. xi; Donald Winch, *Adam Smith's Politics: An Essay in Historiographic Revision* (Cambridge: Cambridge University Press, 1978), p. 5.

167. *WN,* pp. 137, 648, 660.

168. "Réflexions sur la jurisprudence criminelle," in *OC,* 7:5–15; *WN,* p. 904.

169. *Procès-Verbal,* pp. 4–5, 16, 30, 63, 65, 67, 78. The institution of the *Lit de Justice,* as a solemn political proceeding, was itself an invented tradition of the sixteenth century; see Sarah Hanley, *The Lit de Justice of the Kings of France* (Princeton: Princeton University Press, 1983), pp. 41–51. Turgot, Malesherbes, and the king were the supporters, within the Council of Ministers, of the use of the procedure. Edgar Faure, *La disgrâce de Turgot* (Paris: Gallimard, 1961), p. 447.

170. Barruel, *Mémoires pour servir a l'histoire du Jacobinisme,* 1:383. Condorcet was supposed to have refused to admit a priest to d'Alembert's deathbed.

171. Augustin de Lamet and Germain Fromageau, *La dictionnaire des cas de conscience* (Paris: Coignard, 1733), 2:1569–70.

172. Richard Burn, *The Justice of the Peace, and Parish Officer* (London: A. Miller, 1758), 1:247–250; *WN,* p. 154.

173. "Mémoire sur les prêts d'argent," in *OT,* 3:180–181.

174. *TMS,* p. 9. Smith's luxuriant language of sentiments, senses, feelings, and emotions is more conspicuous in the 1759 edition of the *Theory of Moral Sentiments* than in the final, 1790 edition, and more so in either than in the *Wealth of Nations.* The words "sentiment," "emotion," and "passion" are well over twice as frequent in the 1759 text as in the additions of 1790; the word "emotion" has almost disappeared in the new additions. On the differ-

ent "voices" of the *Theory of Moral Sentiments* and the *Wealth of Nations,* see Vivienne Brown, *Adam Smith's Discourse* (London: Routledge, 1994), chap. 2.

175. *TMS,* p. 319.

176. [Levesque de Pouilly], *Théorie des Sentimens Agréables* (London: Brakstone, 1750), pp. 5, 83.

177. On Condorcet's philosophy of history, and his conception of the history of ideas as a contribution to political identity, see Jennifer Paige Montana, "Intellectual Subversion in Eighteenth-Century Political Thought: Condorcet's Philosophy of History" (Ph.D. diss., Harvard University, 1994).

178. François Guizot, *Cours d'Histoire Moderne: Leçons du cours de 1828* (Brussels: Hauman, Cattoir, 1838), pp. 17, 25–26.

179. See Bailyn, *On the Teaching and Writing of History,* pp. 55–58.

180. *Corr.,* p. 313.

181. *Esquisse,* in *OC,* 6:196.

182. Letter of February 2, 1770, in *OT,* 3:373–374.

183. Hume to Smith, August 1776; Smith to Thomas Cadell, October 1780; and Smith to Andreas Holt, October 1780, in *Corr.,* pp. 205, 248, 251.

184. "Playfair's *Edition of Wealth of Nations,*" *Edinburgh Review,* 7, 14 (January 1806), 470–471.

185. "Illustration of relations of contract by the conceptions of money and a book," in Immanuel Kant, *The Philosophy of Law,* trans. W. Hastie (Edinburgh: T. & T. Clark, 1887), pp. 125–131.

186. Letter of August 24, 1815, in *The Adams-Jefferson Letters: The Complete Correspondence between Thomas Jefferson and Abigail and John Adams,* ed. Lester J. Cappon (Chapel Hill: University of North Carolina Press, 1959), 2:455. This observation is taken by Bernard Bailyn as the epigraph to the first chapter of *The Ideological Origins of the American Revolution;* the observation about sentiments is in a letter of 1818 from John Adams to Hezekiah Niles, also quoted by Bailyn. Bernard Bailyn, *The Ideological Origins of the American Revolution,* enl. ed. (Cambridge, Mass.: Harvard University Press, 1992), pp. 1, 160.

187. Tocqueville, *L'Ancien Régime et la Révolution: Fragments et notes,* 2:33, 45; letter to Tocqueville of November 5, 1853, quoted in Lady Eastlake, *Mrs. Grote: A Sketch* (London: John Murray, 1880), pp. 133–134.

188. *WN,* p. 8.

189. Letter of April 1771, in *Correspondance de Condorcet et Mme. Suard,* pp. 26–27.

190. *LRBL,* p. 112.

191. "About a week after I was made a Commissioner of the Customs," Smith wrote to his friend William Eden, "upon examining my own wearing apparel, I found, to my great astonishment, that I had scarce a stock, a cravat, a pair of ruffles, or a pocket handkerchief which was not prohibited to be worn or used in Great Britain. I wished to set an example and burnt them all." Letter

of January 1780, in *Corr.*, pp. 245–246; and see Ian Simpson Ross, *The Life of Adam Smith* (Oxford: Clarendon Press, 1995), chap. 19.

192. Marc Bloch, *L'étrange défaite* (Paris: Gallimard, 1990), p. 30.

193. The characteristic of the "mechanical" philosophy of the French—with its "political economy" and its "science of government"—was to provide "an eagle's-eye view, in place of painfully acquired knowledge of the needs and the true circumstances of the country." Johann Gottfried von Herder, *Auch eine Philosophie der Geschichte zur Bildung der Menschheit* (1774), in *Sämtliche Werke*, ed. B. Suphan (Berlin: Weidmann, 1891, rpt. 1967), 5:536.

194. *TMS*, p. 135.

195. *TMS*, p. 195.

196. Paine, *The Rights of Man*, 1:95–97.

197. *TMS*, pp. 233–234.

198. John Stuart Mill, "On the Definition of Political Economy; and on the Method of Investigation Proper to It" (1836), in *Collected Works* (Toronto: University of Toronto Press, 1967), 4:321–323.

199. Giacomo Leopardi, "Dialogo di Tristano e di un amico" (1834), in *Tutte le opere*, 1:184.

200. John Stuart Mill, *Principles of Political Economy with Some of Their Applications to Social Philosophy* (Toronto: University of Toronto Press, 1965), p. 752; idem, *On Liberty* (London: Penguin Books, 1974), pp. 106, 125.

2. Adam Smith and Conservative Economics

1. A slightly shorter version of this chapter was published in the *Economic History Review*, 45, 2 (1992), 74–96.

2. *Annual Register*, 32 (1790), 212–213; *Scots Magazine*, 52 (1790), 363. See also John Rae, *The Life of Adam Smith* (1895) (New York: Augustus M. Kelley, 1965), pp. 435–436; F. W. Hirst, *Adam Smith* (London: Macmillan, 1904), p. 234. Rae quotes a letter of August 20, 1790, from the penal reformer Sir Samuel Romilly—at that time a fervent supporter of the Revolution—in which he compares the "little impression" made by Smith's death with the earlier "panegyrics" to Dr. Johnson: "Scarce any notice has been taken of it." Samuel Romilly, *Memoirs of the life of Sir Samuel Romilly* (London: John Murray, 1840), 1:403.

3. "It is a matter of very natural curiosity to enquire in what manner Dr. ADAM SMITH, who published such a laboured eulogium on the stoical end of David Hume, closed his own life." *The Times*, August 4, 1790, p. 2. The reference is to the letter by Smith, published in 1777 with *The life of David Hume*, of which he wrote, in 1780, that it had "brought upon me ten times more abuse" than his attack, in the *Wealth of Nations*, on the commercial system of Britain. *Corr.*, p. 251.

4. *The Times*, August 16, 1790, p. 4. Smith's system is said in the original edition to be "most [sic] essentially different from that of Count Verri," which

seems to have been a misprint, corrected in the *Gentleman's Magazine* reprint later in 1790.

5. *Gentleman's Magazine*, 60, pt. 2 (July 1790), 673; also ibid., (August 1790), 761–762.

6. *Gazette Nationale, ou Le Moniteur Universel*, August 24, 1790, p. 976; October 25, 1790, p. 1232; May 26, 1791, p. 605. Alengry, in his study of Condorcet, surmises that the notes were never written. Franck Alengry, *Condorcet guide de la Révolution française* (Paris: Giard and Brière, 1904), pp. 20, 693; see also Eugène Daire, "Notice sur Condorcet," in *Mélanges d'économie politique*, ed. Daire (Paris: Guillaumin, 1847), 1:458, n. 2; Gilbert Faccarello, "Presentation," in *Condorcet mathématicien, économiste, philosophe, homme politique*, ed. Pierre Crépel and Christian Gilain (Paris: Minerve, 1989), pp. 123–125.

7. *Bibliothèque de l'homme public; ou analyse raisonnée des principaux ouvrages françois et étrangers*, ed. M. de Condorcet, M. de Peysonel, M. Le Chapelier (Paris: Buisson, 1790), 3:108. Smith appears in the series after Aristotle but before Plato. The point of the library was "as far as it will be possible, to put the science of government and of administration within the reach of everyone," since, "according to the new constitution, there is no one who cannot be called to discuss and to defend the interests of their canton, their province, and even of the entire kingdom." Political economy was therefore of the first importance: "This study will become that of all good spirits" (1:iv–vi). In Spain, Condorcet's summary was apparently considered less subversive (in 1792) than Smith's own work: a translation was published with Condorcet's name but without Smith's, and with a note by the translator explaining that while the original author sometimes made regrettably "improper applications of his theories," the abridgement offered "all the advantages without the inconveniences." Ernest Lluch, "Condorcet et la diffusion de la *Richesse des nations* en Espagne," in Crépel and Gilain, *Condorcet*, p. 192.

8. "Both man's moral nature, and his mental processes, were the subject of much general intellectual inquiry, and some controversy, in the middle of the century; of bitter partisan strife in the French Revolutionary period . . . Writers of the 1790s looked back on their predecessors of the earlier generation, and saw subversion in work that in its day was at most mildly reformist." Marilyn Butler, *Jane Austen and the War of Ideas* (Oxford: Clarendon Press, 1987), pp. 7–8.

9. Letter to Lord Craig of February 20, 1794, in *The Collected Works of Dugald Stewart*, ed. Sir W. Hamilton (Edinburgh: Thomas Constable, 1858), 10:lxxiii.

10. "Had Mr. Burke possessed talents similar to the author of 'On the Wealth of Nations,' he would have comprehended all the parts which enter into, and by assemblage, form a constitution." Thomas Paine, *The Rights of Man*, pt. 1 (1791) (London: J. M. Dent, 1958), p. 53.

11. Mary Wollstonecraft, *Vindication of the Rights of Woman* (1792) (London:

Penguin Books, 1982), pp. 148–150, 252; *Vindication of the Rights of Men,* in *The Works of Wollstonecraft,* ed. Janet Todd and Marilyn Butler (London: Chatto & Pickering, 1989), 5:24–25. See *TMS,* pp. 61–62, 256.

12. James Mackintosh, *Vindiciae Gallicae: Defence of the French Revolution and its English admirers, against the accusations of the Right Honourable Edmund Burke* (London: G. G. J. and J. Robinson, 1791), p. 30.

13. Elie Halévy, *La formation du radicalisme philosophique,* vol. 2, *L'évolution de la doctrine utilitaire de 1789 à 1815* (1901) (Paris: Presses Universitaires de France, 1995), p. 75; see also note 82 below on Halévy's view of Smith and Burke.

14. [T. Archard], *Suppression of the French nobility vindicated, to which is added a comprehensive view of Dr. Smith's system* (London: J. Debrett, 1792), p. 69.

15. Edmund Burke, *Reflections on the Revolution in France* (1790) (London: Penguin Books, 1982), pp. 189, 197, 351; see also J. G. A. Pocock, "The Political Economy of Burke's Analysis of the French Revolution," in *Virtue, Commerce, and History* (Cambridge: Cambridge University Press, 1985), p. 199.

16. Both words were little more than general terms of abuse; see, for example, Burke, *Reflections,* pp. 213–214, 299–300. Dugald Stewart's Victorian biographer could thus write that "in no part of his political writings" did Stewart show "higher moral courage than in his estimate of the doctrines of the French Economists . . . at a time when their general doctrines were subjected in this country to the indiscriminating obloquy of an alleged revolutionary tendency." Stewart's commitment to his newborn godson, in 1793, was quite bold: "I promise to do all I can to make him a Philosopher and an Economist," and to give him a snuffbox "with the *Rights of Man* inscribed on the lid." John Veitch, "A Memoir of Dugald Stewart," in Stewart, *Works,* 10:l, cxxxv.

17. In the first pages of the *Reflections,* Burke refers to the pro-Revolutionary duke de la Rochefoucauld, with whom Smith was on friendly terms until the end of his life; see Dugald Stewart, "Account of the Life and Writings of Adam Smith, LL.D," in *EPS,* p. 303, and *Corr.,* p. 279. Smith was also on good terms with Earl Stanhope (*Corr.,* p. 278), and with Burke's detested Lord Lansdowne (Shelburne): *Corr.,* pp. 137–138, 278, 295.

18. Edmund Burke, *The Correspondence of Edmund Burke,* ed. A. Cobban and R. A. Smith (Cambridge: Cambridge University Press, 1967), vol. 6 (1789–1791), pp. 364, 478. Condorcet criticized Burke's views on the French Revolution before the publication of the *Reflections,* and compared him unfavorably with the English feminist Mrs. Macaulay: she was "as enthusiastic for liberty as Mr. Burke could be for tyranny" and would not have stooped to "the absurd and disgusting galimatias by which the famous rhetorist" had attacked the French constitution. "Sur l'Admission des Femmes au Droit de Cité" (1790), in *OC,* 10:123–124.

19. Burke, *Reflections,* p. 183; for Smith's observations on prejudice, see, for ex-

ample, *WN*, pp. 124, 340, 361, 474–475, 503, 517, 533, 555, 640, 663, 772, and 944, and *TMS*, pp. 228–229.

20. Burke, *Reflections*, pp. 187, 189, 192; see Smith's discussion of religious instruction, *WN*, pp. 788–814, and Chapter 5.

21. Burke, *Reflections*, p. 181.

22. *The Parliamentary History of England* (hereafter *PH*), vol. 30 (February 1, 1793), cols. 329–330. Lansdowne was at the time one of the leading British supporters of the French Revolution. He later sent Stewart the comment on Smith quoted in the 1810 edition of Stewart's "Account": "I owe to a journey I made with Mr. Smith from Edinburgh to London, the difference between light and darkness through the best part of my life." "Account," n. 1, p. 347.

23. "To trace the errors of the French to these causes was manifestly fallacious," Loughborough (the former Alexander Wedderburn) went on. "The Old Man of the Mountains," by contrast, "had every quality to entitle him to shine as a French hero." *PH*, vol. 30, cols. 333–334.

24. The pseudonymous contributors to *The Bee* reported in 1791 that Smith was contemptuous of Dr. Johnson (except when he described "the madness of modern wars"), had doubts about Shakespeare, and "regarded the French theatre as the standard of dramatic excellence" ("Amicus"); and that his affection for Hume "hindered him from being a Christian" ("Ascanius," or Lord Buchan). *The Bee*, 3 (1791), 2, 3, 5, 7, 165, 166. The report of Smith's respect for Rousseau, at least, is unconvincing. Smith did translate parts of Rousseau's *Discourse on Inequality* in 1756, but he later described him, in a letter to Hume, as a "hypocritical pedant." *Corr.*, pp. 112–113.

25. *Corr.*, p. 313.

26. *Adam Smith's Library: A Catalogue*, ed. Hiroshi Mizuta (Oxford: Clarendon Press, 2000), p. 62. Mizuta also shows that Smith owned a presentation copy, from the author, of Condorcet's 1785 essay on probability and voting, and a copy of Condorcet's *Vie de M. Turgot*, published in England in 1786. Condorcet makes the remark about Smith in the English constitutional chamber in his "Examen sur cette question: est-il utile de diviser une assemblée nationale en plusieurs chambres?" (1789), in *OC*, 9:358.

27. *TMS*, pp. 61, 228. The additions, which Smith completed in the winter before his death, amount to about one third of the complete edition. Stewart, "Account," p. 328; *Corr.*, p. 310; D. D. Raphael and A. L. Mcfie, "Introduction," in *TMS*, p. 43. In the "Advertisement" to the edition, Smith says that his remaining "great work" is to be a "theory of jurisprudence," of which "I have not altogether abandoned the design." *TMS*, p. 3. See also Laurence Dickey, "Historicizing the 'Adam Smith Problem': Conceptual, Historiographical and Textual issues," *Journal of Modern History* 58 (September 1986), 579–609.

28. *TMS*, pp. 231–233.

29. Dupont enclosed a book he had just written about commercial reform. In his

letter, he apologizes for its moderate tone, and speaks of his efforts to "persuade" people—the opponents of the commercial treaty—who were "animated even to fanaticism" ("animés jusqu'au fanatisme"); Smith speaks of the spirit of system which takes over the more gentle public spirit, "always animates it, and often inflames it even to the madness of fanaticism." "I have avoided shocking directly the prejudices of my readers . . . All public opinion deserves to be treated with respect," Dupont says; Smith says of the man of humanity that "when he cannot conquer the rooted prejudices of the people by reason and persuasion, he will not attempt to subdue them by force." *Corr.*, pp. 312–313; *TMS*, pp. 232–233.

30. Smith's last explicit political comment is in a letter to Henry Dundas of March 25, 1789, in which he strongly supports the "propriety and prudence of every part of" Pitt's conduct in the crisis. *Corr.*, pp. 318–319. Burke and Fox were Pitt's great opponents, whom he accused of "factious opposition" and "desperate faction or cabal." *PH*, vol. 27, col. 1007. The supposedly "French" paragraphs in *TMS* (pp. 231–233) are concerned largely with "civil faction." Smith's language echoes in striking respects the parliamentary disputes of 1788–89: he mentions leaders who mean "their own aggrandisement"; efforts to change the "constitution or form of government" (*PH*, vol. 27, cols. 959, 1117); proposals to "new-model the constitution" (cols. 856, 948); hopes for "internal tranquillity" and happiness (cols. 988, 990); the objective of "proper temper and moderation" (col. 713): debates of December 10 and 26, 1788, and January 16, 19, and 26, 1789.

31. *TMS*, pp. 233–234. Smith's description of the "royal reformer," with his "general, and even systematical, idea of the perfection of policy and law," seems to be based on Frederick's memoirs, of which he owned the edition published posthumously in Berlin in 1788. *Adam Smith's Library: A Catalogue*, p. 97. Frederick describes the efforts of "the prince" to achieve "complete perfection," and he proposes that sovereigns "should act from a determinate system of politics, war, finance, commerce, and laws"; he writes of the prince that "he must see, think, and act for the whole community." "Essai sur les formes de gouvernement, & sur les devoirs des souverains" (1781), in *Oeuvres Posthumes de Frédéric II, Roi de Prusse* (Berlin: Voss and Decker, 1788), 6:68, 69, 87.

32. On the interpretation of Smith as increasingly conservative and critical of France, see Walther Eckstein, "Einleitung," in Adam Smith, *Theorie der ethischen Gefuhle*, trans. Eckstein (Leipzig: Felix Meiner, 1926), pp. xlii–xliii; see also Raphael and Macfie, "Introduction," in *TMS*, pp. 18–19. Donald Winch's description—of Smith's "remarkably unruffled comments on the revolution"—is more convincing. Winch, "The Burke-Smith Problem and Late Eighteenth-Century Political and Economic Thought," *Historical Journal*, 28, 1 (1985), 233.

33. Letter of June 1777, in James Boswell, *Life of Johnson* (Oxford: Oxford University Press, 1980), p. 810.

34. Walter Bagehot reproduces the viceregal tone of the late eighteenth-century Anglo-Scottish ascendancy in his odd essay "Adam Smith as a Person": "Lord Mansfield is said to have told Boswell that he did not feel, in reading either Hume or Adam Smith, that he was reading English at all; and it was very natural that it should be so. English was not the mother tongue of either . . . Hume is always idiomatic, but his idioms are constantly wrong; many of his best passages are, on that account, curiously grating and puzzling; you feel that they are very like what an Englishman would say, but yet that, after all, somehow or other, they are what he never would say . . . [Smith] adheres to the heavy 'book' English which he had found in the works of others, and was sure that he could repeat in his own." Walter Bagehot, *Biographical Studies* (London: Longmans, Green, 1889), pp. 272–273.

35. Alexander Carlyle, *Autobiography of the Rev. Dr. Alexander Carlyle* (Edinburgh: William Blackwood and Sons, 1860), pp. 281, 283, 430–431. Carlyle's memoir covers the period until 1770, and was written between 1800 and 1805. Carlyle was opposed to Smith's skeptical view of militias and national military spirit in Book 5 of the *Wealth of Nations*. Ibid., p. 283; and see R. B. Sher, *Church and University in the Scottish Enlightenment* (Edinburgh: Edinburgh University Press, 1985), pp. 236–239.

36. Carlyle, *Autobiography,* p. 547.

37. Lord Cockburn, *Memorials of His Time* (Edinburgh: Adam and Charles Black, 1856), pp. 46, 80. See also Bianca Maria Fontana, *Rethinking the Politics of Commercial Society: The Edinburgh Review, 1802–1832* (Cambridge: Cambridge University Press, 1985).

38. Stewart, "Account," p. 339.

39. "We had then no popular representation, no reformed burghs, no effective rival of the Established Church, no free press, no public meetings, no trial by jury at all in civil actions"; it was only the "steadiness" of a few Whig lawyers which saved Scotland from the prostration of Austrian or Russian provinces. Lord Cockburn, *An Examination of the Trials for Sedition which have hitherto occurred in Scotland* (Edinburgh: David Douglas, 1888), 1:76–77.

40. *A Complete Collection of State Trials,* ed. T. B. Howell and T. J. Howell (London: T. C. Hansard, 1817), 23:117, 182, 231–238 (hereafter *State Trials*); Cockburn, *Examination,* 1:159, 176; "Trial of Mr Muir," *Scots Magazine,* 55 (1793), 417–424, 484–490. The indictment against Muir says that he set out to "represent the government of this country as oppressive and tyrannical, and the legislative body of the state as venal and corrupt"; he compared France and Britain "with respect to the expenses necessary for carrying on the functions of government"; and he represented the monarchy as "useless, cumbersome and expensive" (col. 118).

41. *State Trials,* 23:346, 348, 351; Cockburn, *Examination,* 1:188.

42. *State Trials,* 23:573, 721.

43. Letters from Lord Craig to Mr. Stewart, and from Mr. Stewart to Lord Craig, February 1794, in Stewart, *Works,* 10:lxx–lxxv. Veitch comments: "On

the back of one of the letters there occur, in Mrs. Stewart's handwriting, the following words:—'Scotland in the 1794. From two persons who were at least three evenings in the week in our house.'"

44. The memoir was read on January 21 and March 18, 1793; the first group of sedition trials began on January 7–11, and continued until March. Stewart's letter of January 1793 is in Stewart, *Works,* 10:cxxxv–cxxxvi.

45. Stewart, "Account," n. G, p. 339. The hint was in a footnote to the original edition: "The length to which this Memoir has already extended, together with some other reasons which it is unnecessary to mention here, have induced me, in printing the following section, to confine myself to a much more general view of the subject than I once intended." Ibid., p. 309.

46. Ibid., pp. 311, 312, 319, 330.

47. Ibid., pp. 330–331.

48. Thomas Starkie's treatise on libel of 1813, quoted in Cockburn, *Examination,* 1:18; ibid., p. 85.

49. Stewart, "Account," pp. 310–311.

50. Cockburn, *Memorials,* pp. 85, 175.

51. *State Trials,* 23:218.

52. All these phrases are taken from Stewart's "Account," pp. 315–319.

53. Quoted in H. W. Meikle, *Scotland and the French Revolution* (Glasgow: Routledge, 1912), p. 249.

54. *The Friend,* in *The Collected Works of Samuel Taylor Coleridge* (Princeton: Princeton University Press, 1969), vol. 4, pt. 1, pp. 217–218.

55. *The Notebooks of Samuel Taylor Coleridge,* ed. Kathleen Coburn (London: Routledge and Kegan Paul, 1962), vol. 2, *Text (1804–1808),* p. 2578.

56. "Sur la liberté de la circulation des subsistances" (1792), in *OC,* 10:364.

57. "Sur le sens du mot révolutionnaire" (1793), in *OC,* 12:622.

58. *Mémoires de l'Abbé Morellet* (Paris: Ladvocat, 1821), 2:10.

59. Ibid., pp. 75–76. Morellet survived the denunciation and the Revolution; his interrogation improved when he produced a book attacking Necker, who was by then extremely unpopular. Morellet's effort to obtain his certificate "can be considered a confrontation between the Revolution and the Enlightenment," in Robert Darnton's words. Robert Darnton, *Gens de lettres Gens du livre,* trans. Marie-Alyx Revellat (Paris: Odile Jacob, 1992), p. 146.

60. See, among the extensive discussions of these debates, Halévy, *La formation du radicalisme philosophique,* vol. 2, chap. 2; J. R. Poynter, *Society and Pauperism: English Ideas on Poor Relief, 1795–1834* (London: Routledge & Kegan Paul, 1969), chap. 3; Gertrude Himmelfarb, *The Idea of Poverty: England in the Early Industrial Age* (London: Faber and Faber, 1985), chaps. 2 and 3; Winch, "The Burke-Smith Problem."

61. *PH,* vol. 32, cols. 700–705, 714–715 (December 9, 1795; February 12, 1796): "The situation of the labouring poor in this country," Whitbread said, was hardly "such as any feeling or liberal mind would wish"; "the

wretched manner in which the poor are lodged," in particular, "is such as ought not to be suffered in a country like this, proud of its freedom, and boasting of the equal rights of its subjects."

62. Ibid., col. 703.

63. *WN*, pp. 157–158.

64. Smith comments that "whenever the legislature attempts to regulate the differences between masters and their workmen, its counsellors are always the masters." *WN*, pp. 157–158; *PH*, vol. 32, col. 705; and see Chapter 4.

65. *WN*, p. 96.

66. *PH*, vol. 32, cols. 704–712.

67. *WN*, pp. 91–96.

68. The example he gives is of a law which obliged masters "to pay their workmen in money and not in goods." *WN*, p. 158.

69. The Reverend J. Howlett, *Examination of Mr Pitt's Speech, in the House of Commons, on Friday, February 12, 1796* (London: W. Richardson, 1796), pp. 22–23.

70. Stewart, "Account," p. 318.

71. *WN*, pp. 91, 96.

72. *WN*, p. 99; "An Early Draft of Part of *The Wealth of Nations*," in *LJ*, p. 567.

73. *An Essay on the Principle of Population* (1798), in *The Works of Thomas Robert Malthus*, ed. E. A. Wrigley and David Souden (London: William Pickering, 1986), 1:107.

74. *Principles of Political Economy considered with a view to their practical application*, in Malthus, *Works*, 5:63–64, 181.

75. *WN*, p. 157.

76. Whitbread, Lechmere, Charles James Fox, and Pitt, in *PH*, vol. 32, cols. 704, 708, 712, 702.

77. Smith and Burke are thought to have met first in 1777. See Jacob Viner, "Guide to John Rae's Life of Adam Smith," in Rae, *The Life of Adam Smith*, p. 27; *Corr.*, p. 47. They exchanged four friendly letters in 1782–83, met in Scotland in 1785, and corresponded in 1786 about a letter of recommendation for Burke's cousin. *Corr.* pp. 258–259, 265, 268, 297–300; William Windham, *The Diary of the Right Hon. William Windham, 1784–1810*, ed. Mrs. H. Baring (London: Longmans, Green, 1866), pp. 59–64. There is no evidence of later relations, and the two took opposing views of current issues. Burke was, for example, critical in 1787 of the Anglo-French commercial treaty; Smith was strongly opposed, as was seen earlier, to Burke's faction in the crisis over the king's illness.

78. Burke, *Reflections*, pp. 235–236, 371–372. Reverence is here a sort of intermediate good: "To be enabled to acquire, the people, without being servile, must be tractable and obedient" (p. 372).

79. Burke's "Memorial" for Pitt was prepared in November 1795. Burke, *Correspondence*, vol. 8, letters of November 7 and 17, 1795 (pp. 337, 344). The pamphlet *Thoughts and Details on Scarcity* was published by Burke's execu-

tors in 1800. It was said to be composed of the memorial for Pitt, together with another letter written at approximately the same time; "fragments" of the second letter, the editors say, were "inserted . . . where they seemed best to cohere." "Preface," in Edmund Burke, *Thoughts and Details on Scarcity* (London: F. and C. Rivington, 1800), p. ix. The comments quoted are in *The Works of the Right Honourable Edmund Burke* (Boston: Little, Brown, 1894), 5:138, 154, 156–157.

80. *Thoughts and Details on Scarcity*, in Burke, *Works*, 5:135, 139, 141, 145, 151, 166; *WN*, pp. 83, 91–93, 793; and see, on Burke and Smith, Donald Winch, *Riches and Poverty: An Intellectual History of Political Economy in Britain, 1750–1834* (Cambridge: Cambridge University Press, 1996).

81. Burke "was also consulted, and the greatest deference was paid to his opinions by Dr Adam Smith, in the progress of the celebrated work on the Wealth of Nations." *Thoughts and Details on Scarcity*, p. vi. Burke's only known communication with Smith over the relevant period was a letter asking Smith to intervene with the duke of Buccleuch in support of a Bristol china manufacturer's application for a patent renewal. Letter of May 1, 1775, in *Corr.*, pp. 180–181.

82. *Gentleman's Magazine*, 70 (1800), 1270; *Monthly Review*, 33 (1800), 392–393. The reviewers were only the first of many who saw Burke as a follower of Smith. Halévy describes Burke as Smith's "disciple," the first to "interpret political economy in the sense of a purely conservative orthodoxy." Halévy, *La formation du radicalisme philosophique*, 2:98. F. Y. Edgeworth writes of the pamphlet that "here Burke enunciates general principles worthy of the *Wealth of Nations*." Edgeworth, "Burke," in *Dictionary of Political Economy*, ed. R. H. Inglis Palgrave (London: Macmillan, 1901), 1:195.

83. Thomas Hodgskin, *Popular Political Economy* (London: Charles Tait, 1827), pp. 2, 6.

84. Lord Acton, *Letters of Lord Acton to Mary, Daughter of the Right Hon. W. E. Gladstone* (London: George Allen, 1904), pp. 91–92.

85. Beatrice (Potter) Webb, "Diary," July 30, 1886, Passfield Mss., London School of Economics.

86. Carl Menger, *Untersuchungen über die Methode der Socialwissenschaften, und der Politischen Oekonomie insbesondere* (1883) (London: London School of Economics, 1933), pp. 207–208; idem, *Investigations into the Method of the Social Sciences with Special Reference to Economics*, trans. Francis J. Nock (New York: New York University Press, 1985), p. 177.

87. Carl Menger, "Die Social-Theorien der classischen National-Oekonomie und die moderne Wirthschaftspolitik" (1891), in *Kleinere Schriften zur Methode und Geschichte der Volkswirtschaftslehre* (London: London School of Economics, 1935), p. 223.

88. Anton Menger, *The Right to the Whole Produce of Labour*, trans. M. E. Tanner (London: Macmillan, 1899), p. 56.

89. James Bonar, "The Revolutionary Element in Adam Smith," *National Liberal Club Transactions*, pt. 99 (1924), 6–7.

90. See Donald Winch, *Adam Smith's Politics: An Essay in Historiographic Revision* (Cambridge: Cambridge University Press, 1978).

91. Dupont de Nemours, "Observations sur les points dans lesquels Adam Smith est d'accord avec la théorie de M.Turgot, et sur ceux dans lesquels il s'en est écarté" (1809), in *Oeuvres de Turgot*, ed. Eugène Daire and Hippolyte Dussard (Paris: Guillaumin, 1844), 1:68–69. Dupont charges Smith with the same principled timidity to which he himself confesses in his letter to Smith of June 1788, which was quoted earlier. His description of Smith as a fellow "disciple" of Quesnay is a reflection of his own "spirit of sect" more than of any extensive association with Smith, during the period in the late 1760s when Smith was in Paris. On Smith's travels, see Ian Simpson Ross, *The Life of Adam Smith* (Oxford: Clarendon Press, 1995), chap. 13.

92. Dupont's first edition of Quesnay's *Physiocratie* appeared in 1767 with the dateline "Pékin." Luigi Einaudi, "À propos de la date de publication de la 'Physiocratie,'" in *François Quesnay et la Physiocratie* (Paris: Institut National d'Études Démographiques, 1958), 1:6.

93. This is Smith's prescription for "equitable regard" to the interest of a manufacturer whose home markets are "suddenly laid open to the competition of foreigners." *WN*, p. 471.

94. Ibid., p. 788.

95. *TMS*, pp. 233–234.

96. Burke, *Reflections*, p. 183; and see Chapter 7. The point of Condorcet's second chamber—the Locke-Hume-Smith-Price constitutional assembly—was indeed to introduce hesitation, delay, skepticism, and irresolution into political decisions.

97. Stewart, *Works*, 10:lxxiii. The remark of Condorcet's which Stewart quoted could hardly be more cautious, or more Solon-like: "If we wish to secure the perfection and the permanence of freedom, we must patiently wait the period when men, emancipated from their prejudices, and guided by philosophy, shall be rendered worthy of liberty, by comprehending its claims." Ibid., 2:237.

98. The process of restriction—"the reduction of the *Wealth of Nations* to a book whose single overarching concern was seen to be driving home the doctrine of free trade"—was already under way in the 1780s, as Richard Teichgraeber shows; it assumed new political importance in the period considered here. See Richard F. Teichgraeber III, "'Less Abused than I had Reason to Expect': The Reception of the *Wealth of Nations* in Britain, 1776–90," *Historical Journal*, 30, 2 (1987), 340.

99. Nathan Rosenberg, "Adam Smith as a Social Critic," *Royal Bank of Scotland Review*, 30 (June 1990), 17–33.

100. Burke, *Reflections*, p. 188.

101. Stewart, "Account," p. 316; Stewart quotes Smith's description of the "sneaking arts of underling tradesmen" in *WN*, p. 493.

102. *WN*, pp. 796–797; and see Chapter 5. Smith's view, in the opinion of one critic, was that atheism is "the proper antidote against the fear of death."

[George Horne], *A Letter to Adam Smith LL.D. on the Life, Death and Philosophy of his friend David Hume Esq, By one of the People called* CHRISTIANS (Oxford: Clarendon Press, 1777), p. 29.

103. Alengry, *Condorcet,* p. 704.
104. *WN,* pp. 342, 344, 920, 926.
105. *TMS,* pp. 228, 230, 239.
106. Burke begins the *Reflections* by telling his French interlocutor about the English supporters of the French Revolution, and about Richard Price's famous sermon of November 4, 1789, on "the Love of our Country." Smith was not an admirer of Price, and Raphael and Mcfie suggest that he "may possibly" have been criticizing the sermon in the *TMS* passages; see fnn. 2 and 6 in *TMS,* pp. 229, 231, and *Corr.,* p. 290. Smith does describe "the love of our own country" as a "noble principle," and one which "seems not to be derived from the love of mankind." But Smith's and Price's views are not in great conflict in these texts. Both try to distinguish the "just love of country" from the "blind and narrow principle" of national faction (Price), or "the mean principle of national prejudice" from "the noble one of the love of our own country" (Smith). Smith says that "nations, having no common superior to decide their disputes, all live in continual dread and suspicion of one another"; Price looks forward to the time when nations "will find out better ways of settling their disputes." *TMS,* pp. 219–230; Richard Price, *A Discourse on the Love of our Country* (London: T. Cadell, 1789), pp. 4–10, 30. "We very weakly and foolishly, perhaps, call the French our natural enemies," Smith says; Price, in his toast to the French Revolution on July 14, 1790, says that "in this kingdom we have been used to speak of the people of France as our natural enemies," but that peace is now at hand. Price, *A Discourse on the Love of our Country,* 4th ed. (London: T. Cadell, 1790), p. 36.
107. *PH,* vol. 33 (16 May 1797), col. 563.
108. *LJ,* pp. 208, 341, 540.
109. *WN,* p. 725.
110. *WN,* p. 527; and see Chapter 3.
111. "Lettres au Contrôleur Général (abbé Terray) sur le commerce des grains" (1770), in *OT,* 3:267; *Réflexions sur le commerce des blés* (1776), in *OC,* 11:161. For a somewhat different interpretation, see Istvan Hont and Michael Ignatieff, "Needs and Justice in the *Wealth of Nations:* An Introductory Essay," *Wealth and Virtue: The Shaping of Political Economy in the Scottish Enlightenment,* ed. Hont and Ignatieff (Cambridge: Cambridge University Press, 1983), pp. 1–44.
112. *WN,* pp. 400, 412. See also Duncan Forbes, "Sceptical Whiggism, Commerce, and Liberty" in *Essays on Adam Smith,* ed. Andrew S. Skinner and Thomas Wilson (Oxford: Oxford University Press, 1975), pp. 186–187.
113. *TMS,* p. 290.
114. *Réflexions sur le commerce des blés,* in *OC,* 11:179; *Esquisse d'un Tableau*

Historique des Progrès de l'Esprit Humain (1793–94), in *OC,* 6:191; and see Chapter 7.

115. Sophie Grouchy, "Lettres sur la Sympathie," in Adam Smith, *Théorie des Sentimens Moraux,* trans. Sophie Grouchy Condorcet (Paris: F. Buisson, 1798), 2:403.

116. *Refléxions sur le commerce des blés,* in *OC,* 11:178–179.

117. Smith's ideas provide little support, in these circumstances, for Hayek's account of Hume, Smith, and Burke as the "typical representatives in England" of a "liberalism" which is to be "clearly distinguished from . . . the tradition of Voltaire, Rousseau, Condorcet and the French Revolution"; or of the "British" and the "French" traditions, between which "there is hardly a greater contrast imaginable." F. A. Hayek, *Studies in Philosophy, Politics, and Economics* (Chicago: University of Chicago Press, 1967), p. 160; idem, *The Constitution of Liberty* (London: Routledge and Kegan Paul, 1960), p. 56. James Buchanan's description of the "libertarian socialist" is more true to Smith, and also to Condorcet: "The person who shares this perspective places a primary value on liberty, as such. He personally disputes, rejects, resents, opposes attempts by others to exercise control or power over his own choice behaviour . . . There is an exhilaration in simply being free." James M. Buchanan, *Liberty, Market, and State: Political Economy in the 1980s* (Brighton: Harvester Press, 1986), p. 4.

118. "Early Draft," in *LJ,* p. 564; and see Chapter 4.

3. Commerce and the State

1. A shorter version of this chapter was published in the *Economic Journal,* 102, 414 (September 1992), 1197–1210.

2. This is the phrase that Smith uses in a letter of October 1780. See *Corr.,* p. 251, and Chapter 1.

3. *WN,* pp. 538–539, 687.

4. The changing interpretation of Smith's views is discussed in Chapter 2; see also Srinivasan Ambirajan, *Classical Political Economy and British Policy in India* (Cambridge: Cambridge University Press, 1978); Salim Rashid, "The Policy of Laissez-Faire during Scarcities," *Economic Journal,* 90 (September 1980), 493–503; Amartya Sen, *Poverty and Famines: An Essay on Entitlement and Deprivation* (Oxford: Clarendon Press, 1981); Donald Winch, *Adam Smith's Politics: An Essay in Historiographic Revision* (Cambridge: Cambridge University Press, 1978).

5. "Lettres au Contrôleur-Général (abbé Terray) sur le commerce des grains," in *OT,* 3:326, 334.

6. *WN,* pp. 90–91, 204, 209–210, 526–527.

7. Ibid., pp. 524–527, 534. Smith describes free commerce in corn as the "best palliative" of dearth (pp. 527, 532, 538), the "best preventative" of dearth (p. 532), and the "best thing that can be done" (p. 534).

8. "Turgot," in John Morley, *Critical Miscellanies* (London: Macmillan, 1886), 2:112.

9. See, for example, *Correspondance inédite de Condorcet et de Turgot, 1770–1779*, ed. Charles Henry (Paris: Didier, 1883), pp. 210–211, 232, 285. In his life of Turgot, Condorcet expressed the hope that Turgot's letters "may eventually become a means of salvation for the people," and he may later have assisted in their publication. *Vie de M. Turgot* (1786), in *OC*, 5:41; and see Peter Groenewegen, "Introduction," in *The Economics of A. R. J. Turgot*, ed. Groenewegen (The Hague: Nijhoff, 1977), pp. xx–xxi.

10. "Lettres sur le commerce des grains," in *OT*, 3:267, 347.

11. *Réflexions sur le commerce des blés* (1776), in *OC*, 11:187.

12. "Sur la liberté de la circulation des subsistances" (1792), in *OC*, 10:362.

13. *WN*, p. 534; "Lettres sur le commerce des grains," in *OT*, 3:300.

14. *WN*, p. 526; *Réflexions*, in *OC*, 11:212, 214.

15. *WN*, pp. 524, 534; *Réflexions*, in *OC*, 11:101–102, 202.

16. *LJ*, p. 525; *Vie de M. Turgot*, in *OC*, 5:41.

17. "Lettres sur le commerce des grains," in *OT*, 3:273, 313.

18. Letter to the Controller-General of December 16, 1769, in *OT*, 3:125; of February 27, 1770, in *OT*, 3:132–133; of October 25, 1770, in *OT*, 3:144.

19. For Turgot and Condorcet, as for Smith, the word "market" had the generally concrete connotation of a particular physical structure, and indeed one which was protected by oppressive government regulations, as when merchants were forced to sell their corn "in markets." See, for example, "Circulaire aux officiers de police des villes" (1766), in *OT*, 2:473–475; *Réflexions*, in *OC*, 11:232–234; and see Chapter 1.

20. Letter to the Controller-General of February 27, 1770, in *OT*, 3:132–133. Smith makes a similar point in his unpublished lectures: "When the price of corn is doubled the wages continue the same as before, because the labourers have no other way to turn themselves." *LJ*, p. 497.

21. "Lettres sur le commerce des grains," in *OT*, 3:267, 288, 340, 347.

22. Letter of March 29, 1770, in *OT*, 3:384.

23. "Lettres sur le commerce des grains," in *OT*, 3:315, 334.

24. *WN*, p. 525.

25. "Lettres sur le commerce des grains," in *OT*, 3:324–328. The "Lettres" were Turgot's last work on economic theory, and he did not develop his notion of *tâtonnement* further. But it is interesting that the word had some mathematical connotation at the time; see Chapter 6.

26. Letter of December 16, 1769, to the Controller-General, in *OT*, 3:119.

27. "Avis sur l'imposition pour l'année 1771," in *OT*, 3:358; see Régis Deloche, "Turgot, Condorcet et la question de l'affectation des ressources," in *Condorcet: mathématicien, économiste, philosophe, homme politique*, ed. Pierre Crépel and Christian Gilain (Paris: Minerve, 1989), pp. 150–159.

28. "Lettres sur le commerce des grains," in *OT*, 3:288.

29. *Réflexions*, in *OC*, 11:197, 201, 208.

30. Ibid., p. 103.
31. *Vie de M. Turgot*, in *OC*, 5:40.
32. *Réflexions*, in *OC*, 11:104–105.
33. Ibid., p. 155.
34. Ibid., pp. 111, 198–199.
35. Ibid., pp. 167, 231.
36. Letter of March 23, 1770, in *OT*, 3:382.
37. Letter of May 4, 1770, in *OT*, 3:386. On the criticisms of Turgot for inconsistency, see Steven L. Kaplan, *Bread, Politics, and Political Economy in the Reign of Louis XV* (The Hague: Nijhoff, 1976), 2:505; and M. C. Kiener and J.-C. Peyronnet, *Quand Turgot régnait en Limousin* (Paris: Fayard, 1979), pp. 274–278.
38. Ordinances of March 23 and April 4, 1770, in *OT*, 3:260–263.
39. Letter of December 16, 1769, to the Controller-General, in *OT*, 3:125–126; "Instruction lue à l'Assemblée de charité de Limoges," February 11, 1770, in *OT*, 3:212, 216–217; "Supplément," in *OT*, 3:250.
40. "Instruction," in *OT*, 3:214–215; "Circulaire" of February 16, 1770, in *OT*, 3:225.
41. Letter to the Controller-General of January 9, 1770, in *OT*, 3:131. The amounts eventually spent in 1770 were 85,009 livres for public works, including roads, ramparts, and spinning instruction, and 36,420 livres for purchases of rice. "Compte rendu," in *OT*, 3:435–436.
42. "Compte rendu," *OT*, 3:459.
43. *Vie de M. Turgot*, in *OC*, 5:41.
44. Letter to the Controller-General of October 25, 1770, in *OT*, 3:151; "Instruction," in *OT*, 3:207–208; "Ordonnance," in *OT*, 3:234–235; "Avis," in *OT*, 3:360–362.
45. "Instruction," in *OT*, 3:212; "Ordonnance imposant aux propriétaires de nourrir leurs métayers jusqu'à la récolte," February 28, 1770, in *OT*, 3:243–244.
46. "Lettre au Chancelier" of May 14, 1770, in *OT*, 3:249.
47. See Kiener and Peyronnet, *Quand Turgot régnait en Limousin*, p. 267.
48. *Vie de M. Turgot*, in *OC*, 5:40.
49. "Arrêt du Conseil établissant la liberté du commerce des grains," September 13, 1774, in *OT*, 4:202–205, 212–214; "Mémoire au Roi" (six draft Reform Edicts), January 1776, in *OT*, 5:155.
50. Letter of September 7, 1766, in *OT*, 2:503.
51. *WN*, p. 526.
52. See Condorcet, *Vie de M. Turgot*, in *OC*, 5:45; Siegmund Feilbogen, *Smith und Turgot* (Vienna: Hölder, 1892); Peter D. Groenewegen, "Turgot and Adam Smith," *Scottish Journal of Political Economy*, 16 (1969), 271–287; Terence W. Hutchison, "Turgot and Smith," in *Turgot, économiste et administrateur*, ed. C. Bordes and J. Morange (Paris: Presses Universitaires de France, 1982), pp. 33–45.

53. *Corr.*, p. 286; see Chapter 1. Turgot praised Smith (together with Tucker) as one of the two "political writers on commerce" in Britain who did not support "the system of monopoly and exclusion." Letter of 1788 to Richard Price, in *OT,* 5:533.

54. *Vie de M. Turgot,* in *OC,* 5:45; *Adam Smith's Library: A catalogue,* ed. Hiroshi Mizuta (Oxford: Clarendon Press, 2000), pp. 62, 206.

55. *WN,* pp. 157–158; see Chapter 2.

56. *WN,* p. 842. Condorcet's main difference with Smith is indeed over his tolerance for government intervention in the form of indirect taxes. *Vie de M. Turgot,* in *OC,* 5:45, 125.

57. *The Correspondence of William Wilberforce* (London: Murray, 1840), 1: 40–41.

58. Feilbogen, *Smith und Turgot,* pp. 157–163.

59. *WN,* p. 539; Donald Winch, "Science and the Legislator: Adam Smith and After," *Economic Journal,* 93 (September 1983), 506.

60. *An Essay on the Principle of Population* (1798), in *The Works of Thomas Robert Malthus,* ed. E. A. Wrigley and David Souden (London: William Pickering, 1986), 1:107.

61. Smith's new reputation was established firmly in 1798–1800, during a period when corn prices in England increased faster than at any time in the past century. See B. R. Mitchell and Phyllis Deane, *An Abstract of British Historical Statistics* (Cambridge: Cambridge University Press, 1962), pp. 486–487, and Chapter 2.

62. The policy is similar to that proposed in the Indian Famine Codes after the Famine Commission Report of 1880, on the basis of a similar analysis that "distress arises, not so much from an actual want of food, as from a loss of wages—in other words, money to buy food." See Jean Drèze, "Famine Prevention in India," in *The Political Economy of Hunger,* ed. Jean Drèze and Amartya Sen (Oxford: Clarendon Press, 1990), 2:17.

63. *WN,* p. 528; *Réflexions,* in *OC,* 11:200.

64. *Réflexions,* in *OC,* 11:148, 200; and see Chapter 6.

65. Letter to Trudaine de Montigny of October 28, 1767, in *OT,* 5:697.

66. *Réflexions,* in *OC,* 11: 235.

67. "Arrêt du Conseil," in *OT,* 4:205–206; letter of 1774, in *OT,* 4:225.

68. *Réflexions,* in *OC,* 11:231.

69. "Lettres sur le commerce des grains," in *OT,* 3:352.

70. *Réflexions,* in *OC,* 11:244–245. Condorcet's argument is that "personal" rights, such as the right to levy charges on inheritance or sales, are owned not by landlords in their role as proprietors, but rather on the grounds that they once exercised a part of sovereignty: "It is a portion of tax revenue which the nation has allowed them to enjoy, and which it can take away from them subject to compensation."

71. *Apologie de l'abbé Galiani,* in Denis Diderot, *Oeuvres,* ed. Laurent Versini (Paris: Robert Laffont, 1995), 3:133.

72. "Lit de Justice," in *OT,* 5:291.
73. Smith talks about the "trouble, vexation, and oppression" associated with "the frequent visits, and the odious examination of the tax-gatherers" (*WN,* p. 827); the "vexation" of customs regulations and the even "more vexatious" laws of excise (pp. 898–899); and, in connection with fermented molasses, "the odious visits and examination of the tax-gatherers" (p. 936). See Chapter 1 and also Chapter 4.
74. "Mémoire au Roi," in *OT,* 5:154–155.
75. "Ordonnance," in *OT,* 3:243–244.
76. *Réflexions,* in *OC,* 11:167.

4. Apprenticeship and Insecurity

1. Letter of February 26, 1776, in *Lettres d'André Morellet,* ed. Dorothy Medlin, Jean-Claude David, and Paul Leclerc (Oxford: Voltaire Foundation, 1991), 1:312. Morellet adds, self-importantly, that he is himself at least as worthy of censorship as Smith: "Je me flatte bien qu'il n'y aura pas une page de mon livre qui ne soit au moins aussi brulable que l'extrait de Smith."
2. Letter of February 22, 1776, ibid., 1:310. The reference is presumably to Smith's observations on the inefficiency of apprenticeships—"long apprenticeships are altogether unnecessary"—and on "the art of the farmer." *WN,* pp. 138–140 and 143–144.
3. *Lettres d'André Morellet,* 1:311, n. 1.
4. See Chapter 1.
5. Beatrice (Potter) Webb, "The History of English Economics" (1885), Passfield Mss., London School of Economics, 3:5, 3:16–17; see also Beatrice Webb's diary entry of 1886, quoted in Chapter 2.
6. *WN,* pp. 96, 138, 530.
7. K. D. M. Snell, "The Apprenticeship System in British History: The Fragmentation of a Cultural Institution," *History of Education,* 25, 4 (1996), 303–304.
8. *WN,* pp. 79, 135–136, 140, 151, 470.
9. The compulsory apprentice clauses of the Elizabethan statute of artificers—5.Eliz.c.4—were repealed in 1814; they had been suspended in relation to the woollen trade from 1803, and repealed in 1809. See O. Jocelyn Dunlop, *English Apprenticeship and Child Labour: A History* (London: T. Fisher Unwin, 1912), chap. 15; T. K. Derry, "The Repeal of the Apprenticeship Clauses of the Statute of Apprentices," *Economic History Review,* 3 (1931–1932), 67–87.
10. *An Inquiry into the Nature and Causes of the Wealth of Nations,* 11th ed., ed. William Playfair (London: T. Cadell and W. Davies, 1805), 1:195, 207, with references to Smith's comments on clockmakers in *WN,* pp. 139–140, and on incompetent workers in incorporated towns, *WN,* p. 146; see also 3:243–246.

11. William Playfair, *Political portraits in this New Aera* (London: C. Chapple, 1813), 1:364, 385; idem, *An Inquiry into the permanent causes of the decline and fall of powerful and wealthy nations* (London: Greenland and Norris, 1805), pp. 219–220.

12. William Playfair, *A Letter to the Right Honourable and Honourable the Lords and Commons of Great Britain, on the Advantages of Apprenticeships* (London: Sherwood, Neely, and Jones, 1814), pp. 15, 30–31.

13. See, for example, Committee of Manufacturers of London and Its Vicinity, "The Origin, Object and Operation of the Apprentice Laws; with their application to Times Past, Present, and To Come," in *The Pamphleteer*, 3, 5 (March 1814), 228, 235; Smith's arguments are at *WN*, p. 137.

14. Committee of Manufacturers, "The Origin," p. 237.

15. *Report from the Committee on the Woollen Manufacture of England; &c.* Comnd. no. 268 (1806), pp. 15, 17.

16. Sir Frederick Eden, *The State of the Poor* (London: Davis, 1797), 1:436, 3:ccccxxvi. Eden's reference, like Playfair's, is to *WN*, p. 146: "If you would have your work tolerably executed, it must be done in the suburbs, where the workmen having no exclusive privilege, have nothing but their character to depend upon, and you must then smuggle it into the town as well as you can."

17. Dugald Stewart, "Account of the Life and Writings of Adam Smith, LL. D.," in *EPS*, p. 339; see Chapter 2.

18. "Substance of the Speech of Mr. Serjeant Onslow," in *The Pamphleteer*, 4, 8 (November 1814), 303–304; Committee of Manufacturers, "The Origin," p. 231; *The Parliamentary Debates* (hereafter *PD*), 1st ser., vol. 27, April 27, 1814, col. 572.

19. Onslow, "Speech," p. 309; see also, on the origins of Onslow's clause, Derry, "Repeal," p. 79.

20. *WN*, pp. 84, 96, 99, 114; see also p. 599, on the contribution of the "high profits of British stock" to "raising the price of British manufactures."

21. *WN*, pp. 115, 599.

22. Lujo Brentano, *On the History and Development of Gilds, and the Origin of Trade-Unions* (London: Trubner, 1870), p. 100.

23. *PD*, vol. 27, April 27, 1814, cols. 572–573.

24. *WN*, p. 141, 146, 151–152.

25. *WN*, pp. 119, 134, 141, 152, 644.

26. *WN*, p. 144; on Smith's sympathy for landed property and country labor, see John Dwyer, "Virtue and Improvement: The Civic World of Adam Smith," in *Adam Smith Reviewed*, ed. Peter Jones and Andrew S. Skinner (Edinburgh: Edinburgh University Press, 1992), pp. 190–216.

27. Committee of Manufacturers, "The Origin," pp. 221–222. The manufacturers' secretary was John Richter, one of Horne Tooke's co-defendants and Francis Place's close associate. Place himself was actively engaged in the enterprise, writing in January 1814 that "the affair of Serjeant Onslow partly

originated with me," and "I never was so intensely occupied in my life as I have been lately with . . . the statute of Elizabeth." Graham Wallas, *The Life of Francis Place, 1771–1854* (London: Longmans, Green, 1898), pp. 95, 159. See also E. P. Thompson, *The Making of the English Working Class* (London: Penguin Books, 1988), esp. pp. 303, 506, 565.

28. Serjeant Onslow himself said in the House of Commons that "the case of the female sex"—of women working illicitly in trades to which they had not been apprenticed, "though many have been driven from them by threats of prosecution"—was one "that presses most strongly on my mind." Committee of Manufacturers, "The Origin," pp. 231–232; Onslow, "Speech," p. 306.

29. The *Wealth of Nations,* Godwin wrote, "makes me feel . . . a painful contraction of the heart." It was "refreshing," nonetheless, after "the perusal of such a book as that of Mr. Malthus." William Godwin, *Of Population: an Enquiry concerning the power of increase in the numbers of mankind, being an answer to Mr. Malthus's Essay on that subject* (London: Longman, 1820), p. 611; see also Wallas, *Francis Place,* p. 157.

30. Arnold Toynbee, *Lectures on the Industrial Revolution in Britain* (London: Rivington, 1884), p. 16.

31. *WN,* pp. 139–140, 143, 151–152.

32. "If masters would always listen to the dictates of reason and humanity, they have frequently occasion rather to moderate, than to animate the application of many of their workmen." Smith argues here that "the liberal reward of labour" is itself something which "increases the industry of the common people." *WN,* pp. 99–100, 139.

33. *WN,* pp. 138–139, 146.

34. Committee of Manufacturers, "The Origin," p. 229.

35. *Report from the Committee on the Woollen Manufacture,* p. 14; "Minutes of the Committee," pp. 373–374.

36. Playfair, "Supplementary Chapter," in *The Wealth of Nations,* 3:243, 251.

37. Playfair, *An Inquiry into Decline,* p. 223; idem, *Political Portraits,* 2:450–451. On Samuel Whitbread's evocation of Smith as a friend of the laboring poor in the debates of 1795–96 over minimum wages, see Chapter 2.

38. *WN,* pp. 28–29; and see Chapter 1.

39. *WN,* pp. 28, 782, 784.

40. *LJ,* pp. 539–540.

41. *WN,* pp. 785, 788; see also Andrew S. Skinner, "Adam Smith and the Role of the State: Education as a Public Service," in *Adam Smith's Wealth of Nations: New Interdisciplinary Essays,* ed. Stephen Copley and Kathryn Sutherland (Manchester: Manchester University Press, 1995), pp. 70–96.

42. *WN,* p. 788; and see Chapter 8.

43. His emphasis on public education, he told two of the Edinburgh Law Lords, came rather "from an anxious desire to prevent the danger of such an evil." See Chapter 2.

44. *WN,* pp. 785–786; *LJ,* p. 540.

45. Playfair, *Inquiry into decline*, p. 222; idem, *Letter*, pp. 11–13.
46. *Report from the Committee on the Woollen Manufacture*, p. 14.
47. *PD*, 1st ser., vol. 9, July 13, 1807, cols. 798, 800.
48. Onslow, "Speech," p. 305; Committee of Manufacturers, "The Origin," p. 233.
49. *TMS*, pp. 220–222.
50. *Report from the Committee on the Woollen Manufacture*, p. 17.
51. Playfair, *Letter*, p. 31.
52. *Essai sur la constitution et les fonctions des assemblées provinciales* (1788), in *OC*, 8:275, 471, 473; "Sur l'instruction publique" (1791–92), in *OC*, 7:455–456.
53. *WN*, pp. 138, 143.
54. *WN*, pp. 154–157, 660.
55. *WN*, pp. 100–101, 119, 139.
56. "La suppression des jurandes," in *OT*, 5:242–244.
57. *Vie de M. Turgot*, in *OC*, 5:68, 77; Brentano, *The History and Development of Gilds*, p. 100.
58. "Lit de Justice," in *OT*, 5:278, 287–288, 291; see Chapter 1, and, on working for collective utility without willing it, Chapter 5.
59. Derry, "Repeal," pp. 78–79.
60. Committee of Manufacturers, "The Origin," p. 238.
61. *WN*, p. 119.
62. *Report from the Committee on the Woollen Manufacture*, p. 10.
63. *PD*, 1st ser., vol. 9, April 23, 1807, cols. 535–536. See also, on the replacement of calico workers—"at once after the expiration of their apprenticeship," or "immediately on their sight beginning to fail them"—by young children, Brentano, *The History and Development of Gilds*, pp. 122–123. The children, Brentano says, were "partly parish apprentices, partly children of workmen, who were forced by their employers by threats of instant dismissal in case of refusal to apprentice their children" (p. 122).
64. "Minutes," p. 43.
65. Playfair, *Letter*, p. 21; see also obituaries of Playfair, in the *Gentleman's Magazine*, 93, pt. 1 (June 1823), 564, and the *Dictionary of National Biography*.
66. "Minutes," p. 102.
67. Dorothy Marshall, *The English Poor in The Eighteenth Century: A Study in Social and Administrative History* (London: George Routledge and Sons, 1926), pp. 182, 189.
68. Indenture reproduced in Dunlop, *English Apprenticeship*, p. 353.
69. "It is plain that seven years apprenticeship cannot be legally served at any age, and it is equally plain that it must be performed in a state of nonage"; this is the conclusion to be drawn, according to one of the documents quoted by the committee, from the decision of Lord Kenyon in the case of Mary Ann Davis, who bound herself for seven years at the age of seventeen, but was described at the time as only fourteen. "Minutes," p. 36.

70. *PD*, 1st ser., vol. 27, April 27, 1814, col. 573.
71. They were rediscovered, yet again, much later in the nineteenth century. W. S. Jevons thus quotes Smith at length in 1882, in a powerful denunciation of "Apprenticeship or Industrial Slavery of Youths." He called the Elizabethan statute "a monstrous law"; "from beginning to end it aimed at industrial slavery," in which the local magistrates, "if they chose to exert their powers, could become the industrial despots of their district." The statute was only completely repealed, as he pointed out, by the Conspiracy and Protection of Property Act of 1875 (an act of which it was said, by a supporter, that "everybody must feel that it was extremely desirable that there should be one law for both the rich and the poor"). But even under the current common law, Jevons said, "the apprentice is in the position of a slave to his master," protected only, if at all, by the "merciful discretion of the justices." Children are in the power, and subject to the will, of both parents and masters. "The child is bound at an age when he can have no sure judgment," Jevons says, citing the "greatest authorities," and "Adam Smith especially"; "his nominal consent, even at a very tender age, is held sufficient to consign him to industrial slavery." See W. S. Jevons, *The State in Relation to Labour* (London: Macmillan, 1887), pp. 34, 36, 75–81; *PD*, 3rd ser., vol. 225, July 12, 1875, col. 1342.
72. *PD*, 1st ser., vol. 28, June 8, 1814, col. 14.
73. *PD*, 3rd ser., vol. 17, May 14, 1833, cols. 1193–94, 1222; *Annual Register*, 75, 202.
74. *PD*, 3rd ser., vol. 17, May 14, 1833, col. 1230; W. L. Burn, *Emancipation and Apprenticeship in the British West Indies* (London: Jonathan Cape, 1937), pp. 108–120, 374.
75. *PD*, 3rd ser., vol. 18, May 30, 1833, col. 142; Burn, *Emancipation,* p. 145.
76. Stephen Hobhouse, *Joseph Sturge: His Life and Work* (London: J. M. Dent, 1919), p. 45.
77. *PD*, 3rd ser., vol. 18, June 3, 1833, col. 313.
78. *PD*, 3rd ser., vol. 17, May 14, 1833, cols. 1235, 1245.
79. *The Gladstone Diaries,* ed. M. R. D. Foot (Oxford: Clarendon Press, 1968), 2:358 (March 30, 1838); W. E. Gladstone, *Speech delivered in the House of Commons on the motion of Sir George Strickland, for the abolition of the Negro Apprenticeship, March 30, 1838* (London: J. Hatchard, 1838), pp. 12–13.
80. Gladstone, *Speech,* pp. 8, 49.
81. *WN*, pp. 136–137, 152–153.
82. Letter of October 26, 1780, in *Corr.,* p. 251.
83. See, for example, *WN*, p. 136, 142, 143, 734.
84. Eden, *The State of the Poor,* 1:436–437.
85. R. H. Campbell and A. S. Skinner, "General Introduction," in *WN*, pp. 53–54, 138, n. 14, and 152, n. 50; see also K. D. M. Snell, *Annals of the Labouring Poor: Social Change and Agrarian England, 1660–1900* (Cambridge: Cambridge University Press, 1985), pp. 228–269.

86. Annotation at p. 207 of the first volume of Pryme's copy of Playfair's *Wealth of Nations*, Cambridge University Library, Rare Books Room.
87. Onslow, "Speech," p. 303.
88. Godwin, *Of Population*, pp. 607–611; Brentano, The *History and Development of Gilds*, p. 113; Toynbee, *The Industrial Revolution*, pp. 15–16; Webb, "History," 3:15.
89. *WN*, pp. 157–158; and see Chapter 2.
90. Brentano, *The History and Development of Gilds*, p. 113.
91. *WN*, p. 158.
92. Gladstone, *Speech*, p. 25; Joseph Sturge and Thomas Harvey, *The West Indies in 1837* (London: Hamilton, 1838), pp. lxxxv, 350–351.
93. Webb, "History," 3:16.
94. He is speaking here of the "masters of coal works." *LJ*, p. 192. In the *Wealth of Nations*, too, he says in his account of slavery that "the pride of man makes him love to domineer, and nothing mortifies him so much as to be obliged to condescend to persuade his inferiors." *WN*, p. 388.
95. *WN*, pp. 827, 899, 927, 936; and see Chapter 1.
96. Onslow, "Speech," p. 308.
97. *WN*, p. 145.
98. Dunlop, *English Apprenticeship*, pp. 234–235.
99. This is Smith's own description of his disposition. See letter of March 25, 1789, in *Corr.*, p. 318.
100. *WN*, p. 145.
101. *WN*, p. 412.
102. "Mémoire sur les prêts d'argent," in *OT*, 3:155.
103. *Vie de M. Turgot*, in *OC*, 5:43.
104. Playfair, "Supplementary Chapter," in *The Wealth of Nations*, 3:519.
105. *WN*, pp. 793, 797.
106. *TMS*, p. 225.
107. Walter Bagehot, *Economic Studies* (London: Longmans, Green, 1908), p. 129.
108. *LRBL*, pp. 106, 164; Thucydides, *History of Peloponnesian War*, vol. 1, trans. Charles Forster Smith (Cambridge, Mass.: Harvard University Press, 1980), 1.22, p. 41.
109. Bagehot, *Economic Studies*, p. 22.
110. *Report from the Committee on the Woollen Manufacture*, p. 12.

5. The Bloody and Invisible Hand

1. A short summary of this chapter was presented at a session organized by Robert Nozick at the 1994 meetings of the American Economic Association, and published in the *American Economic Review*, 84, 2 (May 1994), 319–322. I am very grateful to Robert Nozick, and also to Stephen Martin, Amélie Rorty, Gloria Vivenza, and A. C. Waterman, for helpful discussions and comments.

2. Kenneth Arrow, "Economic Theory and the Hypothesis of Rationality," in *The New Palgrave: A Dictionary of Economics* (London: Macmillan, 1987), 2:71; Kenneth Arrow and Frank Hahn, *General Competitive Analysis* (San Francisco: Holden-Day, 1971), p. 1; James Tobin, "The Invisible Hand in Modern Macroeconomics," in *Adam Smith's Legacy: His Place in the Development of Modern Economics*, ed. Michael Fry (London: Routledge, 1992), p. 117.

3. See James Bonar, *Philosophy and Political Economy in Some of Their Historical Relations* (London: Sonnenschein, 1893), pp. 150, 173; Alec Macfie, "The Invisible Hand of Jupiter," *Journal of the History of Ideas*, 32, 4 (October–December 1971); 595–599; Gloria Vivenza, *Adam Smith e la cultura classica* (Pisa: Il Pensiero Economico Moderno, 1984), pp. 15–16.

4. "The History of Astronomy," in *EPS*, pp. 49–50. Wightman suggests that while the "History" may have been written in several parts, even the "'last part' was written *before* 1758." W. P. D. Wightman, "Introduction," in *EPS*, pp. 5–11.

5. *TMS*, pp. 184–185.

6. "Nor is it always the worse for society that it was no part of it," Smith continues. "By pursuing his own interest he frequently promotes that of the society more effectually than when he really intends to promote it. I have never known much good done by those who affected to trade for the public good. It is an affectation, indeed, not very common among merchants, and very few words need be employed in dissuading them from it." *WN*, pp. 453, 456, 462, 471.

7. Macfie, "The Invisible Hand," pp. 595, 598.

8. Macfie notes that "the invisible hand appears only once in the *Wealth of Nations* in a rather slight way," that the reference in the "History of Astronomy" is also slight, and that even the passage in the *Theory of Moral Sentiments* is not especially emphatic. A. L. Macfie, *The Individual in Society* (London: George Allen and Unwin, 1967), p. 103. Macfie and D. D. Raphael, too, observe in their introduction to the Glasgow edition of the *Theory of Moral Sentiments* (*TMS*, p. 7) that "commentators have laid too much stress on the 'invisible hand.'"

9. In the centenary celebrations in London for the *Wealth of Nations* in 1876—organized by the Political Economy Club, with W. E. Gladstone in the chair, and with eight speeches, including by Léon Say, then French minister of finance—the invisible hand is not mentioned; nor is it mentioned in articles about the occasion in the *Economist*, the *Times*, the *Daily News*, the *Pall Mall Gazette*, and *Capital and Labour*. Political Economy Club, *Revised Report of the Proceedings held in celebration of the 100th year of the publication of the "Wealth of Nations"* (London: Longmans, 1876). No mention is made in the record of a similar event organized in New York by the International Free Trade Alliance. "The Adam Smith Centennial," in *New Century* (New York: Randolph, 1876). August Oncken, in 1874, does quote the invisible hand passage from the *Wealth of Nations*, but comments that "this principle of re-

alistic philosophy is not original." August Oncken, *Adam Smith in der Culturgeschichte* (Vienna: Faesy and Frick, 1874), p. 19. The idea seems to have edged toward its present prominence by the end of the nineteenth century, and is noted by James Bonar in his article on Smith in the 1892 *Palgrave. Dictionary of Political Economy,* ed. R. H. Inglis Palgrave (London: Macmillan, 1892), 3:413, 415.

10. Cliffe Leslie, in his attack on Smith's "abstraction," quotes the invisible hand passages from both the *Wealth of Nations* and the *Theory of Moral Sentiments,* and concludes that "the clerical system of deductive reasoning certainly runs through and warps the whole philosophy of Adam Smith"; "the mischief done in political economy by this assumption respecting the beneficent constitution of nature, and therefore of all human inclinations and desires, has been incalculable." Thomas Edward Cliffe Leslie, *Essays in Political and Moral Philosophy* (Dublin: Hodges, Foster and Figgis, 1879), pp. 154–155, 158. Ingram is even more suspicious: "There is another vicious species of deduction which, as Cliffe Leslie has shown, seriously tainted the philosophy of Smith . . . This theory is, of course, not explicitly presented by Smith as a foundation of his economic doctrines, but it is really the secret substratum on which they rest." Ingram's usual charge against Smith is of subversion: "a certain deadness to the high aims and perennial importance of religion," and a failure to "keep in view the moral destination of our race." But he is prepared, on this occasion, to add the supplementary charge that Smith is in fact *too* concerned with the importance of religious conceptions: Smith "is secretly led, as we have seen, by *a priori* theological ideas." John Kells Ingram, *A History of Political Economy* (1888) (New York: Augustus M. Kelley, 1967), pp. 89–90, 102, 104.

11. Carl Menger, "Die Social-Theorien der classischen National-Oekonomie und die moderne Wirthschaftspolitik" (1891), in *Kleinere Schriften zur Methode und Geschichte der Volkswirtschaftslehre* (London: London School of Economics, 1935), pp. 219–245; idem, *Untersuchungen über die Methode der Socialwissenschaften, und der Politischen Oekonomie insbesondere* (1883) (London: London School of Economics, 1933), pp. 200–207.

12. Marshall is retranslating, here, from the German of Adolf Held. He writes that "some misunderstanding of Adam Smith's position has been imported into this country from Germany; but unfortunately the corrections of those mistakes, which have been made in Germany, have not been noted here." Held, in Marshall's account, objects to the emphasis by Smith's critics on "natural and necessary harmony," and the "laying excessive stress on occasional passages in which he speaks of 'the unseen hand which leads a man to this end, though he has not intended it himself.'" Alfred Marshall, *Industry and Trade* (London: Macmillan, 1923), pp. 747–748; and see Adolf Held, *Zwei Bücher zur socialen Geschichte Englands* (Leipzig: Duncker and Humblot, 1881), p. 160.

13. See Ernest Campbell Mossner, *Adam Smith: The Biographical Approach*

(Glasgow: University of Glasgow, 1969); and Ian Simpson Ross, *The Life of Adam Smith* (Oxford: Clarendon Press, 1995).

14. Letter of July 21, 1757, in *The Complete Works of Voltaire*, vol. 102 (Oxford: Voltaire Foundation, 1971), p. 106; and see John Morley, *Voltaire* (London: Macmillan, 1888), p. 339.

15. *Macbeth*, 3.2.47–51. Davenant's "simplified" version of *Macbeth*, much favored in the eighteenth century, preserves the invisible hand, but substitutes:

> Come dismal Night,
> Close up the Eye of the quick sighted Day
> With thy invisible and bloody hand

Quoted in Dennis Bartholomeusz, *Macbeth and the Players* (Cambridge: Cambridge University Press, 1969), p. 23. In the Piave libretto for Verdi's *Macbeth*, the speech about night ("light thickens . . .") is given to Lady Macbeth, and the hand of night becomes the hand of the husband:

> Notte desiata, provvida veli
> La man colpevole che ferirà.

Giuseppe Verdi, *Macbeth*, ed. Eduardo Rescigno (Milan: Mondadori, 1983), 2.2, p. 94.

16. James C. Dibdin, *The Annals of the Edinburgh Stage* (Edinburgh: Richard Cameron, 1888), pp. 89, 95. In Paris and London, Smith had theatrical acquaintances; David Garrick wrote to Smith's friend Mme. Riccoboni in 1767 that "I have seen and [co]nvers'd with Your friend Mr. Smith. He is a most agreeable Man." *The Letters of David Garrick*, ed. David M. Little and George M. Kahrl (Oxford: Oxford University Press, 1963), 2:552.

17. See, on "the tragedy of Mahomet, one of the finest of Mr. Voltaire's," and "that beautiful tragedy of Voltaire, the Orphan of China," *TMS*, pp. 177, 227.

18. The High Priest is vengeful:

> Tremblez, malheureux roi, votre règne est passé;
> Une invisible main suspend sur votre tête
> Le glaive menaçant que la vengeance apprête

and Oedipus pathetic:

> Pour la première fois, par un don solennel,
> Mes mains jeunes encore enrichissaient l'autel:
> Du temple tout-à-coup les combles s'entr'ouvrirent;
> De traits affreux de sang les marbres se couvrirent;
> De l'autel ébranlé par de longs tremblements
> Une invisible main repoussait mes présents

Voltaire, *Oedipe*, 3.4.69, and 4.1.128. Voltaire does acknowledge the influence of Sophocles on these two scenes. See "Lettres sur Oedipe" (1719), in

Oeuvres complètes de Voltaire (Paris: Firmin-Didot, 1876), 1:69, and, on Sophocles' coarseness, or "grossièreté," 1:66. The function of Jocasta's old romantic interest—the same Philoctetes, keeper of the arrows of Hercules in the Trojan Wars, whom Sophocles in his *Philoctetes* had abandoned on a desert island with an excruciating foot wound—is, Voltaire writes, to make her less "insipid" by giving her "at least the memory of a legitimate love," as well as some "passion," in the form of anxiety as to the fate of someone she once loved (1:72). Smith, who was a student of Sophocles, and who was fascinated at the end of his life by the "piacular guilt" of Oedipus and Jocasta, would certainly have been familiar with Voltaire's play; see *TMS,* pp. 30, 107, and *LRBL,* pp. 121–124. Voltaire's preface to *Oedipe* of 1730, in which he discusses two of the literary topics with which Smith was most concerned— the three dramatic unities, and the shortcomings of blank verse—is likely to have influenced Smith's lectures on poetry and his essays on syllables and rhymes, and on the imitative arts. *LRBL,* pp. 117–127; *EPS,* pp. 176–213, 220–225. Dugald Stewart indeed refers, in his biography of Smith, to the account of the "difficulté surmontée" in "the Preface to Voltaire's *Oedipe*" as "probably" the source of Smith's view of "the difficulty of the imitation." Dugald Stewart, "Account of the Life and Writings of Adam Smith, LL.D" (1793), in *EPS,* pp. 305–306. *Oedipe* and its hands (4.1.165–166) are certainly notable instances of the shortcomings of the twelve-syllable rhyming couplet:

> La main des dieux sur moi si long-temps suspendue
> Semble ôter le bandeau qu'ils mettaient sur ma vue.

19. Ovid, *Metamorphoses,* trans. Frank Justus Millar (Cambridge, Mass.: Harvard University Press, 1984), 12.492–493, p. 215.

20. Smith, according to Mizuta's catalogue, owned the 1662 Leyden edition of Ovid's works. See Ovid, *Opera omnia,* ed. Heinsii (Leyden, 1662), vol. 2, plate opposite p. 574; *Adam Smith's Library: A Catalogue,* ed. Hiroshi Mizuta (Oxford: Clarendon Press, 2000), p. 183.

21. "And from behind Zeus thrust him on with exceeding mighty hand." Homer, *The Iliad,* trans. A. T. Murray (Cambridge, Mass.: Harvard University Press, 1985), 15.695, p. 159.

22. Arthur Darby Nock, *Essays on Religion and the Ancient World* (Cambridge, Mass.: Harvard University Press, 1972), 1:146.

23. *Macbeth,* 2.3.129.

24. "Éloge de Pascal" (1776), in *OC,* 3:619; *TMS,* p. 139.

25. "Recherches sur les causes des progrès" (1748), in *OT,* 1:133; *Zum ewigen Frieden* (1795), in Immanuel Kant, *Werkausgabe,* ed. Wilhelm Weischedel (Frankfurt: Suhrkamp, 1968), 11:198.

26. Joseph de Maistre, *Considérations sur la France* (1797) (Paris: Complexe, 1988), p. 49. Napoleon, in St. Helena, arrived at a similarly dismal metaphor, in an extended comparison of the English and the French Revolutions, and

the regicides of Charles I and Louis XVI: "In England, the affair was led by an invisible hand; it had more reflection and calm. In France, it was led by the multitude, whose fury was without limits." Emmanuel de Las Cases, *Mémorial de Sainte-Hélène,* ed. Joël Schmidt (Paris: Éditions du Seuil, 1968), p. 614.

27. The Latin adjective *invisibilis,* according to Lewis and Short, is first used, other than by Celsus, in Tertullian and Lactantius; see, for example, Lactantius, *De divino praemio,* 7; Augustine, *City of God,* 10.12–13.

28. See David Hume, *The Natural History of Religion* (Stanford: Stanford University Press, 1957), pp. 27, 30, 32, and more than a dozen other references. "The term *invisible* is conspicuously emphasised throughout *The Natural History.*" Peter Jones, *Hume's Sentiments: Their Ciceronian and French Context* (Edinburgh: University Press, 1982), p. 82. Hume and Smith were already friends by the early 1750s, and the "History of Astronomy" is one of the most "Humean" of Smith's writings. *Corr.,* pp. 8–11, 16–18; D. D. Raphael, "'The True Old Humean Philosophy' and Its Influence on Adam Smith," in *David Hume: Bicentenary Papers,* ed. G. P. Morice (Edinburgh: University Press, 1977), pp. 23–38. In his essay on superstition, too, Hume speaks of the invisible in false religion. "Of Superstition and Enthusiasm," in David Hume, *Essays Moral, Political, and Literary,* ed. Eugene F. Miller (Indianapolis: Liberty Classics, 1987), p. 74. Miracles are ascribed to "the interposition of some invisible agent" in Hume's *Enquiry;* he attributes the dislike of "jarring elements" to his stylized Stoic; he is concerned, in his discussion of causes, with the explanation of "irregular events." "The Stoic," in Hume, *Essays,* p. 154; David Hume, *Enquiries concerning Human Understanding and concerning the Principles of Morals,* ed. L. A. Selby-Bigge (Oxford: Oxford University Press, 1975), pp. 87, 115. Smith's phrase about fire and water, immediately before the reference to the invisible hand of Jupiter, is itself distinctively Humean, and recalls an observation from the *Treatise:* "In all the incidents of life we ought still to preserve our scepticism. If we believe, that fire warms, or water refreshes, 'tis only because it costs us too much pains to think otherwise." David Hume, *A Treatise of Human Nature,* ed. L. A. Selby-Bigge (Oxford: Oxford University Press, 1978), p. 270.

29. *LRBL,* pp. 68, 71. There are many similar uses of the word "invisible" elsewhere in the writings of Smith's acquaintances; Lord Kames, for example, complains at length about "the introduction of invisible powers" such as "deities, angels, devils, or other supernatural powers" into epic poetry. Lord Kames, *Elements of Criticism* (Edinburgh: A. Millar, 1762), 3:239, 248.

30. *TMS,* pp. 107, 251.

31. Smith, *EPS,* p. 42; there are at least a dozen other references in the "History of Astronomy" to chains of either intermediate or invisible events, including at pp. 44, 45, 50, 58, 91, 92.

32. *EPS,* p. 75; see also *EPS,* pp. 45–46, 119; *LRBL,* pp. 145–146; A. S. Skinner, "Adam Smith: Science and the Role of the Imagination," in *Hume and the*

Enlightenment, ed. W. B. Todd (Austin: University of Texas Press, 1974), pp. 164–188; D. D. Raphael and A. S. Skinner, "General Introduction," in *EPS,* pp. 12–13.

33. It is in some respects reminiscent of the invisible bodies, motions, and blows in Lucretius, *De rerum natura,* 2.128, 136, 714–715. Lucretius also makes fun of Jupiter's thunderbolts, and of the theories of storms believed in by savages, whose ignorance of causes compels them to refer events to the dominion of the gods rather than seeking to understand, for example, the "invisible bodies of the wind" (1.295, 6.55, 387).

34. *EPS,* pp. 42, 50, 90–92.

35. "Review of Johnson's *Dictionary,*" in *EPS,* pp. 233–238.

36. Macfie, *The Individual in Society,* p. 156.

37. I am grateful to Istvan Hont and Sylvana Tomaselli for discussion on this point. As Knud Haakonssen has written, of the section in the *Theory of Moral Sentiments* in which the invisible hand appears, "In this passage, Smith strikes that perfect equipoise between irony and encomium which is so characteristic of him." Knud Haakonssen, *The Science of a Legislator: The Natural Jurisprudence of David Hume and Adam Smith* (Cambridge: Cambridge University Press, 1981), p. 91.

38. For an account of the modern invisible hand, see Karen I. Vaughn, "Invisible Hand," in *The New Palgrave,* 2:997–999, and the discussion later in this chapter.

39. *TMS,* pp. 183–185. The title of the chapter is "Of the beauty which the appearance of UTILITY bestows upon all the productions of art, and of the extensive influence of this species of Beauty." *TMS,* p. 179.

40. Dugald Stewart, *Elements of the Philosophy of the Human Mind* (1792), in *Collected Works,* ed. Sir William Hamilton (Edinburgh: Constable, 1854), 2:248.

41. Robert Nozick, *Anarchy, State, and Utopia* (Oxford: Basil Blackwell, 1974), pp. 18–19.

42. Arrow and Hahn, *General Competitive Analysis,* p. 1.

43. "History of Astronomy," in *EPS,* p. 46.

44. Thus Caeneus: "caecamque in viscera movit / versavitque manum vulnusque in vulnere fecit." Ovid, *Metamorphoses,* 12.492–493.

45. Robert Nozick, *Philosophical Explanations* (Oxford: Clarendon Press, 1981), pp. 343, 347.

46. Ferguson goes on immediately to say that "nations stumble upon establishments, which are indeed the result of human action, but not the execution of any human design." Adam Ferguson, *An Essay on the History of Civil Society* (1767) (Edinburgh: Edinburgh University Press, 1966), p. 122; F. A. Hayek, *Studies in Philosophy, Politics, and Economics* (London: Routledge and Kegan Paul, 1967), p. 96.

47. See Chapter 1.

48. Jeremy Bentham, *The Theory of Legislation,* ed. C. K. Ogden (London:

Kegan Paul, 1931), p. 368; *Traités de législation civile et pénale par M. Jérémie Bentham,* ed. Étienne Dumont (Paris: Bossange, 1802), 3:19.

49. "One cannot help noticing that Smith always tends to exaggerate 'the weakness and folly of man,' when in the presence of his invisible hand," Alec Macfie writes. He also sees some tension in Smith's apparent presumption that providence is "deceiving" men: "'Deception' seems strange, as it is consistent neither with a perfect Deity nor with a proper recognition of human dignity." Macfie, *The Individual in Society,* pp. 122–123, 125. If the invisible hand is invisible of necessity (because it is the hand of God), then the individual is not blind by virtue of his or her incapacity to see it; I am grateful to A. C. Waterman for emphasizing this point. But the invisible hands of social theory, including those in the *Wealth of Nations* and the *Theory of Moral Sentiments,* are not invisible in this sense; they are visible, in fact, to social theorists. The hand of God is itself something to be glimpsed, in the view of some theologians; this is one of the implications, presumably, of the use of the metaphors of "revelation" and "revealed" religion. When Adolf Held translates "invisible" as *unsichtbar,* and Alfred Marshall translates it back into English as "unseen" (of which the more usual German translation would be *ungesehen*), then the meaning of the phrase changes; the invisible hand was not in fact seen (just as the hand of Caeneus/Caenis was not seen by the centaurs), but it could be seen, under other circumstances or by other people. The relationship between God's knowledge and man's, or between the all-seeingness of God and the limited vision of men, was indeed one of the continuing preoccupations of the sect of enlightenment. The new empire of light and reason aspired to illuminate the pleasing illusions of power, and it also aspired to illuminate the secrets of the universe. There was nothing, in principle, which could not be seen by men. "To attribute sovereignty to the people . . . to make man eternal is to make him God," Felicité de Lamennais wrote of Condorcet's ideas of political reform and physiological perfectibility. To make men enlightened, too, is to make them like gods; Felicité de Lamennais, "Influence des doctrines philosophiques sur la société" (1815), in *Réflexions sur l'état de l'église en France* (Paris: Tournachon-Molin, 1819), p. 156.

50. *TMS,* p. 234; on resemblances between Frederick and Smith's "royal reformer," see Chapter 2.

51. Epictetus, *The Discourses,* trans. W. A. Oldfather, (Cambridge, Mass.: Harvard University Press, 1925), 1.19.13–15; Vivenza, *Adam Smith e la cultura classica,* pp. 69–72.

52. See *TMS,* pp. 104–107, 288, 338.

53. *WN,* p. 678; *TMS,* p. 234. On Smith's views of Quesnay, see Istvan Hont, "The Political Economy of the 'Unnatural and Retrograde' Order: Adam Smith and Natural Liberty," *Französische Revolution und Politische Ökonomie,* 41 (1989), 122–149. Smith's language here echoes Lucian's description of the foolish Stoic in "Philosophies for Sale." The Stoic who is about to be

sold is described by Hermes as imagining that he is "the only wise man . . . the only just man, brave man, king, orator, rich man, lawgiver, and everything else that there is." *The Works of Lucian*, vol. 2, trans. A. M. Harmon (Cambridge, Mass.: Harvard University Press, 1915), p. 487.

54. *Vie de Voltaire* (1789), in *OC*, 4:20, and see Chapter 1.

55. "Idea for a Universal History with a Cosmopolitan Purpose" (1784), in *Kant's Political Writings*, ed. Hans Reiss (Cambridge: Cambridge University Press, 1970), pp. 41–42; Kant, *Werkausgabe*, 11:34. Kant was familiar with the *Theory of Moral Sentiments*, and there is some similarity of cadence between his individuals—with their ends "an welcher, selbst wenn sie ihnen bekannt würde, ihnen doch wenig gelegen sein würde"—and Smith's, who pursue ends "without intending it, without knowing it." Kant concludes, a little later in the essay (p. 39), that the cunning of nature leads one to infer the design of a wise creator, and not "die Hand eines bösartigen Geistes" (the hand of a malicious spirit). On Kant, Smith, and the "marketplace of feelings," see Samuel Fleischaker, "Philosophy in Moral Practice: Kant and Adam Smith," *Kant-Studien*, 82, 3 (1991), 249–269.

56. G. W. F. Hegel, *Vorlesungen über die Philosophie der Geschichte* (Stuttgart: Reclam, 1961), pp. 78–79. Hegel does go on to exempt a certain side of the lives of individuals, seen as an end and not as a means: their "Moralität, Sittlichkeit, Religiosität." The idea of reason, or nature, as cunning is characteristically Stoic, as in Balbus' description, in *De natura deorum*, of "naturam, qua nihil potest esse callidius." Cicero, *De natura deorum*, 2.142.

57. This is the phrase Smith uses in the *Theory of Moral Sentiments* (*TMS*, p. 158).

58. Immanuel Kant, *Observations on the Feeling of the Beautiful and Sublime* (1764), trans. John T. Goldthwait (Berkeley: University of California Press, 1960), p. 74.

59. See, on the interests which lie behind ostentatiously public-spirited or pious-spirited actions, Smith's remarks on the Quakers, who would never have agreed to free their slaves if the slaves had "made any considerable part of their property." *WN*, pp. 388–389; see also, for comments in a similar tone, pp. 51–52 (on the interest of princes in adulterating the coinage), p. 141 (the interest of manufacturers in incorporated towns), p. 144 (the sophistry of merchants and manufacturers in conveying that the general interest of the country is identical with their own private interests), p. 153 (the interest of parish worthies in making it difficult for the poor to become settled), p. 188 (the interest of dukes of Cornwall in offering mineral rights to the people who discover tin mines), p. 393 (the interest of proprietors, who were also legislators, in passing laws to restrict the rights of tenants), pp. 401–402 (the interest of medieval kings in granting privileges to wealthy burghers, as the "enemies of [their] enemies"), pp. 455–456 (the "invisible hand" passage), pp. 728–729 (the interest of the "proud minister of an ostentatious court" in executing conspicuous public works), p. 737 (the lack of interest, by direc-

tors of regulated colonial companies, in the companies' "general trade"), p. 760 (the interest of university teachers in performing their functions in a "careless and slovenly" manner), pp. 797–798 (the interest of established clergy in maintaining their authority, through the menace of "eternal misery"), pp. 802–803 (the interest of medieval clergy in perpetuating "the grossest delusions of superstition").

60. *WN,* pp. 663–664.

61. Frank Hahn, "Reflections on the Invisible Hand," *Lloyds Bank Review,* 144 (April 1982), pp. 17, 20.

62. Smith wrote later, of Turgot's economic reforms, that they "did so much honour to their Author, and, had they been executed without alteration, would have proved so beneficial to his country." See *Corr.,* p. 286, and Chapter 1.

63. "Lit de Justice" of March 12, 1776, in *OT,* 5:288–289.

64. *WN,* pp. 266–267, 459, 467, 660, 662.

65. "Lit de Justice," in *OT,* 5:288.

66. Note (f), in *An Inquiry into the Nature and Causes of the Wealth of Nations,* 11th ed., ed. Playfair (London: T. Cadell and W. Davies, 1805), 2:559; comment on Book 4, chap. 8 (*WN,* p. 660).

67. Lionel Robbins, *The Theory of Economic Policy in English Classical Political Economy* (London: Macmillan, 1952), p. 56.

68. *WN,* pp. 454–456.

69. *WN,* pp. 144, 157, 471–472.

70. *WN,* p. 267; and, on competition and policies of economic and political reform, see Chapter 6.

71. Jacob Viner, *The Role of Providence in the Social Order* (Philadephia: American Philosophical Society, 1972), pp. 81–82; Macfie, "The Invisible Hand of Jupiter," p. 595. Macfie refers on several other occasions to the "theological" character of the invisible hand, and to the "very general theological framework" in which it should be seen, as part of "a seventeenth century, almost Newtonian picture." Macfie, *The Individual in Society,* pp. 49, 54, 56, 69.

72. "Doctor SMITH, when the hour of his departure hence shall arrive, will copy the example of the BELEIVER, or the INFIDEL, as it liketh him best." [George Horne], *A Letter to Adam Smith LL.D. on the Life, Death, and Philosophy of his friend David Hume Esq. By one of the people called CHRISTIANS* (Oxford: Clarendon Press, 1777), pp. 29, 36.

73. On the circumstances of Stewart's "Account," see Chapter 2. Hume wrote, in 1759: "Three Bishops called yesterday at Millar's shop to buy Copies, and to ask Questions about the Author: The Bishop of Peterborough said he had passed the Evening in a Company, where he heard it extolled above all books in the World. *You may conclude what Opinion true Philosophers will entertain of it, when these Retainers to Superstition praise it so highly.*" The sentence emphasized is the one which Stewart chose to omit. The other passage in Hume's letter which Stewart omitted is similarly incautious: "Voltaire has

lately published a small Work called *Candide, ou L'optimisme. It is full of Sprightliness and Impiety, and is indeed a Satyre upon Providence, under Pretext of criticizing the Leibnitian System.* I shall give you a Detail of it." *Corr.,* pp. 34–35; Dugald Stewart, "Account of the Life and Writings of Adam Smith, LL.D" (1793), in *EPS,* pp. 297–298.

74. John Dunn, "From Applied Theology to Social Analysis: The Break between John Locke and the Scottish Enlightenment," in *Wealth and Virtue: The Shaping of Political Economy in the Scottish Enlightenment,* ed. Istvan Hont and Michael Ignatieff (Cambridge: Cambridge University Press, 1983), pp. 119–120. "It would certainly be a profoundly implausible claim to make in relation to either [Hume or Smith] that the *framework* of their thinking was in any sense 'theocentric,'" Dunn writes. It is interesting that John Stuart Mill, in a letter of 1852 in which he objects to the charge that political economy "unless connected with Xtianity is 'a true child of the devil,'" says of "A. Smith, Turgot, Say, Ricardo & my father not one of whom was a believer in Xtianity," that they were in no respect concerned to justify universal selfishness. Letter to John Lalor of July 3, 1852, in *The Later Letters of John Stuart Mill, 1849–1873,* ed. Francis E. Mineka and Dwight N. Lindley (Toronto: University of Toronto Press, 1972), p. 93.

75. See, for example, *TMS,* pp. 92, 111, 166, 171, 178, 305; also Raphael and Macfie, "Introduction" and Appendix 2.

76. "The laws concerning corn may every where be compared to the laws concerning religion," Smith writes; both show the power of "prejudices" and unreason. He criticizes "great sects" and ecclesiastical establishments, which he describes in the characteristically scornful language of "incorporation" and "plan," reserved in general for manufacturers and merchants: "The clergy of every established church constitute a great incorporation. They can act in concert, and pursue their interest upon one plan." The church, for Smith, is a part of government. But it is also an outside influence on government, imposing its interests in much the same way as merchants and monopolists; its worldly power is simply strengthened, from time to time, by "all the terrors of religion." *WN,* pp. 539, 797. Jacob Viner describes the "virtual disappearance from the *Wealth of Nations* of the doctrine of an order of nature designed and guided by a benevolent God"; he says that "there are only a few minor passages in the later work which can be adduced as supporting evidence of the survival in Smith's thought of the concept of a divinity" who promotes economic welfare, and concludes that "such general statements" as the one about the invisible hand "play a much more modest role" in the *Wealth of Nations.* Jacob Viner, "Adam Smith and Laissez Faire," in *The Long View and the Short* (Glencoe, Ill.: Free Press, 1958), pp. 126–129. A. C. Waterman, by contrast, interprets Smith's use of the word "nature," in the *Wealth of Nations,* as evidence of a continuing theological framework; see A. C. Waterman, "'Pure and Rational Religion': A Theological Reading of Adam Smith's *Wealth of Nations,*" University of Manitoba, 1997.

77. See Walther Eckstein, "Einleitung," in Adam Smith, *Theorie der ethischen Gefühle*, ed. Eckstein (Leipzig: Felix Meiner, 1926), 1:xlv–l, and also notes at 1:300–301; Macfie, *The Individual in Society*, pp. 108, 111; Raphael and Macfie, "Introduction," pp. 19–20 and Appendix 2 in *TMS*.

78. One such passage is Smith's discussion of the relative contributions of "the duties of devotion, the public and private worship of the Deity," of "futile mortifications," and of "a whole life spent honourably," to prospects of reward and punishment in "the life to come." See *TMS*, pp. 132–134, and notes to this passage in the Raphael-Macfie and Eckstein editions. A second is also concerned with eternal punishment and with the doctrine of atonement, where Smith's successive emendations, and his eventual deletion of an extended exposition of orthodox views of atonement, suggest a declining concern with what Raphael and Macfie describe as "pious sentiments." See *TMS*, p. 91, and Appendix 2 in *TMS*, p. 383. Smith's discussion of religious fanaticism is similarly harsh: "Even to the great Judge of the universe, they impute all their own prejudices, and often view that Divine Being as animated by all their own vindictive and implacable passions." *TMS*, pp. 155–156. In his minor emendations, too, he sometimes seems to be emphasizing his differences with religious thought, as when he inserts the words "whining and"—the adjective "whining" being particularly associated, apparently, with Christianity—into his description of "melancholy moralists"; he refers here to Pascal, the object of Condorcet's distaste over the heavy, all-powerful hand of the Christian God. *TMS*, p. 139.

79. Smith's description of religion in the new additions to the *Theory* is reminiscent of the statements of both Cleanthes and Philo in the last part of Hume's *Dialogues:* religion is a "consolation" to men (Cleanthes), and it is also an object of "contemplation," as of "so extraordinary and magnificent a question" (Philo). David Hume, *Dialogues concerning Natural Religion* (1779) (London: Penguin Books, 1990), pp. 136–138. Like Hume, Smith is interested in religious belief as the expression of the emotional and intellectual needs of men. His account of faith is more profound than Hume's—and also, perhaps, more sympathetic to the foundations of religious feeling—in that he describes belief as a way of making sense of the world as it is. For Hume, man is made miserable by the prospect of eternal punishment: "When melancholy, and dejected, he has nothing to do but brood upon the terrors of the invisible world, and to plunge himself still deeper into affliction." *Dialogues*, p. 137. For Smith, he is melancholy because he cannot bring himself to believe that the world is orderly and just. The two extended new discussions of religion in Parts 3 and 6 of the *Theory*, concerned with eternal justice and with universal benevolence, take the form of dismal choices between impossible optimism and frightful loneliness. On the one hand, Smith says, the idea of universal benevolence is the source "of no solid happiness" to "any man who is not thoroughly convinced that all the inhabitants of the universe, the meanest as well as the greatest, are under the immediate care and protection

of that great, benevolent, and all-wise Being, who directs all the movements of nature; and who is determined, by his own unalterable perfections, to maintain in it, at all times, the greatest possible quantity of happiness." This idea, Smith says, repeating that the "divine Being" has contrived the universe "so as at all times to produce the greatest possible quantity of happiness," "is certainly of all the objects of human contemplation by far the most sublime." On the other hand, for Smith "the very suspicion of a fatherless world, must be the most melancholy of all reflections; from the thought that all the unknown regions of infinite and incomprehensible space may be filled with nothing but endless misery and wretchedness." *TMS*, pp. 235–236. The dilemma is characteristically Humean. One possibility is to be convinced of something quite unconvincing, that is to say, of the existence of a super-eternal and super-utilitarian God. The other possibility is to be endlessly gloomy, unconsoled by the sort of conviction which almost everyone, ever, has held.

80. Smith's resolutely secular language in the *Wealth of Nations* is in some contrast to the language of the contemporaries by whom he was influenced (such as Quesnay), and whom he in turn influenced (such as Burke). Quesnay thus says of the natural law that "all men and all human powers should be subject to these sovereign laws, instituted by the Supreme Being; they are immutable and beyond question, and the best possible laws . . . It is only the knowledge of these supreme laws which can constantly assure the tranquillity and prosperity of an empire." François Quesnay, "Le Droit Naturel" (1765), in *François Quesnay et la Physiocratie* (Paris: Institut National d'Études Démographiques, 1958), 2:740–741. For Burke, later, it is an error for governments to interfere with "the Divine Providence" which occasionally imposes bad harvests: "We, the people, ought to be made sensible that it is not in breaking the laws of commerce, which are the laws of Nature, and consequently the laws of God, that we are to place our hope of softening the Divine displeasure to remove any calamity under which we suffer or which hangs over us." Edmund Burke, "Thoughts and Details on Scarcity" (1800), in *The Works of the Right Honourable Edmund Burke* (Boston: Little, Brown, 1894), 5:157.

81. See Duncan Forbes, "Hume's Science of Politics," in Morice, *David Hume: Bicentenary Papers,* pp. 39–50; Deborah A. Redman, "Adam Smith and Isaac Newton," *Scottish Journal of Political Economy,* 40, 2 (May 1993), 210–230.

82. "We all know, Sir," Bishop Horne wrote in his letter to Smith, "what the word SUPERSTITION denotes, in Mr HUME's vocabulary, and against what Religion his shafts are levelled, under that name . . . [H]e so often sate down calmly and deliberately to obliterate from the hearts of the human species every trace of the knowledge of GOD and his dispensations; all faith in his kind providence, and fatherly protection." [Horne], *A Letter to Adam Smith,* pp. 12–13, 16. It was his friendship with Hume, under these circumstances, that was held against Smith, as evidence of his subversive beliefs. "Ascanius" (Lord Buchan, who was James Steuart's nephew) wrote of Smith that "when

he met with honest men whom he liked, and who courted him, he would believe almost anything they said . . . Smith's well placed affection for Hume, as a man, hindered him from being a Christian, from the same foible I have described . . . O venerable, amiable, and worthy man, why was you not a Christian!" "Ascanius," *The Bee*, June 8 1791, pp. 165–167. Archbishop Magee, as D. D. Raphael has shown, attributed Smith's backsliding on the doctrine of atonement to "the infection of David Hume's society." Appendix 2, in *TMS*, p. 384.

83. The Reverend John Sinclair, *Memoirs of the Life and Works of Sir John Sinclair* (Edinburgh: Blackwood, 1837), 1:39–40.

84. There is no reason to infer from the circumstance that Smith was Hume's "dearest friend" that they agreed on all subjects. Smith indeed alluded to minor differences, saying, of the philosopher John Bruce, that "he and I differ a little, as David Hume and I used to do." *Corr.*, pp. 208, 296. Smith and Hume differed in public over utility and virtue, as well as over strategies for good temper in religion. But the tone of Hume's and Smith's correspondence, over a period of more than twenty years—the sense of intimacy and complicity, or of Sinclair's "identity of sentiment"—is difficult to reconcile with the presumption of serious religious differences. Smith's letters to Hume have something of the sprightliness which Hume admired in Voltaire, and which is characteristic of Hume's own letters to Smith. Of his pupil the duke of Buccleuch, Smith writes: "He has read almost all your works several times over, and was it not for the more wholesome doctrine which I take care to instill into him, I am afraid he might be in danger of adopting some of your wicked Principles. You will find him very much improved"; of Hume's opponent John Oswald, "The Bishop is a brute and a beast." *Corr.*, pp. 105, 131. Smith's letter to Alexander Wedderburn about Hume's last weeks, which is an early version of the letter later published to so much "clamour," is hardly pious: "Poor David Hume is dying very fast, but with great cheerfulness and good humour and with more real resignation to the necessary course of things, than any Whining Christian ever died with pretended resignation to the will of God." The changes that Smith himself made in the published version of the letter are again interesting: to Wedderburn he quotes Hume as asking Charon to have patience until "I have the pleasure of seeing *the churches shut up, and the Clergy sent about their business,*" and in the published letter as having patience until "I may have the satisfaction of seeing the downfall of some of the prevailing systems of superstition." *Corr.*, pp. 203–204, 219 (italics added). Hume entrusted to Smith the posthumous publication of his most profoundly skeptical work, the *Dialogues concerning Natural Religion*, and Smith had earlier entrusted to Hume the posthumous publication of his "History of Astronomy," which was also relatively subversive. See *Corr.*, pp. 168, 251; Ernest Campbell Mossner, *The Life of David Hume* (Oxford: Clarendon Press, 1980), pp. 323–328; Ross, *The Life of Adam Smith*, chap. 17.

85. *LRBL,* pp. 23, 50–51. The editors add that the sentence is "in large letters in MS." The conjunction of Lucian, with his ridicule of such "solemn and respectable characters, as Gods, Goddesses, Heroes, Senators, Generals, Historians, Poets, and Philosophers," and Swift with his more severe irony was for Smith a system of ridicule and also of instruction: "Both together form a System of morality from whence more sound and just rules of life for all the various characters of men may be drawn than from most set systems of Morality." *LRBL,* pp. 50–51. The evidence about Hume's preferences—"since Lucian is your favourite author and since you know that I like him as much as you do"—is in a letter of 1767 from Morellet, in *The Letters of David Hume,* ed. J. Y. T. Greig (Oxford: Clarendon Press, 1932), 2:158. Hume was also reading Lucian's dialogues before he died, as Smith pointed out in his published letter. *Corr.,* pp. 219, and also pp. 203–204.

86. Ernest C. Mossner, "Hume and the Legacy of the *Dialogues,*" in Morice, *David Hume: Bicentenary Papers,* p. 13; John Valdimir Price, *The Ironic Hume* (Austin: University of Texas Press, 1965). Mossner does add "a word of caution: although Hume is a consummate ironist, one has to learn not to be overzealous and to see irony lurking around every corner."

87. *TMS,* p. 339. Turgot said of Hume, in a letter to Condorcet, "I know that there are men who are very insensitive ("très peu sensibles") and who are at the same time honest, such as Hume, Fontenelle, etc.; but they all have as the basis of their honesty *justice,* and even a certain degree of *goodness.*" Letter of December 1773, in *Correspondance inédite de Condorcet et de Turgot, 1770–1779,* ed. Charles Henry (Paris: Didier, 1883), p. 144.

88. *LRBL,* p. 50.

89. Macfie, *The Individual in Society,* pp. 108, 111.

90. Raphael and Macfie, "Introduction," in *TMS,* pp. 6–7, 10; Macfie, "The Invisible Hand of Jupiter," p. 599.

91. "Adam Smith's main references are in fact to Cicero, *De Officiis* and *De Finibus* . . . [which] would be fairly familiar to his young audiences," Macfie writes. Peter Jones says of Hume that "he names Cicero more than fifty times," and that "explicit allusion was often unnecessary since Cicero was the one classical writer familiar to and admired by almost every educated person in France and England in the late seventeenth and early eighteenth centuries." Macfie, *The Individual in Society,* p. 44; Jones, *Hume's Sentiments,* p. 30.

92. Cicero, *De natura deorum,* 1.10.

93. The imperfect virtues of the Stoics, Smith says, were "proprieties, fitnesses, decent and becoming actions, for which a plausible or probable reason could be assigned, what Cicero expresses by the Latin word *officia,* and Seneca, I think more exactly, by that of *convenientia.*" *TMS,* p. 291. It was decent, in this sense, to try not to make other people distressed, as they would be, for example, by the publication of Hume's *Dialogues.* The word "tranquillity," which Smith uses amazingly often—fifteen times in five paragraphs, in the new discussion of duty in the sixth edition of the *Theory of Moral Sentiments,*

four times in two paragraphs in his discussion of friendship, three times in his discussion of Epicurean virtue—is associated, after all, with the "quiet" which he wished to preserve in the months after Hume's death: a "locus quietis et tranquillitatis plenissimus." Cicero, *De oratore*, 1.1.2.

94. Vivenza, *Adam Smith e la cultura classica*, pp. 90–91.

95. "It was desirable, not merely as the means of procuring the other primary objects of natural desire, but as something which was in itself more valuable than them all." *TMS*, p. 300.

96. *TMS*, p. 277.

97. See, for example, on vices as part of the plan of the universe, *TMS*, p. 36; on suicide, *TMS*, pp. 279–288; on Stoic astronomy, *EPS*, p. 62; and on the paradoxes of the Stoics, *TMS*, pp. 289–291; see also Vivenza, *Adam Smith e la cultura classica*, pp. 66, 76–78. The Stoical wise man enjoys his own self-applause, has a "breast in which dwells complete self-satisfaction," and "enjoys his own complete self-approbation." *TMS*, pp. 143, 147–148. This endlessly happy wise man is common, in fact, to Stoic and Epicurean thought; Cicero's Epicurean "derives no inconsiderable pleasure from comparing his own existence with the life of the foolish." Cicero, *De finibus*, 1.62.

98. "The stoical apathy is, in such cases, never agreeable, and all the metaphysical sophisms by which it is supported can seldom serve any other purpose than to blow up the harsh insensibility of a coxcomb to ten times its native impertinence." The "sense of propriety," for Smith, is "much more offended by the defect, than it ever is by the excess of that sensibility" which "we naturally feel for the misfortunes of our nearest connections." *TMS*, p. 143. Smith does not accept the Stoic apathy, Vivenza says: "Apathy tends to make man indifferent to the success or failure of the action undertaken; Smith by contrast is anything other than unaware of consequences . . . such arguments lead to a passivity in human behavior which is totally foreign to Adam Smith's thought." Gloria Vivenza, "Elementi classici nel pensiero di Adam Smith: giurisprudenza romana e morale Stoica," in *Gli Italiani e Bentham*, ed. R. Faucci (Milan: Franco Angeli, 1982), 1:161.

99. The other doctrine is the "contempt of life and death"; on these two, Smith says, "rested the whole fabric of Stoical morality." *TMS*, p. 288.

100. See, on Stoic "indifference," *TMS*, pp. 273, 275, 277, 290, 292. Smith seems to have been rereading Arrian's *Discourses of Epictetus*, in considerable irritation, when he was preparing the sixth edition of *Theory of Moral Sentiments*. See *TMS*, pp. 277–293. Epictetus compares Socrates to a skillful ballplayer: "So ought we also to act, exhibiting the ballplayer's carefulness about the game, but the same indifference about the object played with, as being a mere ball" (*Discourses* 2.5.21).

101. See Smith's references to the "direction of conduct" at *TMS*, pp. 274, 277 (twice), 280, and 281 (twice): "The directors of my conduct never command me to be miserable . . . Whether we are to be drowned, or to come to a harbour, is the business of Jupiter, not mine" (p. 277).

102. "The plan and system which Nature has sketched out for our conduct, seems

to be altogether different from that of the Stoical philosophy . . . By the perfect apathy which it prescribes to us . . . it endeavours to render us altogether indifferent and unconcerned in the success or miscarriage of every thing which Nature has prescribed to us as the proper business and occupation of our lives." *TMS,* pp. 291–293; see also pp. 143, 235. In Smith's anti-utilitarian and anti-contractarian theory, Vivenza writes, "the principle which unites men in society is of a nature to do with sentiments . . . [S]ociety emerges from a relationship which is in some sense affective." Gloria Vivenza, "Studi classici e pensiero moderno: la sintesi di Adam Smith," *Atti e Memorie della Accademia di Agricoltura, Scienze e Lettere di Verona,* 6, 41 (1989–90), 128.

103. *TMS,* pp. 278, 289, 292; on ridicule and the mock heroic, see *LRBL,* pp. 44–47; and on "paranomasia, when we don't name but describe a person, as the Jewish lawgiver for Moses," *LRBL,* p. 32.

104. Stoicism had the function, in England and France in the eighteenth century, of a substitute religion; a deism for the pious, or a demonstration of respect for virtue. Samuel Clarke thus praises the Stoics for their defense of virtue, but chides them for their failure to proceed to "a firm belief and expectation of a future state of rewards and punishments, without which their whole scheme of morality cannot be supported." Samuel Clarke, *A Discourse of Natural Religion,* in *British Moralists, 1650–1800,* ed. D. D. Raphael (Oxford: Clarendon Press, 1969), 1:215–216. To be demonstratively Stoic was to be a safe deist. See Gunter Gawlick, "Hume and the Deists: a Reconsideration," in Morice, *Hume: Bicentenary Papers,* pp. 128–138. It was also to be demonstratively opposed to Epicureanism. Smith seems to have been characteristically prudent in avoiding any suspicion of promoting "licentious systems"; of being accused, like Hume, of Epicurean tendencies. See Richard B. Sher, "Professors of Virtue: The Social History of the Edinburgh Moral Philosophy Chair in the Eighteenth Century," in *Studies in the Philosophy of the Scottish Enlightenment,* ed. M. A. Stewart (Oxford: Clarendon Press, 1990), pp. 110–111. Smith says of Epicurus that his "system is, no doubt, altogether inconsistent with that which I have been endeavouring to establish," and he distinguishes the prudence he himself favors from the "inferior prudence" of the Epicurean. *TMS,* pp. 216, 298. He rejected, without irony, the Epicurean view of sentiments as the objects of moral action, in relation to which virtue is no more than an instrument. But his descriptions of the sentiments of friendship, of sympathy with our friends' pain, of guilt, of affection for places and things, are distinctively Epicurean. Sentiments are of moral importance even when they are not the objects of morality; the morality without sentiments of the Stoics is for Smith a sort of delusion. *De finibus* is one of Smith's principal sources in the *Theory of Moral Sentiments,* and there are striking similarities between his description of sentiments and the descriptions in the account of the Epicurean system in Book 1 of *De finibus:* the dread of being seen of the guilty (1.51, *TMS,* p. 118); the anxiety and torment of the man who dreams of wealth and station (1.60, *TMS,* pp. 181–183); the tranquillity

of the man with friends, and the secret brooding of the solitary man (1.66–67, *TMS*, pp. 22–23); our partiality to our own surroundings (mostly people, for Smith, and places, for Torquatus, 1.69, *TMS*, p. 227). Vivenza says that there is "a certain Epicurean coloration" to Smith's Stoic-inspired ideas; she speaks, too, of the closeness of Epicurean and Stoic positions in the period of Smith's sources. Vivenza, "Elementi classici," 1:169–170. Smith, she concludes, adopts "a position in part Stoic and in part Epicurean." Vivenza, *Adam Smith e la cultura classica*, pp. 64–66.

105. On Stoic insensibility, *TMS*, pp. 140–143 and 147–149; on suicide, pp. 278–288; on providence, pp. 288–293; and on the Stoic paradoxes, pp. 289–291. Smith's reorganization of the material on Stoic doctrines also tends to reduce its importance; as Raphael and Macfie say, the arrangement in the earlier editions has a greater impact, and "shows up more clearly the pervasive character of Stoic influence." "Introduction," in *TMS*, p. 5.

106. Letter of September 10, 1759, in *Corr.*, p. 47; it is this picture of Stoic philosophy which Smith deletes in the sixth edition, restoring it in part at the end of the volume.

107. In Lucian's "Zeus Catechized," Zeus tries unsuccessfully to explain the Stoic doctrines of destiny and providence; in "The Tragic Zeus," he looks on with mounting irritation as the Stoic Timocles is vanquished by the Epicurean Damis in a public debate about the order of nature, providence, and the evidence of divine design; in the "Parliament of the Gods," he is told that if he goes on turning himself into gold, he is at risk of being made into a bracelet; in the "Double Indictment," he complains about the wearying business of dispensing hail and lightning, watching battles in Babylon and banquets in Ethiopia, and not being able to sleep, lest Epicurus should be confirmed in his denial of divine providence, and the supply of sacrifices and oblations should come to an end. "This notion of providence, as the foundation of Socratic and Stoic theology, was in that capacity most specifically singled out for Lucian's attacks," the Lucian scholar Maurice Croiset concluded in *Essai sur la vie et les oeuvres de Lucien* (Paris: Hachette, 1882), p. 228. "By contrast with the Epicureans, their traditional enemies the Stoics are perhaps Lucian's favorite butt," C. P. Jones writes; "he is clearly influenced by philosophic debates . . . and above all by attacks on Stoic views of providence." C. P. Jones, *Culture and Society in Lucian* (Cambridge, Mass.: Harvard University Press, 1986), pp. 28, 40–41. It is interesting that the work of Lucian's which Smith singles out for its "Gaiety"—and of which he says that "few things are more entertaining"—is his account of the false prophet Alexander of Abonoteichos. *LRBL*, p. 52. This is Lucian's most powerful defense of Epicurus, and of those, "atheist or Christian or Epicurean," who resisted Alexander, while "the followers of Plato and Chrysippus and Pythagoras were his friends." Epicurus, Lucian wrote, was a man who set men free; who brought them peace and tranquillity, freeing them "from terrors and apparitions and portents, from vain hopes and extravagant cravings, developing in them

intelligence and truth, and truly purifying their understanding, not with torches and squills and that sort of foolery, but with straight thinking, truthfulness and frankness." "Alexander the False Prophet," 25, 38, 47, in *The Works of Lucian,* 4:209, 225, 235.

108. See, on "the business of Jupiter" in Epictetus' ship, *TMS* p. 277. In the "History of Ancient Physics," Smith speaks of "this almighty Jupiter, who, at a destined period, should, by an universal conflagration, wrap up all things." In his lectures on rhetoric, he describes a poem by John Harvey, the author of *The Bruciad,* in which Harvey omits "the effects of the Music on Jupiter himself, the thunder bolt falling from his hand and the eagle[s] settling herself at that particular moment on his hand." *EPS,* p. 117; *LRBL,* p. 67. This is in the spirit of Lactantius, whose works Smith owned, and presumably lectured from; *De falsa religione,* for example. In his lectures on jurisprudence, Smith asks, "What had Jupiter who dwelt in the Capitol to do with a slave who came from Syria or Cappadocia. Besides, the deities then could never be addressed empty handed; whoever had any request to ask of them must introduce it with a present. This also entirely debarred the slaves from religious offices as they had nothing of their own to offer." *LJ,* p. 179; there is some resemblance here to Oedipus' providence, whose "invisible main repoussait mes présents."

109. "All his affections were absorbed and swallowed up in two great affections; in that for the discharge of his own duty, and in that for the greatest possible happiness of all rational and sensible beings . . . His sole anxiety was about the gratification of the former; not about the event, but about the propriety of his own endeavours." *TMS,* p. 277, and, on Epictetus, p. 288. The Stoic, here, unites the least charming characteristics of several different ethical personalities: the self-obsession of the deontologist; the insensitivity of the utilitarian; the quietude of the pietist.

110. To deny the sincerity of public spirit and the disinterestedness of private friendship, Hume says, is to be deficient in self-knowledge. The philosopher of universal self-love "does not know himself: He has forgotten the movements of his heart; or rather he makes use of a different language from the rest of his countrymen, and calls not things by their proper names." "Of the Dignity or Meanness of Human Nature," in Hume, *Essays,* p. 85.

111. Hume, *Dialogues,* p. 128.

112. Cicero, *De natura deorum,* 2.17.

113. The world is so imperfect, Philo responds, that it might be taken to be "the work only of some dependent, inferior deity"; in some circumstances, too, "its origin ought rather to be ascribed to generation or vegetation than to reason or design." Hume, *Dialogues,* pp. 66, 79, 86.

114. *TMS,* p. 185. "If you see a spacious and beautiful house, you could not be induced to believe, even though you could not see its master, that it was built by mice and weasels," Balbus says; when a man goes into a house, or into a gymnasium, or into the forum, "and observes in all that goes on arrange-

ment, regularity, and system, he cannot possibly suppose that these things come about without a cause: he realizes that there is someone who presides and controls." It is interesting that the passage in Smith's "History of Astronomy" about the invisible hand of Jupiter recalls the immediately preceding discussion in *De natura deorum.* This is the account, attributed by Balbus to "our master Cleanthes," of the origin of ideas of the gods. One explanation is "the awe inspired by lightning, storms, rain, snow . . . all of which alarming portents have suggested to mankind the idea of the existence of some celestial and divine power." The more powerful explanation, however, is "the uniform motion and revolution of the heavens . . . [the] ordered beauty of the sun, moon, and stars, the very sight of which was in itself enough to prove that these things are not the mere effect of chance." *De natura deorum,* 2.14–17.

115. *The Leibniz-Clarke Correspondence,* ed. H. G. Alexander (Manchester: Manchester University Press, 1956), p. 14.

116. It is easier, evidently, to show that an idea or simile was important in the thought of a theorist than that it was unimportant; that he or she referred to it frequently, that it was consistent with other parts of his or her work, and so forth. The infrequency of references to the invisible hand in comments of contemporaries (and of nineteenth-century scholars) on Smith's work provides some supporting evidence of unimportance. But the proposition that references of a particular sort are infrequent in a population of which the size is unknown, but known to be very large—in this case, the population of comments about Smith—is quite elusive. There could be other explanations, too, for the apparent paucity of references; for example, that ideas of providential order were so obvious, to contemporaries, as to require no comment.

117. Macfie, *The Individual in Society,* p. 122. Viner suggested, in "Adam Smith and Laissez Faire," that the "doctrine of a harmonious order of nature, under divine guidance"—or what Macfie calls the "theistic invisible hand type of argument"—is far more important in the *Theory of Moral Sentiments* than in the *Wealth of Nations,* and he describes its "virtual disappearance" in the later book. Jacob Viner, "Adam Smith and Laissez Faire," p. 127. One of Viner's early commentators, Henry Bittermann, extended the argument in that he questioned the importance of harmonious order even in the *Theory of Moral Sentiments.* "It is contended further that Smith's theory of ethics did not rest directly on the doctrine of the order of nature, that this order contained no implications of specific standards or policies, which had to be found in phenomena directly." Henry Bittermann, "Adam Smith's Empiricism and the Law of Nature," pt. 2, *Journal of Political Economy,* 48 (1940), 717–718. Macfie, too, accepts Viner's argument about the unimportance of natural harmony in the *Wealth of Nations;* he, too, shows that the invisible hand was of only minor importance in the *Theory of Moral Sentiments,* and goes on to question the contrast Viner draws between the two works. Having noted all

the references to "Nature, the Deity or the invisible hand," in the *Theory of Moral Sentiments*, Macfie concludes that "it is quite remarkable how little relation they have with the main sympathy-spectator argument." Macfie, *The Individual in Society*, p. 102. Raphael sees the "more metaphysical elements in Smith's ethics and economics" as of only hypothetical importance: "He does not in fact need them for his causal explanations . . . [T]he 'invisible hand' is not to be understood literally as the hand of God." D. D. Raphael, "Adam Smith: Philosophy, Science, and Social Science," in *Philosophers of the Enlightenment: Royal Institute of Philosophy Lectures*, vol. 12, ed. S. C. Brown (Atlantic Highlands, N.J.: Humanities Press, 1979), p. 92. Gloria Vivenza, in her discussion of Smith's relations to Stoic ethics, speaks of the "fundamental problem" posed by the "need to find some accord between a theological model of Stoic origin (the providentialist concept of universal harmony, applied in some fashion by Smith also to the economy), which is optimistic, and definitely—despite Smith's generally antidogmatic orientation—to a substantial extent aprioristic," on the one hand, and, on the other, "a philosophy of practice which begins with the individual," and which recognizes both natural instincts and the "exquisitely social character" of people's motives. Vivenza, *Adam Smith e la cultura classica*, p. 91. The sequence of these arguments, over most of the past century, seems to be as follows: it is recognized that the invisible hand, while of evident importance to Smith's thought, is in some tension with this thought; it is suggested, by Viner, that providentialist conceptions are important only in the *Theory of Moral Sentiments*, and not in the *Wealth of Nations*; it is further shown, by Macfie and others, that these conceptions are not even important in Smith's ethics. The suggestion in this chapter has been of a next step in the sequence: to question whether the invisible hand is indeed in some sense important to Smith, as distinct from being important in nineteenth- and especially in twentieth-century interpretations of his work. The principal difference with Macfie's account, thereby, is over his description of the invisible hand as an "overruling concept," or as the "energizing power of the whole system." Macfie, *The Individual in Society*, p. 54; idem, "The Invisible Hand of Jupiter," p. 599. If the invisible hand is seen, instead, as a concept of only unimpressive power, then its ontology—whether it is to be understood "in the wider context of [Smith's] ultimate faith," as it is for Macfie, or as a useful conceit, as has been suggested here—is itself a matter of relatively minor importance.

118. David Hume, *Dialogues concerning Natural Religion*, p. 84; "History of Astronomy," in *EPS*, p. 105.

119. Immanuel Kant, *Critique of Pure Reason* (1787), trans. N. Kemp Smith (New York: St. Martin's Press, 1965), pp. 147–148. It is interesting that one of the charges advanced against Hume by Bishop Horne, in his open letter to Smith, is of glorifying the understanding: Hume believed, he said, "that the nature of all things depends so much upon man, that two and two could not be equal to four, nor fire produce heat, nor the sun light, without an act

of the human understanding." [Horne], *Letter,* pp. 42–43. The editors of Smith's "History of Astronomy" in 1795—of whom one, Joseph Hutton, had been criticized for the quasi-atheistical tendencies evinced in his geology, and the other, Joseph Black, was closely involved, as the attending physician, in the suspect episode of Hume's happy and composed death—add a note at the end of the *History* saying that Smith "left some Notes and Memorandums, from which it appears, that he considered this last part of his History of Astronomy as imperfect," and explaining that it "must be viewed, not as a History or Account of Sir Isaac Newton's Astronomy." *EPS,* p. 105. One object of this gloss could have been to defend Smith against the posthumous charge of glorifying the imagination, to the detriment of the glory of God's order; or of presenting Newton's system as one philosophical system among others, to the detriment of its dignity as the description of God's celestial clockwork.

120. *WN,* p. 456. As Richard Schüller wrote, if Smith's point is no more than that private interests coincide "as a general rule" with the interests of society, then he is asserting nothing with which his historicist critics (such Wilhelm Roscher and Karl Knies) would disagree. The "dubious" point in Smith's position would be if he were to assert that the harmony of public and private interests holds "without exception." But this he is careful not to do. The historical economists, Schüller writes, cite Smith "without consideration for the context, and even falsely"; Bruno Hildebrand, for example, following Smith's German translator Max Stirner, in his account of the invisible hand passage "leaves out the word 'frequently,' which is here of decisive importance." Richard Schüller, *Die Klassische Nationalökonomie und ihre Gegner: Zur Geschichte der Nationalökonomie und Socialpolitik seit A. Smith* (Berlin: Carl Heymann, 1895), pp. 42–44. See also Alfred Marshall's comments, cited in note 12 above.

121. See, for example, *TMS,* pp. 186, 336; see also Macfie, *The Individual in Society,* p. 115; Vivenza, "Studi classici," p. 113.

122. *TMS,* pp. 183–187.

123. "Monopole et monopoleur" (1775), in *OC,* 11:46; and see Chapter 6.

124. "History of Astronomy," in *EPS,* pp. 77, 105.

125. Vaughn, "Invisible Hand," p. 998.

126. Bernard Williams, *Shame and Necessity* (Berkeley: University of California Press, 1993), pp. 50–52; see also, on the "unprofound" quality of the insight that actions can have unintended consequences, Amartya Sen, "The Profit Motive," in *Resources, Values, and Development* (Oxford: Basil Blackwell, 1984), pp. 92–93.

127. *TMS,* pp. 104, 107, 338–339; the two discussions of "piacular guilt" were added in the sixth edition.

128. Vaughn thus writes that the unintended consequences "may, given the right circumstances, result in an order that . . . appears as if it were the product of some intelligent planner." Vaughn, "Invisible Hand," p. 998.

129. "The notion that a social system moved by independent actions in pursuit of different values is consistent with a final coherent state of balance, and one in which the outcomes may be quite different from those intended by the agents, is surely the most important intellectual contribution that economic thought has made to the general understanding of social processes." Arrow and Hahn, *General Competitive Analysis*, p. 1; Vaughn, "Invisible Hand," p. 998.

130. Hayek, *Studies in Philosophy, Politics, and Economics*, p. 97.

131. In the "ancient wisdom," in Proudhon's description, everything depended on an arbitrary divinity, and on the "terror of an invisible master." P.-J. Proudhon, *Système des contradictions économiques ou philosophie de la misère* (1846), in *Oeuvres complètes*, ed. C. Bouglé and H. Moysset (Paris: Marcel Rivière, 1923), 1:52–53.

132. *EPS*, p. 77; Smith speaks of bestowing coherence at *EPS*, pp. 63, 69, and 76.

133. See Amartya Sen, "Internal Consistency of Choice," *Econometrica*, 61, 3 (May 1993), 498–499. As Hayek says, in his criticism of Schumpeter's "positivism" (in which valuations of factors of production are "implied in" the valuation of consumers' goods), "Implication is a logical relationship which can be meaningfully asserted only of propositions simultaneously present to one and the same mind." F. A. Hayek, "The Use of Knowledge in Society," *American Economic Review*, 35, 4 (September 1945), 530. In one sense of what Arrow and Hahn describe as the "equilibrium concept," the equilibrium is coherent (or the acts of agents are compatible) in that there is no excess demand at nonnegative prices; no goods are unsold in the "final coherent state of balance." In a different concept, it is the disposition of household utility which is coherent; there is no household which is unsatisfied in the sense that it has fallen below "the minimum guaranteed utility level." Arrow and Hahn, *General Competitive Analysis*, pp. 1, 23, 120. Order is in both cases, here, a characteristic of events, and not of propositions. But the order is bestowed by the theorist in the sense that she has a theory (a concept) of demand and supply, or of household utility.

134. "History of Astronomy," in *EPS*, pp. 43–44.

135. The theorist starts, in Nozick's account, with the idea of a "realm," which may be "some overall pattern or design." To provide a "fundamental explanation" of the realm is to explain it in terms which are not its own; to "make no use of any of the notions of the realm." In the social investigations which are the principal subject of "invisible hand explanations," the initial realm or pattern is the sort of thing which tends to be thought of, by present consensus, as having been designed or invented. (It is the sort of thing which "one would have thought had to be produced by an individual's or group's successful attempt to realize the pattern," which "one would have thought could arise only through intelligent design," or which "looks to be the product of someone's intentional design.") But the pattern turns out to have arisen as the result of actions which, while they are intentional (and therefore conscious), do not include among their objectives the establishment of this

particular pattern or realm. Nozick, *Anarchy, State, and Utopia,* pp. 18–19.

136. Hayek, *Studies in Philosophy, Politics, and Economics,* pp. 104–105.

137. F. A. Hayek, "Scientism and the Study of Society, Part III," *Economica,* 41 (February 1944), 31.

138. Marcus Aurelius, *The Communings with Himself of Marcus Aurelius,* trans. C. R. Haines (Cambridge, Mass.: Harvard University Press, 1930), 7.48.

139. Hayek thus defended the effort to understand social life from the "inside," to start from "our knowledge of the inside of these social complexes," or of "what things *mean* to the acting men," and to think about other people as if "we have a mind like theirs." F. A. Hayek, "Scientism and the Study of Society, Part II," *Economica,* 38 (February 1943), 40–41, 47.

140. "Discours de Réception prononcé dans l'Académie Française" (1782), in *OC,* 1:392.

141. Jacques Necker, *Sur la législation et le commerce des grains* (1775), in *Oeuvres complètes* (Paris: Treuttel and Würtz, 1820), 1:4; and see Chapter 1.

142. Stewart, *Elements of the Philosophy of the Human Mind,* 2:248.

143. Nozick, *Philosophical Explanations,* pp. 347–348, and n. 56, p. 714.

144. Ibid., p. 347. It is possible that economic agents have multiple intentions, of different sorts: that they intend to increase their own profits, that they also (although this is, as Smith says, "an affectation, indeed, not very common among merchants") intend to increase the economic well-being of the society, and that they even intend to influence the behavior of other merchants, with a view to improving the norms of the economic system. The controls exercised in a decentralized "invisible hand" order are, as Geoffrey Brennan and Philip Pettit have suggested, "contingently non-intentional": "The consumers intentionally go elsewhere for a better price, and, while it is not intentional on their part that doing so punishes the original vendor for non-competitive pricing, they might also have performed the action intentionally under that description." The device is invisible because "those who remain mere participants in the system, those who fail to adopt a theoretical stance on what happens, will necessarily fail to recognise what is going on . . . [T]hey lack any sense of the aggregate shape of things." Brennan and Pettit are concerned with "essentially non-intentional" controls—the "intangible hand," in their description—in which the sanctions on certain kinds of behavior take the form of being disapproved of, or of attitudes rather than actions. Geoffrey Brennan and Philip Pettit, "Hands Invisible and Intangible," *Synthese* 94 (1993), 196, 200. There is an additional, quite different sense in which the patterns or orders which are the outcome of invisible hand explanations are "essentially non-intentional" from the point of view of the individuals who are their subjects. An order could thus never be among the purposes or intended objects of "mere participants" if it were to exist, or to be expressed, only in the mind of the theorist; of the Kantian investigator, bestowing order upon nature. The orders which are contingently non-intentional, in this sense, are ones which are sufficiently widely known, or which have been discussed sufficiently extensively, that they could, at least, form

part of the intentions of individuals. The imaginative orders of the theorist are not written on her forehead; if she keeps them to herself, they are of necessity invisible. But if these imaginative orders, or social objectives, are indeed the subject of extensive public discussion—as is the case for Smith's own two "invisible hand" outcomes, of equitable distribution of goods (in the *Theory of Moral Sentiments*) and of increased national income (in the *Wealth of Nations*)—then they are, by virtue of their publicness, the sort of objectives about which people tend to reflect, or which they tend to discuss, in much the same way that they discuss political or moral choices. They are associated with the sort of behavior which is self-conscious, reflective, and discursive; the behavior, in fact, which is in Nozick's account particularly unsusceptible to invisible hand explanations.

145. Vaughn, "Invisible Hand," p. 998.

146. The invisible hand is indeed often interpreted, in the post–Second World War economic literature, as little more than a depiction of the particular body of economic analysis constituted by general equilibrium theory; the authors of a 1990 history of the invisible hand describe it as "a theoretical system based on the idea of economic equilibrium": Bruna Ingrao and Giorgio Israel, *The Invisible Hand: Economic Equilibrium in the History of Science*, trans. Ian McGilvray (Cambridge, Mass.: MIT Press, 1990), p. ix.

147. "You take refuge in the principle of 'equilibrium' (for so with your consent we will translate *isonomia*)"; this is the Academic Cotta's accusation in *De natura deorum* against the Epicurean Velleius, who has been talking about "forces of preservation." *De natura deorum*, 1.109, and see also 1.50. Cicero is credited by Lewis and Short with coining the word "aequilibritas," as a translation of Epicurus' *isonomia;* "aequilibrium" they attribute to Seneca. Turgot and Condorcet use the word "équilibre" fairly frequently in their economic writings, in a wide variety of senses. See Jacques Bourrinet, "Les prodrômes de l'équilibre économique," *Revue d'économie politique*, 76 (1966), 255–277; Ingrao and Israel, *The Invisible Hand*, pp. 42–54; and Chapter 3. Turgot refers to equilibrium five times in a letter to Hume of 1767, with which Smith may have been familiar. The letter, which is about economic value, begins with advice to Hume in his quarrel with Rousseau, and is in this respect part of a joint effort of Smith and Turgot—whom Smith describes as "a friend every way worthy of you"—to dissuade Hume from further public dissension. Letter of March 25, 1767, from Turgot to Hume, in *OT*, 2:658–665; letter of July 6, 1766, from Smith to Hume, in *Corr.*, pp. 112–114.

148. *WN*, pp. 488–489; Fred R. Glahe, ed., *Adam Smith's An Inquiry into the Nature and Causes of the Wealth of Nations: A Concordance* (Lanham, Md.: Rowman and Littlefield, 1993).

149. *TMS*, pp. 235–237.

150. *WN*, pp. 455–456. Smith does refer to social maximization—"the greatest possible neat produce," the "greatest possible" annual reproduction—in his

account of the "system" of the sect of Economists, but with considerable skepticism as to the prospects for an "exact regimen of perfect liberty and perfect justice." *WN,* pp. 673–674, 678.

151. *WN,* p. 456. Turgot says much the same thing in his "Éloge de Vincent de Gournay" of 1759. Gournay's principles, he says, "seemed to him to be no more than the maxims of the simplest good sense. The whole of this supposed *system* was founded on the following maxim: a man knows his own interest better than another man to whom this interest is entirely indifferent . . . It is pointless to prove that each individual is the only judge of the most advantageous use of his land and his labor. He alone has the local knowledge without which the most enlightened man reasons only blindly. He alone has that experience which is the more sure because it is limited to a single object." *OT,* 1:602, 605–606; and see Chapter 1. Dugald Stewart quotes part of this passage in the notes to his account of Smith's life, adding that Turgot's memoir "till lately, was very little known, even in France." Stewart, "Account," in *EPS,* p. 344.

152. Note (p), in *The Wealth of Nations,* ed. Playfair, 2:253; comment on Book 4, chap. 3 (*WN,* p. 493).

153. The system of equilibrium is a model. It is not a description of the ordinary, imperfectly competitive conditions of particular economies. But it is also an ideal. It identifies an outcome, or an order, which is optimal in a quite precise sense. It is (or would be) beneficial for the individuals by whom it is constituted. The "point of equilibrium" is in Turgot's description, as was seen in Chapter 3, such as to "procure for the entire society the greatest sum of production, enjoyment, wealth, and strength." "Lettres sur le commerce des grains," in *OT,* 3:315, 334. Competitive equilibrium, in modern theory, yields an optimal or efficient allocation of resources, in which "there is no way of making everyone better off." See Arrow and Hahn, *General Competitive Analysis,* p. 91.

154. F. A. Hayek, *The Road to Serfdom* (1944) (Chicago: University of Chicago Press, 1972), pp. 39, 42.

155. Necker, *Sur la législation et le commerce des grains,* p. 173.

156. Robbins, *The Theory of Economic Policy,* pp. 56–57; see also Macfie's review of Robbins's book, in Macfie, *The Individual in Society,* pp. 156–158.

157. Hahn, "Reflections on the Invisible Hand," pp. 17, 20. Hahn talks of reasons for actions in his discussion of the incentive structure and reward differentials in market economies: "If one wants people to act in a certain way one must give them a reason for doing so" (p. 18). But the agent, here, is the policy maker, the person who wants other people to act in particular ways. The "reasons" of these other people are not the outcome of their own reflection; they are no more than rewards.

158. Necker, *Sur la législation et le commerce des grains,* p. 321.

159. The "optimal economic policy" in such a social order (or the criterion for ordering different policies) is a matter, rather, of efficiency in the sense of in-

creasing the chance, for any randomly selected member of society, of having a high income. Hayek, *Studies in Philosophy, Politics, and Economics,* p. 173.

160. Hayek, *Studies in Philosophy, Politics, and Economics,* pp. 87–88, 160–161; F. A. Hayek, *The Constitution of Liberty* (London: Routledge and Kegan Paul, 1960), p. 56.

161. Hayek, *Studies in Philosophy, Politics, and Economics,* pp. 161–162.

162. Hayek, "Scientism and the Study of Society, Part III," pp. 28–29.

163. Hayek, *Studies in Philosophy, Politics, and Economics,* p. 164; idem, *The Constitution of Liberty,* pp. 61, 63.

164. Stewart, "Account," p. 311, n. G, p. 339; and see Chapter 2.

165. Stewart, *Elements of the Philosophy of the Human Mind,* 2:226, 235.

166. *WN,* pp. 385, 418, 776.

167. *LJ,* p. 5.

168. *TMS,* p. 210.

169. Menger, *Untersuchungen,* pp. 201, 207; and see Chapter 2; Hayek, *Studies in Philosophy, Politics, and Economics,* pp. 99–101.

170. Lawrence H. White, "Introduction," in Carl Menger, *Investigations into the Method of the Social Sciences with Special Reference to Economics,* trans. Francis J. Nock (New York: New York University Press, 1985), p. xvi.

171. Hayek, *Studies in Philosophy, Politics, and Economics,* p. 100.

172. James Buchanan, "Public Goods and Natural Liberty," in *The Market and the State: Essays in Honour of Adam Smith,* ed. Thomas Wilson and Andrew S. Skinner (Oxford: Clarendon Press, 1976), p. 274.

173. Hayek, *The Road to Serfdom,* pp. 73–74; on Condorcet's political thought, see Chapters 6 and 7.

174. *WN,* pp. 687, 708.

175. Hayek, *The Road to Serfdom,* p. 87.

176. Hayek, "The Use of Knowledge in Society," pp. 526–527.

177. Edmund Burke, *Reflections on the Revolution in France* (1790), ed. Conor Cruise O'Brien (London: Penguin Books, 1982), pp. 119–120, 183. Among the "fathers" of the genuinely historical approach, Hayek writes, "Edmund Burke is one of the most important and Adam Smith occupies an honourable place." Hayek, "Scientism and the Study of Society, Part II," pp. 50–51.

178. *Max Weber's Science as a Vocation,* ed. Peter Lassman, Irving Velody, and Herminio Martins (London: Unwin Hyman, 1988), pp. 13–14.

179. F. A. Hayek, "Scientism and the Study of Society, Part I," *Economica,* 35 (August 1942), 286.

180. "Éloge de Vincent de Gournay," in *OT,* 1:605–606. It is interesting that Turgot contrasts local experience, here, to the wisdom of the state, and also to the wisdom of speculators; the local individual "instructs himself by repeated attempts, by his successes, by his losses, and acquires a subtlety of which the refinement, sharpened by the sentiment of need, by far surpasses all the theory of the indifferent speculator."

181. *WN,* pp. 782, 788.

182. Hume, *Dialogues concerning Natural Religion*, p. 58. There is some irony in Hume's insistence on the puniness of individual knowledge, to which he indeed draws attention. "Let us become thoroughly sensible of the weakness, blindness, and narrow limits of human reason," Philo says at the outset of the *Dialogues*. The devout Demea reacts to this exhortation with "unreserved satisfaction." The more subtle Cleanthes, by contrast, adopts "an air of finesse; as if he perceived some raillery or artificial malice in the reasonings of Philo" (pp. 41–42).

183. "History of Astronomy," in *EPS*, p. 104; and see Chapter 8.

184. "Of Commerce," in Hume, *Essays*, p. 254.

185. These are qualities "by which we are capable of discerning the remote consequences of all our actions, and of foreseeing the advantage or detriment which is likely to result from them." *TMS*, p. 189.

186. "Of Refinement in the Arts," in Hume, *Essays*, p. 271.

187. *WN*, pp. 25, 782, 784, 787–788, 796; and see Chapter 4. The particular advantage of the study of science and philosophy, together with "the frequency and gaiety of public diversions," is to "correct whatever was unsocial or disagreeably rigorous in the morals of all the small sects into which the country was divided," and notably of the small religious sects which the "common people" tend to join when they live in great cities. *WN*, pp. 795–796.

188. Burke, *Reflections*, pp. 124, 171, 183.

189. *The Friend*, in *The Collected Works of Samuel Taylor Coleridge* (Princeton: Princeton University Press, 1969), vol. 4, pt. 1, p. 189.

190. Benjamin Constant, "De la force du gouvernement actuel" (1796) and "Des réactions politiques" (1797), in *De la force du gouvernement actuel de la France et de la nécessité de s'y rallier* (Paris: Flammarion, 1988), pp. 95, 134, 151–152. On the "slow" and "almost imperceptible" reform of "old establishments," as against those who "commence their schemes of reform with abolition and total destruction," see Burke, *Reflections*, pp. 279–280.

191. Hayek, *The Road to Serfdom*, p. 18.

192. *The Contest of Faculties*, in *Kant's Political Writings*, p. 183; and see Chapter 7. De Maistre's gardener, with his invisible hand and his pruning tools, is a spectacularly less agreeable figure. "The adept gardener directs his pruning less toward absolute vegetation than toward the fructification of the tree: it is fruits, and not wood and leaves, that he demands from the plant. Now, the true fruits of human nature, the arts, the sciences, the great enterprises, the lofty conceptions, the masculine virtues, are associated, above all, with the state of war." De Maistre, *Considérations sur la France*, pp. 49–50.

193. Hayek, *Studies in Philosophy, Politics, and Economics*, p. 166; and see Chapter 8.

194. Burke, *Reflections*, p. 151.

195. Hayek, *The Road to Serfdom*, p. 75; idem, *Studies in Philosophy, Politics, and Economics*, p. 162; idem, "The Use of Knowledge in Society," p. 527.

196. Hayek, *Studies in Philosophy, Politics, and Economics*, pp. 174–175.

197. *LJ*, p. 403.
198. See, on independence and autonomy as the basis of obligations, *Kant's Critique of Practical Reason*, trans. Thomas Kingsmill Abbott (London: Longmans, Green, 1889), p. 122.
199. On Kant's inquiry "What is money? . . . What is a book?" see Chapter 1.
200. *De natura deorum*, 2.57.
201. This is the phrase Vaughn uses of her second step, about the understandability of unintended consequences. Vaughn, "Invisible Hand," p. 998. Vaughn is herself admirably free of blind confidence in the desirability of unintended orders: "One could easily imagine a spontaneous order in which people were led as if by an invisible hand to promote a perverse and unpleasant end. The desirability of the order that emerges . . . depends ultimately on the kind of rules and institutions within which human beings act," and "how one views the institutions of society makes a difference not only to one's political views, but also to how one evaluates an economic system."
202. Proudhon, *Système des contradictions économiques*, p. 53.
203. Macfie, *The Individual in Society*, p. 102.
204. Cicero, *De finibus*, 1.62–70.
205. Macfie, *The Individual in Society*, p. 111.

6. Economic and Political Choice

1. *WN*, p. 26.
2. Joseph A. Schumpeter, *History of Economic Analysis* (New York: Oxford University Press, 1954), p. 135. Keith Baker provides a full account of Condorcet's economic writings in *Condorcet: From Natural Philosophy to Social Mathematics* (Chicago: University of Chicago Press, 1975), esp. pp. 55–72 and 197–263; see also the section "Économie" in Pierre Crépel and Christian Gilain, eds., *Condorcet: mathématicien, économiste, philosophe, homme politique* (Paris: Minerve, 1989), pp. 121–195.
3. Letter of November 1, 1776, in *Voltaire's Correspondence*, ed. Theodore Besterman (Geneva: Institut et Musée Voltaire, 1964), 95:145–146. Voltaire was at the same time reading Condorcet's observations on Pascal, and he was particularly surprised to find himself interested by Condorcet's work on the regulation of the corn trade when "his head was still full" of such elevated subjects as "sublime metaphysics," "the uncertainty of our knowledge of nature, Epictetus and Montaigne." Voltaire's eulogy of Condorcet, in a letter to Amélie Suard a few months later—"For myself, I will admit to you in confidence that I place him ahead of almost all the men of his century. I admire the loftiness of his soul and the simplicity of his manners; the fineness and force of his mind; his singular eloquence, and the depths of his knowledge. At the moment I am reading a work of his which inspires me with veneration"—may well, as Besterman points out, refer to the *Réflexions*. Letter of January 25, 1777, in *Voltaire's Correspondence*, 96:45. Voltaire chose his

confidante with his usual care, for Mme. Suard was still Condorcet's intimate friend and correspondent. But it seems plausible that the reference was indeed to the *Réflexions,* which was at the time Condorcet's most extended work.

4. See, for example, Franck Alengry, *Condorcet Guide de la Révolution Française* (Paris: Giard and Brière, 1904), pp. 703–704; Léon Cahen, *Condorcet et la Révolution française* (Paris: Alcan, 1904), pp. 42–43.

5. "Lettres au Contrôleur Général (abbé Terray) sur le commerce des grains," in *OT,* 3:315, 326, 334; and see Chapter 3.

6. "Valeurs et monnaies," in *OT,* 3:91–92, 97–98.

7. "Tableau général de la science, qui a pour objet l'application du calcul aux sciences politiques et morales" (1794), in *OC,* 1:558.

8. "Lettres sur le commerce des grains," in *OT,* 3:326.

9. Letter of December 9, 1766, to Dupont de Nemours, in *OT,* 2:519.

10. See Joseph Louis Lagrange, *Oeuvres,* ed. J. A. Serret (Paris: École Polytechnique, 1882), 2:383, 553; Condorcet, "Indéterminés," in *Supplément à l'encyclopédie* (Amsterdam: Rey, 1777) 3:571; Condorcet, *Essai sur l'application de l'analyse à la probabilité des décisions rendues à la pluralité des voix* (1785) (New York: Chelsea House, 1972), p. 171.

11. "Lettres sur le commerce des grains," in *OT,* 3:324, 327–328, 354. On Quesnay's polemics with the court doctor Jean-Baptiste Silva, see Jean Sutter, "Quesnay et la médecine," and Jacqueline Hecht, "La vie de François Quesnay," in *François Quesnay et la Physiocratie* (Paris: Institut National d'Études Démographiques, 1958), 1:197–210 and 211–294.

12. *Réflexions sur le commerce des blés* (1776), in *OC,* 11:104–105, 149.

13. "Sur le préjugé qui suppose une contrariété d'intérêts entre Paris et les provinces" (1790), in *OC,* 10:136.

14. "Que toutes les classes de la société n'ont qu'un même intérêt" (1793), in *OC,* 12:650.

15. "Fragment de l'histoire de la Xe époque," in *OC,* 6:528–529, 537.

16. *TMS,* p. 185.

17. "Monopole et monopoleur" (1775), in *OC,* 11:46, 48; *Réflexions sur le commerce des blés,* in *OC,* 11:145–146, 200.

18. *Réflexions sur le commerce des blés,* in *OC,* 11:148.

19. Ibid., 127, 235.

20. *Vie de M. Turgot* (1786), in *OC,* 5:27–28.

21. *Réflexions sur le commerce des blés,* in *OC,* 11:201.

22. "Monopole et monopoleur," in *OC,* 11:41–42.

23. Jacques Necker, "Éloge de Jean-Baptiste Colbert" (1773), in *Oeuvres complètes* (Paris: Treuttel and Würtz, 1821), 15:42, 45–46; and see Condorcet's letters to Voltaire of November 14 and 28, 1776, in *Voltaire's Correspondence,* 95:175–176 and 202–203. Necker says of Colbert that "the virtue necessary for an administrator of finances knows no limits," and—in a metaphor of the invisible hand quite unlike Smith's, and a metaphor of an indis-

soluble chain quite unlike Condorcet's—that he must be inspired "by the idea of a God who holds in his hands the first links in that vast chain, which has allowed us to glimpse the harmony of the universe." "The faculties of mind which must form the genius of the administrator" are so immense, for Necker, as to be "so to speak, beyond the dominion of language," and thus, "confronted with the way of thinking of administration, all others disappear." Necker, "Éloge," 15:11–12.

24. Dugald Stewart, "Account of the Life and Writings of Adam Smith, LL.D." (1793), in *EPS*, p. 318.

25. *Réflexions sur le commerce des blés*, in *OC*, 11:241.

26. "But it is not a question of the interests of the administrator, it is a question of the interests of the nation," Condorcet adds. "Monopole et monopoleur," in *OC*, 11:50–51.

27. "Monopole et monopoleur," in *OC*, 11:46; *Réflexions sur le commerce des blés*, in *OC*, 11:204, 240–241.

28. "Monopole et monopoleur," in *OC*, 11:46–47, 50.

29. "Éloge de Gournay" (1759), in *OT*, 1:608.

30. Alexis de Tocqueville, *L'ancien régime et la Révolution* (1856), ed. J.-P. Mayer (Paris: Gallimard, 1967), pp. 187, 212–213; and see Chapter 1; for Tocqueville's notes on Turgot, see *L'Ancien Régime et la Révolution: Fragments et notes inédites sur la Révolution*, ed. André Jardin, in Tocqueville, *Oeuvres complètes*, ed. J.-P. Mayer (Paris: Gallimard, 1952–1953), vol. 2, pt. 2, pp. 377–439.

31. *Réflexions sur le commerce des blés*, in *OC*, 11:146.

32. "Mémoire sur les prêts d'argent" (1770), in *OT*, 3:167.

33. "Monopole et monopoleur," in *OC*, 11:45; *Réflexions sur le commerce des blés*, in *OC*, 11:197, 200–202.

34. "Fragment de l'histoire de la Xe époque," in *OC*, 6:528.

35. "Éloge de Gournay," in *OT*, 1:603.

36. "Lettres sur le commerce des grains," in *OT*, 3:323.

37. "Instead of buying horses, people will buy hangers-on and places; for expenditures on taste . . . they will substitute expenditures on intrigue." *Essai sur la constitution et les fonctions des assemblées provinciales* (1788), in *OC*, 8:391.

38. *Réflexions sur le commerce des blés*, in *OC*, 11:146.

39. On Lamet and Fromageau's *Dictionnaire des cas de conscience*, see Chapter 1.

40. "Fragment de l'histoire de la Xe époque," in *OC*, 6:570.

41. "Réflexions sur l'esclavage des nègres" (1781), in *OC*, 7:126. The pamphlet was written in the assumed person of "Joachim Schwartz," a Swiss Protestant pastor, who refers the reader to "mon *Sermon sur la fausse conscience,* imprimée à Yverdun en 1773."

42. "Éloge de Gournay" (1759), in *OT*, 1:620.

43. "Sur la liberté de la circulation des subsistances" (1792), in *OC*, 10:367.

44. *Réflexions sur le commerce des blés*, in *OC*, 11:144–145.

45. "Monopole et monopoleur," in *OC*, 11:51.

46. *Vie de M. Turgot,* in *OC,* 5:42.
47. "Fragment de l'histoire de la Xe époque," in *OC,* 6:536.
48. *Réflexions sur le commerce des blés,* in *OC,* 11:191–192.
49. Ibid., p. 180.
50. "Réflexions sur l'esclavage des nègres," in *OC,* 7:64.
51. "De l'influence de la révolution d'Amérique sur l'Europe" (1786), by "un habitant obscur de l'ancien hémisphere," in *OC,* 8:19, 41–42.
52. *Réflexions sur le commerce des blés,* in *OC,* 11:251.
53. "De la nature des pouvoirs politiques dans une nation libre" (1792), in *OC,* 10:607; and see Chapter 1.
54. *Réflexions sur le commerce des blés,* in *OC,* 11:167.
55. Ibid., p. 111; letter to Count Pietro Verri, November 7, 1771, in *OC,* 1:282.
56. See Cahen, *Condorcet et la Révolution française,* pp. 83–87; Baker, *Condorcet,* pp. 252–267; Jean-Paul Joubert, "Condorcet et les trois ordres," in Crépel and Gilain, *Condorcet,* pp. 305–312.
57. *Sur les assemblées provinciales* (1788), in *OC,* 8:453–454, 458–459. This argument might be compared to Ricardo's later and much better known chapter "On Machinery" in his *Principles:* David Ricardo, *On the Principles of Political Economy and Taxation* (1821) (Cambridge: Cambridge University Press, 1975), pp. 386–397.
58. "Calculate how much the Poor Rate, in England, has cost for supplying their consumption, and see what an enormous difference there would be in the effects if this same capital had been employed to support industry." "Que toutes les classes de la société n'ont qu'un même intérêt," in *OC,* 12:648.
59. *Sur les assemblées provinciales,* in *OC,* 8:453–454, 461, 477; *Esquisse d'un tableau historique des progrès de l'esprit humain,* in *OC,* 6:246–248. See also Emma Rothschild, "Social Security and Laissez Faire in Eighteenth-Century Political Economy," *Population and Development Review,* 21, 4 (December 1995), 711–744.
60. The development of the intellectual faculties is important, Condorcet wrote in his account of the causes of poverty, even for those of whom "it is imagined that they do not need to make use of them." *Sur les assemblées provinciales,* in *OC,* 8:460.
61. "Sur l'instruction publique" (1791–92), in *OC,* 7:320–321.
62. *Réflexions sur le commerce des blés,* in *OC,* 11:165.
63. *Vie de M. Turgot,* in *OC,* 5:147–148.
64. *Sur les assemblées provinciales,* in *OC,* 8:513–515.
65. "Fragment de l'histoire de la Xe époque," in *OC,* 6:521–522.
66. *Vie de M. Turgot,* in *OC,* 5:130–136; *Sur les assemblées provinciales,* in *OC,* 8:624, 634–635. This "work" of Condorcet's—a footnote extending over seven pages—is indeed the only one to earn a mention in Jevons's "Survey of Mathematico-Economic Books," in W. S. Jevons, *The Theory of Political Economy* (London: Macmillan, 1888), p. 278.

67. "Sur l'impôt personnel" (1790), in *OC*, 11:477; "Sur l'impôt progressif" (1793), in *OC*, 12:632.
68. *Sur les assemblées provinciales*, in *OC*, 8:280; *Vie de M. Turgot*, in *OC*, 5:185–186; "Sur l'impôt progressif," in *OC*, 12:629.
69. "Discours sur les finances" (1792), in *OC*, 12:97–98.
70. "Sur la constitution du pouvoir chargé d'administrer le trésor national" (1790), in *OC*, 11:543–544. One "should not even hope to ever be able to attain this end in a rigorous manner, and the only perfection consists in continuing to get nearer and near to it." On Condorcet's work on public finance, see Régis Deloche, "Turgot, Condorcet, et la question de l'affectation des ressources," and Gilbert Faccarello, "Présentation," both in Crépel and Gilain, *Condorcet*, pp. 121–149, 150–159; Gilbert Faccarello and Philippe Steiner, *La pensée économique pendant la Révolution française* (Grenoble: Presses Universitaires de Grenoble, 1990).
71. Letters of 1771 and 1773 to Count Pietro Verri, in *OC*, 1:282, 287; Pietro Verri, *Meditazioni sulla Economia Politica* (Naples: Giovanni Gravier, 1771), p. 22.
72. Letters to Verri, in *OC*, 1:287. The problem was of determining the movement of three bodies projected into space, and subject to the force of reciprocal attraction. See Condorcet, "Problème des trois corps," in *Supplément à l'encyclopédie*, 4:533–535, and Michelle Chapront-Touzé, "Condorcet et le problème des trois corps," in Crépel and Gilain, *Condorcet*, pp. 29–35. It is interesting that the comparison between price relationships and the three-body problem later occurred to Léon Walras; Henri Poincaré, however, warned Walras that his "results" may be "deprived of all interest, because they will be subordinated to the arbitrary conventions introduced initially." For Walras, in contrast to Condorcet, the "analogy between economics and celestial mechanics"—or between the fundamental differential equations describing the marginal utilities of three commodities A, B, and C, and those describing the attractions of three celestial bodies T, L, and S—was a decisive example showing that the procedures of economics were "rigorously identical" to those of the physical-mathematical sciences; that it was a "mathematical science with the same claim as mechanics or astronomy." Léon Walras, "Économique et mécanique," *Metroeconomica*, 12 (1960), 3–13. Poincaré's position, in correspondence with Walras, was closer to Condorcet's. "Satisfaction is a quantity," he wrote, "but not a quantity that can be measured." He was therefore concerned by the initial "arbitrary conventions" which Walras's system required: "I have no way of comparing the satisfactions felt by two different individuals. This increases even further the number of arbitrary functions to be eliminated." Henri Poincaré, "Lettre à M. Léon Walras" (1901), in Walras, "Économique et mécanique," pp. 12–13. The ensuing results, Poincaré warned Walras, may be "deprived of all interest, because they will be subordinated to the arbitrary conventions introduced initially. You must therefore make an effort to eliminate these arbitrary functions, and this

is what you are doing." He added that "in mechanics, one often ignores friction and considers bodies as infinitely polished. As for you, you consider men as infinitely egotistical and infinitely farsighted."

73. Letter to Verri, in *OC*, 1:288; Jean d'Alembert, "Application," in *Encyclopédie, ou dictionnaire raisonné des sciences, des arts et des métiers* (Paris: Briasson, 1751), 1:553.

74. He later restated the entire argument—the long footnote on fiscal transitions from the *Vie de M. Turgot*—using arithmetic alone. *Sur les assemblées provinciales*, in *OC*, 8:609–610.

75. "Sur la constitution du pouvoir," in *OC*, 11:543–544. Like Smith, more than like Turgot, Condorcet is parsimonious in his references to economic equilibrium, and firmly imprecise. His description of the advantages of removing the fetters of regulation from the "industry of the people," at the beginning of the *Réflexions sur le commerce des blés*, is thus conditional: "If there could be some equilibrium between those who have everything and those who have nothing . . ." *Réflexions sur le commerce des blés*, in *OC*, 11:104–105.

76. *Esquisse*, in *OC*, 6:191; "Tableau général de la science," in *OC*, 1:567.

77. This was in his proposals for the reform of public education, including the establishment of a special chair in the application of mathematics to the political and moral sciences, and in political economy. "Sur l'instruction publique," in *OC*, 7:536–537, 564.

78. "Discours sur les sciences mathématiques," February 15, 1786, in *OC*, 1:469, 479.

79. "Éloge de M. Buffon" (1788), in *OC*, 3:340–342.

80. See, on Condorcet's conception of social mathematics, Baker, *Condorcet*, esp. pp. 225–244, 330–342.

81. "Éloge de M. d'Alembert" (1783), in *OC*, 3: 79.

82. "For there are reliable means of reaching a very great probability in many cases, and, in a large number of cases, for evaluating the degree of this probability." "Remarques sur les Pensées de Pascal" (1776), in *OC*, 3:641.

83. *Réflexions sur le commerce des blés*, in *OC*, 11:207–208.

84. "Tableau général de la science," in *OC*, 1:543.

85. *Esquisse*, in *OC*, 6:183, 217.

86. David Hume, *A Treatise of Human Nature*, ed. L. A. Selby-Bigge (Oxford: Clarendon Press, 1978), pp. 185, 265, 273. On Hume's influence on Condorcet, see Baker, *Condorcet*, pp. 138–155.

87. *Esquisse*, in *OC*, 6:220, 260.

88. "Tableau général de la science," in *OC*, 1:558–572. This is Condorcet's last, incomplete, work on political economy; see Baker, *Condorcet*, pp. 336–339. Condorcet gives the examples, here, of international comparisons of real incomes, and of comparisons of real incomes over time. If one knows the relative prices of silver and rice in China and Europe, he writes, then one can conclude that there is a profit to be made by sending silver to China and

bringing rice to France; one, however, "learns nothing about the mass of needs which are satisfied with this quantity of rice." If one knows the relative prices of flour in Athens and modern France, similarly, then one can ascertain how much its value has changed in terms of silver; one learns nothing about the satisfaction of needs, or about the "price which, in different countries and at different periods, people attach to the enjoyments which can result from the possession of given things" (p. 562).

89. "Otherwise, each time that one wishes to obtain a different kind [of result], whether out of curiosity or from a motive of utility, one would be obliged to manipulate again the entire mass of these facts, in order to use them, to classify them according to the order which the new use requires." "Sur l'instruction publique," in *OC,* 7:558.

90. "Tableau général de la science," in *OC,* 1:554.

91. *Sur les assemblées provinciales,* in *OC,* 8:487.

92. "Sur les élections" (1793), in *OC,* 12:639.

93. Condorcet, *Essai sur l'application de l'analyse,* p. i; Hiroshi Mizuta, *Adam Smith's Library: A Catalogue,* ed. Hiroshi Mizuta (Oxford: Clarendon Press, 2000), p. 62; see also Gilles-Gaston Granger, *La mathématique sociale du marquis de Condorcet* (1956), rev. ed. (Paris: Odile Jacob, 1989), pp. 97, 144.

94. "Sur les élections," in *OC,* 12:639.

95. Condorcet, *Essai sur l'application de l'analyse,* pp. lii–liv, lxxix, 113–119.

96. Vincent de Gournay had been confronted, Turgot wrote, with a "false unanimity" against reform, in that "in rejecting each particular exception, he had a majority of votes with him; but in rejecting all exceptions at the same time, he aroused against himself all the votes of the people who each wanted one exception, even though they did not agree on the sort of exception they wanted." "Éloge de Gournay," in *OT,* 1:620.

97. *Sur les assemblées provinciales,* in *OC,* 8:214–216, 268–271.

98. Letter of May 2, 1785, to the king of Prussia, in *OC,* 1:305–306.

99. "Sur l'instruction publique," in *OC,* 7:562.

100. See, for example, Duncan Black, *The Theory of Committees and Elections* (Cambridge: Cambridge University Press, 1958), pp. 163–164; Kenneth J. Arrow, "Formal Theories of Social Welfare," in *Collected Papers of Kenneth J. Arrow,* vol. 1, *Social Choice and Justice* (Cambridge, Mass: Harvard University Press, 1983), pp. 126–127; James M. Buchanan and Gordon Tullock, *The Calculus of Consent* (Ann Arbor: University of Michigan Press, 1962), p. 327; but compare Granger, *La mathématique sociale du marquis de Condorcet,* pp. 100–102.

101. "Lettres sur le commerce des grains," in *OT,* 3:343; "Tableau général de la science," in *OC,* 1:563; *Sur les assemblées provinciales,* in *OC,* 8:577.

102. "What in fact should one be looking for?" Condorcet asks: "Is it the expression of the will of an assembly? No, without doubt; it is a result which one can regard as being in conformity with truth, because it is that of the majority

of voters, who are supposed to pronounce in favor of truth rather than in favor of error." *Sur les assemblées provinciales,* in *OC,* 8:601.

103. See Kenneth J. Arrow, *Social Choice and Individual Values* (New Haven: Yale University Press, 1963), pp. 81–86.

104. "Aux amis de la liberté, sur les moyens d'en assurer la durée" (1790), in *OC,* 10:177–178. On Condorcet's views of political legitimacy, see, for example, *Sur les assemblées provinciales,* in *OC,* 8:221–229. Condorcet's idea of the truth of laws is certainly influenced by conceptions of natural law; by the view, for example, that a law is true if it corresponds to "nature," or to natural justice. But these conceptions are themselves probabilistic in Condorcet's usage. It is possible, Condorcet concedes, that a law which has been decided upon in a free procedure is contrary to natural law. But this outcome is not particularly probable; it is less probable, in any case, to the extent that people are enlightened, instructed, and well informed about their own and other people's rights. I am grateful to Philip Pettit for comments on this point.

105. Jean-Jacques Rousseau, *Du contrat social* (Paris: Flammarion, 1992), pp. 64–65, 137.

106. *Esquisse,* in *OC,* 6:176–177; "De l'influence de la révolution d'Amérique sur l'Europe," in *OC,* 8:4–7; and see Chapter 7.

107. Rousseau, *Du contrat social,* p. 37.

108. "Aggrégation," in *Encyclopédie, ou dictionnaire raisonné des sciences, des arts et des métiers,* 1:173.

109. One can hardly imagine, Condorcet adds, that "all the citizens should have eaten every day at these republican tables, and even that they should not have lived habitually with their families." "Fragment de l'histoire de la IVe époque," in *OC,* 6:413–419.

110. "Sur l'abolition des corvées" (1776), in *OC,* 11:89; *Esquisse,* in *OC,* 6:140–141; *Du contrat social,* pp. 122, 135.

111. "Aux Germains" (1792), in *OC,* 12:166; "Sur l'instruction publique," in *OC,* 7:329; and see Chapter 7.

112. *Esquisse,* in *OC,* 6:224–225; and, on the modest enlightenment needed in a future, calmer society, "Fragment de l'histoire de la Xe époque," in *OC,* 12:572–573.

113. This will in turn "preserve them from that perfidious art whereby their passions are captured in such a way that they are led into error and into crime." "Tableau général de la science," in *OC,* 1:543.

114. Edmund Burke, *Reflections on the Revolution in France* (London: Penguin Books, 1982), p. 188; idem, *An Appeal from the New to the Old Whigs* (London: J. Dodsley, 1791), p. 133.

115. Joseph de Maistre, *Considérations sur la France* (1797) (Paris: Complexe, 1988), p. 121.

116. "Réflexions sur le protestantisme," in *Oeuvres complètes de Joseph de Maistre* (Lyon: Vitte-Perrussel, 1884), 8:91.

117. *Sur les assemblées provinciales,* in *OC,* 8:213. It is interesting that Condorcet

here anticipates the objection raised by James Buchanan against Arrow's impossibility result: that democracy or "'government by discussion' implies that individual values can and do change in the process of decision-making," and that if values in the sense of orderings of social alternatives are unchanging, "discussion becomes meaningless." James M. Buchanan, *Fiscal Theory and Political Economy* (Chapel Hill: University of North Carolina Press, 1960), p. 85.

118. *Sur les assemblées provinciales,* in *OC,* 8:213–216, 601.

119. Léon Walras, *Éléments d'économie politique pure ou théorie de la richesse sociale* (1871) (Paris: R. Pichon, 1926), pp. 129–130.

120. John Stuart Mill, *A System of Logic Ratiocinative and Inductive* (1843), in *Collected Works* (Toronto: University of Toronto Press, 1974), 8:832, 908–910.

121. John Stuart Mill, *On Liberty* (London: Penguin Books, 1974), pp. 69, 79–80.

122. "Fragment de l'histoire de la Xe époque," in *OC,* 6:643.

123. C.-A. Sainte-Beuve, "Oeuvres de Condorcet," in *Causeries du Lundi* (Paris: Garnier, 1868), 3:345–346.

124. "Sur l'instruction publique," in *OC,* 7:193, 324–326, 360–361.

125. "Fragment de l'histoire de la Xe époque," in *OC,* 6:534.

126. John Morley, "Condorcet," in *Critical Miscellanies* (London: Macmillan, 1886), 2:163.

127. Condorcet, *Essai sur l'application de l'analyse,* p. clxxxv.

128. "Sur l'instruction publique," in *OC,* 7:434–435.

129. Immanuel Kant, "Der Streit der Fakultäten" (1798), in *Werkausgabe,* vol. 11, ed. Wilhelm Weischedel (Frankfurt: Suhrkamp, 1968), pp. 359–360; *Kant's Political Writings,* ed. Hans Reiss (Cambridge: Cambridge University Press, 1970), pp. 183–184.

130. "Fragment de l'histoire de la Xe époque," in *OC,* 6:585, 595.

131. *Réflexions sur le commerce des blés,* in *OC,* 11:191–194.

132. François Quesnay, "Despotisme de la Chine" (1767), in *François Quesnay et la Physiocratie,* 2:918, 923.

133. "Mémoire sur les municipalités" (1775), in *OT,* 4:580–581, 621; Tocqueville, *L'ancien régime et la Révolution,* pp. 257–258; and see Chapter 1.

134. Letter of December 21, 1770, in *OT,* 3:398–399.

135. *Vie de M. Turgot,* in *OC,* 5:205, 207.

136. "Sur l'instruction publique," in *OC,* 7:211, 214; "Fragment de l'histoire de la Xe époque," in *OC,* 6:549, 579; and see Chapter 7.

137. *Vie de M. Turgot,* in *OC,* 5:196.

138. "Fragment de l'histoire de la Xe époque," in *OC,* 6:527–529.

139. Mill, *On Liberty,* p. 69.

140. "Fragment de l'histoire de la Xe époque," in *OC,* 6:515, 518.

141. Morley, "Condorcet," p. 254.

142. "Fragment de l'histoire de la Xe époque," in *OC,* 6:527–529.

7. Condorcet and the Conflict of Values

1. A version of this chapter was published in 1996 in the *Historical Journal*, 39, 3 (September 1996), 677–701.

2. C.-A. Sainte-Beuve, *Causeries du Lundi* (Paris: Garnier, 1851), 3:265, 268, 277.

3. *Esquisse d'un tableau historique des progrès de l'esprit humain* (1795), in *OC*, 6:263.

4. Isaiah Berlin, *Against the Current: Essays in the History of Ideas* (New York: Viking Press, 1980), pp. 3–4.

5. Bernard Williams, "Introduction," in Isaiah Berlin, *Concepts and Categories: Philosophical Essays* (Oxford: Oxford University Press, 1980), p. xvi; Isaiah Berlin, *The Crooked Timber of Humanity: Chapters in the History of Ideas* (London: John Murray, 1990), p. 13.

6. Isaiah Berlin, *Four Essays on Liberty* (Oxford: Oxford University Press, 1969), pp. 167–168.

7. Milan Kundera, *The Art of the Novel*, trans. Linda Asher (London: Faber and Faber, 1988), pp. 160–161.

8. Václav Havel, *Living in Truth*, ed. Jan Vladislav (London: Faber and Faber, 1989), pp. 159, 177; idem, "Planting, Watering, and Waiting," *International Herald Tribune*, November 13, 1992. "The rational reorganisation of society," in Berlin's words, "would create the happy, free, just, virtuous, harmonious world which Condorcet so movingly predicted," and "this kind of omniscience was the solution of the cosmic jigsaw puzzle." Berlin, *The Crooked Timber*, pp. 5–6.

9. Benjamin Constant, "De l'uniformité," in *De l'esprit de conquête et de l'usurpation* (1814), in *Écrits politiques*, ed. Marcel Gauchet (Paris: Gallimard, 1997), p. 168.

10. Edmund Burke, letter of 1791 or 1792, in *The Correspondence of Edmund Burke*, ed. A. Cobban and R. A. Smith (Cambridge: Cambridge University Press, 1967), 6:478; Louis-Gabriel-Ambroise de Bonald, "Observations sur un ouvrage posthume de Condorcet," in *Oeuvres complètes*, ed. J.-P. Migne (Paris, 1864), 1:721–723; Joseph de Maistre, *Considérations sur la France* (1797) (Paris: Complexe, 1988), p. 76.

11. Thomas Robert Malthus, *An Essay on the Principle of Population, as it Affects the Future Improvement of Society, with Remarks on the Speculations of Mr. Godwin, M. Condorcet, and other Writers* (1798), in *The Works of Thomas Robert Malthus*, ed. E. A. Wrigley and David Souden (London: William Pickering, 1986), 1:7, 63.

12. Charles Taylor, *Hegel* (Cambridge: Cambridge University Press, 1975), p. 10; idem, *Sources of the Self: The Making of Modern Identity* (Cambridge, Mass.: Harvard University Press, 1989), p. 319.

13. Destutt de Tracy, *A Commentary and Review of Montesquieu's Spirit of Laws* (Philadelphia: William Duane, 1811), p. 258.

14. See the "avertissement" of the first editors and the report of the first distributors (the Parliamentary Committee of Public Instruction of 1795), in *OC,* 6:4, 8. Arago himself, in his biographical introduction to the edition of the 1840s (which is still the only extensive edition of Condorcet's non-scientific works), describes his mission as the rehabilitation of a fellow academician, "scientific, literary, philosophical, and political." "Biographie de Condorcet," in *OC,* 1:vi. On the striking concentration on the *Esquisse,* and on "utopianism," in modern readings of Condorcet, see Keith Baker, *Condorcet: From Natural Philosophy to Social Mathematics* (Chicago: University of Chicago Press, 1975), pp. 343–344; and Franck Alengry, *Condorcet Guide de la Révolution Française* (Paris: Giard and Brière, 1904), pp. 835, 854.

15. Alexis de Tocqueville, *L'ancien régime et la Révolution* (1856), ed. J.-P. Mayer (Paris: Gallimard, 1967), p. 44.

16. "Éloge de M. D'Alembert" (1783), in *OC,* 3:78–79; Baker, *Condorcet,* pp. 176–189.

17. "Tableau général de la science" (1793), in *OC,* 1:567.

18. *Réflexions sur le commerce des blés* (1776), in *OC,* 11:242; "Sentiments d'un républicain sur les assemblées provinciales et les états généraux" (1789), in *OC,* 9:142–143.

19. Condorcet, *Essai sur l'application de l'analyse à la probabilité des décisions rendues à la pluralité des voix* (1785) (New York: Chelsea House, 1972); Condorcet uses the word "impossibility" himself, in his letter presenting the *Essay* to Frederick II of Prussia. *OC,* 1:306; and see Chapter 6.

20. *Essai,* pp. lxv–lxviii, 116–117; *Essai sur la constitution et les fonctions des assemblées provinciales* (1788), in *OC,* 8:581–582, 594. The question of "bad reasons" for political preferences arises, here, when individuals, confronted with three different constitutional proposals, prefer both "extremes" to the "center" position.

21. "Sur les élections" (1793), in *OC,* 12:643.

22. "Sur l'instruction publique" (1791–92), in *OC,* 7:201–202.

23. *Réflexions sur le commerce des blés,* in *OC,* 11:145.

24. "Dissertation philosophique et politique, ou réflexions sur cette question: s'il est utile aux hommes d'être trompés?" (1790), in *OC,* 5:371.

25. Letters of December 4 and 13, 1773, in *Correspondance inédite de Condorcet et de Turgot, 1770–1779,* ed. Charles Henry (Paris: Didier, 1883), pp. 141, 148.

26. "If he is speaking of the reflective, calculated interest, by which man compares himself to others and prefers himself, it is false that even the most corrupted men always behave according to this principle." Letter of December 1773, ibid., pp. 143–144.

27. *Vie de M. Turgot* (1786), in *OC,* 5:175.

28. "Sur l'instruction publique," in *OC,* 7:234.

29. *Vie de M. Turgot,* in *OC,* 5:175, 194.

30. On Helvétius and Bentham, see John Morley, *Diderot and the Encyclopaedists* (London: Macmillan, 1886), 2:136–141.

31. "Sur l'instruction publique," in *OC*, 7:235–236.
32. *Vie de M. Turgot*, in *OC*, 5:187.
33. *Réflexions sur le commerce des blés*, in *OC*, 11:155; see Chapter 3.
34. "Sur l'admission des femmes au droit de cité" (1790), in *OC*, 10:126.
35. A nation is an "abstract being," and as such it "can be neither happy nor unhappy." "Thus, when one speaks of the happiness of a nation collectively, one can understand only two things: either a sort of median value, seen as the result of the happiness or unhappiness of individuals; or the general means of happiness, that is to say of tranquillity and well-being, which the land, laws, industry, and relations with foreign nations can provide for the citizens generally. It is enough to have some idea of justice to feel that one should hold to the latter sense. Otherwise, one would have to adopt the maxim, too prevalent among ancient and modern republicans, that the few can legitimately be sacrificed to the many." "De l'influence de la révolution d'Amérique sur l'Europe" (1786), in *OC*, 8:4–5.
36. "Réflexions sur l'esclavage des nègres" (1781), in *OC*, 7:80–81, 120.
37. *Réflexions sur le commerce des blés*, in *OC*, 11:145, 161, 191.
38. Ibid., in *OC*, 11:179.
39. Condorcet, *Esquisse*, in *OC*, 6:191; "Plan d'un emprunt publique" (1789), in *OC*, 11:361.
40. "Réflexions sur l'esclavage des nègres," in *OC*, 7:122.
41. This is from a fragment published by Léon Cahen, "Un fragment inédit de Condorcet," *Revue de métaphysique et de morale*, 22 (1914), 590.
42. "Sur l'instruction publique," in *OC*, 7:201–202.
43. Ibid., 7:202; Benjamin Constant, "De la liberté des anciens comparée à celle des modernes" (1819), in *Écrits politiques*, p. 596.
44. "Sur l'instruction publique," in *OC*, 7:203, 211–213, 326; "Discours sur les conventions nationales" (1791), in *OC*, 10:209.
45. Condorcet questions Pietro Verri, in one of his very first writings on political economy, about the enlightened self-interest of despots. You are trying, he says, "to make them understand that their true interest lies in making the people happy . . . But are you not afraid that you will degrade the people a little in the eyes of their masters, that they will come to see them as beasts of burden who are worth no more than what they bring in?" Letter to Count Verri of 1771, in *OC*, 1:285.
46. "Sur l'instruction publique," *OC*, 7:215, 327. The characteristic of true morality, Condorcet says in his "Lettres d'un théologien" of 1774, is that it "orders the powerful to regard the weak as his brother, and not as an instrument which at his will he can use or break." *OC*, 5:334. In his *Vie de Voltaire* (1789), too, he denounces those who seek to make of other men "the blind instruments of their ambition and their greed." *OC*, 4:181.
47. "Sur l'instruction publique," in *OC*, 7:215; *Sur les assemblées provinciales*, in *OC*, 8:482.
48. *Esquisse*, in *OC*, 6:263.
49. "This purported opposition of interests . . . has until now been one of the

principal causes which has slowed the progress of liberty, of peace, of the true equality which is still so little known." "Sur le préjugé qui suppose une contrariété d'intérêts entre Paris et les provinces" (1790), in *OC*, 10:134. If people's interests were really opposed, Condorcet wrote, "society would be perpetually disturbed by a silent war between these enemy classes." "Que toutes les classes de la société n'ont qu'un même intérêt" (1793), in *OC*, 12:646.

50. Condorcet, *Essai*, p. iii. It is not entirely clear which "ancients" Condorcet had in mind; Cicero, perhaps.

51. One of Condorcet's continuing preoccupations was with the competing uses of political nouns; with "the words which console and reassure men." *Réflexions sur le commerce des blés*, in *OC*, 11:167; and see Chapter 3. His principal argument for some sort of instruction in moral reflection, during the Revolution, is that it will make it possible for people to defend themselves against "seduction": "plunder in the name of justice, tyranny in the name of liberty or equality, barbarism in the name of humanity." "Sur l'instruction publique," in *OC*, 7:329.

52. One illustration of the problem is taken from preferences over constitutional arrangements: voters must choose between outcomes in which distinct orders have distinct chambers, in which different orders have distinct arrangements in a single chamber, and in which different orders sit without distinction in a single chamber. *Sur les assemblées provinciales*, in *OC*, 8:589–598.

53. Ibid., p. 574.

54. Lord Acton, "Sir Erskine May's *Democracy in Europe*" (1878), in *Essays in the History of Liberty* (Indianapolis: Liberty Classics, 1985), p. 82.

55. "Examen sur cette question: est-il utile de diviser une assemblée nationale en plusieurs chambres?" (1789), in *OC*, 9:358.

56. "Avis aux Espagnols" (1792), in *OC*, 12:131.

57. "Sur les élections," in *OC*, 12:643.

58. "De la nature des pouvoirs politiques dans une nation libre" (1792), in *OC*, 10:607.

59. The decision would follow a "reasoned discussion" of "all the opinions and all the grounds on which these opinions could be based"; it would consist of successive rounds of voting on propositions; and it would—in the case of a decision which might in any way violate individual rights, including property rights—require a plurality of three fourths or more. This method might at first sight seem, Condorcet says, to entail "des lenteurs insupportables." *Sur les assemblées provinciales*, in *OC*, 8:213–216, 601.

60. See Arago, "Biographie de Condorcet," in *OC*, 1:clxii–clxiii; Elisabeth Badinter and Robert Badinter, *Condorcet: un intellectuel en politique* (Paris: Fayard, 1988), p. 42; letter of May 1774 from Turgot to Condorcet, in Henry, *Correspondance*, pp. 175–176; *Oeuvres de Maximilien Robespierre* (Paris: Presses Universitaires de France, 1967), 10:456. See also, on Condorcet's writings of the Revolutionary period, Hélène Delsaux, *Condorcet journaliste (1790–1794)* (Paris: Honoré Champion, 1931).

61. Antoine Diannyère, "Notice," in Condorcet, *Esquisse d'un tableau historique des progrès de l'esprit humain* (Paris: Agasse, 1797), p. 54.
62. Bonald, "Observations," pp. 721–722.
63. Morley, *Diderot,* 2:229.
64. Voltaire's support for Russian over Turkish despotism, for example, could have been inspired by political principles as well as by the desire to charm the empress Catherine, Condorcet says. One can be against despotism because it violates the rights of individuals, including the rights of individuals as women, oppressed in the "tyrannical customs of the East, which condemn an entire sex to a shameful slavery"; "this is what Voltaire should have thought; this is what Turgot did think." *Vie de Voltaire,* in *OC,* 4:145–146.
65. John Stuart Mill, "Autobiography," in *Collected Works* (Toronto: University of Toronto Press, 1981), 1:115.
66. "Universalism" is in fact one of the nouns (like "rationalism" and "nationalism") which is mostly used, at least in its secular sense, by people who are opposed to the positions which it denotes.
67. See, on universalism, Berlin, *The Crooked Timber,* pp. 85, 175–177, 245; Arthur O. Lovejoy, *The Great Chain of Being* (1936) (Cambridge, Mass.: Harvard University Press, 1970), pp. 290–293.
68. *Esquisse,* in *OC,* 6:86–87; David Hume, *A Treatise of Human Nature,* ed. L. A. Selby-Bigge (Oxford: Clarendon Press, 1978), pp. 272–274. See, on the influence of Hume on Condorcet, Baker, *Condorcet,* pp. 138–155; Keith Baker, "L'unité de la pensée de Condorcet," in *Condorcet: mathématicien, économiste, philosophe, homme politique,* ed. Pierre Crépel and Christian Gilain (Paris: Minerve, 1989), pp. 515–524; Richard Popkin, "Condorcet and Hume and Turgot," in *Condorcet Studies,* vol. 2, ed. David Williams (New York: Peter Lang, 1984), pp. 47–62.
69. Myles F. Burnyeat, "Can the Skeptic Live His Skepticism?" in *The Skeptical Tradition,* ed. Burnyeat (Berkeley: University of California Press, 1983), p. 129.
70. "Dogmatism" in general does not pose problems of this sort. It is not incoherent in the same sense that skepticism seems to be; one can conceive of fully coherent dogmatists, so attached to themselves that they do all they can, all the time, to promote their own dogmas. The difficulties arise with Condorcet's particular version of dogmatism, in which the belief (the "dogma") to be asserted is a belief that one's beliefs should not be asserted, or at least not if one will thereby interfere with the rights of others to determine their own beliefs. The incoherence of belief and life is a problem for all skeptics, and for some dogmatists.
71. Bernard Williams, "Conflicts of Values," in *Moral Luck: Philosophical Papers, 1973–1980* (Cambridge: Cambridge University Press, 1981), p. 71. The history of liberalism shows, as Williams points out, that the consequences of believing in the plurality of values "need not be quietist or conservative," and "the business of reaffirming and defending the plurality of values is itself a political task."

72. Séance du 18 Floréal An II (1794), in *Oeuvres de Robespierre*, 10:442–464. Stoicism, for Robespierre, was so evidently superior, or "sublime," as to merit a special Revolutionary holiday—along with "Malheur" and the Supreme Being, the festival "au Stoïcisme." Condorcet does indeed discuss Zeno and Epicurus in the *Esquisse;* he speaks of "two new sects, who founded morality on opposing principles, at least in appearance," adds that both sects were infiltrated by men who were, respectively, "hard, proud, and unjust" and "voluptuous and corrupt," and concludes that "the philosophy which aspired to elevate itself above nature, and that which wished to do no more than obey it, the morality which knew no other good than virtue, and that which found happiness in voluptuousness, led to the same practical consequences." *OC*, 6:89–92.

73. Edmund Burke, *Reflections on the Revolution in France* (1790) (London: Penguin Books, 1982), p. 183; Bonald, "Sur l'économie politique" (1810)—an attack on Adam Smith—in *Oeuvres*, 2:299.

74. "Lettres d'un bourgeois de New-Haven à un citoyen de Virginie, sur l'inutilité de partager le pouvoir législatif entre plusieurs corps" (1787), in *OC*, 9:14.

75. "Sur l'admission des femmes," in *OC*, 10:122. Condorcet gives a similar definition in the letters from "New Haven" (*OC*, 9:14), and in the *Esquisse* (*OC*, 6:176).

76. In the Aristotelian schemes with which he was familiar, Condorcet was following the order in which children are supposed to develop, but reversing the order of nature: the state is not prior by nature to the individual, and the emotions are not subject by nature to the governance of the mind. Aristotle, *Politics*, 1253a, 1254b, 1334b.

77. *Vie de M. Turgot*, in *OC*, 5:207.

78. This is in his extended argument in favor of equal instruction for women, "Sur l'instruction publique," in *OC*, 7:219.

79. It is "not the present sensation or momentary pain or pleasure, which determines the character of any passion, but the general bent or tendency of it from the beginning to the end," Hume writes; "the passions, therefore, must depend upon principles." Hume, *Treatise*, pp. 384–385, 387; and see Chapter 1. Condorcet's sentiments are much closer to Hume's than to the sensations (or "vibrations") of Hartley or Condillac; on Condorcet's differences with Condillac, see Baker, *Condorcet*, pp. 114–117.

80. Victor Cousin, *Philosophie écossaise* (Paris: Librairie Nouvelle, 1857), p. 151.

81. Plato, *Protagoras*, 322C–323C. Condorcet's version of this thought, with its emphasis on the details of domestic conduct, is in something of the same spirit as Bernard Williams's: "The capacity for creative emotional response has the advantage of being, if not equally, at least broadly, distributed." Bernard Williams, *Problems of the Self* (Cambridge: Cambridge University Press, 1973), p. 229.

82. Condorcet is close, here too, to Hume: in Baier's description, "at the very

heart of Hume's moral theory lies his celebration of family life and of parental love. Justice, the chief artificial virtue, is the offspring of family cooperativeness and inventive self-interested reason." Annette Baier, *Moral Prejudices: Essays on Ethics* (Cambridge, Mass.: Harvard University Press, 1994), pp. 57–58.

83. "Sur l'instruction publique," in *OC*, 7:234–236. "The American forgets that the negroes are men; he has no moral relation with them," Condorcet writes of the colonial plantation owner; he must also make special efforts to harden the hearts of his children, for example, by making his daughters watch slave trials. "Remarques sur les Pensées de Pascal" (1776), in *OC*, 3:647–648.

84. "Sur l'instruction publique," in *OC*, 7:198; *Vie de M. Turgot,* in *OC*, 5:181–182.

85. "Sur les Pensées de Pascal," in *OC*, 3:640.

86. *Esquisse,* in *OC*, 6:91. The phrase "hors d'oeuvre" had by then, in fact as early as the *Encyclopédie* of 1765, taken on the modern culinary connotation of "small dishes which accompany big dishes." *Encyclopédie, ou dictionnaire raisonné des sciences, des arts et des métiers* (Neufchâtel: Faulche, 1765), 8:313.

87. *Esquisse,* in *OC*, 6:92.

88. Ibid., pp. 261–265; *Vie de M. Turgot,* in *OC*, 5:195.

89. Sainte-Beuve, "Causeries," p. 267.

90. Max Rouché, *La philosophie de l'histoire de Herder* (Paris: Presses Universitaires de France, 1940), p. 538.

91. Ernst Cassirer, *The Philosophy of the Enlightenment,* trans. Fritz C. A. Koelln and James P. Pettegrove (Princeton: Princeton University Press, 1951), p. 233.

92. Thus, on society as a *Maschiene,* Johann Gottfried Herder, "Auch eine Philosophie der Geschichte zur Bildung der Menschheit" (1774), in *Sämtliche Werke,* ed. B. Suphan (Berlin: Weidmann, 1891), 5:516, 529, 533–536, 538, 546, 549, 564; or on man as a mere *Werkzeug,* pp. 524, 526, 547, 564. Are we "beings destined to do something for ourselves in the world," Herder asks, or are our "needs, our ends, and our decisions the objects of a political calculation: everyone in the uniform of his estate, a machine?" (p. 539).

93. This is Posa speaking to King Philip in *Don Carlos.* Friedrich Schiller, *Don Carlos* (1787), trans. James Kirkup (Garden City, N.Y.: Doubleday, 1959), 3.10.3051–53, p. 161. The scene was Hölderlin's "favorite." Friedrich Hölderlin, *Oeuvres,* ed. Philippe Jaccottet (Paris: Gallimard, 1967), p. 98.

94. On the state as *Sittenschule,* see Friedrich Hölderlin, *Hyperion oder der Eremit in Griechenland* (Stuttgart: Reclam, 1976), p. 35.

95. Immanuel Kant, "Beantwortung der Frage: Was ist Aufklärung?" (1784), in *Werkausgabe,* ed. Wilhelm Weischedel (Frankfurt: Suhrkamp, 1968), 11:53; idem, "Der Streit der Facultäten" (1798), in *Werkausgabe,* 11:359–360; *Kant's Political Writings,* ed. H. Reiss (Cambridge: Cambridge University

Press, 1970), pp. 54, 183–184. The metaphor of the enlightened ruler oblig-
ing his subjects to move, like a flock of animals, to a richer pasture is in fact
Diderot's, in one of the fragments he contributed to the *Histoire des deux
Indes* of 1774 (as well as in his *Réfutation d'Helvétius*). Denis Diderot,
Oeuvres (Paris: Robert Laffont, 1994–1995), 1:862, 3:590, 660. It is interesting that Diannyère described Condorcet, at the end of his life, saying of
his earlier uncordial relations with Diderot that "I was wrong . . . [He] was
the best of men." Diannyère, "Notice," p. 59.

96. "Éclaircissements sur la versification allemande" (1761), in *OC*, 1:631–665;
see, on Hume in Germany, "Hume and the Sources of German Anti-rational-
ism," in Berlin, *Against the Current*, pp. 162–187.

97. Immanuel Kant, *Critique of Pure Reason* (1787), trans. N. Kemp Smith
(New York: St. Martin's Press, 1965), p. 412.

98. "Moral philosophy divides itself in the eighteenth century into three principal schools, which are themselves divided between the three principal countries of Europe: France, Great Britain, and Germany," Paul Janet writes; the
(French) doctrine of pleasure and interest is counterposed to the (Anglo-
Scottish) doctrine of moral sentiments and to the (German) doctrine of pure
understanding. Paul Janet, *Histoire de la science politique dans ses rapports
avec la morale* (Paris: Alcan, 1913), 2:574.

99. "Zibaldone di pensieri" (1821), in Giacomo Leopardi, *Tutte le opere,* ed.
Walter Binni (Milan: Sansoni, 1993), 2:1213–16.

100. Tocqueville, *L'ancien régime,* p. 43.

101. Ibid., p. 257.

102. See, on Diderot's concern with emotion, Roger Hausheer, "Introduction,"
in Berlin, *Against the Current*, p. xxxiii.

103. "J'y retrouvais une foule de sentiments que j'avais crus nés de la Révolution."
Tocqueville, *L'ancien régime,* pp. 44–46, 231.

104. Tocqueville, *L'ancien régime,* pp. 259–261, 309.

105. François Furet, *Penser la Révolution française* (Paris: Gallimard, 1978),
pp. 36, 280.

106. Quoted in Furet, *Penser la Révolution française,* pp. 280–281.

107. Tocqueville, *L'ancien régime,* p. 231.

108. It is quite inappropriate, Condorcet wrote early in 1789, to judge Voltaire on
the basis of positions—"une disposition des esprits"—which are subsequent
by ten years to his death, and by half a century to his philosophy; to condemn
him, for example, for "having distinguished the good which can exist without freedom, from the happiness which comes from liberty itself." *Vie de Voltaire*, in *OC*, 4:182; and see Chapter 1.

109. Tocqueville said that the Économistes, of all the men of the 1750s, would be
most at home in the socialism of the mid-nineteenth century, and for Furet,
their ideas "prefigured" the tyranny of 1793 rather than the liberalism of
1789. Tocqueville, *L'ancien régime,* pp. 261–262; Furet, *Penser la Révolution française,* p. 248; and see Chapter 1.

110. One consequence of Tocqueville's journey, for his modern exegetes, is to show the unimportance of the Revolution in the genesis of revolutionary thought. But there is a different consequence as well: it is to suggest that the counter-Revolution, or the political thought of the Revolution's critics, is similarly unimportant in the genesis of liberal, "diversitarian" individualism. The critique of centralizing uniformity is to be found within the ancien régime and within the enlightenment; within the disputes, well before Burke's *Reflections*, over the economic theories of the first Économistes.

111. Benjamin Constant, "Des réactions politiques" (1797) and "Des effets de la terreur" (1797), in *De la force du gouvernement actuel de la France et de la nécessité de s'y rallier* (Paris: Flammarion, 1988), pp. 124, 173, 176, 178.

112. They are the rights to fair judicial procedures, and to the innocent exercise of one's faculties. Constant, *Réflexions sur les constitutions et les garanties* (1814), which he quotes in the preface to his *Principes de politique* of 1815. Constant, *Écrits politiques*, pp. 305–306.

113. Constant, "De la liberté des anciens comparée à celles des modernes," p. 617.

114. Tocqueville, *L'ancien régime*, p. 256; *Esquisse*, in *OC*, 6:191.

115. Tocqueville, *L'ancien régime*, pp. 255–262, 267; *Réflexions sur le commerce des blés*, in *OC*, 11:178–179.

116. John Stuart Mill, *On Liberty* (1859) (London: Penguin Books, 1974), pp. 75, 97, 99, 178, 187.

117. John Morley, *Recollections* (London: Macmillan, 1918), 1:57.

118. John Morley, "Condorcet," in *Critical Miscellanies* (London: Macmillan, 1886), 2:254–255.

119. François Guizot, *Mémoires pour servir à l'histoire de mon temps* (Paris: Michel Lévy, 1858), 1:291.

120. John Morley, "A Few Words on French Models," in *Studies in Literature* (London: Macmillan, 1891), pp. 157, 169.

121. C.-A. Sainte-Beuve, "M. Fauriel" (1846), in *Portraits contemporains* (Paris: Calmann-Lévy, 1889), 4:126–127, 179; J.-B. Galley, *Claude Fauriel: Membre de l'Institut, 1772–1843* (Saint Étienne: Imprimerie de la Loire Républicaine, 1909).

8. A Fatherless World

1. "Fragment de l'histoire de la Xe époque," in *OC*, 6:595.

2. David Hume, *An Enquiry concerning the Principles of Morals* (1751) (Oxford: Clarendon Press, 1961), pp. 283–284.

3. John Stuart Mill, "On the Definition of Political Economy; and on the Method of Investigation Proper to It" (1836), in *Collected Works* (Toronto: University of Toronto Press, 1967), 4:310.

4. *TMS*, p. 30. Philoctetes was the excruciatingly crippled weapons keeper of Hercules, left by Odysseus on the wild, wooded, and deserted island of

Lemnos. Smith's view of *Philoctetes* was that "it is not the sore foot, but the solitude, of Philoctetes which affects us, and diffuses over that charming tragedy, that romantic wildness, which is so agreeable to the imagination." Voltaire in his *Oedipe* reveals that Philoctetes, rescued from the wilderness, and with his foot restored, was Jocasta's long-lost lover, and could thus evoke "at least the memory of a legitimate love." Philoctetes was no "poor groom of Hercules," Voltaire adds; "it is certain" that he was "a prince of Greece, famous for his exploits." "Lettres sur Oedipe" (1719), in *Oeuvres complètes de Voltaire* (Paris: Firmin-Didot, 1876), 1:72; and see Chapter 5.

5. Carl Menger, *Investigations into the Method of the Social Sciences with Special Reference to Economics,* trans. Francis J. Nock (New York: New York University Press, 1985), pp. 168–169.

6. "Fragment de l'histoire de la Xe époque," in *OC,* 6:528; see Chapter 6.

7. The essay was later retitled "Of Refinement in the Arts." David Hume, *Essays Moral, Political, and Literary,* ed. Eugene F. Miller (Indianapolis: Liberty Classics, 1987), pp. 269–273.

8. "Of Commerce," in Hume, *Essays,* p. 260.

9. *WN,* p. 788; *LJ,* p. 540.

10. "Of Refinement in the Arts," in Hume, *Essays,* p. 280.

11. *TMS,* pp. 335–336.

12. Dugald Stewart, "Account of the Life and Writings of Adam Smith, LL.D.," in *EPS,* pp. 316, 331; and see Chapter 2.

13. See Ian Simpson Ross, *The Life of Adam Smith* (Oxford: Clarendon Press, 1995).

14. See Elisabeth Badinter and Robert Badinter, *Condorcet: un intellectuel en politique* (Paris: Fayard, 1988).

15. *TMS,* p. 231.

16. *Vie de M. Turgot* (1786), in *OC,* 5:45, 125.

17. *Corr.,* p. 286.

18. The story of the competition is told in Ian Ross and David Raynor, "Adam Smith and Count Windisch-Grätz: New Letters," *Studies on Voltaire and the Eighteenth Century,* 358 (1998), 171–187. Smith's comment about the Scottish-style books is in a letter of July 1785, quoted on pp. 179–182. Ross and Raynor comment (p. 175) that Smith's discouraging response indicates both his own ill health and "some waning of the Enlightenment, a rejection of the agenda of cosmopolitan engagement with intellectual issues" which had been expressed, earlier, in his writings on rhetoric and economics.

19. *WN,* pp. 96, 98.

20. *Vie de M. Turgot,* in *OC,* 5:42.

21. *The Notebooks of Samuel Taylor Coleridge,* ed. Kathleen Coburn (London: Routledge and Kegan Paul, 1962) vol. 2, *Text (1804–1808),* p. 2578.

22. "Discours préliminaire," in Jean-Baptiste Say, *Traité d'Économie Politique, ou simple exposition de la manière dont se forment, se distribuent, et se consomment les richesses* (Paris: Deterville, 1803), p. iii; George Pryme, *An Introductory*

Lecture and Syllabus, to a course delivered in the University of Cambridge, on the principles of political economy (Cambridge: Smith, 1823), pp. 3, 5; and see Chapter 1.

23. *WN*, pp. 127, 827.

24. "Lettre d'un laboureur de Picardie" (1775), in *OC*, 11:7, 21; the laborer, who was born into a rich but undistinguished family, had been spending his Sundays reading Necker's book aloud to his six children (pp. 3–4, 30).

25. *WN*, p. 528; *Réflexions sur le commerce des blés* (1776), in *OC*, 11:201.

26. Mathurin Gillet, *L'utopie de Condorcet* (Paris: Guillaumin, 1883), p. 42; on Condorcet's correspondence with Turgot, see Chapter 7.

27. "Political Economy and Sociology," in Thomas Edward Cliffe Leslie, *Essays in Political and Moral Philosophy* (Dublin: Hodges, Foster, and Figgis, 1879), pp. 385, 387.

28. *WN*, pp. 782, 787–788; and see Chapters 4 and 5.

29. *Essai sur la constitution et les fonctions des assemblées provinciales* (1788), in *OC*, 8:476–477.

30. "Sur l'instruction publique" (1791–1792), in *OC*, 7:192.

31. François de Fénelon, *Les aventures de Télémaque* (Paris: Garnier, 1994), pp. 166, 169, 348; and see Chapter 1; see also Emma Rothschild, "Condorcet and Adam Smith on Education and Instruction," in *Philosophers on Education: Historical Perspectives*, ed. Amélie Oksenberg Rorty (London: Routledge, 1998), pp. 209–226.

32. *WN*, pp. 28–30; *LJ*, p. 540. On Smith's ideas of education, see Mark Blaug, "The Economics of Education in English Classical Political Economy: A Reexamination," in *Essays on Adam Smith*, ed. Andrew S. Skinner and Thomas Wilson (Oxford: Clarendon Press, 1975), pp. 568–599; and Andrew S. Skinner, "Adam Smith and the Role of the State: Education as a Public Service," in *Adam Smith's Wealth of Nations: New Interdisciplinary Essays*, ed. Stephen Copley and Kathryn Sutherland (Manchester: Manchester University Press, 1995), pp. 70–95.

33. "Sur l'instruction publique," in *OC*, 7:259, 284–285.

34. *WN*, pp. 787–788, 796–797.

35. "Of Refinement in the Arts," in Hume, *Essays*, pp. 271–274.

36. "Fragment de l'histoire de la Xe époque," in *OC*, 6:549; "Sur l'instruction publique," in *OC*, 7:211–213; and see Chapter 7.

37. *WN*, p. 768.

38. One of Smith's illustrations of the changing disposition to wonder, in his "History of Astronomy," is of the artisan—"such as dyers, brewers, distillers"—whose imagination becomes accustomed to the strange appearances of his art. "History of Astronomy," in *EPS*, p. 44.

39. *Réflexions sur le commerce des blés*, in *OC*, 11:127; and see Chapter 6.

40. *WN*, pp. 622–623.

41. "Lettres au Contrôleur Général (abbé Terray) sur le commerce des grains," in *OT*, 3:324, 327–328.

42. "Of Commerce," in Hume, *Essays,* p. 254.

43. "Éloge de M. D'Alembert" (1783), in *OC,* 3:79.

44. "The Platonist," in Hume, *Essays,* p. 155. On the enemies of "Reason . . . in possession of the throne, prescribing laws, and imposing maxims, with an absolute sway and authority," see David Hume, *A Treatise of Human Nature,* ed. L. A. Selby-Bigge (Oxford: Clarendon Press, 1978), p. 186.

45. "History of Astronomy," in *EPS,* pp. 45–46; and see also the "General Introduction" by D. D. Raphael and A. S. Skinner in *EPS,* esp. pp. 12–14.

46. "History of Astronomy," *EPS,* p. 105; and see Chapter 5.

47. James Beattie, *An Essay on the Nature and Immutability of Truth, in Opposition to Sophistry and Scepticism* (1776) (London: W. Baynes, 1823), pp. 148, 271; see also the discussion of Beattie and Hume in Edgar Wind, *Hume and the Heroic Portrait: Studies in Eighteenth-Century Imagery,* ed. Jaynie Anderson (Oxford: Clarendon Press, 1986).

48. See, for example, Lucretius, *De rerum natura,* 2.1054–63: "Seeds innumerable in number in the unfathomable universe are flying about in many ways driven in everlasting movement . . . the seeds of things themselves of their own accord, knocking together by chance, clashed in all sorts of ways, heedless, without aim, without intention." *On the Nature of Things,* trans. W. H. D. Rouse, rev. Martin F. Smith (Cambridge, Mass.: Harvard University Press, 1992), p. 177.

49. David Hume, *Dialogues concerning Natural Religion* (1779) (London: Penguin Books, 1990), p. 75; Lucretius, *De rerum natura,* 2.1095–96; *On the Nature of Things,* p. 181.

50. *TMS,* p. 235; and see Chapter 5.

51. Hume, *Treatise,* pp. 181–182, 269.

52. William Wordsworth, *The Prelude,* 3.62–63.

53. Stewart, "Account," p. 279. Smith and Hume agree with Hutcheson in deriving moral distinctions from sentiment rather than from reason, but reject his hypothesis of a simple, and therefore unexplainable, or unanalyzable, moral sense.

54. Stewart, "Account," p. 279; *TMS,* pp. 318–327.

55. *TMS,* pp. 18, 159–165; Hume, *Treatise,* pp. 146, 581.

56. Smith is less of a consequentialist than Hume, in modern terms, but he is not thereby a deontologist, for whom morality consists in a rational obedience to duty. "Philosophers have, of late years, considered chiefly the tendency of affections, and have given little attention to the relation which they stand in to the cause which excites them. In common life, however, when we judge of any person's conduct, and of the sentiments which directed it, we constantly consider them under both these aspects," Smith writes; two of the last passages he added to the *Theory of Moral Sentiments* are concerned with the "fallacious sense of guilt" of Oedipus and Jocasta, innocent in their sentiments, but "tending" to fatal consequences. *TMS,* pp. 18, 107, 338–339.

57. *TMS,* p. 143.

58. Letters of December 1773, in Charles Henry, ed., *Correspondance inédite de Condorcet et de Turgot, 1770–1779* (Paris: Didier, 1883), pp. 143–144, 155. On the importance of conversation in Smith's moral philosophy, see Henry C. Clark, "Conversation and Moderate Virtue in Adam Smith's *Theory of Moral Sentiments*," *Review of Politics*, 54, 2 (Spring 1992), 185–210.

59. This is the phrase which Kant uses to describe the metaphysics of morality, "scrupulously cleansed of everything empirical." Immanuel Kant, *The Moral Law: Kant's Groundwork of a Metaphysic of Morals* (1785), trans. H. J. Paton (London: Hutchinson, 1948), p. 55.

60. Stewart, "Account," p. 287. Stewart expresses some doubt about Smith's efforts to evade any hypothesis of "the existence of some moral faculty which is not borrowed from without," and he indeed says of the *Theory of Moral Sentiments* that "for my own part I must confess, that it does not coincide with my notions concerning the foundations of morals" (pp. 287, 290); on the circumstances in which Stewart's "Account" was first read in Edinburgh, and its role in protecting both Smith's and Stewart's reputations in the turbulent times of the anti-Jacobin repression, see Chapter 2.

61. Letter of May 18, 1774, in *OT,* 3:670–671.

62. "Fragment de l'histoire de la Xe époque," in *OC,* 6:595.

63. *WN,* p. 775.

64. *LJ,* pp. 142–143; *WN,* p. 772.

65. "Of Refinement in the Arts," in Hume, *Essays,* p. 274.

66. Duncan Forbes, *Hume's Philosophical Politics* (Cambridge: Cambridge University Press, 1978), p. 65.

67. *WN,* pp. 51–52, 188, 402, 729. On the sovereign prince, who seeks, like Frederick the Great, to act upon "some general, and even systematical, idea of the perfection of policy and law," and "to erect his own judgment into the supreme standard of right and wrong," see *TMS,* p. 234, and Chapter 2.

68. David Hume, *History of England,* quoted in Forbes, *Hume's Philosophical Politics,* p. 309.

69. For Smith and for Hume, as for Hobbes, in Richard Tuck's description, "the route to agreement must lie through *politics.*" Richard Tuck, *Hobbes* (Oxford: Oxford University Press, 1989), p. 57. But their confidence in political discussion, and their dislike of political fear, are quite unlike Hobbes. "The bonds of words are too weak to bridle mens ambition, avarice, anger, and other Passions, without the fear of some coercive power," Hobbes wrote in *Leviathan;* for Smith, in the *Wealth of Nations,* writing of the dissenting clergy, "fear is in almost all cases a wretched instrument of government, and ought in particular never to be employed against any order of men who have the smallest pretensions to independency. To attempt to terrify them, serves only to irritate their bad humour." *WN,* pp. 798–799; and Hobbes, *Leviathan,* chap. 14, quoted in Tuck, *Hobbes,* p. 68.

70. Donald Winch, *Adam Smith's Politics: An Essay in Historiographic Revision* (Cambridge: Cambridge University Press, 1978), p. 177.

71. "Lit de Justice" (1776), in *OT,* 5:288.
72. "Of the Independency of Parliament," in Hume, *Essays,* pp. 42–43.
73. "Of the Middle Station of Life," ibid., pp. 546–547; "Of Refinement in the Arts," ibid., p. 277.
74. Letter to Condorcet of July 16, 1771, in *OT,* 3:529.
75. *TMS,* pp. 190–191, 233–234.
76. On the "gloomy and melancholy" character of superstition, and the "confidence," "presumption," and "surprising flights of fancy" of enthusiasm, see "Of Superstition and Enthusiasm," in Hume, *Essays,* pp. 73–74.
77. "Discours de réception à l'Académie Française" (1782), in *OC,* 1:401.
78. On Smith's opinions, or rather absence of opinions about democratic politics, see Winch, *Adam Smith's Politics,* esp. chaps. 1 and 8, and Duncan Forbes, "Sceptical Whiggism, Commerce, and Liberty," in Skinner and Wilson, *Essays on Adam Smith,* pp. 179–201.
79. "Fragment de l'histoire de la Xe époque," in *OC,* 6:579.
80. *Rapport sur l'Instruction Publique, Fait au nom du Comité de Constitution, par M. Talleyrand-Périgord* (Paris: Assemblée Nationale, 1791), pp. 4, 11–12.
81. "Fragment de l'histoire de la Xe époque," in *OC,* 6:552.
82. Benjamin Constant, *De la force du gouvernement actuel de la France et de la nécessité de s'y rallier* (Paris: Flammarion, 1988), pp. 41–42.
83. *Vie de M. Turgot,* in *OC,* 5:181.
84. "Of Refinement in the Arts," in Hume, *Essays,* p. 271. Condorcet, similarly, says of the earliest "progress toward moral perfecting," in the Fourth Epoch of Greek antiquity, that "the greater equality enjoyed by women had made the domestic virtues more common" (even though men still lived separately from women, and were thus deprived of their "common society"). "Fragment de l'histoire de la IVe époque," in *OC,* 6:463–464.
85. "Discours de réception," in *OC,* 1:395.
86. "Sur l'instruction publique," in *OC,* 7:226–228.
87. C.-A. Sainte-Beuve, "Oeuvres de Condorcet," in *Causeries du Lundi* (Paris: Garnier, 1868), 3:345–346.
88. "Fragment de l'histoire de la Xe époque," in *OC,* 6:596.
89. "Lettres sur le commerce des grains," in *OT,* 3:327–328.
90. "Éloge de Vincent de Gournay" (1759), in *OT,* 1:618–619.
91. "Tableau général de la science" (1793), in *OC,* 1:567.
92. *Esquisse d'un tableau historique des progrès de l'esprit humain,* in *OC,* 6:178–181.
93. G. W. F. Hegel, *Philosophy of Right* (1821), trans. T. M. Knox (Oxford: Oxford University Press, 1967), pp. 126–127.
94. Say, "Discours préliminaire," pp. vi, xxiv–xxvi.
95. "Éloge de Vincent de Gournay," in *OT,* 1:602, 618–619.
96. *TMS,* pp. 231–234.
97. *TMS,* pp. 180, 183, 185, 233–234.

98. This is the dilemma of the natural philosopher that Smith describes in relation to the "system of Sir Isaac Newton." *EPS*, pp. 104–105.
99. *Esquisse*, in *OC*, 6:181.
100. *WN*, p. 723.
101. *TMS*, p. 231.
102. "Of the Original Contract," in Hume, *Essays*, p. 465.
103. *LJ*, pp. 89, 403; "Of the Original Contract," in Hume, *Essays*, pp. 465–487; and see Winch, *Adam Smith's Politics*, pp. 51–54.
104. James Anderson, "To Foreign Correspondents," *The Bee, or Literary Weekly Intelligencer*, 1 (1791), xvii–xxviii; and see Chapter 1.
105. *TMS*, p. 136.
106. "Lettres sur le commerce des grains" (1770), in *OT*, 3:119.
107. *WN*, pp. 204, 321, 412, 421–422, 454–456, 526, 920.
108. Comte de Las Cases, *Le Mémorial de Sainte-Hélène*, ed. Joël Schmidt (Paris: Éditions du Seuil, 1968), 2:1441–42.
109. "Lettres sur le commerce des grains," in *OT*, 3:352, and see Chapter 3.
110. "Mémoire sur les prêts d'argent," in *OT*, 3:163–164; *Réflexions sur le commerce des blés*, in *OC*, 11:148; and see Chapter 6.
111. Letter of Smith to Andreas Holt of October 1780, in *Corr.*, p. 251.
112. *WN*, pp. 152–158.
113. Richard Burn, *The Justice of the Peace, and Parish Officer* (London: A. Millar, 1758), 1:443–5, 516–522, 2:472.
114. "Lit de Justice," in *OT*, 5:295.
115. *WN*, pp. 341–345.
116. "Lit de Justice," in *OT*, 5:287, 290.
117. *WN*, pp. 26–27.
118. Seneca, *De beneficiis*, in *Moral Essays*, vol. 2, trans. J. W. Basore (Cambridge, Mass.: Harvard University Press, 1989), 1.xiv.1; the description of Seneca is Smith's, in *TMS*, p. 48.
119. *WN*, pp. 26–27.
120. The soul, in a commercial society, "comes out of itself, is no longer isolated, comes to know the universe." "Plan d'un ouvrage sur le commerce, la circulation et l'intérêt de l'argent, la richesse des états" (1753–54), in *OT*, 1:380.
121. Jane Austen, *Mansfield Park* (1814) (London: Penguin Books, 1985), p. 90.
122. Tacitus, *The Histories*, trans. Clifford H. Moore (Cambridge, Mass.: Harvard University Press, 1968), 1.vii, xv, xx, pp. 14–15, 30–31, 39; on the necessity of self-interest and the greed of the human race, as observed in the reign of the emperor Nero, see Seneca, *De beneficiis*, 5–7.
123. See, for example, *WN*, pp. 118, 128; "Lettres sur le commerce des grains," in *OT*, 3:323.
124. *TMS*, p. 83.
125. *WN*, pp. 126–127, 145, 729–730, 782. The seaport conversations are imagined by the young boy's "tender mother, among the inferior ranks of people"; she is "afraid to send her son to school" in such a place.

126. "Mémoire sur les prêts d'argent" (1770), in *OT*, 3:175; John Stuart Mill, *On Liberty* (1859) (London: Penguin Books, 1974), pp. 163–164. Individuals often cause "pain or loss" to others, in the course of their pursuit of a "legitimate object," Mill writes; "society admits no right, either legal or moral, in the disappointed competitors to immunity from this kind of suffering, and feels called on to interfere only when means of success have been employed which it is contrary to the general interest to permit—namely, fraud or treachery, and force."

127. "Fragment de l'histoire de la Xe époque," in *OC*, 6:527–529.

128. *LJ*, pp. 538–539.

129. *WN*, p. 130.

130. *Réflexions sur le commerce des blés*, in *OC*, 11:170–171.

131. François-René de Chateaubriand, *Mémoires d'outre-tombe* (1849) (Paris: Le Livre de Poche, 1973), 3:712–720.

132. Las Cases, *Le Mémorial de Sainte-Hélène*, 2:1441, 1526; and see Chapter 1.

133. G. W. F. Hegel, *Phenomenology of Spirit* (1807), trans. A. V. Miller (Oxford: Oxford University Press, 1977), pp. 329, 331, 349; and see Chapter 1.

134. This is the language of the Paris Peace Treaty of 1814; see *Acten des Wiener Congresses*, ed. J. L. Kluber (Erlangen, 1819), 1:9, 36; and Emma Rothschild, "What Is Security?" *Daedalus*, 124, 3 (Summer 1995), 53–98.

135. Quoted in François Furet, "Bonaparte," in *Dictionnaire critique de la Révolution française*, ed. François Furet and Mona Ozouf (Paris: Flammarion, 1988), p. 222.

136. They saw "effects without causes, abysses without foundations; they wandered with a somber uncertainty like shadows isolated and floating in space," and nature "offered nothing to their confused imagination but the vast silence, and the eternal night of chaos." Jean-Etienne-Marie Portalis, *Éloge d'Antoine-Louis Séguier, avocat-général au Parlement de Paris* (Paris: Nicolle, 1806), pp. 50–51, 54–58, 76–78.

137. Letter of November 13, 1815, in *The Adams-Jefferson Letters: The Complete Correspondence between Thomas Jefferson and Abigail and John Adams*, ed. Lester J. Cappon (Chapel Hill: University of North Carolina Press, 1959), 2:456.

138. John Morley, "Condorcet," in *Critical Miscellanies* (London: Macmillan, 1886), 2:212.

139. Alexis de Tocqueville, *L'ancien régime et la Révolution* (1856), ed. J.-P. Mayer (Paris: Gallimard, 1967), pp. 249–251.

140. This was in one of his newspaper contributions; see *Chronique de Paris*, December 8, 1792, p. 1369.

141. "The words *peace* and *commerce* are in England what *peace* and *glory* are for France," Fiévée wrote, after studying the ribbons produced by London merchants to celebrate the Treaty of Amiens; the English were nonetheless far more insistent than the French on their own national superiority. Joseph Fiévée, *Lettres sur l'Angleterre, et réflexions sur la philosophie du XVIIIe siècle* (Paris: Perlet, 1802), pp. 30–31, 48.

142. Benjamin Constant, "De M. Dunoyer et de quelques-uns de ses ouvrages" (1826), in *Écrits politiques,* ed. Marcel Gauchet (Paris: Gallimard, 1997), pp. 668–669.

143. On the religion of utopian revolution, see Gareth Stedman Jones, "Before God Died: The Rise and Fall of Socialist Utopia, 1789–1989," Carlyle Lectures, Centre for History and Economics, King's College, Cambridge, 1998.

144. Constant, "De M. Dunoyer," p. 674; on Condorcet's description of the pretension of some men to be "guides" of others, see Chapter 7.

145. Friedrich Engels, "Preface to the English Edition of 1888," in Karl Marx and Friedrich Engels, *The Communist Manifesto* (1848), trans. Samuel Moore, ed. A. J. P. Taylor (Harmondsworth: Penguin Books, 1977), p. 63.

146. Say, "Discours préliminaire," pp. vi–vii.

147. Edmund Burke, *Reflections on the Revolution in France* (1790), ed. Conor Cruise O'Brien (London: Penguin Books, 1982), p. 175.

148. Benjamin Constant, "De la liberté des anciens comparée à celle des modernes" (1819), in *Écrits politiques,* p. 605.

149. Constant, "De la liberté," p. 611; "Sur l'instruction publique," in *OC,* 7:201.

150. Constant, "De la liberté," pp. 598, 613, 616.

151. Alexis de Tocqueville, *Voyages en Angleterre et en Irlande,* ed. J.-P. Mayer (Paris: Gallimard, 1967), pp. 205–206.

152. Tocqueville, *L'ancien régime et la Révolution,* pp. 51–52.

153. The ten or fifteen years which preceded the French Revolution, Tocqueville wrote in his notes for *L'ancien régime et la Révolution,* were ones of "great prosperity," in which industry and commerce were improved and extended. "One might think, that with men's lives becoming in this way more busy and more sensuous, the human mind would have turned away from abstract studies which have as their object man and society, to concentrate more and more on the contemplation of petty daily affairs. This is what has been seen only too much in our own times, and it is the opposite of what was seen then." The "spectacle" of those pre-Revolutionary years, of the bankers and merchants of Hamburg, for example, with their high-minded conversations and their discussions of philosophy and politics, was "after all, one of the greatest which humanity has ever displayed, in spite of the errors and absurdities of the period." Alexis de Tocqueville, *L'Ancien Régime et la Révolution: Fragments et notes inédites sur la révolution,* ed. André Jardin, in *Oeuvres complètes,* ed. J.-P. Mayer (Paris: Gallimard, 1952–1953), vol. 2, pt. 2, pp. 37–38; Constant, "De la liberté," p. 617.

154. Morley, "Condorcet," p. 255.

155. In "bourgeois society," François Furet wrote in *Le passé d'une illusion,* "inequality is an idea which circulates as contraband, in contradiction with the manner in which individuals imagine themselves." The idea of the equality and universality of men, which is claimed as the foundation of modern society, is "constantly denied by the inequality of property and wealth, produced

by competition among its members. Its movement contradicts its principle, its dynamism, its legitimacy." François Furet, *Le passé d'une illusion: essai sur l'idée communiste au XXe siècle* (Paris: Robert Laffont, 1995), pp. 21–22.

156. "Of Commerce," in Hume, *Essays*, p. 265.

157. Mona Ozouf, "Égalité," in Furet and Ozouf, *Dictionnaire critique de la Révolution française*, p. 709.

158. *LRBL*, p. 88.

ACKNOWLEDGMENTS

I would like to thank Gavin Alexander, Bernard Bailyn, Keith Baker, Myles Burnyeat, Nancy Cartwright, Aida Donald, Penny Janeway, Stefan Klasen, Melissa Lane, Anne Malcolm, Stephen Martin, Merav Mack, JoEllyn Moore, Joakim Palme, Marten Palme, Asha Patel, Amy Price, Tanni Mukhopadyay, Martin Rees, Victoria Rothschild, Elaine Scarry, Amartya Sen, John Shaw, Noala Skinner, Gareth Stedman Jones, Jonathan Steinberg, Richard Tuck, Gloria Vivenza, Patricia Williams, Donald Winch, and the late Judith Shklar for many extremely helpful discussions. I am particularly grateful to Amartya Sen, Melissa Lane, Gareth Stedman Jones, Richard Tuck, Amanda Heller, Penny Janeway, Merav Mack, and Rosie Vaughan for comments on the manuscript.

Chapter 2 of the book appeared, in a slightly shorter version, in the *Economic History Review* for March 1992, Chapter 3 in the *Economic Journal* for June 1992, and Chapter 7 in the *Historical Journal* for May 1996. Versions of Chapters 5 and 6 have been discussed in the History and Economics Seminar at the Centre for History and Economics, King's College, Cambridge. I am grateful to participants in the seminar for helpful comments, and to the John D. and Catherine C. MacArthur Foundation for support to the Centre for History and Economics.

INDEX